NOTES

NOTES

Instructor's Manual and Test Bank

for

Personality Theories
Development, Growth, and Diversity

Fourth Edition

Bem P. Allen
Western Illinois University

Boston   New York   San Francisco
Mexico City   Montreal   Toronto   London   Madrid   Munich   Paris
Hong Kong   Singapore   Tokyo   Cape Town   Sydney

Table of Contents

Preface

This manual accompanying *Personality Theories: Development, Growth, and Diversity* is designed to help college and university teachers go beyond the usual lecture so that classroom experiences are interactive and cooperative in nature. As a member of a major higher-education teachers' organization I have come to realize that modern, post-secondary teachers are recognizing the need to do more than simply lecture to students. Higher education teachers recognize that, while their skills as expert lecturers are frequently needed, they have other roles to play as well. Today's college instructor is taking the responsibility to communicate the newest findings in his or her field, information that is so new it could not be included in the text. Contemporary teachers also understand that it is frequently necessary to cover extra-text material in class and to give a different slant to certain text material, because its essential nature is such that full appreciation requires multiple perspectives. Most of all, today's post-secondary teachers are realizing that students must become involved with the course material and participate in the educational enterprise by teaching each other, if they are to fully integrate the material in a way that will have an impact on them lasting beyond the end of the semester. That is why special procedures that will draw students into classroom involvement are becoming highly valued by modern instructors.

The contents of this manual provide some of those special procedures by fully exploiting exercises and sources of classroom discussion found in the text. But there is more. Each manual chapter begins with a *Chapter Outline* that instructors can use to help organize classroom activities. *Objectives* follow for teachers who wish to provide students with a bit more structure in approaching course materials. Like the chapter outlines, the objectives are reasonably short so that they could be written into the course syllabus, made into transparencies, or copied and distributed to students.

Classroom Discussion: Beyond the Text and the Lecture items are next. Each discussion item provides a detailed guide to full exploitation of an issue raised in or implied by the text. Some items relate to critical thinking questions or running comparison segments. By use of this manual section, you can bring course material to life in class, thereby infecting students with the kind of intellectual enthusiasm that will promote lasting learning. Further, discussion items can be altered or expanded to touch on issues raised in lectures. These discussion items can take from minutes of class time to entire class periods, depending on the item and how instructors approach it.

Next are the *Classroom Exercises: Practical Applications.* They are designed to make classroom activities out of the individual exercises in the text's boxes, but now also include exercises not found in the text. Many of these are personality tests that will provide individual students with personal insight, and will be edifying to the class as a whole when group results are reported in class. These practical, hands-on exercises will aid students in learning more about individual differences and about personality testing. Classroom analyses of test scores will help students interpret their individual scores. Opportunities to learn more about experimentation are also included. Many exercises can be geared to take part or all of a class period.

Discussion items and some exercises have a special feature that compensates for the lack of attention to multicultural issues that characterized many theorists. Most of the theorists covered in the text are deceased and some of those who are still alive formed their basic ideas years ago, before the change in the populations of North America, Australia, and Europe made multicultural considerations critically important. Classroom activities provided by this manual come from my experience as a multicultural teacher and give instructors the opportunity to celebrate our diversity and our many cultures. Several of these activities take remote implications and subtle nuances of theories and turn them into classroom interactions that will create better understanding of diverse cultures.

Two other manual sections are for instructor and student support. *Suggested Readings for Lecture Support* selects for instructors the two most helpful readings for vitalizing and expanding lectures. Readings are in accessible books, magazines, and journals and are chosen, in part, for their clarity. Individual readings are accompanied by statements indicating why they are useful. Each will aid instructors in efforts to go beyond the text.

Suggested readings for students is a selection of two short, clear, enjoyable, and interesting articles, many from popular sources, that will help interested students expand their education. Each includes a statement telling instructors why students will benefit from reading the article.

A case history of a young Latino named Estella Monroe supplements the text and is printed here in its entirety. A picture of her life is painted on a sufficiently broad canvas to allow each theorist a chance to "analyze" her. The case includes the hypothetical analyses of the various theorists and a summary of their concepts used in analyses. You may introduce Estella to the class early in the semester and have students speculate on how each theorist would analyze her personality as each is covered or wait until the end of the semester and entertain speculations about the projected analyses of all the theorists at once.

This edition includes an on-line student guide. Students can access it at my Web site which also contains others links: http://www.wiu.edu/users/mfbpa/bemjr.html The guide contains hints at where to focus study efforts, practice multiple choice items and links to relevant web sites.

These suggestions for using the manual chapter sections and the Estella Monroe chapter are just that, suggestions. Any of the activities can be changed to fit your own personal orientation. Your own creativity is more important than any suggestions I might make. You may want to use manual activity write-ups as stimuli to help you conjure up your own activities.

Adopters of *Personality Theories* are encouraged to use the activities included in this manual for the sake of enriching classroom experiences. Those who do use the activities should feel free to contact the text author with reports of particularly interesting experiences or problems. Write Bem Allen, WIU, 110, Macomb, IL 61455, or use e-mail: mfbpa@wiu.edu . That you are happy with the text and this manual means a great deal to me. I'll help you in any way I can.

Preface: Multiple Choice Test Item Bank

Not long ago I presided over a workshop on writing effective multiple choice items. Among the themes that emerged from the workshop was the necessity and the difficulty of writing plausible incorrect alternatives for items. It requires a great deal of thought and work, but it can be done if a simple rule of reiterative learning is followed: both within and between theories, ideas of theorists are compared and contrasted, so that differences and similarities are discerned. Each alternative for an item is either a correct statement about whatever theorist is featured in the main body of the item, a statement about the theorist that is incorrect or not consistent with the main body, or a statement about another theorist. A constraint on this method is that there must be clearly only one correct alternative among those offered to students for consideration. There are, by the way, four alternatives per item. "All of the above," "none of the above," and "both a and b" are never used. These devices lower the number of legitimate alternatives and confuse students. Finally, while "which one of the following is not [something or other]" is not used, for some items students are asked to pick out an alternative that is an exception in some way. Use of these items allows the presentation of correct information in more than one alternative and requires students to discriminate between correct and incorrect information. Items of this sort are phrased (for example) "All except one of the following are among Freud's psychosexual stages. Which is *NOT* among Freud's psychosexual stages?" (note that "not" is emphasized). In this way, students are told exactly what the question requires, and are reminded twice that an exception is sought, rather than being confronted with a single unemphasized "not."

Testing should be a learning experience, not just an opportunity to evaluate students. Typical multiple choice tests usually include only one bit of correct information per item: the single correct alternative. In contrast, this file includes many items that contain correct information in the main body of the question as well as in more than one alternative. Throughout the test bank, students are reminded of differences and similarities among theories, because alternatives of a question addressing one theory may contain several correct statements about other theories. Again, this is a reiterative learning approach. However, even when several theories are mentioned in an item, students can still respond correctly if they possess information concerning the theory featured in the main body of the item, but not the others mentioned. Just the same, it will be easier for students, and more edifying, if they can remember how other theorists' ideas contrast with the idea that is the focus of the item.

Another property of these items is that they are relatively free of cues allowing students to respond on the basis of other than knowledge of text materials. I have, for example, been careful to avoid revealing information in one item that will give away the answer to another item, over-use a given alternative ("c"), and making the correct alternative typically the longest one. Also, except for a rare attempts at humor (it keeps students awake during tests), I have tried to make all alternatives serious candidates for selection by students.

As this is the fourth edition, items left over from the earlier editions have been "battle tested." Left-over items that have proven good discriminators between students who did well and students who did poorly on tests were retained. Other left-over items were rewritten to eliminate problems and still others were deemed inadequate and dropped. Lessons learned from the earlier files were applied to this file.

The fourth edition test item bank includes an "Extra Items" section. Thus, there are now 100 or more items covering each theorist-chapter. The new items are added at the end of the main item file. A chapter's new items cover issues found in all parts of the chapter (i.e., these item sections are comprehensive). Because they span whole chapters, new items can be used for make-up and final exams, preserving the other items for during-the-semester-tests. By the way, new items tend to cover broader, more global issues, rather than specific concepts. They fit the "critical thinking" mold better than typical multiple choice items.

Preface

A computerized version of this test bank is available that will allow you to choose exactly the items you wish to use and print them out (contact your Allyn and Bacon representative). Alternatively, if you wish to copy items from this manual, I've made it as easy for you as I possibly could. Each item is labeled in the right margin with the chapter designation and the item number (e.g., 12.23, for chapter 12, item number 23). Also, the number for the text-page from which the item is drawn appears just below the chapter-designation/item number. These numbers will not mean anything to students and will not give away answers (answers are separately listed at the end of each file).Thus, you can copy whole pages (items are *NOT* split across pages), cut and paste if need be, and renumber to the left of each item.

There are now a total of more than 1700 items, plenty for as many as ten tests and a final (consistent with my belief that tests are a learning experience, I have given up to ten tests per class during most of my career). If you give ten 50 item tests and a 50 item final, you will use only about one-third of the file. Obviously, you have a large number of items to choose from so that you will be able to select only items with which you feel comfortable. To put it another way, if you do not like some items in the file, forget them; there are plenty more to choose from.

I expect that this test bank will help you teach students about theories of personality and provide you with a accurate evaluation of their knowledge. If you have any comments about it, or the text, please write or email me at Western Illinois University, Psychology 110, Macomb, IL 61455; mfbpa@wiu.edu. More generally, please consider steering your students to my web page which they can find at (www.) wiu.edu/users/mfbpa/bemjr.html. There they will find links to everything they may want to know about personality or about psychology. One of the links is to a free student guide. BPA

Appendix: Film-Video List

Edifying and enjoyable videos or films featuring the major personality theorists and their ideas are difficult to find. Most of them were deceased before cameras that record video were readily available. While all of them lived into the motion picture era, few were professionally filmed. Nevertheless, because I collect ads for videos and films, and have made good use of some leads and my long distance telephone service, I have been able to locate several excellent media presentations for your possible use. There are enough so that you can feature two or three videos/films per section of the course (unit covering some number of chapters), even if you divide the course into several sections. Each selected video/film is briefly described in the appendix and an address where you can contact the distributor is provided. Where possible, a toll free telephone number is also included.

Chapter 1

Introduction

Chapter Outline

Preliminary Definition of Personality

  IMPLICATIONS AND CAUTIONS

Methods of Studying Personality

  THE CASE STUDY METHOD

  THE CORRELATIONAL METHOD

  THE EXPERIMENTAL METHOD

Personality Tests: Personologists' Tools

  RELIABILITY AND VALIDITY

  PROJECTIVE AND OBJECTIVE TESTS

Testing and Theorizing About Personality in a World of Human Diversity

A Final Word About "Science"

Chapter Sections

  INTRODUCTORY STATEMENT

  THE PERSON: BIOGRAPHIES

  VIEW OF THE PERSON: GENERAL PHILOSOPHICAL ORIENTATION

  BASIC CONCEPTS: THE HEART AND SOUL OF A THEORY

  EVALUATION: PLACING A THEORY IN PERSPECTIVE

Occasional Sections

Conclusion Section

E-mail Interaction (Section)

Summary Points

Essay/Critical Thinking Questions

E-mail Interaction

Objectives

1. Understand the preliminary definition of personality.

2. Be able to compare and contrast the three methods of studying personality and know the value of case histories.

3. Know the difference between reliability and validity and between projective and objective tests.

4. Be able to discuss the advantages and limitations of the scientific approach.

5. Know the rationale for the various chapter sections including those on diversity.

Classroom Discussion: Beyond the Text and the Lecture

1. There is no better way to start a personality theories class than to consider the question, "What is personality?" Have students offer popular definitions of personality and their own personal definitions. Ask them to relate their definitions to the preliminary definition. It will also be interesting to examine popular notions of personality, such as what is meant by "She has a good personality." What do people mean when they say that someone has a "disturbed" (or sick) personality? Can personalities be immature and mature? Simple and complex? Is personality mostly conscious or mostly unconscious (whatever students choose, ask them to provide experiential evidence to support their positions). To end the discussion, ask students to pose important questions about personality that may be answered during the semester.

2. Discuss some correlations: a positive correlation between head size and the climate/geographical region in which people are born and reared (the hotter the region, the bigger the head size); a positive relationship between being female and doing well in elementary school that turns to a negative relationship by high school; a positive correlation between physiological arousal and task performance that turns negative when arousal rises above a moderately high level; a positive correlation between how long one can resist an eyeblink and how much pain one can tolerate; and others you undoubtedly can concoct. Have students attempt to explain these correlations. Do they imply causation? Are they merely happenstance? Are there "third variables" that may explain these relationships?

3. What is diversity and why do we study it? To answer the first part of the question, have students turn to the Introductory chapter of the text and discuss the definition of diversity found there. To help answer the second part of the question--both parts will be more fully answered as students read the text--try the "Who in the world is here?" exercise. Ask each student to indicate her or his ethnic background. Most students will know whether they are of Native American, Mexican, German, English, Italian, African, Chinese, Indian (or other) heritage, or, more likely, a combination of the several heritages. This exercise has two main pedagogical strengths: (1) students will become aware of their ethnicity and, thus, be primed for discussions on diversity; and (2) students will be covertly told that everyone is a part of diversity (one of two primary principles of diversity; the other being no group has sole rights to the label "oppressed"). You can expand this discussion by asking students to identify their major sources of identity, which would include gender and sexual orientation, as well as ethnicity and anything else they may wish to mention. You can also have them go to my web page (see Preface) and, under the link "Multicultural" lookup their own ethnic group(s).

Classroom Exercises: Practical Applications

1. An exercise I have used in class for years is a favorite of students. I first ask students to pick a public figure with whom all students will be familiar. Examples used in recent years are President Clinton, sports figure Michael Jordan, Malcolm X, and TV personality Oprah.

Next, invite students to select, one at a time, behavioral dimensions along which to place behaviors of the chosen public figure. For example, "conscientiousness" might be selected and Oprah placed at the sixth scale point near the "high conscientiousness" end of a seven point scale. "Self-centered/other-centered" might be selected next, and so forth until the public figure's behavior is located on about six dimensions. Align each successive dimension on the blackboard under the preceding one. Stress that for each dimension, the figure's behavior is placed to one extreme or the other only if she or he shows consistent behavior on the dimension. Also, remind students that only when a person displays consistent behavior assigned to a point near one end or the other of a dimension can that person be said to have the trait corresponding to the point (Oprah would have the trait "highly conscientious").

Finally, draw a line from the selected point on the top most dimension to the point on the next lowest dimension, and so forth until a line connecting all selected dimensional points has been completed. This is the "personality profile" line for the public figure and is a graphic representation of that person's personality. Stress that no person's personality is so simple as to be specifiable on such a small number of dimensions; simplification is necessary in a classroom demonstration.

Point out to students that many people in the room share a given trait with the public figure, but, given enough dimensions, no two people would have exactly the same personality profile. This reminder should lead students to discuss the uniqueness of each individual's personality.

2. Develop a personality test in class. First, have students select a trait or type for assessment. For example, "shyness"

Chapter 1

might be selected. Then have students propose items for their "shyness" scale. "I rarely look people in the eye" scored on a seven point agree-disagree scale, would be an example. After, say, twenty or thirty items have been selected, discuss with students how the validity of the new scale might be established (does it correlate well with existing shyness scales?; does it discriminate well between people nominated by peers as especially shy versus nominees who are especially outgoing?). How would reliability be established (e.g., administer the scale to the same people twice and correlate across administrations)? When I carried out this exercise a number of years ago, the students' scale, composed during a single class session, showed high reliability and was embarrassingly, highly related to established scales.

Suggested Readings for Lecture Support

Perry, W., Sprock, J., Schaible, D., McDougall, A., Minassian, A., Jenkins, M., & Braff, D. Amphetamine on Rorschach measures in normal subjects. *Journal of Personality Assessment,* 1995, 64, 456-465.

This is the article used in the text to demonstrate experimental procedures. By consulting it, you could provide more detail than could be included in the text and, thereby, help students develop a better grasp of how to do an experiment.

Allen, B. P. *Coping with Life in the 21st Century.* New York: Writer's Club Press, 2001.

The first chapter of this book debunks "common sense." Because students may use common sense to understand personality, they may need the information in this brief section. It also contains a discussion of "good" and "bad" critics of research.

Suggested Readings for the Student

Lilienfeld, S. O., Wood, J. M., & Garb, H. N. What's wrong with this picture? SCIENTIFIC AMERICAN, 2000 (May), 81-87.

This popular press article is about the failure of projective tests to show reasonable reliability and validity. It is a palatable way to learn about these concepts and the mysterious Rorschach and TAT tests.

Lesko, W. A. *Readings in social psychology: General, classic, and contemporary selections (2nd Ed.).* Boston: Allyn & Bacon, 1994.

The introductory section of this recent book contains three papers that deal with issues related to science and the use of statistics. One is about lying with statistics, a second concerns the "science" in social science, and the third relates to bias in the subject samples typically employed by psychological researchers.

The Psychoanalytic Legacy: Sigmund Freud

Chapter Outline

Freud, the Person

Freud's View of the Person

Basic Concepts: Freud

PERSONALITY STRUCTURE: THREE INTERACTING
SYSTEMS

FIVE STAGES OF PERSONALITY DEVELOPMENT

A BASIC DIVERSITY ISSUE: FREUD'S VIEW OF
FEMALES

Evaluation

CONTRIBUTIONS

SUPPORTING EVIDENCE: OLDER AND MORE
CURRENT

LIMITATIONS

CONCLUSION

Summary Points

Essay/Critical Thinking Questions

Email Interaction

Objectives

1. Know the evolution of Freud's thought and the reasons
he became one of the greats of the twentieth century.

2. Become familiar with Freud's personality structures.

3. List and discuss Freud's five stages of personality development and be familiar with his famous case histories.

4. Be able to discuss Freud's theoretical notions about females and the apparent emotions behind them.

5. Understand the basic criticisms of Freud's theory and therapy, including the controversies surrounding his famous case histories.

Classroom Discussion: Beyond the Text and the Lecture

1. Freud was shaped by the era during which his ideas took shape, the Victorian Period. Describe that epoch briefly for students: the time of British Queen Victoria was marked by sexual repression, as illustrated by euphemistic language such as "limb" for "leg" because the latter was too risqué. Ask students how that time differs from now. Probe to get them to see that sexual problems would have been prominent then, relative to now. But are sexual problems of no importance now? What is the difference between the handling of such problems then and now? Perhaps this discussion will give students a taste of the criticism that Freudian theory is out-of-date.

2. Students will have fun and inform themselves by considering Freud's oral-aggressive and oral receptive types. Have them look up the text descriptions of these types and come up with illustrations of people they have known who fit these profiles (caution them not to use names or refer to anyone other class members are likely to know, except public figures or fictional people, such as TV characters). An exploration of anal-retentive and anal-expulsive types could be even more interesting. Bring up the Odd Couple TV series that most students have probably seen in re-runs and the recent sequel to the original movie. How do these types, in the extreme, become significant "pains in the backside" for many of us. Such topics as "put-down artists," gullibility, compulsive neatness and orderliness, and extreme messiness and disorderliness should come up. Get ready for laughter and chagrin.

3. Over the years, I've found that women students can get pretty upset with Freud. He seems "to get" females coming and going: identify and become feminine, that is what

8

you're supposed to do, but then you take on neurotic traits; identify less completely, become relatively masculine, adopt high achievement orientation, succeed, than be accused of "pursuing masculine power." What do the women in your class think about Freud's view of females? Maybe you can find some students who will defend Freud and some who will oppose him (the latter may be males). A lively discussion will ensue (I know; I've tried it).

Classroom Exercises: Practical Applications

1. Would some male student be willing to play Sigmund Freud and some female student be willing to play Phyllis Freud? If so, have them train themselves in the orientation of these two "theorists." Then have them field questions from other students about their "theories." It should be amusing and should allow students to etch Freud's masculine perspective in bold relief, as it would surely appear when seen in contrast to Phyllis' feminine perspective.

2. After students have read Freud's famous cases (Box 2.1), but before they have a chance to read "revisiting Freud's famous cases" (Box 2.3), have them attempt to critique Freud's interpretations of those cases (you will probably have to tell them to read only through the discussion of psychosexual stages). You may have to give them some hints, such as "What evidence do you think that Freud had to support his interpretations?" or, more specifically, "How could Freud be sure that Anna O was cured by psychoanalysis?" In general, try to get students to indicate what kind of evidence would be sufficient to support Freud's interpretations. If they can, it may become evident to them that Freud did not have the requisite evidence.

3. Analyze some dreams in class. Ask students to provide some concocted dreams or "dreams of a friend" (it may be best to discourage students from presenting their own real dreams; the public analysis may be embarrassing). You may wish to add dreams that you have read about or that have been related to you by people you know. After a dream has been described, have students suggest which Freudian notions are hidden in the dream in symbolic form. You may wish to have students look at Table 2.3 for some guidance, but they should not be limited to just the Freudian dream symbols. Do the symbols in a given dream have

universal meaning--the same for all people--or are they peculiar to the particular person who had the dream? Lively debates should occur.

Suggested Readings for Lecture Support

MacMillan, M. *Freud Evaluated.* London: MIT Press, 1997.

Here is the most thorough examination of Freud and his ideas ever done. Freud's supporters should read it in order to counter the attacks on Freud. Those who have doubts about Freud will resonate to it.

Esterson, A. *Seductive mirage: An exploration of the work of Sigmund Freud.* New York: Open Court, 1993.

Esterson's book raises some powerful questions about Freud and his theory. By taking a good look at each of them, you can present students with much richer detail on the controversies surrounding Freud than was possible in the text.

Suggested Readings for the Student

Freud, S. *Three case histories.* New York: Collier, 1963.
Freud is not a light read for anybody, but if there are any of his works that can be handled with relative ease by students, it is his description of three of his most famous cases.

Benjamin, L. T. & Dixon, D. N. Dream analysis by mail: An American woman seeks Freud's advice, *American Psychologist,* 1996, 51, 461-468.
This case and the history behind it is very fascinating. The case itself will be intrinsically interesting to students. More importantly, it shows the best side of Freud.

Chapter 3

Personality's Ancestral Foundation: Carl Jung

Chapter Outline

Jung: The Person

Jung's View of the Person

Basic Concepts: Jung

CONSCIOUSNESS AND UNCONSCIOUSNESS

ARCHETYPES

DREAMS AS MESSAGES FROM A WISE

 UNCONSCIOUS

PERSONALITY TYPOLOGY

PERSONALITY DEVELOPMENT

Evaluation

CONTRIBUTIONS

LIMITATIONS

Conclusion

Summary Points

Running Comparison

Essay/Critical Thinking Questions

Email Interaction

Objectives

1. Learn how mystical experiences and contact with Freud laid an early foundation for Jung's unconventional ideas.

2. Be able to compare the personal unconscious and collective unconscious with Freud's conception of the unconscious and to outline the central role of archetypes.

3. Understand the nature of archetypes and be able to describe archetypes that are central to Jung's theory. Also consider the Japanese archetypes (Table 3.1).

4. Become familiar with Jung's typology--the combination of introversion/extraversion and the four psychological functions--and his notions about personality development.

5. Understand the Myers Briggs Type Indicator (MBTI) functions (Box 3.3). Know the problems with Jung's central notions (especially the case of the Sun Phallus man) and the lasting contributions attributed to him.

Classroom Discussion: Beyond the Text and the Lecture

1. You are likely to have several students who are to be big horror movie fans. They may be willing--perhaps for "extra credit"--to rent some of their favorite movies and scan them so that they can locate clips for in-class viewing that illustrate various Jungian archetypes. Alternatively, you could assign students one or more of the movies listed in the text, have them rent the movies and scan them for clips that illustrate archetypes. Still another possibility is to devote a class period to showing a movie that you know to be rich with Jungian archetypical imagery.

2. A contrast of Little Hans and Little Anna will be enjoyable and educational for students. First, have students provide details of the two cases, one at a time, without any analysis. Recording key events on the board may be helpful. Next, analyze each case as it was originally done. Finally, switch analyses: do Little Anna according to Freud and Little Hans according to Jung. If the students do not mention it, point out how Freud dwelled on sexual interpretations and Jung avoided them.

3. What personas do students have? Have individual students indicate what masks they put on periodically. As each student speaks, list their personas on the blackboard. After all those who wish to speak have done so, tally the personas to see which are most popular, then discuss why

the most popular ones are so frequently donned. Finally, initiate a discussion on how and why a person may become one of his or her personas (the professor, her text; the tenor, his voice).

Classroom Exercises: Practical Applications

1. The exercise defined in Box 3.3 could be carried out in class. Have students, by reference to the text, come up with descriptions of people who would fit each of the possible combinations of introversion/extraversion with the several psychological functions. Write these combinations on the blackboard, along with students' consensus description of each combination. Then have each student tell why she or he fits best into one of the eight categories (in a large class you may want to take a random sample of students for the purpose of reporting reasons for self-classification, followed by a tally of the number of students falling into each of the categories). For a more structured exercise, go through my web site, to the "Personality" link, to the "Personality Tests" link (Keirsey Temperament Sorter). You could take the MBTI yourself and discuss the print-out with the class or have some students take it and bring their print-outs to class for discussion (your counseling department will have it). I have participated in an exercise employing those materials and find that participants are quite taken with the uniqueness of each person.

2. Extraversion/introversion is Jung's best known concept and central to his theory. It is also a notion with which students are likely to be familiar. Lead them in writing a set of personality test items that would differentiate between introverts and extraverts. Each proposed item could be rated on a seven-point true-of-me/not-true-of-me scale:

"I prefer to be alone with my thoughts most of the time."

true of me __ __ __ __ __ __ __ not true of me

After there has been general agreement on a set of items, have students discuss the picture of the introvert and extravert that is reflected in the items. Is this portrait true to

Jung's concepts? Is it more a picture of popular notions about the personality dichotomy than a rendering of Jung's ideas? Revision may result from this discussion. Should more involvement be desired, have the items typed into a questionnaire, duplicated, and given to students. They will be intrigued by knowledge of how they scored on their own scale.

3. Lead students in a search for additional archetypes, beyond the ones mentioned in the text. There are a number of universal experiences for which archetypes could be conceived. Is there an archetype for God? For heaven? For hell? For war? For death? For sickness? For joy? For hatred? For friendship? For romantic love? You can think of other possibilities. The point is to have students contemplate experiences that have been common to humans since they emerged from Africa. Coming up with symbols for the archetypes they select should be interesting to students. Clasped hands for friendship? A skull for death? A heart for romantic love? This may be an exercise that you may want to outline in class one day and carry out on another day, so that students have time to think and to browse through books and magazines.

Suggested Readings for Lecture Support

Don, N. W. "The Rhine-Jung letters: Distinguishing parapsychological from synchronistic events": Comments. *Journal of Parapsychology*, 1999, 63,184-185.

Jung's parapsychology is compared with that of parapsychology guru, J. B. Rhine.

Noll, R. *The Jung cult: Origins of a charismatic movement.* Princeton, N J: Princeton University Press, 1994.

Noll's powerful book can inspire a serious consideration of Jungian theory, just as early criticisms of Freud put a hole in the Freudian dam that is now threatening to become a gaping orifice. You can also pick up much interesting information from this book that will fascinate students; for example, Noll covers many little known facts about Jung's childhood.

Suggested Readings for the Student

Jung, C. G. *Flying saucers, a modern myth of things seen in the skies.* (R.F.C. Hull, Trans.) Princeton, New Jersey: Princeton University Press, 1978.

Students are fascinated by the possibility of life on another planet. In fact, as Carl Sagan likes to say, odds are there is intelligent life out there. Jung's theorizing about the meaning of sightings will be interesting to students.

Iaccino, J. F. *Psychological Reflections on cinematic terror: Jungian archetypes in horror films.* London: Praeger, 1994.

This book is an encyclopedia of horror movies. Aside from covering Jung's archetypes, it is an edifying and interesting review of horror films.

Overcoming Inferiority and Striving for Superiority: Alfred Adler

Chapter Outline

Adler, The Person

Adler's View of the Person

Basic Concepts: Adler

DEVELOPING SOCIAL FEELING: SOCIETY, WORK, AND LOVE

STYLE OF LIFE

FUTURE GOALS VERSUS PAST EVENTS

OVERCOMING INFERIORITY

STRIVING FOR SUPERIORITY AND THE SUPERIORITY COMPLEX

FAMILY INFLUENCES ON PERSONALITY

DEVELOPMENT

Evaluation

CONTRIBUTIONS

LIMITATIONS

Conclusion

Summary Points

Running Comparison

Essay/Critical Thinking Questions

Email Interaction

Objectives

Chapter 4

1. Know the events in Adler's early life that not only shaped his personality but also his theory.

2. Be able to state in detail the meanings of Adler's central ideas, social interest and style of life.

3. Understand the relationship between Adler's notions about inferiority, superiority, and compensation.

4. Understand what early recollections really mean, in contrast to mere memories.

5. Consider the controversies surrounding Adler's "birth order." What is the current status of birth order and Adlerianism.

Classroom Discussion: Beyond the Text and the Lecture

1. In many ways, Adler became the mirror image of Freud. A discussion of how the two differed can sharpen students' conceptions of both. Point out that, whereas Jung greatly deemphasized sexualism, Adler virtually eliminated that pillar of Freud's thought altogether. What broad form of motivation did Adler substitute? How did the two see childhood problems differently?

A good topic to get into in this context is sibling rivalry. You could explore how Adler's birth order and "parental over-indulgence" (see Box 4.1) notions relate to sibling rivalry. How would spoiled and neglected siblings get along? Also, have students compare Adler's ideas on this topic with those of the evolutionary theorist (see box 4.2).

2. Discuss the relevance of the Frankenstein story, preferably before the students have had a chance to read about it, and the Adlerian analysis of it. First, you may want class members to provide each other with accurate details of the story. They may want to talk about how Shelley's story differs from the Hollywood versions. Perhaps you could get one class member to read the story early in the semester so that she or he can serve as the "resident expert." You could assume that role if no student wants it. Once the facts are sorted out, you can proceed with an Adlerian analysis.

Emphasize Frankenstein's early life and contrast it with his life away from home. Highlight the reasons he created the monster, the monster's own needs and strivings, and the relationship between the two beings. This discussion can be a way to make Adler's point of view come alive.

3. Discuss birth order experiences. Every class member has thought about the impact of the presence or absence of siblings, and, if they have siblings, each has considered her or his position among siblings. After years of talking about birth order with students, I find that many take this Adlerian idea very seriously, maybe too seriously. Almost without fail, at least a few students will come up to talk with me after a discussion of birth order. They tend to be either disturbed about their birth position or blithely confident that it has shaped their personalities.

Perhaps you should begin with testimonials from students concerning their birth positions and what impact, if any, they feel it has had on their lives. Of course, only-children and last-borns should have their say as well. Are they spoiled? Are first-borns higher in achievement motivation? Are later-borns more adventurous and higher in risk taking? Note where gender differences between a student and her or his siblings makes a difference. Inquire about the significance of spacing of children. If, for example, a person's only sibling is ten years older, is that person equivalent to a first-born? Consider discussing the study of birth order longitudinally and contextually versus studying it cross-sectionally and universally.

Classroom Exercises: Practical Applications

1. Do an Early Recollections (ERs) exercise. In class, have students first conjure up an ER and anonymously record a brief summary of it on notebook paper. Then ask students to indicate whether they would allow their responses to be read in class. A simple "yes" or "no" recorded in the upper right-hand corner of response-sheets would be sufficient.

Let me suggest that you not read example responses without examining them first. Take them home and screen them. Find the most interesting ones, and from that pool, select those that could be read without revealing the identity of the writer. Also, eliminate those that might generate embarrassment either in the writer or in other class members. The remaining set should be fascinating and edifying.

It is important to bring out the relevance of the ERs to the current styles of life of students. What can you assume about the goals and direction of movement of a student based on her or his summary? How does a student's ER relate to the three great problems of life, society, work and love? In general, indicate how an ER is more relevant to "now" than to the time the event in the recollection occurred.

2. Develop a scale to measure Social Interest. The text, at the beginning of the Basic Concepts section, provides information concerning what issues should be assessed. Capacity to develop and maintain friendships is very important to Social Interest. One scale item might be "How many close friends do you have, people to whom you can and do bare your soul?"

--   --   --   --   --   --   --

1   2   3   4   5   6   7

none to 1 2-3 4-5 6-8 9-10 11 12 or more

Another item might assess length of friendship relationships: "On average, how long, in months, have your friendships lasted?" The scale would be similar to that above, but varying between three months and 60 months in intervals that increase in length as above.

Another set of items would assess cooperative spirit. A sample is: "What percentage of the time do you use 'we' instead of 'I' or 'me' in reference to activities that you share with others?" followed by a seven point scale with percentages varying from 15 to 90 (or other set).

In a similar manner, guide students in selecting items relating to work (time invested in work, involvement in work, cooperative spirit shown during work) and love (concern for partner relative to self, time spent meeting partner's needs, dedication to child-rearing). After the scale is completed, you may or may not want to run-off a formal questionnaire and administer it to students. Most of the educational benefits will derive from constructing the scale. Students should come away from that task with a deeper and more lasting understanding of Social Interest.

3. Design a program for losing weight using Carlson's neo-Adlerian methods that are covered in the text under "Adlerian therapy: A going and growing concern." A first step would be to elicit ERs from the client. Knowing what kind of person is seeking help seems essential. Because Adlerian therapy is flexible and

eclectic, methods used to facilitate successful dieting would be different for different clients.

Bearing that caveat in mind, the students might be asked to suggest what first step should the client be encouraged to take. If they need help, perhaps you could suggest that the client might write down reasons for dieting and keep them available for handy reference when the urge to eat between meals becomes strong. What else could the client do to avoid eating other than low-fat, sugar-free, low-calorie foods only at meal times. A suggestion from Carlson's case history is to avoid places where snacking often occurs. Better still, where possible, instruct the client to keep snacks out of his or her living space. Also useful to the client may be relaxation procedures, instructions on more effective use of social support ("Tell friends what you are trying to accomplish and talk to them often about it."), and periodic self-efficacy checks ("On a 100 point percentage-scale, what is the likelihood that you will be able to avoid eating candy today?").

Because students may take this exercise personally, you may want to remind them that they should suggest that "the client" initiate an exercise program. Also, you may be wise to indicate that, if dieting is to have a chance to succeed in the long run, "the client" should resign herself or himself to a life-time of healthy eating and exercising.

Suggested Readings for Lecture Support

Zweigenhaft, R. L. & Von Ammon J. Birth order and civil disobedience: A test of Sulloway's "born to rebel" hypothesis. *The Journal of Social Psychology*, 2000, 140, 624-627.

This straightforward article shows that there are at least some birth order hypotheses that prove out. Also, students will be interested in this student protest article.

Allen, B. P. *Coping With Life In The 21st Century*. New York: Writers' Club Press, 2001

This text contains a chapter on friendship that could spur a strong discussion of this aspect of social interest. It's chapter on romantic love is also applicable. Both strongly take gender into account.

Suggested Readings for the Student

tape. Suggest to students that they check at local video/audio tape rental stores.

Sulloway, F. J. *Born to Rebel: Birth Order, family Dynamics, and Creative Lives.* N. Y., N. Y.: Vintage Books, 1997.

Here's the latest on birth order, a subject that fascinates students.

Chapter 5

Moving Toward, Away From, and Against Others: Karen Horney

Chapter Outline

Horney, The Person

Horney's View of the Person

Basic Concepts: Horney

BASIC ANXIETY: INFANTILE HELPLESSNESS IN A PARENTAL WORLD

COPING BY WAY OF TEN NEUROTIC NEEDS

MOVING TOWARD, AGAINST, AND AWAY FROM PEOPLE

DEVELOPING AN IDEALIZED VERSUS A REAL IMAGE OF SELF

A BASIC DIVERSITY ISSUE: THE PSYCHOLOGY OF WOMEN

Evaluation

CONTRIBUTIONS

LIMITATIONS

Conclusion

Summary Points

Running Comparison

Essay/Critical Thinking Questions

Objectives

1. Learn how Karen Horney's struggles to be "ahead of her time" shaped her personality and created early emotional difficulties.

2. Be able to outline Horney's disagreements with Freud, particularly those relating to his treatment of women.

3. Become familiar with Horney's basic anxiety, neurotic needs, and basic orientations to people as well as the extreme personality manifestations associated with them. Indicate how controllers fit into this framework.

4. Understand Horney's "self" and the concepts surrounding it, including those, such as compartmentalization and cynicism, relating to problems of self-conception. Contrast her view of jealousy with that of the evolutionary theorists.

5. Appreciate Horney's contributions to the modern understanding of jealousy, her pioneering work in the psychology of women, and her novel therapeutic technique, self-analysis.

Classroom Discussion: Beyond the Text and the Lecture

1. This is a good place for a thorough-going discussion of the psychology of women and Freud's treatment of females. Horney believed that Freud's theory, written by a man for men, was often inappropriately applied to women. Induce the students to indicate points of contention between Freud and Horney: on penis envy; on women's alleged biological deficiency; on "Mother's" responsibility for that deficiency; on competitiveness among women; on reasons for clitoral stimulation; on women's "frigidity"; on women's alleged submissiveness and masochism; and on Freud's Oedipus complex and his neglect of culture.

2. The "tyranny of the shoulds" is one of Horney's most creative and useful ideas. It predates Albert Ellis' "musturbation" and related ideas. Students will profit from considering their own tyrannies.

To initially take the discussion out of the potentially embarrassing domain of personal reflection, adopt a general orientation: talk about the "shoulds" that are prominent parts of students' cultures. Here is an opportunity to point out differences in the dictates of the different cultures represented in your class.

Have students list these "shoulds" (perhaps you will want to write them on the blackboard). Do more of them apply to women than to men? Are many of them quite illogical, even ridiculous? After this thawing of the ice, you could heat up the discussion further by suggesting that some students may want to indicate which "shoulds" are particularly problematic for them. A productive way to end the session is to elicit suggestions as to how the chains of these tyrannies might be broken.

3. To better understand Horney's extreme manifestations of her movement orientations--self-effacing, expansive, and resigned--students could conjure up some examples from their experience and report them to the rest of the class. First, of course, remind students that they should not mention any names or provide other identifying information. A good rule is limiting selections to some examples from among people who students knew in the distance past. Most students will have known a self-effacing person: someone who would humiliate him- or herself endlessly in order to give "all the credit" to a person in their lives they could not stand to lose. They will have also known (probably several) "controllers." Finally, some of them are likely to have known one of those volatile individuals who is obsessed with *not* being controlled and with "calling their own shots."

Classroom Exercises: Practical Applications

Chapter 5

1. Have students do a "What's Your Orientation?" exercise. Ask them to pick the four entries best from Table 5.1 that fit them. Make it forced choice: they must choose 4, not less or more. If three of their choices fit one of the orientations, they may cautiously consider that orientation to be their own. Ask them to give you their choices on notebook paper, sans names. You could tally their choices on the blackboard, but you may want to take them home and think about them so that you can be maximally sensitive to students' feelings. In any case, are any of the ten neurotic needs chosen by at least a simple majority? If not, is any one clearly chosen more than the others? Do the three most chosen needs fit one of the orientation patterns? If so, what accounts for this group orientation? Is it that the respondents are college students? Predominantly female (or male)? Mostly young (older) people? A lively discussion should follow.

2. Have the students each choose an attachment style from the three listed in Box 5.3. Urge them to write down their choice so that you can be reasonably sure that they have actually made a selection. You may not, however, want to collect them. If you do collect choices, I suggest that anonymity be preserved. To replicate Shaver's research, tally the number of choices of each of the three styles.

   Next, consider the implications of each style for adult interpersonal relations, perhaps emphasizing romantic relations. What parental practices contribute to developing the secure style and each of the two insecure styles? Is there hope for adults who seem locked into one of the insecure styles? Addressing these three points will generate a spirited discussion.

3. Have the students complete the Jealousy Scale in Box 5.3. I find that students are more fascinated with this scale than any other I have ever used in class, and I've administered many. Have each student calculate his or her individual score. If you want to calculate a class average (median for small classes), have them pass in their scores on an otherwise blank sheet.

Elicit comments from students concerning the experience of completing the scale. Did any items make them uncomfortable? Were any particularly true of individual class members? Any particularly false? Do any items reflect something in addition to or instead of jealousy? Which items best fit Horney's ideas about jealousy? By having students indicate both their scores on the scale and their chosen styles on the blank sheet, you could look at the relationship between the two responses. However, students can do the correlation individually by looking at their own chosen styles in relation to their scores on the scale, as indicated in the Box.

There is one problem with trying to relate style choices with Jealousy Scale responses: discussion of the Jealousy Scale responses alone may take up an entire class period by itself.

Suggested Readings for Lecture Support

Quinn, S. *A mind of her own: The life of Karen Horney.* New York: Addison-Wesley Publishing Co., 1988.

Horney, K. *Self analysis.* New York: Norton, 1942.

Horney, K. The unknown Karen Horney: Essays on gender, culture, and psychoanalysis. New Haven, CT: Yale University Press, 2000.

Horney, K. *Feminine Psychology.* New York: Norton, 1967.

Browsing through any or all of these books, written for popular consumption, would provide you with additional information that would be edifying and enjoyable to students.

Buss, D. M. & Schackelford, T. K. From vigilance to violence: Mate retention tactics in married couples. *Journal of Personality and Social Psychology*, 1997, 72, 346-361.

Chapter 5

This article will give you a good idea of the evolutionary theorists' point of view. A lot of psychologists do not like this position, but it is being taken very seriously. Thus, like it or not, it is a good idea to keep track of where it is going.

Suggested Readings for the Student

Horney, K. *The adolescent diaries of Karen Horney.* New York: Basic Books, 1980.

Seldom has a famous figure in psychology bared her or his soul as completely as has Horney in this delightful, little book. If your students are like most, either still in or just out of their teens, they will be especially enthralled by this book.

Horney, K. *Self analysis.* New York: Norton, 1942.

The case of Clair is summarized in the text, but space limitations forced exclusion of the rich detail contained in this book. *Self-analysis* also includes other case histories that will be easy and provocative reading for students.

Buss, D. M., Larsen, R., Westen, D. & Semmelroth, J. Sex differences in jealousy: Evolution, physiology, and psychology. *Psychological Science*, 1992, 3, 251-255.

Psychological Science is known for its short, pithy, and easy to read articles. This one will intrigue students, who tend to be fascinated with gender differences in jealousy orientation.

Personality From the Interpersonal Perspective:
Harry Stack Sullivan

Chapter Outline

Objectives

1. Appreciate how Sullivan's early experiences shaped the direction his career-path took and his philosophical orientation evolved. Consider why Sullivan was a remarkable example of human diversity.

2. Understand the interpersonal nature of Sullivan's theory and the importance of the relationship between significant others and the self.

Chapter 6

3. Learn the relationship between cognitive development (prototaxic, parataxic, and syntaxic) and emotional development (the evolution of interpersonal security during the six stages of development).

4. Become familiar with how anxiety plays a role in the learning process and in psychotherapy (psychiatric interview and therapy).

5. Know why Sullivan's training and personal problems gave him a fresh, objective point of view and, at the same time, limited his perspectives.

Classroom Discussion: Beyond the Text and the Lecture

1. "Be a good mother" is a social demand that plagues every adult woman who has children (see Box 6.2). First, you may want to examine the expectation of mothers in general. Are they reasonable? Are they as numerous and intense as those made on fathers? Can they ever be fully met? You may also want to examine differences in the demands made on mothers as a function of culture or ethnicity. Of course, you do not want to call on African-American, Latina, or other ethnic group members of the class to "represent their group" in expressing opinions on this matter. You may, however, have the courage to bring up stereotypes of "the Jewish mother," the mother's alleged control of family affairs in the African-American community, or the Mexican-American mother's alleged propensity to have many children and to invest her life solely in them.

Next, if class-time is not exhausted, ask students about how any mother could go wrong through over-use of forbidding gestures and through promoting the "bad mother" personification in her children. How can a mother, instead, promote interpersonal security and satisfy her children's need for tenderness? End on a positive note: help students draw some conclusions concerning what kind of mother would be a reasonable and non-suffocating primary parent who is encouraged to fulfill many other roles as well.

2. "Why is physical contact with a mothering one so important to all primates, including humans?" is probably a question requiring the wisdom of Solomon to answer, but at least you could address the manifestations of receiving or not receiving satisfaction of the need for contact.

A *Primetime* (ABC, June 3, 1993) segment featuring a special program for severely abused children reminded me of the power of positive contact with a mothering one and the fact that the person providing contact need not be the biological mother. For these children, forbidding gestures assumed a highly concrete and monstrous form (one child was tied to the top of the family auto which then was driven at high speed; another was sexual bait to attract boyfriends for her mother). It seemed that nothing would work to save these children who were so violent that one repeatedly attempted to burn everything down and another tried several times to kill its siblings. Yet, being constantly held and even bottle-fed by adult men and women brought most of these terribly disturbed children to normalcy.

Relaying these experiences to students can inspire them to look for other manifestations of need for contact. You may also pose several questions that will get students thinking about the importance of contact. Is it true that the best part of sex for women is being held? [As you may recall from the text, Philip Shaver thinks that women who feel this way may be people who are anxious ambivalent types.] Maybe it is more true for men! Will a waiter or waitress who touches a customer collect bigger tips than one who doesn't? (Yes they will, according to social psychological research). Is someone's willingness to touch you a sign that you are accepted? Is refusal to touch someone a sign of rejection? [Culture may be a factor: The apparent Korean custom to avoid touching a stranger, even when returning change from a grocery sale, caused a rift between Korean and African-American people in Chicago.] Can people become satiated regarding the touches of a particular person? (Couples do a lot of touching early in courtship but not so much later.) Hopefully students can come away from this discussion with an appreciation of how crucial is positive contact with a mothering one and how the need for contact carries over into adult life.

3. Sullivan was alleged to be schizophrenic. He was, of course, definitely a creative thinker. Is there a connection? As you know, there may be. A few minutes of browsing through abnormal psychology texts will turn up examples of art by psychotic artists. Must one be a little bit crazy to see what others cannot see, to conceive of notions that are beyond others, to penetrate the veil that enshrouds understanding of the human condition? Notice that many of the best comics are somewhat disturbed (e.g., Richard Pryor, Woody Allen, Jonathan Winters). A sixth sense with regard to human foibles may be the forte of the great comic.

Bringing up these points should elicit similar ones from students. You can lead them to the realization that being a little "crazy" brings with it an unusual perspective.

Classroom Exercises: Practical Applications

1. Do a personification exercise in the classroom context. Here are some examples of choices from which students may choose: good me, bad me, shy me, mischievous me, altruistic me, not me, worthless me, martyred me, maybe me. You and the students can add more. You may want to tally responses on the board: Students will likely be interested in which choices they share with other students. However, the greatest degree of involvement may come from having students indicate why they chose given alternative personifications. What experiences correspond to a choice?

2. The learning processes exercise in Box 6.3 will likely be intriguing and informative for students. Each student can complete the exercise by simply following instructions (you need not do more than say "do it"). As usual, you can tally results, but anonymity is essential. You may need to take the task home, because showing sensitivity to students feelings may require some contemplation of results.

Perhaps the safest way to elicit anecdotes concerning why students assigned high percentages to given categories of learning processes is to have students write down their stories anonymously. By being cautious you can get students to indicate reasons for their responses that will not reveal too much about themselves, more than they want to disclose. Perhaps you can suggest that student testimonials in class avoid reference to intimate relations, including relations with parents. For example, you would want to avoid testimonials like "I learned not to spy on my parents when they were undressed, because they whipped me with a belt once when I did it' (learn by anxiety process). Examples relating to elementary school experiences will be adequate and will likely avoid embarrassment.

Additional thought provoking questions include: "How many of you assigned at least 40% of your points to just one of the four categories?"; "How many of you had more points in one of the two classes of processes than in the other?" and "How many of you had just as many points in one of the positive categories as in one of the negative categories."

3. There is an exercise that would serve as a stimulating companion to discussion question number 3. You could do what a colleagues required of his students: each student had to complete a drawing as would a person with some kind of psychiatric disorder. It may be necessary that you preface this exercise with a brief description of some of the better known disorders. An alternative is to have students read an introductory psychology book-chapter on abnormal psychology. Of course, if your students are upper-level, this step will not be necessary.

Have the students do the pictures at their leisure and submit them to you before the Sullivan chapter is considered so that you will have time to inspect them before they are discussed in class. My colleague displayed his class' pictures in the halls of the psychology building where they were generally admired. Some of them were very interesting, probably much more interesting than would have been the case had they used their own "normal" perspective. A discussion of these pictures in class could form the basis for an understanding of "craziness and creativity."

Suggested Readings for Lecture Support

Sullivan, H. S. *The Interpersonal theory of psychiatry.* (H. S. Perry and M. L. Gawel, Eds.) New York: Norton, 1953.

This edited work is probably the best and most complete consideration of Sullivan's theory. You probably will not want to read it all--it is relatively short, but quite dense--but you may want to consult it to get a flavor of Sullivan's orientation and to scan it for examples to use in class.

Mullahy, P. *Oedipus, myth and complex.* New York: Grove Press, 1948.

Here is Sullivan clarified...and you, like me, may need clarification. Mullahy is the most accomplished interpreter of Sullivan.

Suggested Readings for the Student

Bower, B. Moods and the Muse: A new study reappraises the link between creativity and mental Illness. *Science News,* 1995, 147 (June, 17), 378-380.

This interesting piece examines the whole matter of madness and creativity. Although it turns out to be more complex than was originally assumed, this nicely written article makes the whole thing understandable and fascinating.

Harlow, H. F. & Harlow, M. K. Love in monkeys. *Scientific American,* 1959, 200, 68-74.

Here is Harlow's work summarized in popular style. This readable article will familiarize students with among the most basic and famous works in modern psychology.

Chapter 7

The Seasons of Our Lives: Erikson

Chapter Outline

Erikson, the Person

Erikson's View of the Person

FREUDIAN?

ON THE TASKS AND POLARITIES OF LIFE

Basic Concepts: Erikson

INFANCY: TRUST AND DISTRUST

EARLY CHILDHOOD: AUTONOMY VERSUS SHAME AND DOUBT

PLAY AGE: INITIATIVE VERSUS GUILT

SCHOOL AGE: INDUSTRY VERSUS INFERIORITY

ADOLESCENCE: IDENTITY VERSUS IDENTITY CONFUSION

YOUNG ADULTHOOD: INTIMACY VERSUS ISOLATION

MIDDLE ADULTHOOD: PRODUCTIVITY VERSUS FUTILITY

MATURE ADULTHOOD: GENERATIVITY VERSUS STAGNATION

OLD AGE: INTEGRITY VERSUS DESPAIR

Theoretical and Empirical Support for Erikson's point of view

LEVINSON: THE MIDLIFE CRISIS

SHEEHY: WOMEN ARE DIFFERENT

EMPIRICAL SUPPORT: RESEARCH CONFIRMING ERIKSON'S VIEW

Evaluation

Chapter 7
CONTRIBUTIONS

LIMITATIONS

Conclusions

Summary Points

Running Comparison

Essay/Critical Thinking Questions

Email Interaction

Objectives

1. Learn how Erikson overcame an early identity crisis and lack of academic credentials to serve in the Freudian camp and rise all the way to a professorship at Harvard.

2. Become familiar with Erikson's evolving view of women, his notions relating to sources of identity, his ideas about the psychosocial orientation and epigenesis, and his concept of "the favorable ratio."

3. Be able to outline Erikson's stages of development, including the polarities of each and the strengths associated with each.

4. Appreciate Levinson's and Sheehy's extrapolations from Erikson's theory regarding the "mid-life crisis."

5. Know the history of support for Erikson's theory, his lasting, general contributions and problems with his point of view, especially regarding the logic of his concepts.

Classroom Discussion: Beyond the Text and the Lecture

1. Erikson makes an interesting assertion as a part of his description of girls at the play age. Girls at this age are supposedly concerned about "being attractive." Students will find it interesting to consider just how early in life

females find themselves facing pressures to be pretty or beautiful. A recent TV essay concerning a certain ethnic group living in a virtually impenetrable compound showed girls as young as six years of age parading before a large audience dressed like adult women, complete with make-up. The alleged reason for this "style show" was to give adult members of families in the audience a chance to barter for the girls as mates for their boys (or men!). Needless to say, this discussion could get into "lookism," the word lovers of politically correct language sometimes use in reference to discrimination against women (and men) who do not "look good." Students may wish to get into how the pressure to "look good" affects and restricts women. Are men also subject to this kind of pressure (the research literature says, "yes")? Given they are, is the pressure on men as great as that exerted on women (the research literature suggests that pressure on men is not as great)?

2. Having students consider what their life-tasks are now and what they will become in one year, five years, ten years, and twenty years from now could be a source of insight for them. People in general, and perhaps young people in particular, tend not to project very far into the future. Imagining what life will be like ten years down the road can be scary. Yet to do so is to help ensure a better future. I once knew a student majoring in hotel management who predicted (correctly) that he would be a hotel restaurant manager within five years of having graduated and a hotel manager within ten years (he didn't get back to me on the ten year prediction).

In looking at life's task, you may even want students to be retrospective. Can they remember what it was like to be a pre-schooler, an elementary school child? You could have them cast their life tasks of the past, present, and future in Eriksonian terms. In any case, encourage students to refer to Erikson's ideas in discussing their life-tasks and, with regard to the future, ask them to take some risks. Urge them to think of their future lives as rather completely different from life now, perhaps even unpleasant at times. End with students conjuring up optimistic and productive futures that fit a more mature perspective than the one that guides them now.

3. "What is love?" is too tough a question to ask, even if "love" is confined to romantic love. It is, however, more feasible to ask the Eriksonian question, "How can you fuse your identity to someone else's without losing it?"

You may want to begin by asking students what it feels like to be "in love," romantically speaking. With enough testimonials, some relatively concrete conceptions of identity fusion will likely emerge. Does fusion with another threaten one's own unique and separate identity? Perhaps the analogy of the salad bowl as opposed to the melting pot, often used in the multicultural context, will be useful here. [Mixed paint, stew pot, and jazz band--doing your own thing while playing with others--are also useful metaphors.] In appropriate and healthy fusion, integration occurs, not assimilation. One meshes with another, like the cogs of a wheel with the gears that give it motion. One does not dissolve into another. Still, fusion with another is tricky business. Perhaps we lose a bit of ourselves whenever we give our hearts to another. Have students realize that one takes identity risks when she of he commits to another human being, but the chances one takes are well worth it.

Classroom Exercises: Practical Applications

1. Examining one's sources of identity may be a troubling task, but it will be enlightening. Have student's do the exercise in Box 7.2. This time, tallying responses for the class as a whole may not be fruitful. Instead, have volunteers tell why a particular source of identity was ranked high or low. Were there any important sources of identity left out (you could preface the whole exercise by telling students to add missing sources, *before* doing the ranking)? For example, heterosexual versus homosexual?

Some students may protest that it is not possible to decide between, for example, being male and being Mexican-American. You may find that some students adamantly refuse to place gender near the top of their ranking. If so, find a student who does place gender at the top and ask for his or her rationale. Students may be denying the truth if they give gender a low rank. If you dare, you might want to ask a student who ranked gender below the top, "would you give up being male (female) in order to retain the identity you have ranked at the top?" [A recent speaker at my university has his students imagine that they awaken one morning to find that they have become the other gender. Some just can not do it.] You may want to end with a discussion of how rankings may change over students' lives. In any case, be cautious. Dealing in identities can be explosive.

2. Resolution of identity crises at the various stages can be made more real. Have students look at previous and present stages--hopefully you will have at least some middle-aged people in class--and judge the degree to which they have resolved crises and attained strengths. To avoid disturbing conclusions individuals may make about themselves, provide them with the following caveats: (1) no one can reasonably conclude that they *absolutely* have or have not resolved the crises associated with given stages; strengths are also attained as a matter of degree; and (3) failures that may be perceived at the present time, whether regarding resolution or attaining strengths, do not mean that success in the future is unobtainable. End by asking students what they can do to deal with unresolved crises and unattained strengths.

3. Construct a scale for measuring the polarities of Erikson's stages by simply making the two extremes at each stage the anchors for seven point scales. An example would be

Initiative is acting on one's desires, urges, and potentials and *guilt* is the harness that restrains pursuit of desires, urges, and potential; the exercise of an overzealous conscious. Indicate toward which of these extremes do you fall?

initiative 7 6 5 4 3 2 1 guilt

Chapter 7
A third of the class could give the scale to older people--
middle-aged and up--a third could give it to teens and
young adults and a third to children. Each student could
give the scale to just one person of the age-group to which
he or she is assigned. The higher the stage with which a
scale is associated, the lower children should score.
Conversely, the higher the stages, the higher older subjects
should score, at least for the polarities of the highest stages.
You could do the analysis informally by just having students
report the age of the her or his respondent and that
person's score, or more formally computing average scores
on the different polarities for the different age groups.
Results should generate some faith, and some reservations,
regarding Erikson's theory.

Suggested Readings for Lecture Support

Erikson, E. Life cycle. In D. Sills (Ed.), *International
Encyclopedia of the Social Sciences.* New York:
MacMillan & Free Press, 1968b, Vol. 9, Pp. 286-292.

Erikson has laid down his most basic ideas in these few
pages.

McAdams, D. P. Attachment, intimacy, and generativity.
Psychological Inquiry, 2000, 11, 117-120.

This current, philosophical article by an expert on Erikson.
tackles the relationship of attachment styles to Erikson's
central ideas.

Suggested Readings for the Student

Woodward, K.L. An identity of wisdom. *Newsweek,* 1994 (May 23), 56.

This tribute to Erikson also traces the roots of his life and
his thinking. It is readable, enjoyable, and informative.

Hall, E. A conversation with Erik Erikson. *Psychology
Today,* June, 1983.

An easy to understand interview of Erikson.

Chapter 8

The Sociopsychological Approach to Personality:

Erich Fromm

Chapter Outline

Objectives

1. Learn how Fromm's early experiences with religion, political ideology, and war shaped his thinking.

2. Understand Fromm's socialist leanings, humanistic orientation, and existential needs.

3. Appreciate Fromm's notions about personality, individual character and social character.

4. Be able to define Fromm's social character types and to name historical figures and societies that fit the types.

5. Know why Fromm has had relatively little impact on modern personality research.

Classroom Discussion: Beyond the Text and the Lecture

1. Here is a topic that students will find fascinating, but may be risky business for you, depending on the degree of openness that characterizes your university. Fromm was a life-time socialist. Some of his concepts were clearly socialist, even communistic (e.g., humanistic communitarian socialism).

You may want to begin the discussion by asking students, "What is socialism?" There are few good examples of successful socialistic societies around, some say none, but Sweden, and perhaps the Netherlands, and maybe even Britain and France might be mentioned to help anchor students' thoughts. Students may confuse socialism with its more specific variety, communism. You may need to help them with the difference.

If socialism worked like its advocates believe it could, what kind of society would result from its operation? What kinds of individuals (Fromm's types) might be over-represented in such a society? Would Fromm's existential needs be better met in a socialist society?

Later students will learn how B. F. Skinner's hypothetical Walden II was translated into a real-life society (actually a commune). Could some of Fromm's ideas be instituted in a socialist society, or are they too vague and ill defined (again, humanistic communitarian socialism may be an example of conceptual ambiguity)? You may want to close with a debate on whether or not Fromm was naive.

2. The necrophilous type is one of Fromm's most unique ideas. Students, who probably have seen every relevant film from the *Addams Family* to the latest slasher video, will be curious about this type. You may want to begin by asking students to define the type so that everyone starts with the

same understanding of Fromm's macabre notion (you will probably have to intervene to make their understanding accurate).

Are there everyday people, as opposed to public figures who are at least somewhat necrophilous? How about morticians? How about physicians who spend their careers doing autopsies (the physician on the late TV series *Picket Fences*)? Students may know people who are preoccupied with death, and not because they are suicidal (warn students not to provide names or other sources of identification). Perhaps these people talk about death excessively. What has created their fascination? As to suicidal tendency, does it or can it relate to necrophilous orientation?

Bringing up additional historical figures may add to the discussion. How about General George Patton who seemed to be really alive only when in combat (one of his favorite admonitions to soldiers was something like "Your job is to kill the poor SOB on the other side before he kills you." Is this characteristic of other military figures? How about General Douglas MacArthur? A relevant movie is *The War Lover* starring Steve McQueen. You could end with a consideration of what contributes to the creation of people who are absorbed by the processes of death and decay. Is it childhood experiences (having to kiss a dead grandparent goodbye?). Or perhaps it is the ultimate power trip: serial killers may be the exemplary necrophilous characters.

3. Few classic personality theorists had truly multicultural experiences. Jung visited native-American tribes, and so did Maslow and Erikson. However, Fromm immersed himself in another culture. He lived for years in the Mexico City area and studied local cultures. Thus, consideration of his chapter is a appropriate occasion to entertain the relationship between culture and personality, especially since his character types are culturally based.

Are there any such things as national characters, personalities that have a stronger presence in certain societies rather than others? The text is somewhat pessimistic about this possibility, but Fromm believed in it and so did Raymond Cattell. It will be interesting and enjoyable for students to discuss how people who partake of different cultures seem to have different personalities. Of course, you don't want to call on ethnic members of your class to give testimonials. However, by beginning with stereotypes like the stoic British, the sexy French, and the hot tempered Italians, you may stimulate Hispanic and African-American (and other) students to discuss how they may see some participants in their culture to be different from Fromm's mostly European based types. These generalizations could well be highly intriguing to students, but, of course, you may want to remind them that no two participants in any culture are totally alike. Further, although some personality types may be over-represented in a given society (Germany: Authoritarians?), there is great diversity within any society. Finally, show students how these generalization may be more a matter of stereotyping than accurate depiction of reality.

Classroom Exercises: Practical Applications

1. Box 8.1 is a straightforward need questionnaire with easy to follow instructions. Have students complete the box in class (if some have already done it, they won't have to sit idly by for long; it is a short exercise). After students have drawn their profile lines, have them put a thin piece of paper over the line and trace it. Passing in these copies will give you the opportunity to show that no two profiles are the same: search through the stack of copies and pick out the few that seem most similar; you can hold them up to show that even the most similar are not identical. Hold up also some that are very different.

Some students may want to indicate why they are high or low on certain needs, but caution them to not be more self-disclosing than their comfort level would dictate. You could end the discussion by asking if the measure is meaningful to students. One index of meaningfulness is whether or not students tended to score themselves to the extremes of the scales. There may be a few or several need scales upon which extreme scoring tended to occur. If so, point them out to students.

2. Students find it interesting to choose from Table 8.1 social character types one that best fits their society. Given a good consensus, you can have students discuss why the type chosen by most class members fits their society. If there is not a good consensus, ask students who differ from the majority why they have made the choices they reported. Fitting types to other societies should also be informative. Perhaps some students in class will not identify with the culture that most students call their own, very likely the culture of mainstream United States society. These students may be non-white, ethnic group members. It will be edifying to have them talk about their cultures. They indicate why some types, other than the ones seen to fit the mainstream United States culture, seem to them a better fit to their cultures.

3. There is much talk, especially among drug and alcoholic abuse counselors, about "enablers," people who unwittingly support substance abuse in a loved one. In effect, substance abusers and their enablers constitute a special kind of symbiotic relationship. One person needs her or his substance of choice and the other needs to keep the peace and avoid the reality that his or her loved one is addicted. Abusers are often "blamers" and enablers are frequently people who are all too willing to accept blame. Perhaps the class could construct a test to discriminate enablers from others. Scales could be in the usual seven point scale format used in previous test construction exercises. Anchors for scales could be simply "agree" and "disagree."

Example items are "Do you feel guilty when someone you love doesn't get what she or he wants?"; "Do you find yourself continually serving someone you love?"; "Are you always trying to keep the peace around your house?"; "Do you continually worry that someone close to you will become upset?" and "Do you have trouble saying no to someone you love?" each rated on the agree-disagree scale.

Students who have lived in households with substance abusers will probably want to take the lead in constructing the "enabler" measure. Perhaps you will want to let them do just that. They are as near to "expert" on the matter as anyone.

Suggested Readings for Lecture Support

Fromm, E. *Escape from freedom.* New York: Holt, Rinehart and Winston, 1941.

This is the book that set Fromm on the road to fame. Reading in it and comparing with the text can provide insights into Fromm's early thinking and how it changed.

May R. The emergence of existential psychology. In Rollo May (Ed.), *Existential Psychology* (pp. 1-48). New York: Random House, 1969a.

If you are interested in existentialism, you will enjoy this book. More importantly, it will help you present the existential position to students.

Suggested Readings for the Student

Fromm, E. *The art of loving.* New York: Harper & Brothers, 1956.

Fromm's book on love is probably his most popular. It is about learning to love in the most general sense of the word. Students will find it moving and enriching.

Fromm, E. On the sources of human destructiveness. In L. Ng. (Ed.). *Alternatives to violence.* New York: Time-Life Books, 1968, 11-17.

Here is a short paper outlining Fromm's thinking on violence. It shows why he was a pioneer in the modern movement to end war and other forms of human destructiveness.

Chapter 9

Every Person is to be Prized: Carl Rogers

Chapter Outline

Rogers, the Person

Rogers' View of the Person

Basic Concepts: Rogers

 ACTUALIZATION: GENERAL AND SPECIFIC

 THE IMPORTANCE OF THE SELF

 PERSONALITY DEVELOPMENT: SOME FAVORABLE CONDITIONS

 PROCEDURES FOR CHANGING PERSONALITY: CLIENT-CENTERED THERAPY

Evaluation

 GENERAL CONTRIBUTIONS

 CARING ABOUT THE PERSON IN HUMAN RELATION-SHIPS

 ROGERS' SCIENTIFIC CONTRIBUTIONS

 LIMITATIONS

Conclusion

Summary Points

Running Comparison

Essay/Critical Thinking Questions

Email Interaction

Objectives

1. Learn how Rogers' fundamentalistic religious background, early interest in agricultural science, time in a seminary, and exposure to Freud's methods, to the medical model, to culturally diverse clients and to cooperative

graduate students shaped his therapeutic style and humanistic thinking.

2. Appreciate how Rogers' exposure to existentialism and phenomenology influenced his humanistic and organismic orientation.

3. Be able to define and relate Roger's other notions to his ideas of actualization and the self.

4. Explore Rogers' thoughts on congruence and incongruence, denial and distortion as well as how Adler may have influenced Roger's client centered therapy that is characterized by empathy and unconditional positive regard.

5. Know how Rogers' pioneered a scientific orientation to therapeutic effectiveness, the research that has confirmed some of his ideas, the virtues of his techniques that some people view as weaknesses, and attacks on him as a person and theorist.

Classroom Discussion: Beyond the Text and the Lecture

1. Here is a good place for reiteration. You could assign a student to lead a discussion on each of the following issues related to ideas Rogers shared with other theorists. Rogers' view is an interesting contrast to that of Freud, and shares some aspects with the positions of Jung and Adler. He shared with Jung the belief in the importance in a cooperative relationship between client and therapist. Rogers, in consistency with Jung, was concerned about "being with" the client, not in "building an equal relationship" (it is hard to imagine the somewhat aristocratic Jung being equal with clients; but he was a mutual participant with clients). The two shared ideas about false fronts: the persona and the facade. "Self-actualization" has some of the same flavor as "individuation." In fact, if students see these coincidences of thought, you could help them get into the similarities and the differences among and between corresponding concepts.

Except for agreement on the observation that people erect defenses to protect the vulnerable underbellies of their psyches, Freud and Rogers' had little in common. Rogers would have nothing to do with Freud's need to guide clients into the "discovery" of traumas rooted in the past. Rogers was present oriented and preferred to have the client call the shots during therapy. Rogers' rejection of the medical model was, in effect, a rejection of Freud. Aside from these points about time perspectives, control in therapy, and assumptions about "causes and "cures," one could add that the expression of an "ideal self" was central to Rogers' thinking, but probably would have been written off as fantasizing by Freud.

Rogers' learned to eschew exhaustive testing and lengthy case histories. Instead, like Adler, Rogers' would be pretty quick about getting down to business with clients. Both would be direct and straightforward with clients. Neither would be deceptive or evasive with individuals in therapy. Like Jung, both were more willing to use whatever works to make things better for the client, a philosophical orientation they shared with Gordon Allport.

Of course, Rogers' shared some ideas with other theorists. Like Sullivan, he referred to empathy. Like Fromm, he was a humanist. There are other parallels that students may see, or to which a discussion may lead them. Recalling previously considered information is an effective aid to their retention processes.

2. Rogers was among the few psychotherapists to work with significant numbers of clients who did not belong to his own cultural group. These are the times when people of color are increasing their proportional representation in the United States and other populations, while "whites" are declining proportionately. Accordingly it is crucial to contemplate the potential importance of ethnic mismatches between clients and therapists.

Rogers was among the first to recognize that a mismatch places limits on the therapist's ability to empathize. Would it be appropriate for a European-American therapist to suggest to an Arab women that she is being too deferential to the men in her life, as therapists of some schools of psychotherapy might do? Would it be good practice for a European-American therapist to show surprise and disapproval when told by a client of Japanese heritage that naughty children should be put out of the house? What if an African-American client told a European-American therapist that two people yelling at each other is a good sign, because verbal abuse is done in lieu of physical attack? How would a devout Catholic from the Philippines react to a therapist's suggestion that it is all right that a close relative is homosexual? Perhaps students of various religious and ethnic backgrounds could come up with examples of potential cultural conflicts arising in the therapist's office. If so it may become evident that it is ideal, if not always practical, that clients and therapists be of the same background. Recognition of the mismatch problem is a reason that some states are mandating that people who do therapy or counseling receive some multicultural training.

3. Are people good and worthy or loathsome and not to be trusted? This, of course, is a question that cannot be answered in any absolute sense. In fact, few of the theorists covered in the text would probably care to attempt an answer. Yet, there has been quite a transition from Freud, in the initial theorist chapter, to Rogers, in this chapter. While Freud might have declined to answer the question, it is implicit in his theory that humans are frail and unable to exercise much control over their impulses. To lesser degrees, some of the theorists covered shared this point of view with Freud.

Perhaps the easiest way to consider the ominous question posed above is to have students review the previously covered theories and decide which were closest to the optimistic and which to the pessimistic end of the human worthiness continuum. Freud could be the standard against which the other theorists would be measured, because his pessimism is hard to deny. Certainly, Horney and Sullivan are candidates for placement toward the pessimistic end. How about Adler and his notions of ingrained inferiority? And Erikson: each stage has its negative pole (e.g., basic mistrust, shame and doubt, inferiority, stagnation)? Is Fromm a candidate for pessimistic because of his emphasis on ideas like the necrophilous and the marketing types? Would Jung be exempted? A thorough discussion at this point in the course could provide students with a useful continuum upon which theorists might be placed for the purpose of differentiating among them.

Classroom Exercises: Practical Applications

1. Have students carry out the simple exercise in Box 9.2. If they have already done it, have them repeat it. After the actual and ideals lists of self-descripters have been completed, have students comment on what they have produced. I have tried this exercise many times. It is one of the most effective that I have used.

Some students will not want to read either of their lists, much less both, thereby allowing others to see that they are not what they would like to be (in practice, I have not often found this to be a problem). However, you may want to prime them with some non-threatening questions, rather than have them immediately reveal what they have recorded. They will likely be willing to indicate the degree to which there is a discrepancy between their two lists. You could ask how many had identical lists (few if any will answer in the affirmative). Then, ask how many had a discrepancy of one word (four words matched across the two lists and one did not). Then ask for discrepancies of two, and so forth. Inquire of students with large discrepancies as to whether they are experiencing a change in their life situations (perhaps they are just out of high school or have just transferred). At this point students should began to open up and talk. If not, you may want to directly indicate that discrepancies are the rule, not the exception. You could do so by creating your own list and pointing to discrepancies on it. I read my own list to students frequently. In any case, talking about the discrepancies should help students realize that the self is continually evolving. The contemporary, actual-self is sure to change and the ideal self is likely to change as well.

2. Creativity was a big concern of Rogers and of other theorists also. A creativity exercise in class would give students a flavor of creativity's essence, an outcome that would be difficult to accomplish by just defining "creativity" or giving a few examples of it.

One simple creativity task is to complete sentences with unique endings. Samples include the following: "The rat jumped onto the _____." ; "After getting a note from Bob, Kara was feeling pretty _____."; "Posed on the edge of _____ _____, Jack began to think of _____."; "It was as big as an elephant and as _____...."

Another is "Tell a story that integrates two unusual objects of beings." Example object pairs are the following: fox and bat; baseball and flower; darkness and color; map and gun; ox and rabbit; artist and wrestler; weasel and worm.

Another creativity exercise is one that I use in my sensation and perception class to help students understand the Gestalt law of good continuation. Doing this exercise will prime students for the consideration of Gestalt principles in the Maslow chapter. On the board, draw three horizontal lines about an inch or two apart. Cross them in their middle with a single vertical line. The law of good continuation dictates that people will tend to see three horizontal lines with a vertical line superimposed on them. But there are other ways to divide this whole into parts. One could mentally cut the vertical line midway between the topmost and middle horizontal line and midway between the center and lower horizontal line. The result is three crosses. One could also cut the lines in the same way, then detach each right-most section of the three horizontal lines. The result is perplexing, but interesting. There are other intriguing possibilities for students to derive.

3. Try a little Rogerian therapy in class. You will need a very open student to play the role of client. Perhaps you had better be the therapist, unless there is someone in the class who you know well enough to trust. In any case, have your "client" repeatedly ask for the therapist's advice and suggestions.

What do students think of the Rogerian orientation: Merely reflect emotions, reiterate clients' comments and refuse to offer advice? Is it frustrating (client Gloria in the *Three Psychotherapists* film expressed considerable frustration at Rogers' refusal to offer advice or suggestions)? Discussion can center on whether the Rogerian approach would be effective with all kinds of clients.

Suggested Readings for Lecture Support

Evans, R. I. *Carl Rogers, the man and his ideas.* New York: E. P. Dutton, 1975.

Here is an efficient way to get a feel for Carl Rogers the person. He is candid and thoughtful in this interview.

DeCarvalho, R. J. Otto Rank, The Rankian circle in Philadelphia, and the origins of Carl Rogers' person-centered psychotherapy. *History of Psychology*, 1999, 2, 132-148.

This is about mysterious, former Freudian Rank and how he influenced Rogers: Important facts that are little known.

Suggested Readings for the Student

Rogers, C.R. & Malcolm, D. The potential contribution of the behavioral scientist to world peace. *Counseling and Values*, 1987, 32, 10-11.

Students will be pleased to know that people are not helpless in the face of seemingly uncontrollable world conflicts.

Hill-Hain, A. & Rogers, C. R. A dialogue with Carl Rogers: Cross-cultural challenges of facilitating person-centered groups in South Africa. *Journal of Specialists in Group Work*, 1988, 13, 62-69.

Here is an opportunity for students to see how person-centered therapy works in a group context and why a

assure other class members that this actual event is not an isolated incident. Perhaps they can offer other relevant examples, such as some in the realm of employment. For example, a person of color applies for a job. Some time after being turned down it is discovered that the employer already had the one or two people of color he needed to evade charges of discrimination while keeping the workforce mostly white. At this point the discussion is likely to grow its own legs, so you will not have to carry it any further (ending it may be the problem). This is a hot topic: handle with asbestos gloves.

3. What would a society be like that fosters self-actualization? First, a discussion on the characteristics of self-actualizers is needed. After students seem to have a grasp of what self-actualizers are like, you may want them to mention some public figures, other than those listed in the text, who fit the consensus "self-actualizer."

Next have them indicate what kind of society would promote self-actualizing (it is, of course, assumed that more people could be self-actualizers if conditions supported self-actualizing to the maximum degree). Would it have an autocratic government? Would quality education be available to everyone? Would wealth be distributed more evenly than in the societies of today? Would religion be strongly represented in the society? Would the arts replace sports as the most valued pursuit? These and other similar questions will get students going. You may want to end with a consideration of how likely it is that such a society could be arranged.

Classroom Exercises: Practical Applications

1. Do the exercise described Box 10.1 as a classroom activity. This exercise could be done with the behaviors listed in Box 10.1, or with some of these behaviors and additional behaviors suggested by the students. For example, "I voted today." "I had sex last night."; "I worked in the garden all day." "I spent the afternoon grooming myself."

To look at intra-individual differences, have individual students each indicate three or four reasons why they would perform one of the behaviors. To make Maslow's point, these reasons should *not* be mutually-exclusive, alternative reasons. Rather they should be compatible reasons that work in concert to produce the behavior. You could do this one behavior at a time until all behaviors have been covered.

There is another point to be made. Different people perform the same behavior for different reasons. For a consideration of inter-individual differences, have students, one at a time, provide *a* reason why they would perform one of the behaviors. Repeating this procedure for each behavior should make it clear that a given behavior is emitted for different reasons by different people.

2. To institute a "Where am I on Maslow's hierarchy" exercise, have students write paragraphs anonymously indicating whether they are at the belongingness and love or esteem level (or other, though they are unlikely to be below or above these levels). After they have completed the paragraphs, have them indicate whether or not they would be willing to have their paragraphs read in class. Take these writings home. There you will have time to choose examples of functioning at different levels of the hierarchy that are clear, meaningful, and devoid of information tending to reveal the identity of the student writers. Reading these in class should provide students with relevant examples of functioning at different levels.

3. Assume that self-actualization is not an all-or-none phenomenon. First, hold a brief discussion concerning "What is a self-actualized person like?" Write the class-generated criteria for being self-actualized on the board. Second, have students, as a group, produce a list of about twenty public figures, each well known to class members. Then have them mediate until they reach consensus on which one of the figures mostly clearly fits the class-generated criteria for being self-actualized. Using the same mediation process have the class decide on the next most actualized public figure, and so forth, until all figures have

been ranked. The exercise can end with a group discussion of why the most actualized figures were given the highest ranks (and, perhaps, why those ranked low received that dubious distinction).

Suggested Readings for Lecture Support

Kiel, J. M. Reshaping Maslow's hierarchy of needs to reflect today's educational and managerial philosophies. *Journal of Instructional Psychology,* 1999. 26, 167-168.

Joan Kiel proposes a very interesting alteration of Maslow's Hierarchy.

Maslow, B. G. (Ed.) *Abraham H. Maslow: A memorial volume.* Monterey, California: Brooks/Cole, 1972.

This final tribute to Maslow captures the warmth and the creativity of a person whose ideas are destined to live on.

Suggested Readings for the Student

Maslow, A. H. Lessons from the peak experiences. *Journal of Humanistic Psychology,* 1962, 2, 9-18.

Students are likely to be intrigued by peak experiences. Here they can get the flavor of these rare occurrences.

Maslow, A. H. Toward the study of violence. In L. Ng. (Ed.), *Alternatives to violence.* New York: Time-Life Books, 1968, 34-37.

This article will interest students who are concerned about violence.

Chapter 11

Marching To A Different Drummer: George Kelly

Chapter Outline

Objectives

1. Learn how Kelly's background was unusual relative to that of other theorists and how that history generated his hard-nosed, scientific orientation.

2. Appreciate Kelly's cognitive approach and his different orientation to time.

3. Know Kelly's central notion, the construct, and the concepts that relate to it.

4. Understand Kelly's ideas about personality development, choices, and the cognitive complexity-simplicity position derived from his theory and revised recently.

5. Be able to indicate how the Role Construct Repertory (REP) test is administered and its results are interpreted, how Kelly's theory has made contributions to business psychology and other fields, how fixed role therapy is conducted, and how limitations of Kelly's approach are traced to the notion of bipolarity and to his personality.

Classroom Discussion: Beyond the Text and the Lecture

1. Go over the use of the scientific method applied a personal problem. The starting point should probably be a student-chosen scenario involving a young adult with a problem. For example, John is having trouble sleeping. He thinks that anxiety over tests is the culprit. How can he test his hypothesis? In this hypothetical case, what "test runs" would be appropriate, what controls would have to be instituted, what data would be collected, what inferences would be made from the data, and what conclusions would be stated?

Given the person in the scenario has posed a correct hypothesis, the class can consider what to do to deal with the person's problem. As an example, suppose that John is correct. A diary he kept confirmed that his sleepless nights tend to be nights before tests; this information controls for extraneous variables, such as loud noise from next door. Assume further that an examination of the diary reveals that obsessive thoughts about the next day's test is the reason John cannot sleep. A corrective step might be to suggest that John avoid studying just before bedtime on nights before tests. Instead he should occupy his mind by reading a novel until he falls asleep from eye fatigue and self-imposed immobility.

2. How was predictability provided students when they were children? Begin this discussion by having students recall childhood situations in which certain modes of behavior brought predictable results. As in the text, many of these examples may revolve around parental responses to "naughty" behavior. If so, encourage students to recall positive behaviors that generated predictable outcomes. For example, bringing home a good report card consistently yielded a trip to the ice cream shop.

Now have students consider predictability in their current circumstances. Do they sometimes find themselves performing socially undesirable behaviors just so they can experience the comfort of predictable outcomes (e.g., tell a friend that she or he "looks ill today," because it consistently offends that person as indicated by an icy stare)? What do they do that leads to comfortingly predictable outcomes. To end the discussion, you may want to examine individual differences in need for predictability. Ask students what level of predictability currently characterizes their lives. For students whose level of predictability is high or low, the question becomes, "How do you *feel* about your level of predictability?" Some students may report regularly experiencing high predictability and leave the impression that an obsession with predictability makes them consistently upset. Others may generally experience low predictability and find that condition to be interesting and challenging. Predictability may be generally important for children, but its value may vary among adults.

3. Examine the degree to which students are characterized by guilt, in Kelly's sense of the word: the perception of being dislodged from some role that is important for relating to significant others. The roles we play are vis-à-vis some other person. In all cases of role playing, an individual playing a certain role has to meet the other person's expectations for that role. Have students come up with examples from their own experience of cases where role expectations for a relationship change. A prime example is role-expectation changes in the course a marriage. Initially in a marriage a husband may expect his wife to "take care of things at home," including childrearing. Further, he may

accurately see her expectations of him as being the bread winner and taking care of external affairs, such as investment of family funds. However, as the children enter school, she begins to see her role differently. Now she wants to share in "winning the bread," and wants to play a part in external affairs. In turn, her expectations of her husband change. She wants him to participate more in home affairs, most especially, child-rearing. Failing to fully appreciate these changes, he may continue to meet old role expectation, thereby experiencing a sense of futility and a feeling of "being dislodged from an important role."

Classroom Exercises: Practical Applications

1. Have students do the exercise in Box 11.3, completion of the REP test. Ask them to note how long it takes to finish the exercise. After students have done the exercise, have them share feelings experienced during completion of the task. Was it easy to do or difficult (they may use time to completion as an index of difficulty: the longer the time, the greater the difficulty)? Students should tell why they found the task easy or difficult. Was it hard because choosing people to fit the roles was difficult? Was choosing two people who were alike in some way and different from the other person the source of the perceived difficulty? Maybe the task was easy because it was self-evident how two of each three persons were seen as alike and different from the third.

Now have students look at the set of constructs that supposedly represent the way each sees his or her world. According to a student's intuitions, does the set for that student seem to encompass the ways he or she sees the world? Students may want to comment on which construct dimensions (under the "emergent" and "implicit" pole labels) elicited by the test are, in fact, not often used by them. What other dimensions would they add? Where the construct system emerging from the test appears not to fit a student well, ask the student what is the problem. Is it that the test's roles (e.g., rejecting person) are inappropriate for the particular student? These and similar questions should bring forth a number of informative self-assessments by students. A more thorough understanding of what is meant by "construction system" should result from this discussion.

2. Of all the ideas inspired by Kelly's theory, none has stimulated more current research than complexity-simplicity. One index of complexity-simplicity is how many constructs a person has available to construe her or his world. If students have completed the first exercise already, it will be relatively easy for them to privately list the number of construct dimensions (e.g., admire-not admire) they typically use. After they have completed this task, ask them to simply turn in the number of dimensions they listed on an unsigned, scrap of paper. Go through these scraps of paper and determine the smallest and largest number of dimensions, as well as the number that divides the distribution into two equal parts, the median: Half of the students' number-of-dimensions fall below the median and half above.

Tell students that you have decided, as a rule of thumb, that scores above the mid-point of the numbers represent relative complexity and those below the mid-point represent simplicity. Of course, the larger and smaller the number of dimensions that students listed, the greater the complexity or simplicity, respectively. Remind students that this test is not diagnostic, just an exercise.

Next, ask students to write down as many words as they can to describe themselves. Also, request that they write down as many words as they can think of to describe an acquaintance, someone they know fairly well, but are not close to. Then, repeat the collection of scraps of paper, but have students turn in two numbers one labeled "number of words used to describe myself" and the other "number of words used to describe an acquaintance." Construct number-of-words distributions and mid-points for both tasks, as you did for the number of dimensions task. Finally, have students observe whether the number of words each used in the self-description task is above or below the mid-point of the class distribution of numbers-of-words used in self-description. Have students make the same observation for number of words used to describe the acquaintance.

Now the critical question can be asked: Is there a tendency for students numbers to end up in the same half of all three distributions? For example, according to complexity-simplicity theory, a student who listed only a few construct dimensions should also be in the lower half of the distributions for number of words used in self-descriptions and for number of words used to describe an acquaintance. If the expected trend tended to occur, students should see evidence supportive of complexity-simplicity theory and should experience further insight into the dichotomy. If the expected trend does not occur, what happened? Was the number of construct dimensions a poor index of complexity-extremity? Is either the number of words used in self-description or the number of words used in describing an acquaintance a poor correlate of complexity-simplicity? Answers may be more enlightening than an observation of the expected outcome.

3. Contemporary research into complexity-simplicity theory has taken an additional turn. Not only is there a current interest in how complex and simple people differ in their perceptions of self and others, researchers are finding that perception of one's own *group* tend to more complex than perceptions of some other group. Have students write down as many words as they can think of to describe "Americans." Then, have them write down as many words as they can think of to describe "Russians." The expected outcome, tested using the scraps of paper method (discussion question 2), is that more words are used in describing one's own group than in describing the other group.

Alternatively, have men describe "males" and "females," and also have women describe both groups. Again, more words should be used to describe one's own group. Another alternative is to have European-American students describe their own group and "people of color," and have students of color describe their own group as well as European-Americans. Again, own-group descriptions should involve more words. Finally, it would interesting to ask students to list sub-groups of their own groups (in-groups) and sub-groups of some other group (out-group). Results should show more sub-groups of each student's own group than of another group (see Park et al, 1992, below). We are more complex about our own group that other groups.

Suggested Readings for Lecture Support

Park, B., Ryan, C.S., & Judd, C. Role of meaningful subgroups in explaining differences in perceived variability for in-groups and out-groups. *Journal of Personality and Social Psychology*, 1992, 63, 553-567.

If you want to know the direction complexity-simplicity theory is currently taking, read this article.

Gruenfeld, D. H. & Preston, J. Upending the status quo: Cognitive complexity in U.S. Supreme Court Justices who overturn legal precedent. *Personality and Social Psychology Bulletin*, 2000, 26, 1013-1022.

When are Supreme Court Justices more complex, when they defend precedent or when they overturn it? Perhaps the answer is counter-intuitive, but it is very interesting.

Suggested Readings for the Student

Uhlemann, M. R., Lee, D. Y., & Hasse, R. F. The effects of cognitive complexity and arousal on client perceptions of counselor nonverbal behavior. *Journal of Clinical Psychology*, 1989, 45, 661-664.

Uhlemann et al is a brief article about how complexity theory might be used to select better counselors. It will provide students with insights into what makes a good counselor.

Viney, L. L., Benjamin, Y. N.., & Preston, C. Mourning and reminiscence: Parallel psychotherapeutic processes for elderly people. *International Journal of Aging and Human Development*, 1989, 28, 239-249.

Students interested in the mourning process will benefit from reading about how Kelly's "guilt" is involved.

Chapter 12

The Social Side of Personality: Walter Mischel and Julian Rotter

Chapter Outline

Mischel: A Challenge to Traits

Mischel, The Person

Mischel's View of the Person

Basic Concepts: Mischel

SUPPORTING EVIDENCE

MISCHEL SUMMED UP: CONSISTENCY OF CROSS-SITUATION BEHAVIORAL PATTERNS

Evaluation

MISCHEL'S CONTRIBUTIONS

LIMITATIONS

Conclusions

Rotter: Internal and External Control of Our Behavior

Rotter, The Person

Rotter's View of the Person

Basic Concepts: Rotter

REINFORCEMENT VALUE, PSYCHOLOGICAL SITUATIONS, AND EXPECTANCY

LOCUS OF CONTROL: INTERNALS AND EXTERNALS

CHARACTERISTICS OF INTERNALS AND EXTERNALS

CHANGING EXTERNALS

Evaluation

CONTRIBUTIONS TO CONTROLLING OUR LIVES

LIMITATIONS

Conclusions

Summary Points

Running Comparisons

Essay/Critical Thinking Questions

Email Interaction

Objectives

1. Outline how Mischel took up Rotter's campaign against mindless "trait" notions, how his cognitive social learning theory emphasizes personal cognitive factors instead of traits, and how he resolved the dilemma surrounding persons' perceptions of behavioral consistency and the limited evidence for consistency.

2. Understand Mischel's unique definition of personality and his conception of "if...then" relations. Tell how Mischel's theory relates to cultural diversity.

3. Know Mischel's basic concepts concerning how people size up a situation and employ their expectancies to generate behavior that will yield desired outcomes. Describe his work on delay of gratification and the implications of his theory for interactionism. Indicate how the summer camp study showed the way that people are consistent from one set of observations of them to the next.

4. Learn how Rotter was influenced by Gestalt psychology, as well as by Adler, and how people's reaction to luck versus skill situations relates to his postulation of a broad disposition regarding the location of control over personal outcomes.

5. Understand Rotter's ideas about reinforcement, expectancies, and locus of control as well as his famous I-E scale. Appreciate evidence regarding the characteristics of

internals and externals, how the external orientation might be changed, and shortcomings of I-E conception.

Classroom Discussion: Beyond the Text and the Lecture

1. Delay of gratification is a topic with numerous important implications. First, have students think back to their childhoods and try to remember the level of delay of gratification they showed then. Next you could ask them what degree of delay ability they show today. Perhaps they would offer personal examples of high or low ability. If they will, some laughter should result, which will introduce a little levity into the discussion.

At this point it is time for a tough question, the answer to which may cause some chagrin, in view of earlier admissions to low ability at delay: Why is ability to delay gratification related to emotional stability and high academic achievement in children? Why is inability to delay related to behavioral problems such as impulse control? Students may have various answers, but they may need prompting. Research on delay of gratification suggests that children who are good at delay are able to devise clever strategies to promote delay. Perhaps children who are able to come up with effective strategies have the intelligence to do well in school. As for emotional stability, stable children are likely to be able to rein in their emotions, which would facilitate delay of gratification by curbing impulsivity. Thus, emotional stability and delay of gratification should go hand in hand. On the other side of the coin, the implusivity that is associated with inability to delay gratification may partially explain behavioral problems such as rejection sensitivity.

Now for a tougher question: If one is an adult with low ability to delay gratification, is she or he doomed to a life of impulsivity, and the accompanying low achievement and emotional stability? First, assure students that high ability to delay gratification is not the only avenue to emotional stability and high achievement. Further, it is possible, even as an adult, to adopt strategies analogous to those mentioned in the text that would promote high delay skill. Suppose, for example, one has a certain dream house in mind and wants it now, but cannot afford it. Instead of grabbing the first approximation to the desired house sold at a premium price and financed it at the prevailing high interest rate, one could spend one's time designing the dream house and lining up reasonable financing. But will becoming better at delaying gratification during adulthood increase achievement and emotional stability and decrease implusivity? The safest answer is "no." Delay of gratification, emotional stability, high achievement and low impulsivity are probably part of one initially small package of abilities that grows larger during childhood. In any case students should learn more about delay of gratification in the process of speculating about these issues.

2. Encourage students to conjure up reasons why people perceive more cross-situational behavioral consistency than actually exists. You may want to start the discussion by indicating a main source of the confusion: temporal consistency is mistaken for cross situational consistency. For example, students see the same person, the Prof., in the same situation, class, every day. Students may laugh about the observation that the Prof. performs the same behavioral ritual upon entering class each day: she places her book on the same desk-top spot each day, turns promptly to the board and writes down the day's topic, turns to the students and says, "Good afternoon!", pulls out her notes, moves her glasses from the top of her head to her nose, mumbles something to herself, then proceeds to lecture while wheeling distinctly on her left heel at the turning point of a continuous march back and forth in front of the black board. They assume her formal but friendly style is how she always is. They also assume that she cannot talk without her "soldier on guard duty" pacing. Their mistaken judgments about her are based on the assumption that the temporal stability she shows--same behaviors in the same situation across time--means she would behave the same in different situations. Have students come up with examples of how a person can behave very consistently in the same situation

across time, but be completely different in a different situation. Work in the notion of "if...then."

What are other sources of the misperception? Guide students to realizing that we may see consistency in a person's behavior simply because we observe the person only in a *series of closely related situations* (Mischel's nominal situation: work). If we interact with a person only at business meetings, during discussion of business in her or his office, gossiping in the hallways or over lunch (work interpersonal situations), we have seen him or her only in one nominal situation, not at home, at a party, caring for children, at a community meeting and so forth.

Once we decide on a person's traits, we tend not to see her or him behave in ways that are inconsistent with our perceptions. We label a person as "aggressive" because that is the way he behaves on the basketball court; his lack of aggression in other settings escapes us. Because of this tendency to see only what confirms our perceptions, we miss variations in the person's behavior as a function of the situations in which he is acting.

In fact, when we observe the behavior of other people, we tend to ignore situational causation of their behavior. As observers of other people's behavior, we tend to perceive that their traits determined whatever they did, while we ignore situational pressures that may have actually determined their behavior. By ignoring situational pressures, we can see people behaving the same at the behest of traits that do not change across situations. (If the "fundamental attribution error" and the "actor-observer effect" are of interest to you, bring them up in this context.)

Guide students in discovering these reasons for apparent but not actual consistency, as well as other reasons you may come up with (e.g., others' inconsistencies make us uncomfortable and invalidate out expectations of their future behavior). If they follow your lead well, they may realize that while behavioral consistency is not entirely illusory, it may be exaggerated in our perceptions.

3. What is wrong with being an external? First ask how many students tend to think that fate, luck, and chance play a very big role in determining their outcomes. Do those who answer affirmatively also often buy lottery tickets? Do they curse the fates when something goes wrong and praise the heavens when good fortune strikes? Many will answer "yes" to these questions.

Then ask them whether their orientation might be bad for their psychological well being. Cases in point include depression. Although it is controversial (what isn't in psychology!) there is accumulating evidence that the external orientation may promote depression. It is easy to imagine that one could get depressed if she or he believes that fate, luck, chance, and powerful others control their lives. Also, high achievement may be less likely for externals. If people do not believe that their own effort and skills determine their outcomes, they will not redouble their efforts and polish their skills.

You may want to add other reasons why being an extreme external is not good. But how does an external change in the direction of being an internal? Here the discussion will be wide open. To launch it, point out that behavior can change cognition: if people force themselves to rely on their own skills and efforts, they may begin to believe in the efficacy of their own resources. To end it, ask them how many famous, successful people can they name who are obvious externals.

Exercises: Practical Applications

1. Ask students to indicate how other people stereotype them (Box 12.1). First, make sure that they know what constitutes a personal stereotype: a trait attributed to a person regardless of situations and irrespective of whether the attribution is at all accurate. Have students list their personal stereotypes on scrap pieces of paper and ask them to indicate whether they would permit you to ask them questions about their stereotypes. You could pick out some of the more interestingly stereotyped students' papers and ask them questions about each of their stereotypes: (1) How

Chapter 12
accurate is this attribution to you?; (2) In which situations do
you act in a way that is consistent with this stereotype, and
in which situations do you act in a way that is inconsistent
with it? (3) How do you feel about being regarded in this
way? This exercise will likely create insight into how it is
restricting, and even oppressive, for people to see each of
us in a monolithic manner: always behaving in only a few
ways.

2. Ask a volunteer student to describe a friend by using
single words. Pick a word from the list (e.g., aggressive) and
inquire of the student as to whether the friend is *always* like
that (aggressive in every situation). The answer is likely to
be "no" and further probing is probably going to reveal that
the friend is aggressive in some situations and not in others.
Alternatively, "if" certain situations prevail, "then" the person
is likely to be aggressive. Repeating this process with
several students will convince most students that
interactionism involving traits (e.g., aggressive) and
situations (e.g., softball game versus wedding reception) is
a very plausible point of view.

3. Have students complete the I-E scale found in Box 12.4
(if they have already done it, they can reconsider responses
while others are completing it). Because the purpose of the
test is understanding internal and external locus of control,
discussion should center on item alternatives that connote
one of those two orientations. Pick an item, ask who
endorsed one of its alternatives, and ask those who
respond why they thought the item alternative was
applicable to themselves. Also, if it is not made obvious by
their answers to your endorsement question, request that
they indicate to which orientation the chosen alternative
refers. You can pose the same question concerning the
opposing alternative for the item you picked, and so on for
other items. The discussion will give students a better grasp
of the I and the E orientations.

Suggested Readings for Lecture Support

Rotter, J. Internal versus external control of reinforcement.
American Psychologist, 1990, 45, 489-493.

Rotter's article summarizing work on his theory is a clear expression of his thinking and the research related to it.

Ayduk, O., Mendoza-Denton, R., Mischel, W., Downey, G. Peake, P. K., & Rodriguez, M. Regulating the interpersonal self: Strategic self-regulation for coping with rejection sensitivity. *Journal of Personality and Social Psychology*, 2000, 79, 776-792.

Rejection sensitive people are a fascinating puzzle. Why are they the way they are? They lack impulse control, and, of course that can be indexed by delay of gratification.

Suggested Readings for the Student

American Psychologist, 1982 award for distinguished scientific contributions to Walter Mischel, 1983, 38, 9-14.

This short piece not only covers Mischel's surprisingly interesting life, it also summarized his contributions.

Phares, E. J. *Locus of control in personality*. Morristown, N. J.: General Learning Press, 1976.

This highly readable book is a bit dated, but it is still probably the most comprehensive and understandable source on locus of control information available. Students can choose parts of the book that relate to matters of particular interest to them, such as locus of control and marriage.

Thinking Ahead And Learning Mastery of One's Circumstances: Albert Bandura

Chapter Outline

Bandura the Person

Bandura's View of the Person

INSIDE/OUTSIDE AND RECIPROCAL CAUSATION

PERSON FACTORS, BEHAVIORS, AND THE EXTERNAL ENVIRONMENT

FREE WILL, PERSONAL AGENCY, AND THE POWER OF FORETHOUGHT

LEARNING

Basic Concepts: Bandura

OBSERVATIONAL LEARNING

LEARNING BY OTHERS' EXAMPLE

GOALS AND SELF-REGULATION

SELF-EFFICACY: AVENUE TO THE CORRECTION OF HARMFUL BEHAVIORS

OTHER THINGS WE LEARN FROM MODELS, BESIDES BEHAVIOR

REWARDS

DEFENSIVE BEHAVIORS

Evaluation

SUPPORTING EVIDENCE

IMPLICATIONS OF SOCIAL COGNITIVE THEORY FOR MORAL FUNCTIONING

SELF-EVALUATION AND SELF-SACRIFICE

LIMITATIONS

Conclusions

Summary Points

Running Comparison

Essay/Critical Thinking Questions

Email Interaction

Objectives

1. Learn about how Bandura's rough-and-ready youth and how chance shaped his thinking; about the reciprocal relations among behavior, feelings, cognitions and neurobiology; and about his notions concerning personal agency and forethought.

2. Know Bandura's ideas concerning observational learning, models, modeling, symbolic modeling, goal setting, resilience, expectations and reinforcement.

3. Contrast Bandura's view with that of other psychologists and outline the evidence he has amassed supporting the importance of self-efficacy. Learn what the Italian studies tell us about academic achievement and moral functioning.

4. Appreciate Bandura's ideas about moral functioning including the cognitive mechanisms we use to justify harming others and relevance to abuse of women.

5. Understand why Bandura's theory is so practically applicable and why it is likely to have a long life.

Classroom Discussion: Beyond the Text and the Lecture

1. Violence is a major and growing problem in our society. It was Bandura's early work that highlighted how easy it is for children to learn aggression by simply watching aggressive models. Practice and reward, long believed to be essential

76

to learning, need not enter the violence learning sequence. To begin this discussion have students recall instances of violence in the media that probably had a profound effect on children. You could prepare for this discussion by having a student watch an evening of prime time TV and report back to the class the number of violent acts per hour of viewing, a figure that will exceed the number of real violent acts occurring in an evening of living in one of our most crime ridden urban areas. You can help your students by mentioning instances such as the violence in Chicago that followed the HBO presentation of *Boys In The Hood*. You could also point out the desensitization that occurs when children repeatedly watch violence in the media and the resulting indifference to violence, as well as possible increased violence proneness, that accompany desensitization.

Consider the solutions that students might suggest: Prohibit children from watching TV or going to the movies; Lobby the networks to clean up their acts (it has been tried, unsuccessfully); Watch TV with children and express disapproval of violence; Point out to children that the violence in the media is fake, just acting. Be sure that children know that, in real life, punching and shooting people can cause brain damage, paralysis, and death (amazingly it appears that some children, even in the pre-teen age range, seem not to understand that shooting someone can profoundly damage them). You will have other questions to raise for students. Hopefully they will come away from this discussion with at least a fledgling desire to curtail media violence.

2. A lively discussion is likely to result from posing the question, "How useful are our friends?" According to social comparison theory, friends should also be rivals. Because they have a life situation similar to our own, we will tend to compare our outcomes to theirs in the hope of doing a little bit better. If we can say that we are a little bit better off than a comparable other, we are doing fine. Should we be doing a little bit worse, it is troublesome. Consistently doing much better or much worse disqualifies the other person as comparable.

Have students examine their own friendships from two perspectives: (1) establish the similarity of their own life situations to that of their friends (both are students, same gender, same family background, same interest, etc.); and (2) explore the competition that probably exists between themselves and their friends. Although it may be hard to admit, do any students remember feeling slightly comforted at some minor misfortune suffered by a friend? This discussion may help students understand their friendships better.

3. The text section on moral functioning carries with it the implicit assumption that humans find harming their own naturally repugnant. Given the assumption is correct, some humans still manage to treat one another horribly anyway. Bandura asserts that people are able to do evil to other humans through the use of self-exonerative processes. Have the class consider each of these processes in turn and attempt to show the unreasonable and immoral nature of each.

For example, dehumanization is a endless process by which one could, in the nth degree, write off most of the world's population as not human, thereby leaving themselves virtually alone. Justifying evil by pointing out the evil of others can be used to excuse any act. It only requires engaging the clear but bogus vision of hindsight. Using phrasing like "ethnic cleansing" does not make rape and torture more acceptable, it only makes it more sinister. In the course of this discussion, students may develop a need to monitor their own thinking more closely so as to avoid the need for self-exonerative processes.

Classroom Exercises: Practical Applications

1. What incentives can students name? Some that you can provide as examples that may stimulate student thought include: an offer of money, a chance to interact with children, an encounter with a person in need, a chance to talk to friends, a chance to impress an important person, an opportunity to confront someone you do not like, an encounter with a person who has psychological problems,

and an opportunity for advancement on the job. After students have listed additional incentives, some important practical questions can be entertained. First, how does an incentive differ from a reward or reinforcement? Answering this question will help students grasp the nature of incentives. Second, how does an incentive differ from a bribe? Bribes are generally considered to be unethical at best. Separating them from incentives would make incentives more attractive as ways to generate desired behavior. Third, how do parents use incentives to shape behavior in their children? After this question is answered, you may want students to consider how to make better use of incentives to generate desirable behavior in children.

2. You can, with the help of your students, demonstrate how people can become more efficacious. For example, in a cooperative learning, group project conducted in one of my classes, students in a group helped one of their own overcome a snake phobia. By providing social support and by modeling snake handling, they induced the phobic to handle a snake in front of the entire class.

Maybe bringing snakes to class is not your thing, but there are less dramatic means of demonstrating increased self-efficacy. For example find a class member who is willing to sing in public and who would like to, but is afraid. After schooling the class on how to be supportive--no laughing, just pleasant, attentive expressions on faces--have your model sing in class then have the reluctant singer follow suit. This and other possible demonstrations may require some outside of class modeling sessions. (The Estella Monroe case in this manual includes a singing-efficacy illustration).

Other possible illustrations of efficacy boosting include lessening fear of insects and lowering fear of speaking in public, two of the most common fears. These demonstrations could follow the format of the singing example. Students may offer other suggestions. Exercises of this sort will be among the events from your class that students will remember years later.

3. Try diffusion of innovation in class. You could be the model or an obviously well-liked and respected student could be recruited to play the role. You probably can come up with a better idea than the following one, but hopefully it will illustrate the point. Bring some Greek worry beads to class and casually manipulate them during lecture (if you cannot find any, they are easy to make: string some plastic beads on a piece of cord; moving them around is believed to attenuate worry). If no student asks you what they are and why you are constantly fingering them, privately recruit a student to pose the question in class. Extol the virtues of the beads and tell how students may have their own. Later check to see how many have adopted your innovation. Alternatively, leave some strings of beads lying around in class and see how many are picked up. Results, of course, should be reported to the class. Another way to go would be to consistently consume an unusual product that is readily available on campus, such as iced coffee, a drink that is popular in Japan, but has yet to catch on here. If it works well, students will gain some insight into how they have come to do some of the things they do.

Suggested Readings for Lecture Support

Bandura, A. Social cognitive theory: An agentic perspective. *Annu Review of Psychology*, 2001, 52, 1-23.

In this interesting, up-to-date article Bandura clarifies and extends his theory and provides research and real-life examples to illustrate his principles.

Bandura, A., Ross, D., & Ross, S. Imitation of film-mediated aggressive models. *Journal of Abnormal and Social Psychology*, 1963, 66, 3-11.

This paper reports one of the most famous studies ever done in psychology. It launched Bandura's career. You may want to detail it in class because students are sure to be fascinated by its simple message: aggression is easy to learn.

Suggested Readings for the Student

Chapter 13

Bandura, A. A sociocognitive analysis of substance abuse: An agentic perspective. *Psychological Science*, 1999b, 10, 214-217.

This short article presents an exciting, optimistic new view of substance abuse. It will be enjoyable and informative reading for students.

Bandura, A. Aggression: A social learning analysis. Englewood Cliffs, N. J.: Prentice-Hall, 1973.

If I had to pick one book on aggression that students would understand and benefit from the most, this would be it.

Chapter 14

It's All a Matter of Consequences: Skinner's Behaviorism

Chapter Outline

Skinner, The Person

Skinner's View of the Person

ENVIRONMENTALISM: THE IMPORTANCE OF CONSEQUENCES

"BEYOND FREEDOM AND DIGNITY"

Basic Concepts: Skinner

OPERANT CONDITIONING

POSITIVE REINFORCEMENT

NEGATIVE REINFORCEMENT AND PUNISHMENT

THE DEVELOPMENT OF HUMAN: LANGUAGE PER-SONALITY, AND CHILD REARING

Evaluation

CONTRIBUTIONS

LIMITATIONS

Conclusions

Summary Points

Running Comparison

Essay/Critical Thinking Questions

Email Interaction

Objectives

1. Analyze Skinner's unusual past and indicate how it both contributed to his hard-nosed, empirical point of view and contradicted his later theoretical and personal orientation.

2. Consider Skinner's central notion, consequences, and his "environmentalism," including his ideas about freedom and dignity.

3. Learn about Skinner's operant conditioning, and his reinforcement processes, including negative reinforcement and punishment.

4. Appreciate Skinner's ideas about language development, childrearing practices, personality development, and creativity, his thoughts on genetic disposition and reinforcement, and his contributions to behavior therapy.

5. Know criticisms lodged against Skinner and his response to critics. Learn needed alterations to Skinner's theory.

Classroom Discussion: Beyond the Text and the Lecture

1. The differences between Skinner and the other theorists covered so far should be obvious to the students and has been the object of much discussion, perhaps too much. Obviously, unlike all the rest, Skinner eschews any kind of mentalism. Unlike most of the others, he emphasizes causative events outside of people. However, less obvious, and often neglected, are the similarities between Skinner and other theorists. Discussing those similarities would strengthen students' memories of previously covered theorists.

Some conclusions about similarities to which you may want to lead students include that Skinner shared with Freud the belief that behavior is pushed from the past rather than pulled by the future. While Skinner would never have used the term "self" in a scientific context, he did acknowledge a kind of Rogerian selfness in a dialogue with one of his daughters. Also, he and Rogers were both interested in creativity. Both he and Sullivan identified kinds of learning. You could also entertain the possibility that some of Fromm ideas, similar to some of Skinner's, referred to the elusiveness of freedom. Finally, like Mischel and Rotter, Skinner had severe reservations about the concept trait. Undoubtedly, you and the students can come up with additional points of similarity, and difference too, if that is of interest.

2. As the students read the chapter, they will not miss the fact that Skinner reared one of his babies in a box. While confining a baby to a box may be too much for many students, they may be able to use some of the principles upon which the baby-box was founded to design a better baby environment.

If confining a nearly naked baby to limited space for reasons of health and comfort is to involve more room than a box, students will have to be creative. A paper floor that can be removed and replenished is a bit much. Perhaps students will have to think in terms of a climate controlled room with an area in which the baby could relieve itself. While children normally cannot learn bowel and bladder control until well after the first year, it may be possible to train a baby, once it is mobile, to urinate and defecate in only one part of a room.

Many questions arise with answers that restrict the attractiveness of a climate controlled, germ free environment. For example, should people wear masks into the room (possibly transparent ones so that faces can be seen)? Should gloves be used to handle the baby, (this practice would limit human contact with the baby)? Should toys be suspended from the ceiling so that the baby can play with them without possibly injuring themselves crawling over or around them?

Maybe a bigger box is the answer. Or maybe no special environment is the best answer. Students may want to ask whether partial freedom from infant illnesses, some caretaking chores, and diaper rash is worth the monetary costs and whether the loss of contact with people negates the health and comfort value of a special environment. You might end with a discussion of ways to "clean up" the usual infant environment as an alternative to creating a special environment.

3. How can one manage a disruptive child in ways that are true to Skinnerian principles? The Skinnerian method called *time out* is applicable here. Time out is a period of non-reinforcement. The child is not necessarily isolated, but may be moved to a place where reinforcement of disruptive behavior is unlikely to occur (in his or her seat at school, while other children are elsewhere in the classroom).

Non-reinforcement can work. Essentially, it is assumed that the child is showing maintenance of disruptive behavior because it is being reinforced for being disruptive. It is much the same thing as saying that the child's behavior is attention-getting: attention is reinforcing disruptive behavior. Thus, the remedy is to avoid paying attention to disruptive behavior. The problem is that non-reinforcement is more difficult than one might think. It is hard to pay no attention to a child who is hitting other children or adults. Likewise it is difficult to ignore a child who is screaming so loud that others cannot converse. Help the students understand that unusual patience and endurance will be needed to institute the non-reinforcement method.

Skinner would almost never suggest that punishment be used, and would rarely if ever advise that negative rein-forcement be employed. However, positive reinforcement might be used. Here is an example that might stimulate other examples from students. While being careful not to reinforce disruptive behavior--timing is all important--one must wait until the disruptive behavior is temporarily discontinued and quickly reinforce whatever the child is doing that is not disruptive, such as simply being quiet. Saying something nice like "Hi [child's name]!" or even offering a favorite treat during the period of non-disruptive behavior will be effective. I have seen it done successfully in a classroom where both the classmates of a disruptive Down's Syndrome child and the teachers offered positive reinforcement for the non-disruptive behavior.

You and the students can contrive other applications of Skinnerian principles. Considering them should alert students to the fact that there are alternatives to punitive methods to control disruptive behavior.

Exercises: Practical Applications

1. Having the students come up with a way to train an animal to do something complex, not just a simple lever press, will help them understand shaping. For example, to get a chicken to discriminate between a red and green panel, first condition panel pecks with the usual methods. Then confront the animal with two panels, one red and one green. Whenever the chicken pecks the green panel, a reinforcer is delivered, but when the animal pecks the red panel, nothing happens. At first, the animal will mistakenly press the red panel as well as the green one. However, after a number of cases of experiencing non-reinforcement associated with the red panel, it will peck only the green panel.

While I have actually done this experiment, it does require at least one chicken and a cardboard box version of the operant chamber. Bringing a dog to class and teaching it a new trick would be more straightforward. A dog could be taught to shake hands or turn in a circle. If the dog does something cute naturally, such as hop on its hind legs, that behavior could be brought under control fairly easily. Ask students if some of them would be willing to bring in their dogs for conditioning. Tell them to also bring in some of their dogs' favorite treats to use as reinforcers.

2. Skinner looked at the use of aversive stimulation with disapproval. Nevertheless, there may be cases when its use is the only available solution to a serious problem. Have students come up with examples of cases where aversive stimulation delivered as punishment may be justified as a way to eliminate undesirable behavior. In each such case have them design a conditioning set-up that would eliminate the undesirable behavior.

An example would be eliminating the self-mutilative behavior of autistic children. Here the child receives a mild electric shock at each performance of a self-mutilating behavior. Research shows that this method works. How could electric shock be used to eliminate attraction to children on the part of child molesters (of course, a prior question would be *should* shock be used for this purpose)? How would it be used to eliminate cigarette smoking and alcohol consumption? Students will be able to provide other cases where shock might be used. This exercise will allow students to consider some ethical questions as well as become more familiar with uses of aversive stimulation.

3. Students seem to confuse negative reinforcement with punishment. Punishment is straightforward: punishing a response by administering aversive stimulation--for example, spanking a child for yelling at a parent--reduces the likelihood of the response. There are an infinite number of good examples of punishment. However, good negative reinforcement examples are harder to come by. In general, anytime a person does something in order to avoid something else what he or she does is negatively reinforced: the absence of what is avoided reinforces the avoidance behavior, making it more likely in the future. To put it another way, any kind of avoidance behavior is likely to be maintained by negative reinforcement.

You can do some negative reinforcing in order to illustrate it. For example, you could tell students "If you will go to see [a movie in town that relates well to one of the topics you are covering] and write a five page paper about it, you won't have to do a term paper." Or you could indicate "I tell you what, if you will make up three excellent essay questions and answer them well, you won't have to take the next test." You can probably come up with other examples that, if implemented, would be carried out by students who then would have demonstrated the principle of negative reinforcement very well.

Suggested Reading for Lecture Support

American Psychologist, vol. 47, #11.

This volume is a tribute to Skinner written mostly by former students and other behaviorists. It is all you will ever want to know about Skinner and how his theory is likely to change in the future. Pick and choose among many interesting articles.

Kimble, G. A. Behaviorism and the unity of psychology. *Current Directions in Psychological Science*, 2000, 9, 208-212.

Famed learning psychologist, Gregory Kimble, tells what alterations of Skinner's theory must be instituted if it is to survive.

Suggested Readings for the Student

Kindade, K. Commune: A Walden-Two experiment. *Psychology Today,* 1973 (January), 6, 35.

Students will find this article on an actual commune based on Skinner's principles to be both interesting and easy to relate to.

Skinner, B. F. Baby in a box. In B. F. Skinner (Ed.), *Cumulative Record: A selection of papers (3rd Ed.),* New York: Appleton Century Crofts,1972, pp. 567-573.

The baby in the box "experiment" is always fascinating to students.

Human Needs and Environmental Press: Henry A. Murray

Chapter Outline

Murray, the Person

Murray's View of the Person

EARLY EXPOSURE TO PSYCHOLOGY

WHY DID MURRAY BECOME A PSYCHOLOGIST?

DEVELOPING A UNIQUE APPROACH TO UNDERSTAND-
ING PEOPLE

Basic Concepts: Murray

PROPOSITIONS

DEFINITION OF NEEDS

VARIETIES OF NEEDS

STRENGTH OF NEEDS AND INTERACTIONS AMONG
THEM

NEED INTEGRATES (COMPLEXES)

ENVIRONMENTAL PRESS

THEMA

Evaluation

CONTRIBUTIONS

LIMITATIONS

Conclusions

Summary Points

Running Comparison

Essay/Critical Thinking Questions

Objectives

1. Describe Murray's unusual regard for his mother and father. Consider his alleged narcissistic character, his despair, his theoretical orientation, his short-lived admiration of Jung, and his competitive relationship with colleagues.

2. Indicate the personal and professional importance of his relationship to Christiana Morgan. Understand the implications of the long unit of the organism, unitary trends, actones, and Murray's special definition of needs.

3. Catalogue and define the varieties of needs--including regnancy, strength, fusions of needs, contrafactions of needs, and need complexes--environmental press, and thema.

4. Understand Paunonen's and colleagues' and Singer's use of Murray's needs to measure personality, Potkay's work with the TAT, the nature and application of the TAT, and its status today.

5. Appreciate how Murray's personality and psychological problems placed limits on his theorizing and outline the short-comings of the TAT.

Classroom Discussion: Beyond the Text and the Lecture

1. Contrasting Murray with the other theorists will help students to integrate the various theories, learning how they are different and how they are similar, a pursuit that is becoming critical as they approach the end of the book.

Murray was Freudian, or was he? Encourage students to argue the point. He was the defender of psychoanalysis at Harvard and he used Freudian language. He was, however, a true scientist grounded in biochemistry and

Chapter 15

neurophysiology, unlike Freud whose ideas were formed prior to the development of these disciplines.

Like Skinner, he believed that organisms are pushed from the past, but Murray disagreed with the behaviorism that was associated with Skinner. His n Succorance is like Horney's basic anxiety. Like Sullivan he was interpersonally oriented. Of course, he and Maslow shared an emphasis on needs. Did Maslow borrow from Murray? This question may start an informative debate that would call for a reconsideration of Maslow. Murray's need integrates were like Jung's archetypes. Finally, looking ahead, Allport was his only defender at Harvard. What did they agree on?

This discussion should prime student for a final synthesis of the theories covered in the text.

2. Have students search popular magazines for need integrates, images that excite needs (video tapes may also be appropriate). These often will be abstract, like clouds molded into an ambiguous form, but can be quite blatant, such as sexual images. Ask them to be especially on the look-out for images that may be particular to a specific culture. For example, students from India may want to search their own publications for need-images that have peculiar meaning for their culture. Native American students may find images in United States magazines that have quite different meanings for them than the same images have for members of society at large (for example, an eagle soaring). Likewise, there may be gender differences in need-related meanings of images and differences among African-American, Mexican-American, and European-American cultures as well. Having students interpret popular images in terms of need symbolism, and thereby inspire others to agree or disagree, will cement "need-integrate" into their minds (and maybe archetypes as well).

3. Classism is one of the most forgotten "isms." People caught in the cycle of poverty that keeps them out of higher education and into low paying jobs are seldom the targets of sympathy because of their social condition. Rather, if they benefit from government programs or are subject to any

91

empathy, it is because of their ethnic status. One way to look at the invisible nature of class is to guide students to realize that being, for example, Latino **and** low socio-economic class is sort of like the double whammy (throw in female, and you have the triple whammy). While one's disadvantaged minority status may be recognized, one's class status and the handicaps associated with it are not likely to be acknowledged. Perhaps the class can come up with ways to separate ethnic status from class standing.

Help in this endeavor may come from considering poor whites. To his credit, Jesse Jackson is one of the few civil rights leaders to mention the plight of poor European Americans. Is white skin sufficient to make the odds high enough that European Americans with family histories of poverty will be able to pull themselves up by their boot straps? Perhaps you have in your class European American students who are the very first in their extended families to attend college and who come from families that have struggled for generations to free themselves from the mire of poverty and unskilled labor. If they are willing to talk about their family histories, stereotypes such as "white trash" and "trailer trash" could be examined. If not, you might lead a discussion of stereotypes targeting lower class whites.

Classroom Exercises: Practical Applications

1. Have the students do the Avoidant/Withdrawn or Approach/Attached exercise in Box 15.1. Ask them to score themselves and to pass scores to you on a scratch pieces of paper (no names). What they will be giving you is simply whether they fall in either of the two categories or neither. You can report to them whether a majority of the class falls into one of the categories, and, if so, ask them what are the implications. Suppose, for example, a majority of the class falls into the avoidant/withdrawn category, is that related to their (likely) young age? To their above average intelligence? To their prominently urban, suburban, or rural residence (whichever applies)? Or is there some other way to explain the outcome? Alternatively, one might expect that

a majority would fall into the approach/attached category because it may be regarded as more socially acceptable.

Individual students may be willing to say why they found particular needs applicable to themselves. Should that be so, additional insights into the nature of Murray's needs will be gained.

2. Are dreams clairvoyant? Some students will think so, even if they have read Box 15.2. Lead an analysis of students' dreams in order to convince them that a dream which appears to be a vision of some future events may be an expression of images that can be more straight-forwardly explained. (Note: Clairvoyant has a broader meaning: perceiving objects, people, or events that are not present; the analyses could assume this broader definition.)

First have students relate dreams that appear to allow perception of future. These would be dreams that occurred on one day and included imagery related to subsequent events. A simple example would be a dream of talking to an old friend followed shortly thereafter by a phone call from the friend. Taking this example as a case in point, if students do not ask "What's the probability that the friend would call you, dream or not?" you may want to do so. Perhaps the old friend calls monthly. If it has been nearly a month since the last calls, the odds of a call are pretty good, regardless of dream content.

Hopefully students will look also at the global nature of dream content which may make it applicable to a number of different future events. For example, a dreamer may say that she or he heard a ringing during a dream, and later the same night, faintly heard a familiar voice. Such content may support interpretations ranging from a "prediction" of a future episode of tinnitus that makes hearing friends difficult to a premonition of a friend's future call.

You can also make some other points should students fail to do so. Do we notice only dreams that seem to be harbingers of future events, while we ignore the vast majority of dreams with no apparent relation to our reality?

Do we dig up dreams retrospectively to match some important event that occurred to us ("Hi Pat!...Not so long ago I had a dream about talking to you on the phone."). You can, of course, think of other alternative explanations of dreams, and so can the students.

3. As suggested by Box 15.3, stories inspired by TAT pictures can be quite fascinating, but may be open to multiple interpretations. If you do not have access to real TAT cards, you can probably find a suitable set of rather ambiguous pictures by scanning magazines or web pages. Any case of people being together in a scene, without it being clear what they are doing together, would qualify. Present these to students and ask them to describe what is happening in the picture. Having several students provide stories about a single picture should convince the class that (1) there are appreciable individual differences in perceptions of content; (2) many, maybe most, of students' stories are routine and without meaningful psychological content; and (3) some pictures will stimulate a consensus story: most students agreeing on what is happening in the scene.

For each student's story have some other students offer a tongue in cheek psychoanalytic interpretation (keep it jocular and in the world of pretend so as to avoid offense) and still other students offer a more straightforward interpretation. Assume a picture of two men facing to the front, shoulder to shoulder, each with a faint frown on his face. A psychoanalytic interpretation might be "these guys are brothers who have been fighting each other for years over who will replace Dad as the apple of Mom's eye." A straightforward interpretation would be "These guys have been waiting for some time to be admitted into some building and are becoming mildly irritated."

To make sure that TAT interpretations are seen as at least potentially helpful in understanding people's personalities and in diagnosing problems, you may want to ask students to provide some stories that might be told by someone who is seriously disturbed. One student could take the perspective of a schizophrenic, another that of a depressed person, and still another that of a person with gender identity problems. They should be able to see that people can read their own motivations into the pictures in ways that shed light on personality and are diagnostic of psychological problems.

Suggested Readings for Lecture Support

Robinson, F.G. *Love's Story Told: A Life of Henry A. Murray.* Cambridge, MA: Harvard University Press, 1992.

This fascinating book probably provides more insight into Murray than anything ever written about him. It is a good read as well as informative.

Lilienfeld, S. O., Wood, J. M., & Garb, H. N. The scientific status of projective techniques. *Psychological Science in the Public Interest,* 2000, 1, 27-65.

This is the "for professionals" version of the Lilienfeld and colleagues' critique of the Rorschach and TAT (the pop version is in Chapter 1 Student Readings). The TAT fares better than the Rorschach.

Suggested Readings for the Student

Murray, H. A. A note on the possible clairvoyance of dreams. In E. S. Shneidman (Ed.) *Endeavors in psychology: Selections from the personology of Henry A. Murray.* New York: Harper and Row, 1981c, pp. 563-566.

Murray, H. A. A method for investigating fantasies: The Thematic Apperception Test (with Christiana D. Morgan). In E. S. Shneidman (Ed.) *Endeavors in psychology: Selections from the personology of Henry A. Murray.* New York: Harper and Row, 1981c, pp. 390-408.

Here are two articles that will be intrinsically interesting to students. Each is a fun read and far too rich in detail for the text author to do them justice.

The Trait Approach to Personality Traits: Raymond Cattell and Hans Eysenck

Chapter Outline

Chapter 16
THE BELL CURVE: RACE AND THE ENVIRONMENT

BIG 5 OR BIG 3?

Conclusions

Summary Points

Running Comparison

Essay/Critical Thinking Questions

Email Interaction

Objectives

1. Indicate how Cattell's relatively privileged childhood and exposure to the early mental testers may have determined his career direction, his interest in the nature/nurture controversy, and factor analysis as well as the orientation implied by his econetic model.

2. Understand Cattell's types of traits and types of intelligence. Discuss Sternberg's, Gardner's and Goleman's theories of intelligence and the relativity conception of intelligence.

3. Appreciate the development of the 16PF and crystallized and fluid intelligence. Know the limitations of factor analysis, the short-comings of the heritability approach, Cattell's use of obscure terms, and the controversies surrounding his loss of a prestigious award.

4. Appreciate how Eysenck's immigrant status and association with Sir Cyril Burt affected his point of view, the relationship of his view to Cattell's, his distinction of traits and types, the central role of the ARAS, his scientific model for studying personality, and the development of tests to measure E, N, and P.

5. Learn how Eysenck's position was supported by several lines of research and the limitations of his position, focusing on deficiencies of the ARAS mechanism and failure to do

truly genetic research. Discuss "race" in the context of the *Bell Curve* and relate early enrichment and IQ inflation to the heritability controversy. Appreciate the number of traits debate.

Classroom Discussion: Beyond the Text and the Lecture

1. Do people study what is important to them personally so that they become advocates for some advantage they have or for the correction of some disadvantage they suffer? Examples would be people with learning disabilities studying learning disabilities, people with good memories studying memory, and relevant to this chapter, people with high intelligence "theorizing" that high intelligence is wired into the brain of a privileged few, and thus, unavailable to others.

First, you may want to take up the general question, do people, perhaps especially in psychology, study what is personally relevant to them. I know a dozen psychologists who are studying what is highly relevant to their own lives. I'll bet you do also. Maybe you could use examples orally, in class, of colleagues who are personally involved with their research, but are not at your university. While there is nothing inherently wrong with this practice, you could ask students about problems with it, such as loss of objectivity. They should be able to come up with some positive aspects of studying personally relevant topics, such as a burning desire to understand the topic.

Now, how about Cattell and Eysenck, two psychologists who were obviously more proud of their assumed, and probably actual, high intelligence than any of their other characteristics (Eysenck, the master of many languages, once summarily dismissed a colleague of mine because he could not speak several languages). By arguing that intelligence is mostly "inherited" and thus presumably not alterable by environmental intervention, are they trying to confirm that they belong to an elite club who are justified in accepting no new members? It is almost like the rich feeling justified in supporting tax breaks for the rich ("We deserve to keep what we have by virtue of our superior intelligence and character."). This could be an explosive discussion, but it would remind students that all kinds of scientists, certainly including psychologists, have their personal axes to grind (Edward Teller the "inventor" of the hydrogen bomb was one of the biggest supporters of nuclear arms). You may also want to consider the possibility that Eysenck and Cattell support the "genetic position" because it makes them look more scientific than others, a position consistent with their self-perceived uniqueness.

2. Genetics is done with populations not traits. Geneticists may look for gene products associated with a characteristic found in a particular population. Breeding to enhance a characteristic may be part of the strategy. For example, behavior geneticist Jerry Hirsch of the University of Illinois has, through breeding of fruit flies, established the existence of two behaviorally different strains, one group of flies that migrate to the top of a container and one that migrates to the bottom. He has shown them to be genetically different at the chromosomal level.

In view of these observations, you could lead the students in designing a research program to search for a genetic disposition to Tourettes Syndrome. First, students need to realize that it is important to sample from the population of Tourettes people. To make this task manageable it would be handy if Tourettes were disproportionately represented in some available, relatively small, population, as bipolar disorder seems to be among the Amish. Lets suppose that Tourettes is highly likely to occur among the Rodarians, a (fictitious) religious group who live together in an small isolated area of the country and intermarry. This group could be studied to determine whether those with Tourettes belong to families who show some marker-characteristic for which there is likely to be a genetic disposition. For example, families with Tourettes do not all have Tourettes, but most may have some kind of motor problem. Motor problems are part of Tourettes people's symptoms and there may well be part of a genetic disposition to such problems. This exercise could teach students that heritability studies are not the only way to investigate the role of the genes in human behavior. In fact, people who do heritability studies might be given the benefit of a doubt concerning their allegedly consistent heritability outcomes, then told "you have your prediction of breeding experiment outcomes, now do the breeding." After all, a heritability index is only a prediction of breeding study outcomes. Therefore, one could argue that, at best, heritability advocates have merely taken the first step in their research program.

3. Discuss how an early enrichment program might be instituted into the public schools. Among the references cited in the Campbell and Ramey (1994) paper (see text references) you will find some that describe the techniques Craig Ramey and his colleagues have used to create enrichment for children. However, you need not go to the trouble of looking up those papers: The students are probably going to show plenty of creativity concerning how to enrich the environments of children. Nevertheless, I have a couple of hints for you. First, remind students that effective enrichment starts very early. Children should spend large parts of each day in enriched environments beginning at a few months of age. Second, every experience in the enriched environment should be a learning experience. For example, when infants are fed, they should be allowed to examine and play with their food. When fingering their food, they are learning about its texture and about interesting shapes they can make of it. Throwing and dropping objects teaches intuitive physics to infants and teaches them that they can make things happen. Like meal time, other experiences, such as bathing, should be extended in time for as long as the infant wants. He or she should be allowed, even encouraged, to play in the water and experience objects floating and appearing and disap-pearing beneath the water. With these hints and your guidance, students should be well on their way to offering many interesting suggestions regarding early enrichment.

Classroom Exercises: Practical Applications

Chapter 16

1. Have students do their own personality profiles by completing the exercise in Box 16.1 with use of Figure 16.3. Here is another opportunity to have students observe that different people have different profiles. Have students place a somewhat transparent piece of paper over their profile line, trace it, and hand the copy in to you. You can hold up different copies to show that they are different. Holding up the two most similar copies will again establish that even the two that are most alike are still different.

Survey students to determine whether there are clusters of dimensions upon which people tend to score high or low. For example, are people who are outgoing also assertive and happy-go-lucky? Are people who are relaxed also placid and sober? This procedure will show that dimensions may be related.

2. Have students fill out the Maudsley Personality Inventory, Short Form (Box 16.3). Determine whether there are any trends. Have students record their scores anonymously and pass them to you. Does the class as a whole tend to be extraverted? Probably the class will report being low on N, unless they fail to see through the relatively transparent N items. Next ask students to indicate whether they scored high or low on E and if either of those extreme results fits their own perceptions of the degree to which they are extraverted or introverted. You can do the same for N, but tread lightly. Students may be embarrassed to admit they are high on N. Perhaps you can protect students' egos by prefacing the question about N scores with a statement concerning the "questionable accuracy of such short tests as the Maudsley." Then high scorers may rush to explain that their score is off the mark. This exercise will further teach students about individual differences and will give them more familiarity with personality testing and its short-comings.

3. Lead students to the design of a hypothetical experiment concerning drug effects on *Is* and *Es* . Perhaps you could have them arrive at the use of pseudoephedrine hydrochloride (brand name, Sudafed): After you have established that they will need to use a mild "upper," ask

them what over the counter products qualify. Of course, informed consent would have to be exercised. Probably accepting as subjects only people who have regularly used Sudafed or its generic equivalent would be a good idea (permits from physicians would be even better).

Lead them to a prediction of an outcome. *Es* who have "down" ARASs should benefit most from taking a dose of Sudafed prior to doing some task requiring concentration. Thus, first, an *E-I* test should be administered to a subject population, and high *Es* and *Is* located and given consent forms indicating "you may be given Sudafed." Half of each group would be given Sudafed and the other half a red piece of candy that looks like Sudafed. In the no-Sudafed condition, there should be no difference between the performance of *Is* and *Es* on, for example, a timed test of arithmetic solving ability, but in the Sudafed condition, *Es* should do better (the Sudafed may actually lower the performance of *Is* as their ARASs are already "up"). [If you really want to run this experiment, use coffee and de-caf coffee and run it through the human subjects committee first.]

Suggested Readings for Lecture Support

Flynn, J. R. Searching for justice: The discovery of IQ gains over time. *American Psychologist*, 1999, 54, 5-20.

In this article, James Flynn lays out the latest information about the fascinating and puzzling implications of the world-wide, on-going increase in IQ.

Cattell, R. B. The 16 PF personality structure and Dr. Eysenck. *Journal of Social Behavior and Personality*, 1986, 1, 153-160.

More clearly than any other source that I know, this paper lays out the differences between the two theorists covered in this chapter.

Suggested Readings for the Student

Eysenck, S. B. G. & Eysenck, H. J. Salivary response to lemon juice as a measure of introversion. *Perceptual and Motor Skills,* 1967, 24, 1047-1053.

Students will find this study especially clear and convincing evidence for the Eysenck's ARAS theory.

Ramey, C. T. & Ramey, S. L. Early intervention and early experience. American Psychologist, 1998, 53, 109-120.

Any would-be parent will be interested in this well written summary of the effects of early enrichment on children and how enrichment is effectively instituted.

Chapter 17

Personality Development and Prejudice: Gordon Allport

Chapter Outline

Allport, the Person

Allport's View of the Person

HUMANISM?

EMPHASIS ON UNIQUE TRAITS AND BEHAVIORAL VARIABILITY

DE-EMPHASIZING THE FREUDIAN UNCONSCIOUS

Basic Concepts: Allport

PERSONALITY DEFINED

TRAITS

CARDINAL, CENTRAL, AND SECONDARY P.D.s

Personality Development

THE PROPRIUM AND THE SEVEN STAGES OF THE DEVELOPING SELF

THE MATURE PERSONALITY

Personality and Prejudice

PREJUDICE DEFINED

SOCIAL DISTANCE

SUBTLE MANIFESTATIONS OF RACISM

Chapter 17
"RACE" DIFFERENCES

STEREOTYPES

PAINTING THE PICTURE OF THE PREJUDICED
PERSONALITY

Evaluation

CONTRIBUTIONS

LIMITATIONS

Conclusions

Summary Points

Running Comparison

Essay/Critical Thinking Questions

Email Interaction

Objectives

1. Learn how Allport's family was very different from that of
any theorist covered earlier and how Allport's family
atmosphere set the tone for his social orientation and open-
minded theorizing.

2. Understand the debate over Allport's alleged humanism,
his view of existentialism, his emphasis on unique traits,
and on behavioral variability, the idiographic approach,
consciousness compared to the Freudian unconscious, and
the eclectic point of view.

3. Appreciate Allport's role in the development of the
Adjective Generation Technique (AGT), his definition of
personality and of trait, his criteria for traits, the difference
between common traits and personal dispositions (P.D.s),
the difference between cardinal, central, and secondary
P.D.s., and whether traits are specific to situations.

4. Be able to define proprium, to outline Allport's stages of personality development and associated concepts, to explain the mature personality--including such issues as functional autonomy, frustration tolerance, and sense of humor. Consider intrinsic and extrinsic religious motivation and its several correlates.

5. Know the interplay between prejudice and racism, the problems with the notion of "race" and with studies of race differences, the definition of stereotypes, results of the recent study on mutual stereotyping by European-Americans and African-Americans, the picture of the prejudiced personality, authoritarianism, the comparison of Allport and Du Bois, and short-comings of Allport's thinking.

Classroom Discussion: Beyond the Text and the Lecture

1. Allport is an appropriate theorist to end with, because his thinking relates well to that of several other theorists. Some important points to cover in this wrap-up discussion include his concern with Freud's alleged over-emphasis on the unconscious. Students may recall that Allport, instead of becoming a hero worshiper upon first encountering the master, had immediate misgivings. Generally he seemed to think that Freud dug too deep too quickly. Sometimes factors closer to the surface are important. Being eclectic and open-minded, Allport did, however, use Freudian ideas when they were appropriate (e.g., id was represented as "body" and superego as "society").

A coincidence with Fromm is worth noting: Allport's "economic orientation" was somewhat equivalent to Fromm's marketing type. He was a defender of Murray, but more because of his openness than because they agreed a great deal. They were particularly at odds concerning the unconscious. But he did think, on an abstract plane, much like Maslow. Both referred to multiple motivations. His approach was idiographic, like Kelly's. However, he emphasized unique traits, unlike Cattell and Eysenck.

Chapter 17

Allport made use of Erikson's identity crisis and his "prejudiced people" were much like Rotter's externals. Finally, like Sullivan and some others, Allport was a stage theorist. These contrasts are only examples of the many that you and the students can conjure up, much to the benefit to the students.

2. After reading the text, I hope that the students are convinced that laughing at themselves is generally good for them. Perhaps you will want to start a discussion on "taking a joke" by reiterating the reasons why laughing at one's self is good. The emphasis should be on communicating that one knows and accepts one's short-comings, but accepts oneself and other people as well.

There are, nevertheless, limitations to joining in the laugher directed to oneself. There is a broad literature that indicates people orient to the negative, because it is more informative. To illustrate, if an individual says something nice about her or himself, it may be true or it may be an attempt at impression management. However, if a person says something negative about him or herself, others may reason "He wouldn't say something *like that* about himself, if it weren't true." That is, negative statements about one's self are less likely to be seen as attempts to manipulate others' opinions of oneself (an important exception is attempts at ingratiation by making negative statements about one's self on trivial issues, thereby looking humble). To put it another way, one is a more credible source when making negative statements about ones' self than when making positive statements.

What does this all have to do with joining in laughter directed at oneself? To laugh at oneself is to admit to deficiencies. That is the virtue of it and also the problem. Too much laughing at oneself can eventually make a person seem to have more deficiencies than strengths. The old adage "kick 'em when they're down" may be apropos. Masochists have little trouble finding people who will pound on them psychologically, because they readily give others' license to "hit" on them. There may be a delicate balance between reasonable humility and psychological masochism. Hopefully students can appreciate that possibility and know that laughing at oneself has its limits.

3. Why does contact between European-Americans and people of color sometimes improve relations between the two groups and sometimes make relations worse? Some people, even some social scientists, naively criticize the psychologists who testified before the Supreme Court prior to the 1954 desegregation decision, because these academics argued that contact between blacks and whites in the schools would improve relations between them. That is exactly what they argued, but that is not all of the argument. Clearly these psychological professionals felt that contact would have positive effects only under certain conditions. Put in summary form, the contact had to be under conditions of equal status, have the support of the powers that be, and occur in a cooperative atmosphere. Obviously those conditions are all too rarely met in the school and elsewhere. Fortunately, recent research indicates that contact may be indirect: Knowing that members of one's own group have friends among the "other" group can go a long way toward smoothing the rough edges of relationships between the groups.

Let me suggest that you start with a question phrased something like this: "Does contact between people of color and 'white' people promote liking and understanding one another better?" You are likely to get arguments on either side, with neither side saying much about the circumstances of contact. Some will refer to their high school experiences of perpetual conflict between "the races," while others will tell how they experienced a decline in personal prejudice once they got to know members of the "other" group. Guide them to a consensus among the opposing debaters by pointing to the conditions that must prevail if friendly, as opposed to hostile, interactions are to occur.

Classroom Exercises: Practical Applications

Chapter 17

1. Have the students use the Adjective Generation Technique (AGT, see Box 17.1) to describe their own group and then another group (e.g. "using a scratch piece of paper, write down five words to describe your own [the other] group"). You may want them to describe a group that is not represented in class (Russians or Iranians), or each other, if, for example, about half the class is Latina(o) and the other is European-American. I would not presume to advise you on this choice.

You may score these descriptions by using using actual FAVorability values (and ANXiety values and FEMininity values) by using the table in the appendix of Allen and Potkay, 1983a. A quicker way is to just assign a valance (+ or -) to each word depending on whether its connotation is positive or negative. In this case a whole description of five words is positive if at least three of the words are assigned pluses, and negative if three minuses are assigned (zeros could be assigned to "ify" words, but this option will give students license to hide bias and may result in no majority of pluses and minuses). You could do the assignment of the valances or have students exchange descriptions and do it themselves. In the latter case, descriptions would be done anonymously, with only the describer's own-group-name coded somewhere on the sheet, perhaps the back (initials or "the last four digits of Grandmother's phone number" could serve as codes, so that students could find their descriptions later, if that is needed).

Did students favor their own group? It is entirely possible that the members of a particular group will not show the in-group bias effect, while the members of another group will show bias. Also, it is possible that one group will show a greater bias than the other (that is what I found in comparing African-Americans' and European-Americans' descriptions). After this consideration, the remaining time on the exercise might be spent comparing descriptions of groups, using some example stereotypic words frequently found on a group's lists of descriptors of another group. For example, I found that European-Americans frequently described African-Americans as "athletic" and the latter described the former as "prejudiced." Should you have African-American and European-American students describe each other, you can expect some interesting comments upon comparing your students' descriptions with those of my student subjects (see Tables 17.2 and 17.3).

2. Help students appreciate that trait expressions may be tied to particular situations. Begin by asking each to think for a minute and come up with the one trait that each is sure he or she posseses. Because students are likely to come up with positive traits, you will probably not encounter difficulties when you ask each in turn to tell the class which trait she of he has chosen. Let us suppose a student chooses "conscientious." First, have the student give examples of behaviors he or she regularly performs that are manifestations of the trait. Now, ask the student, "Are you always conscientious, in all the social and physical situations you encounter?" Students will (almost) all find exceptions to the rule of behavioral consistency, even for their most prominent trait. Pointing to the exceptions will allow students to appreciate that a person's traits are, at least to a degree, specific to particular situations or classes of situations. One may be highly conscientious in situations relating to dress, personal hygiene, and personal property, but be a slob on a camping trip and in the office at work.

3. Have students respond to the Social Distance Scale (SD scale) listed in the text. There are seven items, each of which could be responded to with the use of seven point scales anchored by "yes, I would" and "no I wouldn't." Let the target of responses be some group that is not represented in class and is likely to be held in contempt at the time of the exercise. An example might be Iraqies. Alternatives are a fictitious group with an evil sounding name (Vulturians?) or some group whose oppression is just now coming to our consciousness (e.g., Haitians). Your choice of a target group will greatly shape results.

This exercise should be done anonymously. You need not score the scale formally, but looking over the responses will probably allow you to state that few people would accept the target in close relationships. If so, ask students why they think *the class* rejected the target. Some answers will take the form: "What will my friends (or neighbors or relatives) think if I married one of these people?" The moral: almost everyone shows some discrimination when it comes to choices for intimate, committed, permanent relationships.

Suggested Readings for Lecture Support

Allport, G. W. *The nature of prejudice.* Reading, MA: Addison Wesley, 1954.

This classic book will allow you to share with students additional insights from Allport's fertile mind.

Allport, G. W. *Patterns and growth in personality.* New York: Holt, Rinehart, and Winston, 1961.

This account of Allport's theory is relevant to child rearing, a topic of great interest to many students.

Suggested Readings for the Student

Winter, D.G. Gordon Allport and the legend of "Rinehart". *Journal of Personality,* 1996, 64, 263-273.

Students will resonate to this story of a legendary Harvard student, as undergraduate Allport told it.

Peterson, B. E. & Lane, M. D. Implications of authoritarianism for young adulthood: Longitudinal analysis of college experiences and future goals. *Personality and Social Psychology Bulletin,* 2001, 27, 678-690.

That a tendency to Right Wing Authoritarianism has implications for choices of undergraduate majors should be of considerable interest to students.

Chapter 1

Multiple Choice Items for the Introductory Chapter

1.1
1

Which of the following is a key psychological phrase generally referring to the observation that people differ in a variety of ways? a. personality traits; b. behavioral dimension; c. personality profile; d. individual differences

1.2
1

Which of the following refers to a continuum of behavior analogous to a yardstick? a. personality traits; b. behavioral dimension; c. personality profile d. individual differences

1.3
2

What is the most basic assumption of the preliminary definition of personality?; a. all people are essentially alike; b. a person behaves consistently from one situation to the next; c. each person's personality is entirely different from that of each other person; d. every personality psychologist has his/her own unique definition of personality

1.4
1

Which of the following refers to internally based psychological characteristics that often correspond to adjectival labels such as shy, kind, mean, outgoing, dominant, and so forth?; a. personality traits b. behavioral dimension; c. personality profile d. individual differences

1.5
2

The preliminary definition of personality is a. all those psychological characteristics that encompass emotions, behavior, thought, and psychological problems; b. a set of degrees falling along many behavioral dimensions, each degree corresponding to a trait; c. consciousness and

unconsciousness; d. all psychological factors, including those relating to intellectual functioning 1.6
3

Which of the following is a serious short-coming of the preliminary definition of personality? a. it is too short: it would have to be a page long to accommodate all the concerns of the many personologists; b. it fails to rely on behavioral consistency; c. it emphasizes physiological processes too much; d. it focuses on developmental processes too little
1.7
3

According to Bjork, which of the following is under-appreciated in our assessments of our abilities and characteristics? a. genes; b. our family histories; c. effort; d. attitude
1.8
3

Which of the following theorists has explicitly rejected the basic assumption of the preliminary definition? a. Mischel; b. Eysenck; c. Cattell; d. Murray 1.9
2

Where single behavioral dimensions corresponding to traits are concerned, a. no two people would ever have the same trait;b. all people are likely to have the same trait; c. it is vary rare that two people would have the same trait; d. any two people could have the same trait
1.10
2

Personologists share a belief in a. individual differences; b. the sameness of personalities; c. the inconsistency of behavior; d. personality being secondary to intelligence
1.11
3

Scientific is a. unbiased observations that are quantified; b. any technique that involves the use of numbers; c. techniques that are used solely by people with Ph.D.s; d. methods that yield significant results 1.12
3

People who use unscientific methods tend to select observations on the basis of a. quantifiability; b. ability to manipulate variables; c. convenience; d. ability to systematize results 1.13

The case study method involves a. studying many cases; b. intensive observations on a single case; c. studying people with heavy case loads; d. hypothetical cases instead of real ones   1.14

5

Which of the following is true of a "narcissistic" person with little "social interest." a. people admire because they are not concerned about what others think of them; b. they are treated as "special" by parents c. they typically have low intellectual skills; d. they are disinterested in parties and other social gatherings

1.15

6

A variable is
a. anything that is static or unchanging
b. something for which changes cannot be quantified
c. a phenomenon subject to qualitative analysis only
d. a variation in quantity specified by numbers

1.16

6

Two variables are said to be correlated if a. the two are unrelated; b. variations in one correspond closely to variations in the other; c. one varies and the other one does not; d. both are unchanging   1.17

6

Which of the following is most clearly a variable? a. a dead tree's height; b. a fossilized skeleton's size; c. your birth date; d. intelligence   1.18

6

In the case of correlation, researchers are usually interested in a. whether variation in one variable closely corresponds to variation in another; b. the curvature of the line relating two variables; c. positive relationships, only; d. negative relationships, only   1.19

6

In the case of a positive correlation a. high values on one variable correspond to low values on the other; b. high values on one variable correspond to high values on the other; c. values on one variable do not correspond to values on the other; d. values of the variables are obtusely related   1.20

A correlation coefficient a. is represented by the letter
"c"; b. indicates the degree of curvature of the line
representing the relationship between two variables;
c. is represented by the letter "r"; d. indicates the degree
to which the relationship between two variables departs
from homogeneity

1.21

In a negative correlation a. high values on one variable
correspond to low values on the other; b. high values on one
variable correspond to high values on the other; c. values on
one variable do not correspond to values on the other; d.
values of the variables are obtusely related

1.22

If the correlation between two variables is nil a. high
values on one variable correspond to low values on the
other; b. high values on one variable correspond to high
values on the other; c. values on one variable do not
correspond to values on the other; d. values of the
variables are obtusely related

1.23

Which of the following correlation coefficients represents the
strongest relationship? a. -.89; b. +.65; c. +.02; d. -.45

1.24

In the "stress" and "upper respiratory congestion"
example a. "stress" is the independent variable; b.
"upper respiratory congestion" is the independent
variable; c. the two variables are positively correlated
d. the two variables are negatively correlated

1.25

Among the limitations of the correlational method, one of
the more serious is a. it cannot be scientific; b. even
large correlation coefficients do not imply causation;
c. negation correlations are not as meaningful as positive
correlations; d. nil correlations are extremely rare

1.26

Which of the following relationships may imply cause and
effect? a. the positive relationship between the height of
husbands and the height of wives; b. the negative

relationship between waist size and head size; c. no example is entirely appropriate: correlation does not mean causation; d. the nil relationship between wealth and religious conviction   1.27
7

Despite the limitations of the correlational method a. if two variables are highly correlated, one will predict the other; b. it is still more scientific than all other methods; c. it is not a source of problems, because it is rarely used; d. it is still better than the experimental method

1.28
7

The independent variable a. has variance that is arranged by the experimenter; b. has variance that occurs naturally; c. does not actually vary; d. is free to vary under the influence of the independent variable(s)

1.29
7

The dependent variable a. has variance that is arranged by the experimenter; b. has variance that occurs naturally; c. does not actually vary; d. is free to vary under the influence of the independent variable(s)

1.30
7

In an experiment a. only independent variables are involved; b. the experimenter sets values of independent variables and observes influences on dependent variables; c. the experimenter sets values on dependent variables and observes influences on independent variables; d. the experimental subjects control what happens to all variables in the experiment

1.31
7

Use of the experimental method makes it reasonable to make statements about a. the "truth-value" of results; b. cause and effect; c. linear relationships only; d. curvilinear relationships only   1.32
8

What sort of test did Perry and colleagues (1995) use in their experiment on dextro-amphetamine? a. the TAT: rather ambiguous pictures of people; b. the MMPI 2 (new Minnesota

Multiphasic Inventory); c. The PSA (Personality Specific
Assessor); d. The Rorschach inkblot test   1.33
                                                          8
The procedure of the Perry and colleagues (1995) study of
dextro-amphetamine involved a. all subjects getting the
same amount of the drug; b. all subjects getting some amount
of the drug; c. some subjects not getting any of the drug; d.
testing immediately after dextro-amphetamine ingestion
                                                         1.34
                                                          7-8
In the Perry and colleagues (1995) study of dextro-
amphetamine, the dependent variable was a measure of
a. anxiety; b. attention; c. drug-resistance; d. drug-tolerance
                                                         1.35
                                                          8
When used to describe research results, "Statistically
significant" means _____. a. unlikely to occur by
chance; b. highly meaningful and important; c. having a high
probability of occurrence; d. representing a very crucial
statistic   1.36
                                                          8
Among the problems with the experimental method is that; a.
personality psychologists, like Cattell and Murray, accept it
uncritically; b. it allows no statements about cause and effect;
c. it usually must be used in artificial settings; d. it is a weak
form of science compared with the case study method
                                                         1.37
                                                          9
"Reliability" of a test refers to a. the degree to which the test
measures what it was designed to measure; b. the degree to
which the test constructor can be trusted; c. the importance of
the test results; d. the degree to which test results are
repeatable   1.38
                                                          9
"Validity" of a test refers to a. the degree to which the test
measures what it was designed to measure; b. the degree to
which the test constructor can be trusted; c. the importance of
the test results; d. the degree to which test results are
repeatable   1.39
                                                          9

All of the following are types of validity, except one. Which one is **not** a type of validity? a. convergent; b. predictive; c. test retest; d. construct validity   1.40
                                                                                              9-10

Which of the following is a characteristic of a projective test? a. stimuli are almost always questions; b. scorers all typically agree on the scoring of responses; c. oral responses are atypically made; d. stimulus materials are often ambiguous pictures   1.41
                                                                                              9-10

Which of the following could reasonably be used as a projective test? a. multiple choice questions in written form b. pictures of people interacting in some way; c. oral questions with definite answers; d. requests for the identification of common objects   1.42
                                                                                              9-10

Which of the tests is projective? a. Thematic Apperception Test; b. the SAT or ACT college entrance exams; c. the Adjective Check List personality test d. The Stanford-Binet intelligence test   1.43
                                                                                              11

Which of the following is most clearly characteristic of objective tests? a. stimuli are almost always questions; b. scorers all typically agree on scoring of responses; c. oral responses are typically made; d. stimulus materials are often ambiguous pictures   1.44
                                                                                              11

Which of the following provides the best example of an objective test? a. Rorschach Test; b. the SAT or ACT college entrance exams; c. the Sentence Completion Test ; d. Thematic Apperception Test   1.45
                                                                                              10-11

What did Lilienfeld, Wood and Garb find when they studied the reliability and validity of popular projective tests? a. these tests are all equally strong; b. the tests as a group were weak, some more than others; c. the Rorschach was the strongest; d. the draw a figure tests were the strongest.   1.46
                                                                                              12

Research has shown that Anglos and Latino a. have nothing in common; b. score very differently on the MMPI-2; c. score differently on four MMPI-2 scales; d. are very similar, except for the language difference

1.47
2

In the definition of personality, each behavioral dimension corresponds to a. a profile; b. a trait; c. a social situation; d. an emotion

1.48
2

Why is the assumption of behavioral consistency so important to the preliminary definition of personality? a. without it each person would have the same personality as each other person; b. without it the definition could not be scientific; c. without it one would be unable to infer a trait from observations of behaviors; d. without it personality would be infinitely variable

1.49
4

Why is it difficult to be unbiased in forming "case histories"? a. oneself is usually the "case" in question; b. more biases come out when one rather than many people are considered; c. only one person ever examines a case history for possible biases; d. the "case" may be a patient with whom one is personally involved

1.50
6

Which of the following is most clearly a psychological variable? a. body temperature; b. brain waves c. I.Q.; d. eye color

1.51
6

Which of the following represents a negative correlation? a. the height of husbands and height of wives; b. waist size and body weight; c. I.Q. score and success in school; d. number of sexual partners and length of romantic relationships

1.52
11

All except one of the following were reported by Masling (1997) in his comparison of objective and subjective tests. Which did he NOT report? a. projective tests predict broader behavior better in the long term; b. on objective tests, the genders differ on reports of dependency; c. it is nearly impossible to fake objective test responses; d. objective tests predict behavior best in the short term

1.53
8

Which is a way that a personologist has described experimentation?; a. "brass instrument psychology"; b. "psychology for the unwashed"; c. "fantasy psychology"; d. "Pilsbury Dough Boy psychology"   1.54

12

What did Hibbard et al. find when they compared Asians and whites on TAT scores? a. there were no differences between the groups on any scales; b. Asians scored lower on denial than whites; c. whites scored lower on total scores; d. whites scored higher on identification.   1.55

9

A test is valid if it a. yields the same score each time a person takes it; b. measures a variety of constructs; c. predicts behavior; d. has two halves that are highly correlated with each other   1.56

11

In the context of psychology, diversity refers to a. the same thing as individual differences; b. numerous cultures; c. change within a person on many different dimensions d. the same thing as in the animal kingdom   1.57

12

Which of the following statements about science is most reasonable?; a. science offers the best approach; b. science is cold and hard, too much so for it to be applied to human emotions and thinking; c. clearly science is less meaningfully applied to everything than spirituality; d. science is neither good or bad, it just is   1.58

13

Which of the following is true of well-thought-out philosophical positions, as opposed to scientific theories?; a. they are never as good as scientific theories; b. no matter how well thought out, they will be filled with contradictions; c. only in dealing with mystical problems, will they be better than scientific theories; d. even if abstract, they can have as much or more merit than scientific theories

1.1,d
1.2,b
1.3,b
1.4,a
1.5,b
1.6,d
1.7,c
1.8,a
1.9,d
1.10,a
1.11,a
1.12,c
1.13,b
1.14,b
1.15,d
1.16,b
1.17,d
1.18,a
1.19,b
1.20,c
1.21,a
1.22,a
1.23,a
1.24,c
1.25,b
1.26,c
1.27,a
1.28,a
1.29,d
1.30,b
1.31,b
1.32,d
1.33,c
1.34,a
1.35,a
1.36,c
1.37,d
1.38,a
1.39,c
1.40,d
1.41,b

1.42,a
1.43,b
1.44,b
1.45,b
1.46,c
Extra
Items
1.47,b
1.48,c
1.49,d
1.50,c
1.51,d
1.52,c
1.53,a
1.54,b
1.55,c
1.56.b
1.57,d
1.58,d

Chapter 2

Multiple Choice Items for the Chapter on Freud

2.1
20

How would you characterize the way Freud viewed the disciples and followers who surrounded him? a. with unqualified trust; b. with great familiarity; c. with suspicion; d. with a great sense of humility

2.2
20

Which of the following is an accurate description of Freud's family? a. his father was stern and humorless; b. his family was Jewish; c. his mother had a dull personality; d. they were Russian

2.3
20-21

All of the following are true of Freud's time in medical school except one. Which is NOT true? a. he entered medical school at age 17; b. his grades were rather mediocre; c. his most esteemed professor believed in closed energy systems; d. he invented a technique for staining nervous tissue

2.4
21

During medical school, Freud experimented with a. extrasensory perception ; b. goldfish; c. cocaine; d. bile

2.5
21

Freud became famous for his early book on; a. dreams b. sexual perversion; c. cocaine; d. bile

2.6
22

Early in his career, Freud adopted which philosophical position? a. indeterminism; b. holism; c. psychological determinism; d. nihilism

2.7
22

Upon what did Freud rely in forming his theory? a. ancient Greek philosophy; b. his own personal experiences; c. the teaching of Francis Cobbs; d. Johann Mueller's experiments

2.8
22

Upon the death of his father, what was probably Freud's dominant feeling?; a. guilt; b. indifference; c. chagrin; d. relief

2.9
21

How did Freud feel about religion?; a. he was devout; b. he was a militant atheist; c. he regarded it as an illusion d. he refused even to discuss the topic;

21

2.10
21

Which of the following is true of Freud's relationship with the Nazis? a. they forced to leave Vienna for England; b. they declared him an non-Jew; c. his books were admired by Hitler; d. they captured his daughter Anna and put her to death

2.11
21

Freud died of cancer of the mouth, probably traceable to a. a genetic disposition to cancer in his family; b. his highly unusual diet; c. a distinct lack of oral hygiene d. chain-smoking cigars

2.12
22-3

Which of the follow words best characterizes Freud's view of the human organism?; a. altruistic; b. apathetic c. selfish; d. benevolent

2.13
23

The id is ; a. self-sacrificing; b. beyond conscious awareness; c. a unit that develops after age 3 d. the third personality structure to develop

2.14
23

The id operates according to the _____ principle. a. agnostic; b. operant; c. pleasure; d. antagonistic

2.15
23

The primary process involves; a. needs to become all one can be; b. conscious thoughts; c. attempts to delay gratification; d. wishes that demand immediate satisfaction

2.16
23

Instincts are composed of a. physical needs only; b. physical needs and psychological wishes; c. mechanisms for delaying gratification; d. conscious thought about sex

2.17
23

All of the following are ways to describe "libido" except one. Which is not a way to describe "libido"?; a. an asexual energy; b. sexual desire in the broadest sense c. physical desire; d. erotic tendencies

2.18
23

The instinct "Thanatos" is associated with ; a. life; b. death; c. transcendence; d. apperception

2.19
23

If you wanted to see the id operating in real life, where would you look?; a. at your conscious sexual fantasies; b. at the flirtatious behavior of young people; c. at an infant's behavior; d. at you relationship to your lovers

2.20
23

123

What is needed to protect the infant from its tendency to accept any available object as a means to gratify a need?; a. a superego; b. an id; c. an archetype; d. an ego   2.21
24

The ego operates according to the _____ principle.
a. pleasure; b. primary process; c. secondary process; d. reality   2.22
24

The ego is guided by a higher level of mental functioning than that which guides the id. Which of the following is related to that functioning?; a. displeasure; b. primary process ; c. secondary process; d. surrealism
2.23
24

Which of the following is most true of the ego? a. it is the arm of the id; b. it commands the other personality structures; c. it is wholly conscious; d. it is impractical
2.24
24

Freud's definition of anxiety includes a. a central reference to explicit sexuality; b. a statement of relationship to fear; c. a reference to unpleasant emotional discomfort; d. a proposal for anxiety reduction   2.25
24

Defense mechanisms a. account for cultural pressures on people; b. satisfy id instincts; c. force people to accept their sexuality; d. help people regain control over id instincts
2.26
25

According to Freud, neuroses are a. helpful psychological processes; b. related to an over-control of instincts; c. more common among men than women d. forms of normal behavior   2.27
25

An hysterical neurosis is; a. quite common; b. physical symptoms designed to avoid painful experiences; c. a real tumor caused by psychological problems; d. episodes of crying and screaming or prolonged laughter   2.28
25

The superego is; a. an arm of the id; b. a mechanism for sexual gratification; c. the representation of society in personality; d. a storehouse of instincts   2.29
25

The superego operates according to the _____ principle.
a. reality; b. primary process; c. pleasure; d. morality
2.30
25

One of the superego's aspects or functions is equivalent to a. conscience; b. the devil on one's shoulder; c. rationality;

d. avoidance of addressing id needs   2.31
                                             25

Introjection involves a. searching for an object to satisfy
id instincts; b. repression of threatening experiences;
c. incorporation of the norms of one's culture; d. failure to
identify with parents   2.32
                                             25-26

All of the following are true regarding superego operation,
except one. Which is NOT true of superego operation?; a.
guilt; b. seeking perfection; c. inhibiting sexual and
aggressive needs; d. rejecting parents' renditions of society's
rules   2.33
                                             26

An ego ideal is a. the same as an ideal ego; b. internal
representations of idealized parents; c. consciousness
restricted to peers like oneself; d. a structure that mediates
between the ego and the superego   2.34
                                             27

Erogenous zones are ; a. the body parts that store ergs
b. non-sexual zones of the body; c. sensitive areas related to
instinctual satisfactions; d. parts of the body that are
purposefully ignored because they are insensitive   2.35
                                             27

To Freud, sexual referred to a. stimulation of the genitals
only; b. sexual intercourse; c. erotic interaction involving two
people; d. pleasurable feelings associated with stimulation of
erogenous zones   2.36
                                             27

Psychosexual refers to a. the sexuality of archetypes;
b. stages that are sexual in the broadest sense;
c. functionally autonomous stages of cognitive
development; d. the sexuality that occurs at adulthood
                                             2.37
                                             27

Which of the following stages is associated with oral
gratification?; a. Narcissistic; b. Oedipal; c. Young adulthood;
d. Juvenile   2.38
                                             27

Fixation involves; a. frustration resulting in permanent
investment of libidinal energy in a stage; b. obsessive-
compulsive behaviors in every case; c. effective and efficient
use of libidinal energy; d. lust for non-human objects: animals
and inanimate objects   2.39
                                             27

Regression is ; a. a statistical concept that Freud used to
estimate loss of libidinal energy; b. moving toward people; c.
anti-erotic; d. retreating to behaviors of an earlier fixated state
                                             2.40
                                             28

Which of the following types would tend to be sarcastic and argumentative? a. oral receptive; b. anal retentive; c. anal expulsive; d. oral aggressive   2.41
27

Which of the following types would tend to be suggestible and gullible? a. oral receptive; b. anal retentive; c. anal expulsive; d. oral aggressive   2.42
28

At the anal stage, toilet training often is a ; a. contest of wills; b. time of neglect of the child; c. time when parents disagree on what to do with the child; d. time of unparalleled cognitive expansion   2.43
28

Which of the following types would tend to be orderly, stingy and stubborn? ; a. oral receptive; b. anal retentive; c. anal expulsive; d. oral aggressive   2.44
28

Delaying gratification and retaining objects results from ; a. being oral receptive; b. childhood experiences of having to retain the feces; c. being oral retentive; d. childhood experiences of over-indulgence   2.45
28

Of all the psychosexual stages, which is most central to Freud's thinking?; a. oral; b. intestinal; c. anal; d. Phallic
2.46
29

At the Phallic stage, which question occupies the minds of children?; a. who does mommy favor?; b. are boys meaner?; c. why don't girls have penises?; d. why do mommy and daddy seem so different?   2.47
29

Which of the following involves the boy's attraction to his mother and desire to do his father in? a. Neurotic complex; b. Inferiority complex; c. Oedipal complex; d. Electra complex
2.48
29

Which of the following involves the girl's attraction to her father and desire to eliminate her mother?; a. Neurotic complex; b. Inferiority complex; c. Oedipal complex; d. Electra complex   2.49
29

Which of the following characterizes the boy during the Phallic stage?; a. genital fixation; b. penis envy; c. castration anxiety; d. basic distrust   2.50
29

Which of the following characterizes the girl during the Phallic stage?; a. genital fixation; b. penis envy; c. castration anxiety; d. basic distrust   2.51
29

Which of the following relates to superego development during the Phallic stage? a. successful toilet training; b. introjection of the same-sex parent's values; c. release of libidinal energies dammed up earlier; d. a feeling of awkwardness around the same-sex parent   2.52
25

Repression ; a. makes threatening material unavailable for recall; b. involves casting our unacceptable traits onto other people; c. allows us to excuse unacceptable behavior; d. produces behavior designed to reverse the effects of undesirable behavior   2.53
25

Rationalization ; a. makes threatening material unavailable for recall; b. involves casting our unacceptable traits onto other people; c. allows us to excuse unacceptable behavior; d. produces behavior designed to reverse the effects of undesirable behavior   2.54
25

Projection a. makes threatening material unavailable for recall; b. involves casting our unacceptable traits onto other people; c. allows us to excuse unacceptable behavior; d. produces behavior designed to reverse the effects of undesirable behavior   2.55
25

Undoing a. makes threatening material unavailable for recall; b. involves casting our unacceptable traits onto other people; c. allows us to excuse unacceptable behavior; d. produces behavior designed to reverse the effects of undesirable behavior;   2.56
30

What is the consequence of the girl's alleged greater difficulty in resolving her complex? a. a stronger superego than the boy; b. less ego-strength, on average, than the boy; c. failure to be sexually interested in anyone; d. stronger identification with the mother   2.57
32-33

The Rat man a. had been reared in a rat infested house; b. kept pet rats and trained them to perform circus-like tricks; c. dreamed of rats perched in a walnut tree; d. thought that rats were eating the anuses of his loved ones   2.58
32

Displacement; a. makes threatening material unavailable for recall; b. involves finding a new target for some feelings; c. allows us to excuse unacceptable behavior; d. is thinking intellectually rather than an emotionally   2.59
32

Little Hans liked to play with his a. horse; b. cow; c. widdler; d. argus   2.60
31

Anna O's symptoms included a. neurasthenia; b. hives; c. dissociative personality disorder; d. communication only in English   2.61
31

Dora a. dreamed that her house was on fire; b. married Herr K; c. talked in tongues; d. had a dream about a saber toothed tiger   2.62
32-33

The Wolf man a. saw seven doves in a pear tree; b. had a dream that Freud interpreted as symbolic of having seen his parents engaged in intercourse; c. had a dream that wolves were attacking his father and the woman he was courting; d. had big pointed ears, thus, the nickname "Wolfman"   2.63
30

During the latency period a. children are especially sexually active; b. children are sexually disinterested; c. children regress to pre-Phallic stages; d. children give up their fixations   2.64
30

Sublimation a. reorients instinctual aims in acceptable directions; b. involves casting our unacceptable traits onto other people; c. allows us to excuse unacceptable behavior; d. produces behavior designed to reverse the effects of undesirable behavior   2.65
30

Which of the following represents ancient or modern support for Freud's ideas? a. the Tallensi people of Ghana bend over backwards to avoid dealing with the Oedipus complex; b. the movie "Legends of the Fall" involved Oedipal rivalries among three brothers; c. the Hopi Indians of New Mexico teach about the Oedipus Complex to their children; d. the movie "Godfather" (Part 1) was about Oedipal rivalry   2.66
30

Cathexes involve a. asexual orientations; b. attachment of libidinal energy to objects in the real world; c. repression of sexuality ; d. effective and efficient use of libidinal energy in the real world   2.67
34

During the Genital stage a. boys long for a vagina; b. girls give up their attraction to males, temporarily; c. girls accept the lack of a penis and identify with the vagina; d. boys give up their attraction to females, temporarily   2.68
34-35

Freud's attitude toward females reflected all of the following, except one. Which was NOT reflected in Freud's attitude toward women? a. he implied that women were morally inferior; b. he believed that girls were mainly interested in manipulating the clitoris; c. he believed that women's greater tendency to neurosis was due to their switch from clitoral to

vaginal pleasure; d. he believed, if you read between the
lines, that women were similar to men, but superior   2.69
                                                        36

Phyllis Freud a. was Freud's youngest daughter; b. Freud's
first wife; c. a tongue-in-cheek gender reversal of Freud's
biography; d. an attempt to show that Freud's theory would
have turned out the same had be been a female   2.70
                                                  36

Which of the following was a disorder Phyllis Freud attributed
to many men? a. testyria; b. hysteria; b. asexual neurosis
c. horse phobias   2.71
                                                         35

Free association adopts an orientation that promotes the
spontaneous flow of ideas and images. Further, it allows
patients to experience a. repression; b. identification
c. catharsis; d. intellectualization   2.72
                                                         37

Manifest and latent content refer to a. the content of
dreams; b. sexual and asexual desire, respectively
c. the content of regressed experienced; d. the defense
mechanism, denial   2.73
                                                         40

Which is an important implication of the recent finding that the
Prefrontal Cerebral Cortex is a crucial site for dream
processing? a. it proves that the pons plays no role in
dreaming; b. that it is inhibited during sleeping is consistent
with Freud's conception of dreams; c. that it rides herd over
the emotions during sleeping is consistent with Freud's
dream conceptions; d. it is physically near the pons   2.74
                                                        37

The goal of psychoanalysis is to provide a. insight into
buried, taboo experiences ; b. a reduction of inferior
feelings; c. a restructuring of cognitive processes
d. extinction of phobias and neuroses   2.75
                                                         37

What technique did Freud try and abandon because it
provided only temporary solutions to patients' problems?
a. acupuncture b. hypnosis; c. laying on of hands; d.
astrology   2.76
                                                         38

Transference is to countertransference as a. night is to day;
b.the patients' unconscious needs are to the analyst's
unconscious needs; c. Oedipus complex is to Electra
complex; d. Phallic stage is to Genital stage   2.77
                                                        39

J. McVicker Hunt thought a. there was no evidence for
Freud's theory; b. studies lent support to the special
importance of early experience; c. the evidence
overwhelmingly supported Freud's view of the unconscious;

d. only Freud's conception of countertransference was valid

2.78

39

In a study of narcissism, Gabrial and colleagues found   a. no gender difference on narcissism; b. high narcissistic subjects had high positive illusions of attractiveness and intelligence; c. females tended to be higher than males on narcissism; d. low narcissistic subjects tended to be fixated at the anal stage or the latency stage

2.79

40-41

All of the following are conclusions regarding the degree of empirical support for Freud ideas, except one. Which was NOT a conclusion about support for Freud's ideas? a. there is no evidence for an "unconscious"; b. Motley's spoonerism studies failed to support Freud's "slips of the tongue" in any way; c. Anderson's work with subjects' recollections of others who were partially similar to significant others cannot be stretched to support transference d. Raskin and Shaw showed that persons scoring high on a Narcissism test used "I" and "me" more than low scorers

2.80

41-42

"False Memories"   a. are, in the final analysis, unrelated to Freud's ideas; b. are irrelevant to the psychotherapeutic context; c. can be induced only by an event that is basically the same as a previous event; d. are supported by a large body of research started by Elizabeth Loftus

2.81

42

Where did Anna O. get the idea, which Freud adopted, that one must dredge up traumas of the past and reexperience them in order to be well? a. from Janet b. from folk lore; c. from Breuer; d. from hallucinations

2.82

39

Motley's "slips of the tongue" research involved all of the following, except one. Which was NOT involved? a. a provocatively dressed female experimenter; b. homosexual and heterosexual males; c. some word pairs designed to elicit verbal foul-ups; d. a warning to some subjects that they would receive an electric shock

2.83

44-45

All but one of the following were among MacMillan's criticism of Freud and his ideas. Which was NOT one of his criticisms? a. Freud changed his mind three times about homosexuality; b. Freud was guilty of circular reasoning; c. Freud paid no attention to physiology; d. Freud changed definitions of key terms

2.84

45

All of the following are among MacMillan's reason's for Freud's continued popularity. Which is NOT reason?

a. people are attracted to the irrational; b. psychoanalysis deals with inherently interesting phenomena, such as sex and dreams; c. people think that psychoanalysis is beyond criticism; d. there is no empirical or experiential evidence to support for any form of the unconscious and identification

2.85

45

Which of the following is true regarding Anna O's "cure" via psychoanalysis? a. she spent nearly eight years in asylums after leaving psychoanalysis; b. she was never able to have a career; c. ten years after leaving psychoanalysis she developed full-blown schizophrenia; d. she committed suicide five years after leaving psychoanalysis

2.86

46-47

Which of the following is true regarding Freud's case of Dora? a. Dora stayed in psychoanalysis until she was cured b. Freud invented the episode of Herr K rubbing his erection against Dora; c. Dora finally married Herr K; d. Freud disagree with Dora concerning her belief that "smelling smoke" meant that she wanted to kiss Herr K

2.87

41

Masson has been criticized because a. Freud's early patients never overtly claimed to have been seduced; b. never consulted with Anna Freud; c. he never even looked at Freud's correspondence with Fliess; d. his interview with Freud occurred in 1939, not 1936

2.88

41

Powell and Boer a. claim that Freud placed heavy pressure on his early patients to recover memory of early childhood abuse; b. felt patients overtly reported being seduced, as Masson claimed; c. found some of Freud's former patients and established that they had actually never been seduced d. claim that Freud had always believed in the Oedipal theory

2.89

47

Regarding Little Hans a. he had no real phobia; b. his phobia developed after a horse kicked him; c. Freud correctly interpreted Hans' case with reference to Lamarck's still valid theory; d. Hans' father's castration threat came months before Hans phobia developed

2.90

47-48

All of the following are Freud's misconceptions about the Wolf Man, except one. Which is NOT a Freudian misconception? a. Freud said that the Wolf Man was incapacitated upon entering psychoanalysis, but he wasn't ; b. Freud claimed that the Wolf Man had numerous problems but he actually never had any physical or mental problems; c. Freud at times described the "wolves" in the dream as other kinds of creatures; d. Freud said that the Wolf Man was terrified of

wolves, but he actually hunted wolves   2.91
                                                          48

Which of the following was true of the Rat Man?   a. he loved
rats; b. he had an aversion for women; c. he was punished for
"masturbating" by Freud, not his father; d. he lived a long life
after being cured by psychoanalysis   2.92
                                                          48

Among the lasting contributions of Freud is   a. penis envy; b.
the latency period; c. castration anxiety; d. identification
                                                          2.93
                                                          48

Today Freud is a. of mainly historical significance
b. still having impact; c. second in citations to B. F. Skinner; d.
considered too controversial for inclusion in most personality
texts
Extra Items   2.94
                                                          20

Freud's age when he received his M.D. degree was a. 17
b. 20; c. 25; d. 30   2.95
                                                          21

How long did Freud survive after he arrived in London in
1938?   a. 10 years; b. 5 months; c. 6 years; d. 1 plus years
                                                          2.96
                                                          22

At an early age, Freud was ordered out of his parents bedroom
by a. a protective nanny; b. an outraged mother; c. a jealous
aunt; d. an irate father   2.97
                                                          23

Freud subsumed the several meanings of libido under
a. love; b. lust; c. longing; d. physical striving   2.98
                                                          25

The superego strives for   a. mastery of guilt; b. 100%
perfection; c. love in its purest sense; d. satisfaction of the ego
                                                          2.99
                                                          27-29

What is NOT a major producer of pleasure in the infant?
a. releasing the feces; b. masturbation; c. thumb sucking; d. the
constant input of varied sensory stimulation   2.100
                                                          29

Where does the boy child get his superego? a. from his
mother; b. from interactions with his peers; c. from his
interactions with all other people; d. from his father 2.101
                                                          47

All of the following are true of Freud's relationship to Little
Hans, except one. Which is **not** true? a. Freud sent Hans a
rocking horse; b. Freud teased Hans about losing his penis;
c. Freud advised that Hans be raised as a Jew; d. Freud
advised that Hans be circumcised   2.102
                                                          28

Anal-expulsive individuals a. are noted for their cleanliness; b. retain things; c. are devoted to "the rules"; d. disregard rules of cleanliness   2.103
                                                                    30-33
During the genital stage, energies are directed more toward a. benefiting others; b. pleasure and self-enhancement; c. curiosity seeking; d. oral expression   2.104
                                                                    43
The basic thesis of Esterson's book <u>Seductive Mirage</u> is a. Freud always really believed in the Oedipal theory; b. most of Freud's early patients offered no information pointing to childhood molestations; c. Freud lied about everything; d. Freud's early patients consciously lied about being seduced by their fathers and mothers   2.105
                                                                    38
A room or a table with food is a dream symbol for a. man; b. nourishment; c. woman; d. child   2.106
                                                                    38
Concerning transference a. there is no evidence for it; b. Freud eventually abandoned the concept; c. Freud replaced the notion with "countertransference"; d. there is tentative evidence supporting the concept   2.107
                                                                    40
When is objectivity particularly difficult to achieve?; a. in the laboratory; b. with use of scientific instruments; c. when testing psychiatric patients for research; d. when, in therapy, unknown occurrences to patients and distractions happen   2.108
                                                                    41
During therapy, Freud failed to appreciate the possible impact of a. his insistence that his patients remember their infancy; b. his copious notetaking; c. his failure to interrupt during free association; d. his informal clothing;   2.109
                                                                    39
According to research, "slips of the tongue" may be a. more verbal confusions than evidence for the operation of the unconscious; b. irrefutable evidence for the operation of the unconscious; c. wholly evidence for the verbal mechanisms gone awry and nothing else, including unconscious operations; d. interpretable in too many ways to be meaningful
                                                                    2.110
                                                                    24
Which of the following is solely below awareness (iceberg)? a. erg; b. id; c. ego; d. superego   2.111
                                                                    25
Who may have actually been responsible for the defense mechanisms? a. Adler; b. Jung; c. Anna Freud; d. Josef Freud
                                                                    2.112
                                                                    26
The "ego ideal" is an internal representation of   a. father;

b. mother; c. adults; d. parents   2.113
                                                                    41

The tragedy of Freud's abandonment of the seduction theory is
a. that he lied about the seductions; b. that he fell for his
patient's lies; c. that some of his patients committed suicide
because he failed to believe them; d. that it represented
insensitivity to the suffering of millions of abused children
                                                                    2.114
                                                                    25

Which is the principle of the superego? a. pleasure; b. reality;
c. morality; d. suppression   2.115
                                                                    46

According to Freud, in the long term (years after therapy), her
therapeutic relationship with Breuer helped Anna O to become
functional by generating in her; a. a sense of optimism; b. a
stronger super-ego; c. a stronger ego; d. a compensatory
personality structure   2.116
                                                                    43

Esterson charges in <u>Seductive Mirage</u> that Freud a. actually
never had the early patients he claims to have had; b. never
had the famous "Sun Phallus" man in therapy; c. typically
concocted an interpretation that fit his current theory, whatever
it happened to be; d. forgot that there were no fathers among
seducers   2.117
                                                                    39

"Positive illusions of attractiveness and intelligence" are
characteristics of a. women only; b. people who score high on
repression; c. people who score high on narcissism
d. children relative to adults   2.118
                                                                    43

According to Esterson, who, in his early writings, did Freud
indicate were NOT among the seducers of his young women
patients? a. fathers; b. brothers; c. non-relatives; d. family
members   2.119
                                                                    43

According to Esterson, Freud was a lover of a. soccer;
b. abstract art; c. political argument; d. analogies   2.120
                                                                    40

A poor theory, from a scientific point of view, a. is simple; b.
"explains" observations after they have occurred; c. has too few
concepts; d. is subject to disconfirmation through research
                                                                    2.121
                                                                    40

Freud ignored the impact of _____, a constant
presence in his therapy room? a. his daughter <u>Anna</u>; b. his
student, <u>Erik Erikson</u>; c. his <u>dog</u>; d. his <u>collection of</u>
<u>pornographic pictures</u>   2.122
                                                                    40

According to a recent review of research on the "unconscious"

a. there is no such thing; b. Freud's conception of it has been completely confirmed; c. the evidence is too mixed to draw firm conclusions; d. it exists, but is not quite what Freud thought it was   2.123
20

With regard to his ideas, Freud a. was very open to criticism; b. was very flexible regarding change; c. clung to each of his notions with great tenacity; d. refused to respond to criticisms regarding his ideas   2.124
34-35

According to Freud, women a. have less ego-strength than men, on average; b. are equal to men in all respects; c. were beginning to catch with men at the turn of the century; d. would have little difficulty competing with men if they would abandon vaginal sex   2.125
49

Which was true of Freud's American woman "patient"? a. she was retarded; b. her boy friend was Irish; c. she dreamed of stabbing herself; d. her parents approved of her boy friend

2.1,c	2.58,b	2.113, d
2.2,b	2.59,c	2.114, c
2.3,b	2.60,d	2.115, d
2.4,c	2.61,a	2.116, c
2.5,a	2.62,b	2.117, c
2.6,c	2.63,b	2.118, a
2.7,b	2.64,a	2.119, d
2.8,a	2.65,b	2.120, b
2.9,c	2.66,b	2.121, c
2.10,a	2.67,c	2.122, d
2.11,d	2.68,d	2.123, c
2.12,c	2.69,c	2.124, a
2.13,b	2.70,a	2.125, c
2.14,c	2.71,c	
2.15,d	2.72,a	
2.16,b	2.73,b	
2.17,a	2.74,a	
2.18,b	2.75,b	
2.19,c	2.76,b	
2.20,d	2.77a	
2.21,d	2.78,b	
2.22,c	2.79,c	
2.23,a	2.80,d	
2.24,c	2.81,b	
2.25,d	2.82,b	
2.26,b	2.83,c	
2.27,c	2.84,d	
2.28,c	2.85,a	
2.29,d	2.86,b	
2.30,a	2.87,a	
2.31,c	2.88,a	
2.32,d	2.89,d	
2.33,b	2.90,b	
2.34,c	2.91,c	
2.35,d	2.92,d	
2.36,b	2.93, b	
2.37,a	*Extra*	
2.38,a	*Items*	
2.39,d	2.94, c	
2.40,d	2.95, d	
2.41,a	2.96, d	
2.42,a	2.97, a	
2.43,b	2.98, b	
2.44,b	2.99, c	
2.45,d	2.100, d	
2.46,c	2.101, b	
2.47,c	2.102, d	
2.48,d	2.103, a	
2.49,c	2.104, b	
2.50,b	2.105, c	
2.51,b	2.106, d	
2.52,a	2.107, d	
2.53,c	2.108, a	
2.54,b	2.109, a	
2.55,d	2.110, b	
2.56,b	2.111, c	
2.57,d	2.112, d	

Chapter 3
Multiple Choice Items for the Chapter on Jung

3.1
53

Freud's response to Jung's "curious sensation in his diaphragm" and the "detonation" was; a. "I had the same sensation."; b. "I didn't feel it as strongly as you." c. "Sheer bosh."; d. "It was because you were thinking of corpses."

3.2
52

When Freud asked Jung to make a dogma of Freud's sexual theory a. Jung could not endorse dogma; b. Jung agreed enthusiastically; c. Jung disagreed, but agreed to succeed Freud; d. Jung agreed reluctantly

3.3
53

Jung's family can be described as; a. poor b. well-to-do but uneducated; c. having clergy and professors in it; d. descendants of royalty

3.4
53

What did young Jung experience in a recurrent dream a. an exploding moon; b. a voluptuous, nude young woman beckoning to him; c. an obvious Phallic symbol; d. the image of his father, dead

3.5
53

Which of the following characterized Jung's childhood? a. happy and carefree; b. miserable; he was abused; c. filled with friends; d. lonely

3.6
54

Freud and Jung met because of Freud's interest in Jung's Studies in Word Association. From 1906 to 1913, they exchanged _____ letters. a. 1000; b. 32; c. 869; d. 350

3.7
54

In 1913, Jung had a premonition of a. an invasion of creatures from outer space; b. the start of World War I in 1914; c. the end of his current romance; d. the beginning of a brave new world

3.8
54

Jung suffered what we would now call a mid-life crisis. He called his struggle "the building blocks of psychosis." Which was among the images that flooded his mind? a. the color violet; b. the devil in the form of a cow; c. elderly sage Elijah and blind beauty Salome; d. an Egyptian god

3.9

137

Jung and Freud shared all of the following terms, except one. Which of the following did they NOT share? a. ego; b. Psyche; c. unconsciousness; d. penis envy   3.10
54-55

In comparing Freud's and Jung's therapeutic styles it is clear that a Freud was controlling, Jung participated with patients; b. their styles were nearly identical; c. neither had patients talk freely; d. Freud was informal, but Jung was quite formal
3.11
55

Contrary to Freud, Jung believed a. there are no solutions to patients' problems; b. in guiding patients away from their problems; c. in the connectedness of the minds of people; d. psychological disaster is inevitable   3.12
54-55

Compared to Freud, Jung was a. pessimistic; b. an intellectual giant; c. tactless; d. open to others' ideas   3.13
55

One of Jung's strongest beliefs was a. that all people are created equal; b. that aspects of mentality are arranged in opposites or contrasts; c. that cures could be obtained very quickly with the right kind of therapeutic support; d. that the unconscious contained only repressed material   3.14
55

The personal unconscious contains a. material that was once conscious but has been forgotten; b. the self ideal; c. the id d. ancestral experiences passed down through generations
3.15
55

The collective unconscious contains a. material that were once conscious but have been forgotten; b. the self ideal; c. the id d. ancestral experiences passed through generations
3.16
56-57

Relative to other theories in this book, Jung's might be called a. atheoretical; b. ascientific; c. pan-cultural; d. multidimensional   3.17
55-57

Jung believed in the uniqueness as well as the _____ of all cultures. a. virtues; b. hopes; c. aspirations; d. commonality
3.18
56

Persona is roughly synonymous with a. ego; b. mask; c. sexual intercourse; d. superego   3.19
56

Which of the following best describes Jung's "self" a. totally unconscious; b. very superficial; c. the total personality; d. at the fringe of the personality   3.20

56

Which of the following is "the equalization of differences in order to bring about a balance or equilibrium?" a. self; b. ego; c. entropy; d. equivalence   3.21

57

Archetype means a. pre-existent forms that are innate and represent psychic predispositions; b. symbols of current conflicts and past unresolved interpersonal quarrels; c. energy consumed to accommodate one intention balanced by energy fueling an opposite intention; d. the storehouse of all the actual experiences that occurred to a particular person   3.22

57

Which of the following Archetypes most resembles Freud's id? a. Pestilence; b. Anima; c. Animus; d. Shadow   3.23

58

Which of the following is the representation of woman in man? a. Pestilence; b. Anima; c. Animus; d. Shadow   3.24

58

According to Jung, what is the physical "fact" that lies behind anima and animus?   a. men and women are very different; b. men and women are very similar; c. the minority of genes belonging to the other sex does not disappear; d. the DNA associated with one sex becomes mixed with that of the other sex   3.25

58

Anima is to animus as a. love is to hate; b. Eros is to Logos; c. A priori is to a posteriori; d. sky is to earth   3.26

58

His anima relating to her animus a. happens whenever they meet; b. cannot happen; they are abstractions; c. can be quite humorous; d. is always a very serious matter   3.27

58

Archetypes affect us in a way that is analogous to which experience? a. "the devil on my shoulder"; b. "dark despair" c. "a religious experience"; d. "love at first sight"   3.28

59

According to Jung, unidentified flying objects (UFOs) reflect the archetype of a. wholeness or totality; b. aerial; c. contrariness d. instability   3.29

59

Mandala means a. Irish god; b. revenge; c. circle; d. incongruence   3.30

57

Concerning archetypes a. there is a limited number of them; b. each is short-lived; c. most are a form of sexual symbolism; d. they are potentials rather than actuals   3.31

60

Which of the following is the best example of synchronicity?

a. "I dreamed of you last night."; b. "You feel sad."; c. "It's weird that you called about your sickness; I've taken sick also."; d. "I don't know what to tell you. I don't understand you at all."

3.32
60-61

Which of the following is an example of an movie in which archetypes are prominent? a. King Kong; b. Water World; c. Sense and Sensibility; d. Naked Gun

3.33
61

When Little Anna was asked, "What would you say if you got a little brother tonight?" what was her reply? a. "I'd hug and hug it."; b. "I'd kill it."; c. "I'd hide from it."; d. "I'd want to see its penis."

3.34
61

What did Little Anna dream about after seeing some carpenters working? a. ants eating her; b. that they cut off her genitals c. that she slept with one of them; d. crying out in pain when they cut wood

3.35
61

All of the following were part of Little Anna's experience, except one. Which was NOT a part of her experience? a. curiosity about where babies come from; b. a game involving "getting rid of mother"; c. curiosity about where Grandmother would go after she died; d. a desire to fly like a condor

3.36
61

Which of the following was part of Little Anna's experience? a. dancing with the King; b. dreaming of snow capped mountains; c. asking her uncle if she could sleep with him d. talking to the tigers at the zoo

3.37
61

Little Anna's curiosity about the life and death cycle was manifested in a. killing a little mouse; b. watching a baby ostrich hatch at the circus; c. after Grandmother said she would go to heaven, Anna asked, "And then you will be a baby again?"; d. having seen her father and some other men urinating, she asked her father, "If all of your pee pee comes out, will you die?"

3.38
61

Noting all the "Freudian symbolism" in Little Anna's experience, Jung indicated a. in this case, Freud is right; b. rather than acting at the behest of psychosexual urges, Anna was under the spell of the collective unconscious; c. though she seemed to act as Freud's notions of psychosexuality would dictate, actually she was just developing her sex role; d. that Freud had examined Little Anna's case and had declared it to be devoid of psychosexual symbolism

3.39
62

According to Jung, dreams are a. messages from the wise unconscious; b. virtually useless for diagnosisc. rarely

meaningful; d. meaningful in terms of latent content, but not manifest content   3.40
62

Regarding dreams, Jung believed a. only latent content is meaningful; b. most people's dreams mean little; c. symbols of the collective unconscious are undisguised in a dream; d. the collective unconscious is manifested in dreams in disguised form only   3.41
62

Compensation (Jung) refers to a. dealing with inferiority; b. countering a deficiency, such as an organ defect; c. trying to overcome being born last; d. balancing a conscious experience with an opposing unconscious one   3.42
63

Prospective (Jung) refers to a. mining the unconscious for "golden" nuggets of self-insight; b. searching the forest of philosophy for the truth hidden among the groves; c. dreams foretelling the future; d. the future orientation of the ego
3.43
63

Which of the following is "a readiness of the psyche to act or react in a certain way." a. type; b. internal orientation; c. libido d. attitude   3.44
63

Extraversion is a. outward turning of libido; b. inward turning of libido; c. overflowing of libido; d. a clogging of libidinal canals
3.45
63

Introversion is a. outward turning of libido; b. inward turning of libido; c. overflowing of libido; d. a clogging of libidinal canals
3.46
63

Of the following who is most likely an extravert? a. "I'm sort of indifferent."; b. "I love to party." ; c. "I move in tight circles."; d. "I spend a lot of time daydreaming."   3.47
63

Jung was a self-proclaimed a. compensator; b. procrastinator c. introvert; d. sensation seeker   3.48
63-64

All of the following are among Jung's psychological functions, except one. Which is NOT among his psychological functions? a. thinking; ; b. feeling; c. intuiting; d. winnowing   3.49
63-64

The eight possible combinations of the psychological functions and introversion-extraversion include all of the following, except one. Which is **not** among those combinations?
a. introverted-feeling; b. extraverted-winnowing;
c. extraverted-intuiting; d. introverted-thinking   3.50
64

Individuation is a. separating oneself from others; b. the process by which the person becomes an in-dividual; c. finding the heart of one's psyche; d. a psychological hunt for the dimensions along which others differ from oneself   3.51
68-69

What did Maloney find when he looked at reactions to three different representations of "Hero" and three of "Mother"? a. results were different for the two archetypes; b. the pattern of reactions was consistent across the three varieties of each archetype; c. the pattern of reactions were inconsistent across the varieties of each archetype; d) no consistent patterns were found.
                                                                                                3.52
                                                                                                69

Raya Jones critiqued Maloney's "Hero"/"mother study by, for example, referring to the latter's failure to take culture into account. How did Maloney react to the criticisms? a. he accepted them as correct; b. he simply dismissed the criticisms; c. he pointed out that his subjects were from all over the world; d. he refused to respond to Jones in any way.   3.53
                                                                                                64

Jung's recognition involves a. transference; b. manifest dream interpretation; c. acknowledging previously neglected unconscious contents; d. Oedipus complex   3.54
                                                                                                66

Which two are the functions added to those of Jung on the Myers Briggs Type Indicator? a. altruistic, selfish; b. future oriented, past oriented; c. judging, perceiving d. hoping, aspiring   3.55
                                                                                                64

Which of the following occurs during Jung's "childhood" stage? a. separation from the "psychic womb"; b. Psychic birth; c. Psychic revolution; d. establishing community roles   3.56
                                                                                                65

All except one of the following are events of Jung's "Youth" stage. Which is NOT a youth event? a. separation from the "psychic womb"; b. Psychic birth; c. Psychic revolution d. establishing community roles   3.57
                                                                                                65

Jung's middle-age stage brings with it a. establishing an interrelation between conscious and unconscious; b. an inevitable crisis; c. the destruction of ying and yang; d. the separation of the female and male selves   3.58
                                                                                                65

Jung's old age stage a. brings the end of hope; b. begins the process of generativity; c. has implications for the reincarnation theme of Eastern religions; d. brings conquest of death
                                                                                                3.59
                                                                                                66

When the author of your text took the Myers Briggs Type Indicator, he was scored as a. extraverted, intuitive, feeling, judging; b. introverted, feeling, thinking, perceiving; c. extraverted, sensing, feeling, judging; d. introverted, sensing, feeling, perceiving   3.60
66

In terms of psychology traditions, perceiving should be, but isn't, positively related to which of the following? a. thinking; b. judging; c. feeling; d. sensing   3.61
66

Which of the following characteristics of Bill Cosby make him fit his Myers Briggs Type Indicator score well? a. he is cautious about what he says; b. he likes routine tasks; c. he is quick witted; d. he is more "intuitive" than logical   3.62
65

Which of the following is the most popular measure of Jung's eight combinations? a. the Myers Briggs Type Indicator; b. the Adjective Check List; c. the Minnesota Multiphasic Personality Inventory; d. the Diagnostic and Statistical Manual III-R
3.63
65

What did Clarkadon (1978) find when he investigated Jung's eight fold classification among Mississippi State students? a. extraverts made very infrequent discussion contributions; b. introverts made very infrequent discussion contributions; c. the best classroom contributions came from feelings types; d. students with the highest sensing scores obtained the highest discussion ratings   3.64
67

Which characterized Jung's attitude toward therapy techniques?   a. he dogmatically espoused only his own methods; b. he embraced whatever worked with a particular patient, even Catholic confession; c. he was orthodox Freudian, except that he rejected penis envy; d. he dabbled with other people's methods and never developed his own
3.65
67

Jung a pioneering all of the following, except one. For which was he NOT a pioneer? a. use of catharsis; b. use of projective tests; c. short-term therapy; d. self-help programs
3.66
67

According to Jung, a complex is a. psychological cores around which sexual experiences gather; b. free-flowing libidinal rivers c. mental contents that stick together and take up residence in the personal unconscious; d. a series of psychic conflicts that originate in the collective unconscious and then are projected outward   3.67
67

With use of the Word Association Test a. patients respond to each of a standardized list of 100 words; b. the therapist has patients listen to him or her recite a set of spontaneously generated words; c. associations with words are given to patients and they guess which words corresponds to each associate; d. patients spontaneously generate words to describe themselves   3.68
                                                                                           67

Jung paid particular attention to what kinds of responses when administering the Word Association Text? a. responses to words with multiple meanings; b. responses to words that are emotionally arousing; c. responses that patients gave reluctantly; d. responses to words that have hidden meanings
                                                                                           3.69
                                                                                           68

Amplification refers to a. encouraging patients to express emotions emphatically; b. having patients elaborate on what the therapist said; c. the therapist's tendency to reiterate whatever the patient says; d. enriching dream content through directed association   3.70
                                                                                           68

Jung frequently equipped patients with a. blinders so that could concentrate on the unconscious better. b. thick glasses to distort present reality so that the past became more prominent; c. knowledge of universal archetypal symbols; d. an understanding of basic psychodynamic processes   3.71
                                                                                           70-71

Donn concluded that Rhine's parapsychology and Jung's synchronicity involved only correlation, not causation. Why would Jung not like this conclusion? a. he wanted no association with parapsychology; b. he personally disliked Rhine; c. he had by then abandoned synchronicity; d. he thought synchronicity involves causation
                                                                                           3.72
                                                                                           68

Investigating large numbers of dreams in succession was called a. cataloging dream content; b. differentiating dreams c. dream series analysis; d. dichotomizing dreams   3.73
                                                                                           68

Jung's dream series analysis is most analogous to a. the world series in baseball; b. the spokes of a wagon wheel that all relate to the wheel's hub; c. the arms of an octopus d. the guns of a battleship each trained on a different target
                                                                                           3.74
                                                                                           68

Jung's "active imagination" refers to a. the child-like quality of many adults' imaginings; b. the snake biting its tail: coming full circle; c. simulating dream experiences by engaging the

imagination while awake; d. the dreams of especially creative people   3.75
                                                                    69-71

All except one of the following are short-comings of Jung's thinking. Which is NOT a short-coming? a. many of his concepts are not amenable to scientific testing; b. some of his notions seem mixed up with others; c. even some of his most central concepts were not defined consistently; d. he rejected Lamarck's well-respected belief in the inheritance of acquired characteristics   3.76
                                                                    70

Which archetype was involved in the controversy about the scientific origins of the collective unconscious? a. Wotan b. The Sun Phallus Man; c. Quarternity; d. Trickster   3.77
                                                                    71

How did Freud cast a shadow over Jung? a. after their break, Jung was labeled a mystic; b. no one took Jung seriously because of his former association with Freud; c. Freud's followers hated Jung for deserting the Master; d. Freud saw to it that Jung was blackballed from every psychiatric organization in the world   3.78
                                                                    71

All of the following are reasons why Jung will long be remembered, except one. Which is a NOT a reason why Jung will be remembered? a. some of his ideas have been endorsed by other theorists; b. a journal devoted to his ideas was founded; c. his notion of introversion-extraversion is largely supported by later research; d. his concepts are more scientifically testable than those of any other theorist
Extra Items   3.79
                                                                    57

Which people's culture would more clearly reflect the collective unconscious? a. modern Swiss; b. 19th century Chinese c. Australian Aborigines; d. Brazilians of today   3.80
                                                                    57

People of African heritage could examine what for evidence of humans' connection to numerical precision? a. the Egyptian Pyramids; b. the deserts of the Sudan; c. the animals of Kenya d. the waters of the Nile   3.81
                                                                    60

The "invincible" child is reflected in which movie? a. The Cat People; b. Babe; c. Children of the Corn; d. Clueless

                                                                    3.82
                                                                    70

Jung was disrespected in his early career because a. he had a mistress; b. he was a believer in mysticism and parapsychology; c. he was interested in but eventually rejected ESP; d. he abandoned sex during his mid-life

                                                                    3.83

Little Anna believed a. boys would rather be girls; b. toys should all have some practical use; c. when people die they reborn; d. mud was just like feces;   3.84
61

What did Anna do related to the collected unconscious that children still do today? a. licked an ice cream cone with the tip of her tongue; b. stuffed pillows under her clothes; c. threw rocks at dogs; d. pretended to sleep walk   3.85
60

Jung believed that dreams a. revealed little about the collective unconscious; b. had to be analyzed one at a time; c. were revealing only in their latent content; d. foretell the future   3.86
63

"His own world is a safe harbour....a walled in garden,..." refers to (Jung)   a. sensing function; b. introversion; c. extraversion d. intuitive function   3.87
64

"Instinctive apprehension" refers to (Jung)   a. sensing function; b. introversion; c. extraversion; d. intuitive function   3.88
64

"..a separate indivisible unity of 'whole'..." refers to (Jung) a. introvert; b. transcendental function; c. individuation; d. recognition   3.89
63-64

All of the following are among Jung's functions, except one. Which is NOT among his functions? a. conniving; b. sensing; c. feeling; d. thinking   3.90
69

A major controversy of Jung's career is a. his rejection of science; b. his tendency to change his theory; c. his belief in the inheritance of ideas; d. his transcendentalism   3.91
65

What is the basic difficulty of youth (teenage through young adult)? a. changes in appearance; b. giving up illusions of childhood; c. developing adult aspirations; d. learning to love as opposed to expressing lust   3.92
66

The Myers Briggs Type Indicator (MBTI) a. adds two functions to those posed by Jung; b. is basically a perversion of Jung's point of view; c. has yet to show any usefulness; d. is fading in popularity   3.93
67

Jung's Word Association Test results were analyzed in terms of a. number of words generated by patient; b. length of words generated by patients; c. behaviors (facial expressions) accompanying responses to words; d. Galvanized Skin Responses (GSR) to word presentations   3.94

Jung sometimes encouraged patients to a. interrupt him during his therapeutic monologues; b. terminate a series of session whenever they wanted; c. to try to fool him during their free associations; d. engage in self-analysis   3.95

According to Jung, what was required for dissolution of a complex?   a. insight; b. ego-strength; c. self-discipline d. will power   3.96

Jung's approach to analyzing dreams was a. a form of trial and error; b. laid out according to a generalized plan applicable to all patients; c. haphazard; d. across several dreams   3.97

Which of the following is an example of Jung's "active imagination"? a. pretending to go fishing; b. in a darkened room, imagine descending a stairway; c. pretending to be sleeping walking; d. imagining something that had just happened   3.98

Adopting whose discredited ideas proved a continuing problem for Jung? a. Freud; b. Bismarck; c. Horney; d. Larmarck   3.99

For Jung, what was the problem posed by the Sun Phallus Man? a. there was actually no such patient; b. this patient may have read about the Son Phallus, rather than experiencing visions of it stimulated by the collective unconscious; c. this patient was later interviewed and shown to be a perfectly normal person who willfully lied to Jung; d. Jung actually had this patient in therapy 20 years after he claimed to have treated him   3.100

71

Which is a popular book based on Jung's ideas?   a. WOMEN WHO RUN WITH WOLVES; b. MEN OF THE MINES; c. THE SEXUAL HABITS OF THE WOMBAT; d. CULT AND CULTURE

3.1,c	3.49,b	3.95, b
3.2,a	3.50,b	3.96, d
3.3,c	3.51,b	3.97, b
3.4,c	3.52,c	3.98, d
3.5,d	3.53,c	3.99, b
3.6,d	3.54,c	3.100, a
3.7,b	3.55,a	
3.8,c	3.56,a	
3.9,d	3.57,a	
3.10,a	3.58,c	
3.11,c	3.59,a	
3.12,d	3.60,d	
3.13,b	3.61,c	
3.14,a	3.62,a	
3.15,d	3.63,a	
3.16,c	3.64,b	
3.17,d	3.65,a	
3.18,b	3.66,c	
3.19,c	3.67,a	
3.20,c	3.68,b	
3.21,a	3.69,d	
3.22,d	3.70,c	
3.23,b	3.71,a	
3.24,c	3.72,c	
3.25,b	3.73,b	
3.26,c	3.74,c	
3.27,d	3.75,d	
3.28,a	3.76,b	
3.29,c	3.77,a	
3.30,d	3.78,d	
3.31,c	*Extra*	
3.32,a	*Items*	
3.33,b	3.79, c	
3.34,b	3.80, a	
3.35,d	3.81, c	
3.36,c	3.82, b	
3.37,c	3.83, c	
3.38,b	3.84, b	
3.39,a	3.85, d	
3.40,c	3.86, b	
3.41,d	3.87, d	
3.42,c	3.88, c	
3.43,d	3.89, a	
3.44,a	3.90, c	
3.45,b	3.91, b	
3.46,b	3.92, a	
3.47,c	3.93, c	
3.48,d	3.94, d	

Chapter 4

Multiple Choice Items for the Chapter on Adler

4.1
75

All except one of the following characterized early admirers of Freud who changed their thinking about him. Which did NOT characterize them? a. they objected to the emphasis on infantile sexuality; b. they had new concepts to offer, different from Freud's; c. they felt the unconscious was either non-existent or greatly over-emphasized; d. they wanted to emphasize parent-child relationships

4.2
75

Which of the following was questionable about Adler and those to whom the next several chapters are devoted? a. their ideas related to Freud's in some way; b. all were concerned with early childhood experiences; c. they all were 19th century science; d. the all were Neo-Freudians

4.3
76

Which of the following was true of Adler and his family? a. his childhood was happy; b. he was a robust child; c. he converted to the Jewish religion; d. he nearly died of pneumonia at age five

4.4
76

Which of the following was true of Adler and his family? a. he was a self-proclaimed poor orator; b. he was closer to his father than to his mother; c. he narrowly escaped an epidemic of rickets; d. he favorably impressed several professors

4.5
76-79

Beginning early in his life, all of the following was true of Adler, except one. Which was NOT true of Adler a. he was a socialist; b. he was a life-long communist; c. he had a strong social conscience; d. he recommended that students familiarize themselves with Freud's theory of dreams

4.6
77

Which of the following distinguished Adler, relative to the other theorists? a. he spent some time in a seminary; b. he was one of few who never had anything to do with Freud; c. he married a U. S. citizen; d. he began mental health clinics

4.7
76

Which was true of Adler's orientation to children? a. he was concerned about adult problems, not those of children; b. he

never worked with children or adolescents; c. he was a constant advisor to child-guidance centers; d. he felt uncomfortable around children due to his own childhood experiences and trauma   4.8
78

Which was true of Adler's orientation to people? a. he was rather distant in interactions with; b. he saw the personality as a whole made up of distinctive parts; c. he was very consistent: he did not change his; d. he believed that striving for superiority was the major motive of people   4.9
77

"Subjective perceptions" means a. backward looking; b. our scripts; c. fragmented; d. out of sync   4.10
78-79

Adler worked against a. socialism; b. people who tried to feel superior; c. war; d. attempts to form an international union of nations   4.11
79

"Individual psychology" means a. a conception of a unique human as a interconnected whole; b. the psychology of the individual rather than of the group; c. a psychology of the masses that concentrated on the disenfranchised; d. the vision of a new discipline that would emphasize environmental influences   4.12
79

Which of the following is the best definition of social feeling? a. feelings about social and institutional; b. efforts to develop feelings about social matters; c. the dominance of social considerations over individual concerns; d. concern for the community and the need to associate/cooperate with people
4.13
80

Which of the following is the best definition of social interest? a. feelings about social and institutional matters; b. efforts to develop social feeling; c. the dominance of social considerations over individual concerns; d. concern for the community and the need to associate/cooperate with people
4.14
80

Which of the following was probably Adler's most important and enduring concept? a. birth order; b. social interest; c. shock; d. teleological   4.15
80

Which of the following are among the relatively recently proposed additions to Adler's three tasks that each person must address? a. love; b. work; c. society; d. spirituality   4.16
80

Which of the following is most clearly true to the concept "style of life?" a. the direction taken by the individual in his or

150

her ability to exercise free choice; b. the individual's unique movement toward self-created goals and ideals; c. the manner of behaving that characterized the individual relative to others; d. the socioeconomic level of the individual throughout most of his or her life   4.17
80

Which of the following is most clearly true to the concept "law of movement?" a. the direction taken by the individual in his or her ability to exercise free choice; b. the individual's unique movement toward self-created goals and ideals; c. the manner of behaving that characterized the individual relative to others; d. the socioeconomic level of the individual throughout most of his or her life   4.18
80

Which of the following is an example of how language has been influenced by the personality theorists?   a. Adler's "social feeling" is a widely used phrase in Europe; b. the "collective unconscious" is currently a popular phrase in Austria; c. Adler's "masculine protest" is universally used; d. Adler's "style of life" probably suggested the popular American phrase "life style";   4.19
80

"The creative power of the individual" refers to a. conceptions of self/world formed while developing styles of life for solving the three great problems of life; b. the power to overcome personal and societal problems with the help of teleological direction; c. the capacity to find solutions to other people's problems; d. the need to create works of art   4.20
81

Prototype is to fictional finalism as a. top is to bottom; b. out is to in; c. accepted is to rejected; d. author is to reader
4.21
81

One's prototypical goal appears in a. one's attitude toward others; b. in everything one does; c. in everything but one's vocation; d. in relations with greater power than oneself
4.22
80-81

The individual's style of life is best seen in a. reflections on the future; b. contemplations of the present; c. dreams; d. new situations   4.23
81

Shock is a. an extreme form of reaction; a person's automatic, unknowing exploitation of symptoms; b. experienced when a person's fiction runs head-on into reality; c. what occurs when consciousness and unconsciousness clash; d. experienced when two people in a close relationship develop different prototypes   4.24
81

Neurosis (Adler) is a. an extreme form of reaction to shock a person's automatic, unknowing exploitation of symptoms; b. experienced when a person's fiction runs head-on into reality; c. what occurs when consciousness and unconsciousness clash; d. experienced when two people in a close relationship develop different prototypes   4.25
81-82

Neurosis (Adler) is a. a state in which social interest is ill-developed; b. a reaction to compensation; c. is a rare phenomenon among women; d. is too rare to be a serious problem   4.26
82

Inferiority refers to a. how others feel relative to oneself; b. Adler's phrase for the consequences of an exaggerated form of inadequacy explained in part by deficient social interest c. all those feelings that come from failed attempts at sexual fulfillment; d. the persistent feeling that one does not measure up to one's own or societal standards   4.27
82

Inferiority complex refers to a. how others feel relative to oneself; b. the consequences of exaggerated inadequacy explained in part by deficient social interest; c. all those feelings that come from failed attempts at sexual fulfillment; d. the persistent feeling that one does not measure up to one's own or societal standards;   4.28
82

To compensate is to a. seek revenge on those who have frustrated oneself; b. overcome weaknesses by striving to become superior in some way; c. to fight the natural disposition to superiority over others; d. to bend over backwards to do or become whatever weaknesses deny oneself   4.29
82

To overcompensate is to a. seek revenge on those who have frustrated oneself; b. overcome weaknesses by striving to become superior in some way; c. to fight the natural disposition of superiority over others; d. to bend over backwards to do or become whatever weaknesses deny oneself   4.30
82

All of the following people are living examples of overcoming weaknesses, except one. Who is NOT an example of overcoming weaknesses? a. James Earl Jones (Darth Vader)l; b. Geraldo Rivera (TV host); c. Carl Lewis (several Olympic gold medals); d. John Stossell (ABC's 20/20)
4.31
82

Which of the following is a characteristic of the neglected or over indulged child? a. the over indulged child expects

homage from others ; b. the neglected child compensates by finding problems "too easy"; c. the over indulged child compensates by becoming humble; d. the neglected child grows up to be too trusting   4.32
83

Which of the following is the best definition of "striving for superiority?" a. overcoming an organ defect that is particularly disfiguring; b. exaggerated, abnormal form of striving involving "overcompensation" for personal weakness; c. universal phenomenon that parallels physical growth; the goal of obtaining perfection; d. the faulty method of addressing one's inferiority by literally faking superiority
4.33
83

Which of the following is the best definition of "superiority complex?" a. overcoming an organ defect that is particularly disfiguringb. exaggerated, abnormal form of striving involving "overcompensation" for personal weakness; c. universal phenomenon that parallels physical growth; the goal of obtaining perfection; d. the faulty method of addressing one's inferiority by literally faking superiority   4.34
83

How would Adler likely regard a braggart? a. as successful at overcoming inferiority; b. as someone working hard at compensating for inferiority ; c. as a person who is very likely to achieve superiority; d. as someone who is blowing off steam in order to compensate for a recent failure   4.35
83

Regarding braggarts, Tucibat (1986) found a. they were universally disliked; b. they were not taken seriously by anyone; c. boasting about success in the future yielded favorable ratings for braggarts; d. boasting about success in the past yielded favorable ratings for braggarts   4.36
82

Of family members, who is the most important in the child's development, according to Adler? a. siblings; b. grandparents; c. mother; d. father   4.37
84

Of family members, who is second most important in the child's development, according to Adler? a. siblings; b. grandparents; c. mother; d. father   4.38
84

Birth order refers to a. the orderliness of the birth process in a family ; b. the degree to which particular children's reactions to the birth of a sibling is orderly; c. the importance of the birth of a new child to the order of the household; d. the child's birth position relative to other siblings   4.39
83

Adler thought that the only child was a. the center of attention; b. dethroned from the central position; c. actively struggling to surpass others; d. the most pampered   4.40
84

Since Adler's original conception of birth order, research has shown; a. differences, in so far as they exist, are between first (only) and later borns; b. his original conception was amazingly accurate; c. differences, in so far as they exist, are between first and only borns; d. there has been no support for Adler's original conception   4.41
84-85

Research by Zajonc and a review by Falbo, indicate all of the following, except one. Which is NOT indicated by their work? a. first borns are more likely to end up in the U.S. senate; b. last borns are the most intelligent; c. later borns added to the family dilute the intellectual atmosphere; d. first borns are more likely to actually succeed
4.42
85-86

All of the following support Sulloway's and others; conception of birth order, except one. Which does NOT support it? a. first borns are higher on "separate knowing"; b. later born students are more likely to be arrested; c. researchers showed that biological birth order and rearing order are different; d. in the context of family, later borns are lower in achievement and higher in rebelliousness, etc.   4.43
85-86

According to Freese, Powell, and Steelman, what was wrong with Sulloway's sample upon which he based his conclusions? a. it was too large; b. it was composed of long-dead public figures; c. it was composed of ordinary people; d. it was composed of lower socioeconomic people   4.44
87

All except one of the following were true of Frankenstein. Which was **untrue**? a. he had a pampered childhood; b. his monster began life with human qualities; c. his adopted sister became his plaything; d. his monster was actually created by another scientist, but Frankenstein brought it to life
4.45
87

According to Huber and colleagues (1989), Frankenstein was a. overwhelmed by compensatory striving for god-like superiority;b. a humble man who was sucked into evil by the influence of an overbearing fellow student; c. a grateful adult who only wanted to get away from his troubled childhood; d. an idiot savant who could do only one thing well, create life
4.46
87

According to Huber and colleagues (1989), Frankenstein labored under the delusion that he was a superior human being. What came as a shock to him? a. rejection by his adopted sister; b. the imperfection of his creature's face c. rejection by the townspeople; d. the inattention, implying a lack of respect for his genius, shown by people at his university   4.47
88

Which is the most accurate regarding Frankenstein's monster? a. he never developed the ability to speak; b. he showed no emotional response to others; c. there was no evidence of social feeling in him; d. he read and was affected by <u>Paradise Lost</u>   4.48
88

To what did Huber and colleagues (1989) attribute Frankenstein's remorse at the beginning of his work on the second creation? a. genuine guilt; b. a sudden realization that if there was a second monster, there would be a third, and so forth until he was consumed by making monsters; c. an attempt to appear more sensitive and thoughtful than others; d. a gallant effort to warn others of his monumental error   4.49
88

How did the monster react to abandonment by Frankenstein? a. he fell into a state of despair and retired to the forest forever; b. he left to live with a blind priest; c. he exclaimed, "if I cannot inspire love, I will cause fear."; d. he began for the first time to talk his master into making him a mate   4.50
88

What happened to Frankenstein and his monster at the end of Mary Shelley's book? a. they finally reconciled and the monster lived out his life in an abandoned hovel on the Frankenstein property; b. Frankenstein submitted the monster to an operation and corrected his facial deformities; c. the monster was shot by villagers as he attempted to leap across a yawning canyon and Frankenstein lived a normal life thereafter; d. the pursued each other to the ends of the earth leaving death and destruction in their wake
4.51
88-89

What is the critical point to be made about early recollections? a. recollections say more about the person in the present than the person as a child; b. recollections are the best known way to get at the person's childhood c. recollections provide valuable data regarding child rearing practices; d. measures of early recollection are more valid and reliable that other personality measures   4.52
89

In Adler's brand of determinism a. the present determines the past; b. the past determines the present; c. the past determines the future; d. the present has little determining force   4.53
89

What did the text author remember about cutting his arm during an elementary school recess? a. the blood b. basking in all the attention; c. the pain; d. the fear   4.54
89

Sanitioso, Kunda, and Fong (1990) informed some subjects that it would be better to be introverted and others that it would be better to be extraverted. They found a. "extraverted" subjects performed better in the experiment; b. "introverted" subjects performed better in the experiment; c. "extraverts" performed better than "introverts" only in the incentives condition; d. subjects whose current conception of themselves was extraverted retrieved extraverted memories more quickly   4.55
90

Which of the following was true of early recollections case studies presented by Adler? a. one case involved a man who wished to be President of the U.S.; b. a woman recalled, "at age forty, I was knitting stockings while I watched my mother work around the house"; c. a man recalled, "at about age six, I fell out of the automobile as it was backing out of the driveway"; d. one case involved a woman who competed with her sister for "best horsewoman"   4.56
90

Which of the following was true of early recollections case studies presented by Adler? a. one case involved a man who wished to be President of the U.S.; b. one person recalled, "at age four, my mother was knitting stockings while I watched workers building a house"; c. one person recalled "at about age six, I fell out of the automobile as it was backing out of the driveway"; d. one case involved a woman who competed with her brother for "best baseball catcher"   4.57
90

Which of the following is a quote from Alder's interpretation of one of his early recollection case histories? a. "this man really is not interested in being President. He is just compensating for a missing arm."; b. "she says she is knitting stockings, but in fact, she is trying to weave a style of life."; c. "he reports that he couldn't keep up with his big brother, but really he desires always to be ahead of his brother."; d. "she believes she must be careful or her sister will win, and she will be 'left in the dirt.'"   4.58
90-91

All of the following, except one, are research results or comments pertaining to early recollections (ERs). Which is

NOT one of those research results? a. Using ERs, Burnell and Solomon (1964) predicted outcomes of Air Force recruit training; b. Hafner, Fakouri, and Labrentz (1982) found that more alcoholics than non-alcoholics remembered being externally controlled; c. Hyer, Woods, and Boudewyns (1989) reported that Vietnam veterans with Posttraumatic Stress Disorder showed low social interest on Ers; d. of the 30 studies on ER reviewed by Watkins (1992), few produced statistically significant results   4.59
91

Leak and Williams (1989a) used two superior measures of social interest and found a. males scored higher than females; b. the sexes did not score differently; c. the greater the social interest, the more positive were perceptions of family environment; d. the higher the social interest the lower the extraversion score   4.60
91

Leak and Williams (1989b) related social interest scores to hardiness and alienation. They found a. social interest was negatively related to total hardiness; b. alienation and social interest were unrelated; c. the greater the social interest the greater the hardiness; d. alienation and hardiness were more closely related than either was to social interest   4.61
91-92

Kal (1972) rank ordered beliefs of Adlerian therapists from most frequently mentioned to least frequently mentioned. Which of the following was ranked first? a. belief in use of early recollections; b. belief in the social nature of humans c. belief in the holistic approach; d. belief in the active role of the therapist   4.62
92

Kal (1972) rank ordered beliefs of Adlerian therapists from most frequently mentioned to least frequently mentioned. Which of the following was ranked second? a. soft determinism; b. belief in the social nature of humans; c. belief in the holistic approach; d. belief in the active role of the therapist   4.63
92

To Adler, a brief therapy approach was a. a matter of shortening the length of sessions so that clients would not have to be in an emotionally charged atmosphere for long; b. techniques to solve clients problems in a specifiable and small number of sessions; c. a means of shortening the total relationship between the therapist and patient, regardless of the number of sessions; d. a ridiculous idea that was not in the best interest of the client   4.64
92-93

Carlson's (1989) case of Jim, who wished to stop smoking, was used to illustrate a. the researcher's new measure of

social interest; b. the superiority of the ER method over psychoanalytic free association; c. the use of Adler's omni-associationist method; d. Adlerian brief therapy   4.65
91-92

All except one of the following were true of the case of Jim (Carlson, 1989). Which was untrue of the case of Jim? a. Jim was given Kern's life style scale; b. after he learned of his real father at age, Jim was a "hellraiser"; c. becoming a "hell raiser" may have been a response to feelings of inferiority; d. Jim was told that he would have to work on his self-efficacy and his ability to memorize suggestions made by his therapist
4.66
91-92

All except one of the following were true of the case of Jim (Carlson, 1989). Which was NOT true of the case of Jim?
a. the estimated cost of Jim's smoking was $15,000
b. Jim was afraid of risky pursuits
c. as a child, Jim was pushed off a stump, breaking his arm
d. kidding from friends about his smoking caused Jim to hide in the bathroom

4.67
91-92

All except one of the following were true of the case of Jim (Carlson, 1989). Which was NOT true of the case of Jim? a. the therapist made dietary suggestions to Jim; b. fruits and vegetables were recommended to Jim as a way to maintain proper PH balance; c. Jim was told to increase his caffeine intake to compensate for the loss of the high he previously got from cigarettes; d. Jim was advised to do deep breathing exercises   4.68
91-92

All except one of the following were true of the case of Jim (Carlson, 1989). Which was NOT true of the case of Jim? a. Jim's efforts at increasing self-efficacy were unrelated to striving for superiority; b. Jim was advised to take vitamins because cigarette smoking leaves a person vitamin depleted; c. it was suggested that Jim avoid situations in which he usually smoked; d. after brief training, Jim needed only to check back with the therapist on a few occasions to assess progress   4.69
93

How many session did it take Dinkmeyer and Sherman (1989) to help a disturbed family become more functional?
a. 10; b. 20; c. 30; d. 40   4.70
93-94

Even several years ago, research showed what about Adler's birth notions? a. his notions have held up remarkably well over the years; b. contradictory findings are more the rule than the exception; c. results are highly qualified: Jordon and

colleagues (1982) showed that first born males were the most indifferent to the interpersonal consequences of achievement; d. Toni Falbo was quoted by a writer, "Birth order really explains a lot"   4.71
                                                                   94

Researchers who responded to Zajonc's and Markus' (1975) American Psychologist article felt that a. had revolutionized the study of intelligence; b. had seriously overstated his case; c. had failed to do enough long-term research to draw any meaningful conclusions; d. had it right about position in the family, but not family size   4.72
                                                                   94-95

What is the main complaint that researchers and therapists have about early recollection measures? a. clients don't like the lengthy instructions; b. clients often seriously distort their recollections to make themselves look good; c. measures are open-ended, abstract, and difficult to quantify; d. reliability of early recollections id good, but not validity   4.73
                                                                   94

According to evolutionary theory's alternative to birth order theory a. position in the family is unrelated to anything except innate intelligence; b. the last born has most of the advantages; c. the number of siblings is unimportant; d. the first born competes for resources with helpless, needy later borns   4.74
                                                                   95

Which was most true of Adler? a. he was recognized in his time, but had little influence later; b. he was known for his in-depth, detailed assessments of childhood traumas; c. he believed that questions of morality were beyond the arena of appropriate inquiry for psychologists; d. he was a model of the responsible, humanitarian professional
Extra Items   4.75
                                                                   76

Some of Adler's patients were a. mental giants; b. acrobats c. Nazis; d. movie stars   4.76
                                                                   77

Adler attracted; a. wealthy patients; b. Austrian nationalists c. socially conscious radicals; d. famous actors   4.77
                                                                   77

Adler become; a. quite wealthy; b. rejecting of communism c. an entrepreneur; d. an accomplished violinist   4.78
                                                                   79

Adler was an early advocate of a. environmentalism; b. internationalism c. women's rights; d. long term therapy   4.79
                                                                   95

All except one of the following are notable contributions of Adler. Which is NOT a notable contribution? a. he invented

the technique of word association; b. he anticipated Rogers' and Maslow's holistic approach; c. his emphasis on the presence is mimicked today; d. he was a pioneer in developing brief therapy techniques   4.80
                                                                        79

Adler hated communism because a. it had succeeded too well; b. communists had borrowed his ideas without credit c. they were threatening to overrun Austria; d. they had incarcerated his daughter Vail   4.81
                                                                        80

Another name for social interest is a. prototype; b. fictional finalism; c. Lebensraum; d. Gemeinschaftsgefuhl   4.82
                                                                        79

Relative to Freud and Jung, Adler was a. absent minded; b. authoritarian; c. politically involved; d. politically conservative   4.83
                                                                        79

Adler was especially opposed to a. violence; b. short term therapy; c. work as a social cause; d. free love   4.84
                                                                        80

Although they were defined somewhat differently, Adler tended to equate a. introversion and extraversion; b. love and lustc. work and love; d. social feeling and social interest
                                                                        4.85
                                                                        80

To Adler, what lies behind personality development? a. childhood trauma; b. complexes; c. childhood beliefs d. appetites   4.86
                                                                        80

For Adler, one's prototypical goal a. is a means of adopting to life; b. defines the way one is sure to turn out; c. influences of the opposite sexed parent; d. is how far one has come in the search for selfness   4.87
                                                                        81

Social feeling is not high among neurotics who (Adler) a. come from wealthy families; b. come from poor families; c. report ERs that emphasize social relations; d. have been pampered as children   4.88
                                                                        83

The superiority complex is best explained by a deficiency a. in social interest; b. in sexual immaturity; c. of prototype developments; d. of ER content   4.89
                                                                        83

It is possible that people would reject braggarts; a. brag about future accomplishments; b. brag about anything what-so-ever; c. brag about past accomplishments; d. brag about the accomplishments of rivals

                                                                        4.90
                                                                        84

Early in the history of the "birth order" factor, Adler warned
a. birth order will prove to be THE most important variable
b. birth order will finally prove to be an unimportant factor
when other variables like gender and family wealth are
considered; c. birth order will be important only for last borns
and only children; d. birth order itself is less important than
the individual child's psychological situation   4.91
                                                        85

Where are first borns most likely to be found a. in the
executive board room; b. on the auto race track; c. hang
gliding; d. on the assembly line   4.92
                                                        86

Rodgers et al. and Guo et al. found what when they
compared cross-section with longitudinal birth order research
results? a. Zajonc's expectations were confirmed with both
methods; b. only longitudinal studies supported Zajonc's
expectations; c. only cross-sectional studies supported
Zajonc's expectations; Zajonc's expectations were confirmed
by neither method   4.93
                                                        87

Frankenstein a. was really a monster with a good heart; b.
had an adopted sister who was presented to him as a gift;
c. was a rather poor student; d. came from a humble
background   4.94
                                                        94

According to evolutionary theory, what is the basis of sibling
rivalry? a. jealousy over physical attractiveness; b. fear of
abandonment; c. jealousy over the greater skills of the older
sibs; d. competition for available resources   4.95
                                                        88-89-95

All of the following are properties of early memories (ER),
except one. Which is NOT a property? a. future oriented; b.
highly accurate; c. related to style of life; d. often used by
Adler   4.96
                                                        91-92

All of the following are findings regarding ER, except one.
Which is NOT a finding regarding the ER? a. ERs are favored
by Adlerian therapists today; b. ERs records are difficult to
quantify; c. alcoholics ERs reflected external control;
d. Vietnam vets' ERs reflected low social interest   4.97
                                                        91

Which of the following is the best summary of social interest
research? a. social interest is unrelated to positive personal
attributes; b. social interest research is still in its infancy; c.
social interest is positively related to psychological health; d.
social interest is a concept without empirical support
                                                        4.98
                                                        92

Which of the following was ranked FIRST in frequency of being mentioned by Adlerian therapists? a. use of early recollections; b. therapist's optimism; c. holistic approach d. social nature of man

4.99
95

All except one of the following are problems with the current state of the Adlerian movement, as noted by Freeman. Which was NOT one of those problems? a. Adlerians are growing older; b. membership in the Adlerian Society is dwindling; c. famous figures such as Carl Rogers, Aaron Beck, and Albert Ellis have ignored Adler's contributions; d. the mission of the Adlerian Society is unclear

4.100
94

How would you describe modern-day feelings about "birth order" on the part of researchers who have investigated it? a. elation; b. moderate caution c. discouragement; d. optimism

4.1,a	4.49,c	4.95, b
4.2,a	4.50,d	4.96, a
4.3,d	4.51,a	4.97, c
4.4,b	4.52,a	4.98, d
4.5,b	4.53,b	4.99, c
4.6,d	4.54,d	4.100, c
4.7,c	4.55,d	
4.8,d	4.56,b	
4.9,b	4.57,d	
4.10,c	4.58,d	
4.11,a	4.59,c	
4.12,d	4.60,c	
4.13,b	4.61,b	
4.14,b	4.62,a	
4.15,c	4.63,b	
4.16,b	4.64,d	
4.17,a	4.65,c	
4.18,d	4.66,b	
4.19,a	4.67,c	
4.20,c	4.68,a	
4.21,a	4.69,a	
4.22,d	4.70,b	
4.23,b	4.71,b	
4.24,a	4.72,c	
4.25,a	4.73,d	
4.26,d	4.74,d	
4.27,b	*Extra*	
4.28,b	*Items*	
4.29,d	4.75, b	
4.30,c	4.76, c	
4.31,a	4.77, b	
4.32,c	4.78, c	
4.33,b	4.79, b	
4.34,a	4.80, d	
4.35,c	4.81, d	
4.36,c	4.82, c	
4.37,d	4.83, a	
4.38,d	4.84, d	
4.39,a	4.85, c	
4.40,a	4.86, a	
4.41,b	4.87, d	
4.42,c	4.88, a	
4.43,b	4.89, c	
4.44,d	4.90, d	
4.45,a	4.91, a	
4.46,d	4.92, c	
4.47,d	4.93, b	
4.48,c	4.94, d	

Chapter 5

Multiple Choice Items for the Chapter on Horney

5.1
99
Horney's theory emphasizes a. parent-child interactions
b. repressed attraction to the opposite sex parent; c. present
relationships with siblings; d. long term sibling relations

5.2
99
Horney was a. Canadian; b. Austrian; c. part Norwegian;
d. part Indian (from India)
5.3
99
Horney's father was a a. preacher; b. sea captain; c. professor
d. school teacher
5.4
99
Horney's feelings toward her father were a. warm; b. negative;
c. characterized by indifference; d. mixed
5.5
100
Horney's maternal grandmother a. raised her; b. may have
been her educational role model; c. was Karen's mother
Sonni's real mother, not her stepmother; d. was unable to gain
an education, a factor that affected Karen badly
5.6
100
Horney was a. a slow learner until collegr; b. a beauty;
c. rather plain, she thought; d. a tomboy to the extreme
5.7
100
Horney was aided by; a. her father's support for her
educational endeavors; b. grandmother Minna's generous
financial support; c. her younger sister's willingness to be a
role model; d. an era in Europe during which women could
seek a higher education
5.8
100
During her medical training, Horney suffered from
a. depression; b. asthma; c. inattention from men; d. rickets
5.9
100
During her first semester in medical school, Horney met
a. a young woman who became her role model; b. with
academic difficulties; c. Oscar Horney; d. was elected president
of an all male organization
5.10
100
During medical school Horney a. adopted Dr. Karl Abraham, a
psychoanalyst, as her mentor ; b. had a series of affairs; c.
became violently ill frequently; d. had several conflicts with
male students
5.11

Which of the following were true of Horney during her medical training? a. she received help with the children from her husband, unusual for the day; b. she worked as a research assistant and was able to hire a nanny for the children; c. she tried to balance mother, homemaker, and medical student; d. she suffered a nervous breakdown and had to drop out of medical school for a time   5.12

All except one of the following were true of Horney as she completed her medical training and migrated to the U.S. Which was NOT true? a. although a student at the Berlin Psychoanalytic Institute, she began to doubt Freud; b. she was impressed and influenced by some of Adler's ideas; c. she came to the U.S. to escape the Nazis and probably what remained of her marriage; d. she founded the Psychoanalytic Institute in the U.S. and kicked out members who questioned Freud's ideas   5.13

All of the following, except one, were criticisms that Horney lodged against Freud's ideas. Which was NOT a criticism? a. she had major misgivings about the case study method that Freud embraced; b. she thought culture was a more important factor than instinct; c. she believed that neurotic needs for affection were more crucial than libidinal urges; d. she emphasized anxiety provoking childhood experiences rather than Phallic motivation   5.14

Instead of libidinal satisfactions, Horney emphasized a. strivings for superiority; b. the ancestral past of humans c. safety from feelings of isolation, helplessness, fear, and hostility; d. the need for interpersonal contact with significant others   5.15

Horney quarreled with all of the following Freudian ideas or derivations of those ideas, except one. Which did she NOT quarrel with? a. Oedipus complex; b. penis envy c. women's castrating tendencies; d. neurosis as the predominant form of maladjustment in the early 20th century   5.16

All of the following, except one, were "bones of contention" in Horney's disagreements with Freud. Which was NOT a matter of contention between Horney and Freud? a. the importance of early childhood experiences; b. the importance of culture c. psychoanalysts' extrapolation from their own cultures to all others; d. the emphasize on sexual factor   5.17

All of the following, except one, were among Horney's beliefs about sexuality. Which was NOT her belief about sexuality? a. masturbation is normal; b. some women are repressed homosexuals; c. sex outside of marriage is neurotic, because it becomes a compulsion; d. there are individuals who, finding themselves in anxious circumstances, are attracted to the most prominent person present   5.18
103-104

Which of the following is one of Horney's sexual types? a. neurotic homosexuals: people who are attracted to the same sex to avoid competition; b. Don (and Dawn) Juans who attempt to seduce every member of the opposite sex they; c. homosexuals who are repressed heterosexuals; d. Amazons who overpower the men they encounter   5.19
103

Which of the following derivatives from Freudian theory did Horney dismiss out of hand? a. most homosexuals are not true homosexuals; b. both sexes have the hormones of the other sex; c. women are naturally masochistic; d. women lack true sexual feelings   5.20
103

According to Horney, why might women display frigidity? a. because it is natural to them; b. because the physiological propensity to it is stronger in women than in men; c. because, even after the Victorian era, it is expected of them; d. because they wish to humiliate their men   5.21
104

Which of the following is the best summary statement concerning Horney's attitude toward sexuality? a. orgasm is the heart and soul of sexuality; b. there are psychological reasons for sexual expression that are far more important than physical gratification; c. sexual expression is almost always neurotic in form; d. it is women who are sexual beings, not men
5.22
102

Which is the most serious and fundamental problem that the young child faces (basic anxiety)? a. sexual frustration; b. a feeling of low status relative to siblings; c. being caught in the titanic clash between instinctual and social needs; d. being lonely and helpless in a hostile world   5.23
104

Which is a reason for the child's insecurity, according to Horney? a. hostile home atmosphere; b. sex role ambiguity c. faulty division of labor among parents; d. sibling rivalry
5.24
104

All of the following, except one, are among the sources of the child's insecurity, according to Horney. Which is NOT a source of insecurity? a. forbidding gestures; b. belittling attitudes

c. overprotection; d. unkept promises

5.25
104

To Horney, a neurosis is a. reactions to threats that repressed material will surface; b. disturbances in the unconscious related to failure of the self to balance needs; c. psychic disturbances due to fears and defenses against them and to attempts to find compromise solutions for conflicting tendencies; d. fundamental insecurities arising from a failure to reconcile need for achievement with need for gratification

5.26
104

Neurotic needs are a. the needs of neurotics to overcome their neuroses; b. the ergs and regnancies that conspire to cripple the ego in its fight to fulfill basic needs; c. coping techniques composed of insatiable demands developed in response to basic anxiety; d. a series of symptoms that are set up each to defend against the other in the struggle to satisfy both social and physical needs

5.27
105-108

Which of the following is NOT among Horney's generalized movement trends? a. moving toward people; b. moving against people; c. moving away from people; d. moving into people

5.28
105

All except one of the following are characteristic of neurotic individuals. Which is NOT one of their characteristics? a. inferiority feelings; b. unhappiness; c. hyperactivity; d. distrust

5.29
105

Which of following is a main reason for identifying the characteristics of the individual's dominant needs a. to determine the repressed experiences that have led to the neurosis; b. to allow the individual insight into his or her neurosis; c. to reveal the relative direction the person is likely to take in relationships with others; d. to learn what to expect from the neurosis in terms of future unconscious conflicts

5.30
105-108

All of the following are true, according to Horney, except one. Which is NOT true? a. conflict is an essential part of neurosis; b. contradictory dispositions toward other people constitute an important part of conflict; c. contradictory dispositions toward the self pervade the personality in neurosis; d. people almost never develop a basic, unidirectional orientation to others

5.31
106

Expansiveness refers to a. desire to be "in control" and not admit that one is incorrect; b. believing that winning is everything, how the game is played is nothing; c. being the on-

looker, the non-competitor, the avoider who is hypersensitive to influence attempts; d. seeking accommodation to others at any price   5.32
105

All of the following are among Horney's Ten Neurotic Needs, except one. Which is NOT one of the ten needs a. Affection and approval; b. Exploiting others; c. Social recognition or prestige; d. Self-actualization   5.33
107

Resignation refers to a. desire to be "in control" and not admit that one is incorrect; b. believing that winning is everything, how the game is played is nothing; c. being the on-looker, the non-competitor, the avoider who is hypersensitive to influence attempts; d. seeking accommodation to others at any price
5.34
106

Self-effacing refers to a. desire to be "in control" and not admit that one is incorrect; b. believing that winning is everything, how the game is played is nothing; c. being the on-looker, the non-competitor, the avoider who is hypersensitive to influence attempts; d. seeking accommodation to others at any price
5.35
106

Hyper-competitiveness is a. the desire to be "in control" and not admit that one is incorrect; b. believing that winning is everything, how the game is played is nothing; c. being the on-looker, the non-competitor, the avoider who is hypersensitive to influence attempts; d. seeking accommodation to others at any price   5.36
106-107

All of the following are needs associated with moving away from others, except one. Which is NOT a need of those oriented to moving away from others? a. Personal admiration; b. Self-sufficiency and independence; c. Perfection and unassailability d. Exhibition   5.37
106

All of the following are needs associated with moving against others, except one. Which is NOT a need of those oriented to moving against others? a. Power; b. Exploiting others; c. Personal admiration; d. Personal achievement   5.38
106

All of the following are needs associated with moving toward others, except one. Which is NOT a need of those oriented toward others? a. Succorance; b. Affection and approval c. Having a partner; d. Narrowly restricting one's life   5.39
108

Which best describes the "idealized image of the self" a. the image of the person one would like to; b. the fiction that guides

one's style of life; c. an artificial pride system; d. a projection onto a more powerful person   5.40
107

Controllers a. try to influence people, but avoid heavy-handed methods; b. may try to determine everything the controlled person does and everything that happens to him or her; c. will resort to every technique, short of violence, in order to control someone; d. are difficult to explain in terms of evolutionary theory   5.41
108

Horney's real self is best characterized by a. a need to belong; b. the end of childhood; c. the potential for growth; d. the beginning of individuation   5.42
108

Horney's externalization means
a. external locus of control of reinforcements
b. need to project strengths onto others
c. a feeling that the external world is not to be trusted
d. the tendency to experience internal processes as if they occurred outside oneself   5.43
108

Which of the following is a byproduct of Horney's externalization? a. indifference; b. rage; c. fortitude; d. amplification   5.44
109

The actual self is a. who one might be; b. who one currently is; c. who one should be; d. who one could be   5.45
109

What is a "blind spot?" a. a contradiction about which one manages to remain unaware; b. an hysterical blindness brought on by the idealized image of the self; c. a scotoma--missing portion of the visual field--upon which unwanted stimulation is focused; d. an actual dysfunction of the visual cortex that results from the fear of "seeing" oneself reflected in others   5.46
109

In compartmentalization a. one hides away in a compartment of the mind; b. key aspects of oneself are separated into "logic tight" compartments; c. significant others are categorized into several compartments; d. the mind is divided into compartments analogous to the id, ego, and superego
5.47
109

According to Horney, rationalization is a. a way to reduce cognitive dissonance; b. a tendency to intellectualize instead of emotionalize about intrapsychic conflicts; c. self-deception by reasoning; d. attempting to be rational when irrationality actually characterizes oneself   5.47
109

Excessive self-control is a. a reaction to contradictory emotions involving holding feelings and behavior in a vice-grip; b. controlling the self in order to control others; c. engaging in a game of acting like a self-controlled person in order to induce self-control in others; d. controlling basic urges so that one looks pure and flawless to others   5.49
                                                                                      109

Arbitrary rightness is a. arbitrarily deciding what is the right thing for others to do; b. an arbitrariness in deciding what is morally right; c. a feeling that others are arbitrary in deciding what is right for oneself; d. the strategy of those who see life as a battle, thus, they must be right about everything lest they be controlled by "foreign influence"   5.50
                                                                                      109

Elusiveness is a. evading the conflict between the real self and the idealized image of self; b. hiding from close relations with members of both genders; c. slithering away from conflicts by refusing to take an identifiable stand; d. saying the opposite of what one really feels about relations with significant others
                                                                                      5.51
                                                                                      109

Cynicism isa. hostility directed toward fate b. denying moral values because of uncertainty about them; c. a form of nihilism in which religion and spirituality are rejected; d. inability to believe in anyone, least of all, oneself   5.52
                                                                                      109-110

According to Horney's psychology of women a. women have been restricted to a private, emotional sphere of life ; b. love and devotion "should" come to be regarded as feminine ideals c. love is an unrealistic value for women to pursue; d. only in men's minds are pursuits outside the emotional realm of secondary importance to women   5.53
                                                                                      109-110

All of the following are among Freud's theoretical speculations that Horney challenged, except one. Which is NOT among Freudian ideas that she challenged? a. women feel shame over their biological deficiencies; b. lacking penises, women overvalue relationships with men; c. women seek sexual stimulation through the clitoris because it is penis-like; d. women develop a superego that includes society's script concerning how to behave   5.54
                                                                                      109-110

What aspect of Freudian thought did Horney feel was particularly illogical? a. that the process of identification is similar for the sexes; b. that people built for a specific biological function would be obsessed with obtaining the biological attributes of the other sex; c. that women should be viewed as lesser when, in fact, women are biologically basic: the embryo

is "female" and must be differentiated into "male"; d. the ideas
of repression and denial as applied to women   5.55
                                                                110

The masculine equivalent of "penis-envy" is a. clitoral envy;
b. vaginal envy; c. ovarian envy; d. womb envy   5.56
                                                                110

Horney regretted a. that anyone ever paid any attention to
Freud; b. that the psychology of women had been considered
only from the point of view of men; c. that Freud was ignorant of
women because he had so few as patients; d. that women had
made no real progress from the turn of the century to the 1940s
                                                                5.57
                                                                110

Horney was ahead of her time in that she recognized that
a. jealousy is not a problem in romantic relationships;
b. sexuality is rather completely unimportant in human
relationships; c. European-American culture is dominated by
masculine ideology; d. progress for women would require open
rebellion, such as the bra burning of the 1960s
                                                                5.58
                                                                110

Which of the following is the biggest contributor to female
dependency, according to Horney? a. motherhood; b. the
belief that sexuality was for men; c. the belief that every woman
must have a man; d. household chores   5.59
                                                                110

"Systematic selection by men" refers to a. men's need to select
options for the women in their; b. men's ability to systematically
select options in their own lives while denying the same ability
to women; c. men's right to select outside-the-home interests
while denying that privilege to women
d. men's structuring of their selection of women so as to
compensate for specific male deficiencies
                                                                5.60
                                                                110

According to Horney, what is woman's reaction to society's
demeaning attitude toward them?   a. increasing their over-
evaluation of relationships with "superior" men; b. a tendency
to withdraw from relationships with men where possible; c.
restricting their friendships and other relationships with other
women; d. rationalizing that their roles as mothers and
homemakers is as valued as the roles of men   5.61
                                                                110

In what way did Adler side with Horney in her feud with the
Freudians? a. he acknowledged the greater inferiority of men
b. he accompanied her to a psychoanalytic convention in
Vienna and supported her as she confronted Freud in person;
c. he was one of the women's movement's first male figures;

d. he felt that decisions about birth control and abortion should be left up to women 5.62
111

Among the "firsts" achieved by Horney was the fact that she pioneered a. sexual therapy; b. plain language, self-exploration books; c. rational emotive therapy; d. clinics for children with emotional problems 5.63
111-115

Shaver and colleagues found that secure adults a. were high in interpersonal sensitivity ; b. showed sexuality that was characterized by "one night stands"; c. showed obligatory care-giving; d. were unlikely to experiment sexually 5.64
111

According to Horney, jealousy is a. fear that a rival will steal one's romantic; b. a general fear that others will encroach upon one's personal relationships; c. fear of losing a relationship that is seen as satisfying insatiable needs for love; d. a need to solely possess every significant other in one's life
5.65
112

What did Levy, Blatt and Shaver (1998) find when they had subjects write a description of each parent? a. as expected, anxious-ambivalent women's descriptions of their mothers were the most ambivalent; b. unexpectedly, secure women's descriptions of their mothers at a low (non-complex) level c. unexpectedly, avoidant women's descriptions of their mothers were the most ambivalent; d. avoidant women also described their parents at a low cognitive level 5.66
112

According to Horney, which is true about morbidly jealous people? a. they are almost entirely femaleb. they are suicidal; c. they display a happy-go-lucky Persona; d. their fear of losing a loved one is out of proportion to the real danger 5.67
112

Mikulincer (1998) found all the following except one. Which was NOT among this researcher's findings? a. secure people showed low anger-proneness; b. anxious-ambivalent people displayed lack of anger control; c. avoidant people were high in hostility; d. avoidant people were fully aware of their anger
5.68
111

In consistency with Horney's view, Philip Shaver and his colleagues hypothesized that; a. that there is no link between childhood jealousy and adult jealousy; b. adults who show child-like jealousy are neurotic; c. the link between childhood jealousy and adult jealousy is mediated by the ideal self image in relation to the real self image; d. the way adult persons relate to their lovers may mirror the way those persons related to their parents as children 5.69

Which of the following reflects one of Shaver's attachment styles? a. I find it easy to break off a relationship. b. I feel secure only in relationships with the opposite sex. c. I like to have more than one boy(girl) friend at a time. d. I feel that others are reluctant to get as close as I would like   5.70

112
Cook qualified earlier attachment work by Shaver and others and showed that attachment is very complex when he reported; a. attachment security level can be relationship specific; b. attachment security level is unaffected by with whom one attaches; c. attachment security level is not reciprocated by the target of attachment; d. few attachment security studies are currently found in the literature

5.71

112
The "tyranny of the shoulds" refers to a. an idea that Horney borrowed from Albert Ellis; b. a notion that is more applicable to men than women; c. the belief that one should do whatever a good person would do; d. the belief that the shoulds that others impose on oneself are tyrannical and ought to be cast off

5.72

115
All below are among the shoulds that plague people, except one. Which NOT is a should? a. point out other's faults; b. be dignified; c. be courageous; d. be honest and generous

5.73

115
Self-analysis is a. analysis of the self from an objective point of view; b. analysis of the self from an outsider's point of view; c. analysis of the connection among the various personality structures; d. analysis to gain a better understanding of oneself through one's own efforts   5.74

115
Self-recognition is a. differentiating the self from that of other people, especially parents; b. coming to know one's own neuroses, idealized self-image, and real self; c. recognizing the nature and extent of connections to the selves of significant others; d. recognizing where one is in life and where one is going in terms of development of the self   5.75

116-117
All except one of the following are facts about Clare, the self-analysis case-study subject. Which is NOT a fact about Clare? a. Clare had never had a long-term relationship with a man until Peter entered her life; b. Clare's mother attempted to abort her; c. Clare's father was uninterested in any of his children; d. as an editor, Clare was intensely irritated with an author who had broken a promise   5.76

116

All except one of the following are meaningful dreams that Clare had. Which one was NOT among her dreams? a. she was lost in a foreign city, could not speak the language, and left her money and luggage at the train station; b. she was adrift at sea, but a strong man put his arms around her and saved her; c. a large bird, glorious in color and grace, was flying away; d. Peter had gone off to war and Clare had lost her feelings for him   5.77
117

Which of the following were true of Clare? a. she wondered whether her love for Peter was a compensation for the loss of her father's love; b. she began to realize that her need for Peter was based on something other than affection; c. she was suicidal when she learned that Peter was having an affair d. that a woman's love was merely a screen for exploiting a man was an original conjecture on her part   5.78
117

All of the following are true concerning short-comings of self-analysis, except one. Which is NOT a short-coming? a. people may see something about themselves that is not true; b. everything that people learn about themselves during self-analysis must be unlearned during regular therapy; c. people may come up with correct information about themselves, but misinterpret it; d. even if people analyze an incident correctly, they may not know what to do about it   5.79
118

In Ryckman and colleagues study of Horney's "hypercompet-itiveness," which of the following measures was most closely related to being hypercompetitive; a. Machiavellianism b. narcissism c. Type E orientation; d. sensation seeking
5.80
119-121

According to evolutionary theory, which is correct regarding men's and women's orientation to ensuring that their genes are passed to future generations? a. only women are highly concerned about sexual infidelity; b. both genders are highly concerned about sexual infidelity; c. men are more concerned about emotional infidelity; d. women are more concerned about emotional infidelity
Extra Items   5.81
100

Horney, to escape from under the thumb of her father, a. run away from home at the age of thirteen; b. refused to obey him c. submitted to the protection of her mother; d. at an early age, decided to reject all males   5.82
100

Having attended psychoanalytic sessions at Dr. Carl Abraham's house, Horney was associated with the founding of the a. anti-Freud movement; b. Feminists' League of

Psychoanalysts; c. NeoFreudian Movement; d. Berlin
Psychoanalytic Institute   5.83
                                                            101

Horney knew and interacted with all of the following, except
one. With whom did she NOT personally know and interact?
a. Freud; b. Sullivan; c. Margaret Mead; d. Fromm   5.84
                                                            119

According to Harris and Christenfeld (1996) and DeSteno and
Salovey (1996); a. the evidence in favor of evolutionary theory
is overwhelming; b. both genders find sexual infidelity equally
highly distressing; c. neither gender is particularly concerned
about either emotional or sexual infidelity; d. sexuality infidelity
implies emotional infidelity and vice versa   5.85
                                                            119

Harris (2000) hooked subjects up to a physiological machine
and found what result that fails to support evolutionary theory?
a. men were unreactive to sexual material; b. men reacted to
sexual more strongly than emotional scenarios even when
infidelity was not involved; c. women were more reactive to
sexual than to emotional infidelity; d. there were no gender
differences at all   5.86
                                                            105-106

Which is characteristic of people who "move toward others"?
a. exaggerated modesty; b. cravings for power; c. hyper-
competitiveness; d. being an on-looker   5.87
                                                            108

The real self is a. who one currently is; b. who one might be; c.
who one should be; d. who one could be   5.88
                                                            109-110

According to Horney, for women, love is a. futility; b. what
women are socialized to seek; c. exploitation; d. a kind of
coercion that women direct to themselves   5.89
                                                            114

According to Shaver and colleagues what percentage of
people to be avoidant types?   a. 25%; b. 55%; c. 10%; d. 75%
                                                            5.90
                                                            112

Philip Shaver recently wonder whether the 40,000 people who
wrote Ann Landers proclaiming a preference for hugs over
intercourse were mainly _____ types. a. secure;
 b. disengaged ; c. avoidant; d. anxious   5.91
                                                            111

Which idea of Horney's regarding jealousy ties in with Philip
Shaver's modern conception of jealousy? a. morbid, adult
jealousy can carry-over from an insatiable childhood appetite
for love; b. jealousy of the same sex parent carries-over into
jealousy of same sex adult friends; c. one's adult partner is
likely to be very similar to the parent of the opposite sex; d.
adult jealousy is unlike childhood jealousy   5.92

112

Which is a concept of another theorist that was anticipated by one of Horney's concepts? a. hyper-competitiveness; b. asexuality; c. musturbation; d. radical consumerism   5.93

118&121

All of the following, except one, are reasons why Horney is worthy of consideration by everyone? Which is NOT a reason she should be considered? a. the case of Clare is a remarkable testimony to the consistency of her thought; b. she was an outstanding writer; c. she anticipated modern notions of jealousy; d. she was a fascinating person   5.94

116-117

What gift did Peter give Clare that she valued disproportionate to its worth? a. a scarf; b. a small diamond ring; c. a sweat shirt; d. a bracelet   5.95

118

Ryckman and colleagues (1999) found what adnormal characteristic related to hypercompetitiveness? a. depression; b. schizophrenia c. bipolar disorder; d. eating disorder   5.96

118

Which of the following was Horney's deficiencies that she shared with other theorists covered in the first part of the text? a. over emphasis on infantile sexuality; b. nonscientific training as a physician and psychiatrist; c. too much concern with interpersonal relations; d. too little concern for the "dark" side of people   5.97

121

What orientation of Horney was refreshing in contrast to the gloomy outlook of the psychoanalysts? a. her approach to self-analysis; b. her good sense of humor; c. her "growth" approach; d. he polyannaish view of life   5.98

121

What contribution did Horney make while an adolescent? a. a method for recording on-going social exchanges; b. a piece of music that is still played; c. a concept, elusiveness, that she later included in her theory; d. a lucid and fascinating chronicle of her life during adolescence   5.99

121

For which of her concepts has Horney received little credit by modern psychological researchers and writers a. her notion of jealousy; b. hypercompetitiveness; c. Type E orientation d. basic anxiety   5.100

105

Which of the following is most likely Horney's greatest contribution? a. the "movement toward others" orientation b. rationalization; c. founding of the Association for the Advancement of Psychoanalysis; d. her attention to "neuroses"   5.101

120

Pratto and Hegarty (2000) showed that evolutionary imperatives are not all there is to men's concern about sexuality infidelity and tendency to exercise surveillance over their women partners when they found what measure to be related to these behaviors? a. Extraversion; b. Endorsement of Sexual Myths; c. Endorsement of Rape Myths; d. Social Dominance Orientation

5.102
120

According to Mathes, men's sexual strategy can be boiled down to; a. "watch her every minute"; b. "have as much sex as you can"; c. "watch male rivals every minute"; d. "be faithful to your partner"

5.103
120

To eliminate "paternal uncertainty" as a factor in preferences, Mathes had men and women choose between emotional support and sexual gratification with their partners. He found a. men showed more concern about emotional support; b. women showed more concern about sexual gratification; c. men showed more concern about sexual gratification; d. there were no gender differences in choices

5.1,a	5.49,d	5.95, d
5.2,c	5.50,c	5.96, b
5.3,b	5.51,b	5.97, c
5.4,d	5.52,a	5.98, d
5.5,b	5.53,d	5.99, a
5.6,c	5.54,b	5.100, a
5.7,d	5.55,d	5.101, d
5.8,a	5.56,b	5.102, d
5.9,c	5.57,c	6.103, c
5.10,a	5.58,c	
5.11,c	5.59,d	
5.12,d	5.60,a	
5.13,a	5.61,d	
5.14,c	5.62,b	
5.15,d	5.63,a	
5.16,a	5.64,c	
5.17,c	5.65,c	
5.18,a	5.66,d	
5.19,c	5.67,d	
5.20,d	5.68,d	
5.21,b	5.69,d	
5.22,d	5.70,a	
5.23,a	5.71,c	
5.24,a	5.72,a	
5.25,c	5.73,d	
5.26,c	5.74,b	
5.27,d	5.75,a	
5.28,c	5.76,c	
5.29,c	5.77,b	
5.30,d	5.78,b	
5.31,a	5.79,b	
5.32,d	5.80,d	
5.33,c	*Extra*	
5.34,d	*Items*	
5.35,a	5.81, c	
5.36,d	5.82, d	
5.37,c	5.83, a	
5.38,a	5.84, d	
5.39,c	5.85, b	
5.40,b	5.86, a	
5.41,c	5.87, d	
5.42,d	5.88, b	
5.43,b	5.89, a	
5.44,b	5.90, d	
5.45,a	5.91, a	
5.46,b	5.92, c	
5.47,c	5.93, a	
5.48,a	5.94, a	

Chapter 6

Multiple Choice Items for the Chapter on Sullivan

6.1
125

Like other theorists, Sullivan declined to support Freud's
a. use of stages b. exclusion of women; c. sexual emphasis
d. emphasis on the unconscious   6.2
125

What did Sullivan wish to emphasize a. humans ancestral past
b. childhood anxiet; c. natural inferiority; d. interpersonal relations
6.3
126

Sullivan was a. Jewish; b. Irish; c. English; d. Rumanian 6.4
126

How did the social law of relatively apply to Sullivan's families?
a. the Sullivans and Stacks had equal status in the community; b.
the two families had equally low status; c. the Stacks had
relatively high status; d. The Sullivans had relatively high status
6.5
126

What signified Sullivan's identity problems? a. he never felt
"grown-up"; b. he felt like a woman trapped in a man's body;
c. he did not know who his real mother was; d. he changed his
name more than once   6.6
126-127

Which of the following accurately describes Sullivan? a. he was
probably the most stable theorist covered so far; b. he had the
vulnerable, haunted look of actor James Dean; c. he had affairs
with many women and married three; d. he had a pristine record
as a solid citizen   6.7
128

All except one of the following accurately describes Sullivan as a
symbol of diversity? Which does NOT describe him? a. he may
have been homosexual; b. he was Irish; c. he had Native
American ancestry; d. he may have been schizophrenic

6.8
126

The women in Sullivan's life included all of the following, except
one. Which woman was NOT included? a. his mother; b. his first
cousin; c. Karen Horney; d. Clara Thompson, also a theorist
6.9
127

Which of the following characterized Sullivan's college career? a.
distinguished; b. non-existent (he went from an exclusive prep
school to medical school); c. nondescript (little is known about it)
d. mediocre   6.10

127

Which of the following characterized Sullivan's medical school career? a. distinguished; b. varied (he switched schools several times); c. nondescript (it is not certain where he went to school); d. mediocre   6.11

127

Sullivan described his medical school as a. the best in the mid-west; b. a diploma mill; c. on par with Harvard medical school; d. one of the oldest in the country (it still exists today)   6.12

127

Sullivan's training as a psychiatrist can be characterized as a. thorough; b. non-existent (he never even worked in a Hospital); c. provided by the patients; d. solid   6.13

127

What was the advantage of Sullivan's psychiatric training? a. he learned from experience in the wards, not from the dogmatic professors of his day; b. he had many distinguished professors, including Adler; c. his training was unusually extended: it took him six years to complete his residency; d. he was a Harvard medical school resident   6.14

127

Sullivan's burning interest during his psychiatric, clinical training was a. depression; b. schizophrenia; c. manic depressive (bipolar) disorder; d. induced psychotic disorder

6.15

127

What is ironic about Sullivan's psychiatric training? a. it was thorough, but he seemed ill trained; b. it was minimal, and his skills were also minimal; d. it was varied, but his approach was unitary; d. it was minimal, but he is a central figure in the development of psychiatric training   6.16

128

All of the following are reasons why Sullivan may have committed suicide, except one. Which is NOT a reason Sullivan may have committed suicide? a. he had inoperable cancer; b. the rural community of his youth was suicide ridden; c. he had a heart ailment; d. the day he died was his deceased mother's birthday

6.17

128

Which was certainly true of Sullivan's death? a. he died of cancer; b. he committed suicide; c. he predicted when and how he would die; d. he died of food poisoning   6.18

129

Which of the following fits Sullivan's definition of personality best? a. a system of interrelated psychic structures; b. a symphony of conscious and unconscious forces; c. the coordination of inter- and intra- psychic forces with the external world; d. the enduring pattern of interpersonal situations characterizing a human life

6.19

Whose view is Sullivanianism least related to? a. Freud;
b. Adler; c. Horney; d. Jung   6.20
                                                                129

Significant others are a. another way to say "parents"; b. people
who are most meaningful in our lives; c. include only members of
the extended family; d. is a small circle of intimates whose primary
role is that of confidant   6.21
                                                                129

A self-system is a. the relationship among the id, ego, and
superego; b. a system that unites the ego and the unconscious;
c. the part of personality born out of influences of significant
others; d. a hierarchy of psychic structures with basic physical
needs at the bottom and self-fulfillment at the top   6.22
                                                                129

Relations with significant others are a. on again, off again; b.
sometimes fantasized; c. absent for many people; d. always
troubled   6.23
                                                                129

Which are among the tensions emphasized by Sullivan?
a. sexual anxiety; b. spiritual anxiety; c. archival anxiety;
d. interpersonal anxiety   6.24
                                                                129

Which is true of the "mothering one?" a. always the biological
mother; b. an adult; c. always a woman; d. middle-aged
                                                                6.25
                                                                129

"Need for tenderness" refers to a. a need to be treated tenderly; b.
desires for physical contact, exclusively; c. desire for relief from
various tensions; d. need for self-esteem
                                                                6.26
                                                                129

Which of the following best describes the ideal infant mothering
one relationship, according to Sullivan? a. close; b. characterized
by reciprocal role-taking; c. entirely psychological; d.
unmanageably complex   6.27
                                                                129-130

Which of the following best describes the emotional relationship
between the infant and the mothering one? a. characterized by
distance; b. responses in the mother short-circuit responses in the
infant; c. too complex to decipher; d. anxiety in the mother is
transferred to the infant   6.28
                                                                130

To what does Sullivan's "empathy" refer? a. the emotional
linkage between the infant and significant other people
b. standing in someone else's emotional shoes; c. a kind of
emotional ESP; d. a sophisticated form of non-verbal
communication   6.29
                                                                130

Interpersonal security refers to a. being secure in interpersonal relations; b. relaxation of the tension of anxiety; c. securing many interpersonal relationsd. seeking to make interpersonal relations secure   6.30
                                                                                   130

"Big, blooming, buzzing confusion" describes a. parataxic mode; b. syntaxic mode; c. orthotaxic mode; d. prototaxic mode
                                                                                   6.31
                                                                                   130

"The child uses speech, but still makes few logical connections within the sequence of experience" a. parataxic mode; b. syntaxic mode; c. orthotaxic mode; d. prototaxic mode
                                                                                   6.32
                                                                                   131

"The meaning of words as well as judgments and observations are shared" describes a. parataxic mode; b. syntaxic mode; c. orthotaxic mode; d. prototaxic mode   6.33
                                                                                   131-132

Which mode is associated with the infant stage of Sullivanian personality development?   a. parataxic mode; b. syntaxic mode; c. orthotaxic mode; d. prototaxic mode   6.34
                                                                                   133-134

Which mode is associated with the childhood stage of Sullivanian personality development? a. parataxic mode; b. syntaxic mode; c. orthotaxic mode; d. prototaxic mode   6.35
                                                                                   131

Which mode is associated with the juvenile stage of Sullivanian personality development?   a. parataxic mode; b. syntaxic mode; c. orthotaxic mode; d. prototaxic mode
                                                                                   6.36
                                                                                   131

Personifications are a. facades or personas given a different name by Sullivan; b. human attributes invested in persons or objects that do not possess them; c. accurate descriptions of significant entities in people's lives; d. fantasized connections to other people, often public figures (John Hinkley and Jody Foster)
                                                                                   6.37
                                                                                   131-132

Which of the following is the best indication of the "good mother?" a. hugs and kisses; b. a satisfying nipple; c. satisfying, warm, and comfortable interactions; d. a deep seated spiritual connection between mother and infant   6.38
                                                                                   132

All of the following, except one, are likely to be personifications of a person. Which is NOT a likely personification? a. bad mother; b. good me; c. bad me; d. bad man   6.39
                                                                                   132

"Forbidding gestures" refers to a. the distressed infants communications with the mothering one; b. the distressed

mothering one's attempts to comfort the anxious infant; c. gestures that are mutually employed by angry infants and mothering ones; d. covert cues such as a hesitancy, reluctance, or revulsion
6.40
137

Which of the following is NOT a theory of homosexuality for which there is significance evidence? a. there is a gene for male homosexuality on the X chromosome; b. hormones present in the womb predispose the fetus to homosexuality; c. ring-finger-longer-than-index-finger found in lesbians; d. response to an auditory click greater for lesbians than hetereosexual women
6.41
137

According to Daryl Bem's "exotic is erotic" theory of homosexuality; a. gay men are attracted to exotic other men; b. gays are more erotic than "straight" men; c. boys who spend childhood times with girls find boys exotic; d. gay boys find exotic materials more exotic than "straight" boys
6.42
129

Which is reasonably likely to describe a significant other a. spiritual; b oral.; c. fantasized ; d. skeletal
6.43
132

All except one of the following parental attitudes are mal-adjustive, according to Sullivan. Which is NOT maladjustive? a. believing that the infant must be clean and dry; b. becoming upset when the infant tinkers with its genitals; c. fancying that the infant "takes after" some other person in the family; d. being concerned about taking care of the infants basic physical needs
6.44
133-134

All except one of the following characterize the childhood stage. Which does NOT characterize the childhood stage? a. articulate speech; b. acculturation in what is proper; c. continued development of the self-system; d. sharing of word meanings, judgments and observations
6.45
133

Which of the following helps the self-system maintain normal functioning during the childhood stage?   a. selective inattention; b. intellectualization; c. denial; d. rationalization

6.46
134

Which are among the emotions children are apt to learn during the childhood stage? a. feeling high; b. feeling fulfilled; c. feeling a part of the larger community; d. feeling shame
6.47
134

During the childhood stage, "manifesting the need for tenderness toward potent figures" a. is especially well received; b. may backfire: these figures may make fun of the child; c. is abandoned, as it is immature; d. is done more desperately than in infancy

6.48

134

All except one of the following are commonsensical, widely used terms adopted by Sullivan to account for learning. Which was originated by Sullivan? a. trial and success; b. learn by anxiety; c. rewards and punishments; d. trial and error

6.49

134

The "anxiety gradient" refers to a. variations of anxiety during childhood; b. learning to discriminate increasing from diminishing anxiety; c. gradations of anxiety across people involved in interpersonal relations; d. a steep slope of anxiety

6.50

133

Which of the following best characterizes the relationship between the example "good mother" and her infant? a. they show no reaction when one is not in the presence of the other; b. they sense the feelings and needs of one another; c. they show upset when anyone other than each other is present; d. they seem unaware of the presence of other people

6.51

134-135

Without parental sanity, what will become of the child? a. it will itself become insane; b. it will arrive at later stages with uncertainty about its worth; c. it will be unable to master the anxiety gradient; d. it will, paradoxically, become a resilient and well-adjusted adult, by virtue of its compensatory abilities

6.52

135

Which is of paramount importance to the child during the juvenile period? a. sexual gratification; b. pleasing parents c. advancing educationally; d. peers

6.53

135

During the juvenile stage a. peers become less important b. the child learns that rules applicable to the home may be inappropriate at school; c. parents become "enemies"; d. religious awakening occurs

6.54

136

During the preadolescence stage a. establishing a relationship with a "chum," a same sex friend becomes of primary importance; b. a single friend is embraced; gangs or cliques are shunned; c. children become "reality" based; fantasy is taboo; d. children become temporarily anti-social

6.55

136

Early adolescence is characterized by a. social indifference; b. abandonment of the "best friend" or chum; c. obsession with

extracurricular activities, especially sports; d. the appearance of
lustful feelings   6.56
                                                                    133

What dynamism develops during early adolescence? a. the lust
dynamism; b. the peer dynamism; c. the intimacy dynamism; d. the
spiritual dynamism   6.57
                                                                    136-137

All except one of the following are intimacy expressions. Which is
NOT an intimacy expression?   a. autophilic; b. isophilic; c.
homophilic; d. heterophilic   6.58
                                                                    136

Katasexual means a. attraction to people of a different race
b. bisexual; c. asexual; d. sexual preference for animals or dead
people   6.59
                                                                    136-137

All except one of the following regard use of the genitals. Which is
NOT among uses of the genitals? a. katagenital; b. onanism; c.
amphigenital; d. paragenital   6.60
                                                                    136-137

All except one of the following regard uses of the genitals. Which
is NOT among uses of the genitals? a. mutual masturbation; b.
metagenital; c. orthogenital; d. omnigenital   6.61
                                                                    138

Sullivan said Americans are the most "sex-ridden" people he
knew. All of the following are reasons why he said that, except
one. Which was NOT a reason for his comment? a. early
marriage is discouraged; b. parents insist on sex education
programs; c. adults view teen sexuality from the "just say not" or
the contraceptive perspective; d. society creates a twilight zone
between adolescence and adulthood   6.62
                                                                    138

According to Sullivan, late adolescence is characterized by
a. the end of lust; b. the establishment of a fully mature repertory of
interpersonal relations; c. termination of relations with the
mothering one; d. the belief in magical and imaginary features of
reality and interpersonal relations   6.63
                                                                    138

Sullivan's "late adolescence" is most similar to a. Horney's
ambivalent stage. b. Jung's young adulthood stage;
c. Freud's genital stage; d. Adler's fourth decade stage
                                                                    6.64
                                                                    138-139

Which of Sullivan's ideas is strongly related to some classic
research with institutional infants and some famous monkey
research? a. contact with the mothering one; b. his classification
of sexual orientations and behaviors; c. the notions of parataxic,
prototaxic, and syntaxic; d. his notion of personification 6.65
                                                                    139

"Marasmus" refers to a. an infant form of manic-depressive syndrome; b. what we would now call attention deficit disorder with hyperactivity; c. precocious intellectual development d. wasting away for want of human contact   6.66
139-140

A line of research in developmental or child psychology is well related to Sullivan's theory. Which of the following represents that line of research? a. paraperceptual studies; b. cognitive development studies; c. attachment studies; d. shyness studies
6.67
139-140

In Harry Harlow's famous monkey studies, which mother figure di baby monkeys prefer? a. the mother with the nipple; b. the mother with the simulated beating heart; c. the mechanical mother that could move; d. the terrycloth mother   6.68
133

Which of the following characterizes the infant of the example "good mother"? a. he relaxes when she picks him up but tenses when she puts him down; b. he cries when she leaves him; c. he smiles only when looking at her; d. when she picks him up he moves his body as if to try to get closer to her   6.69
140

The most widely used assessment technique in psychiatry was developed by Sullivan. What is it called? a. the Minnesota Multiphasic Personality Inventory; b. the Thematic Apperception Test; c. The Psychiatric Interview; d. the Rorschach inkblot test
6.70
139-142

All but one of the following are among Sullivan's contributions to understanding people through the interview process. Which is NOT one of those contributions? a. assumptions about the nature of interview data; b. statistical methods for analyzing interview data; c. structural outlines for obtaining and organizing information; d. guidelines for interpreting the interview process and defining the roles of participants   6.71
140

Which was one of Sullivan's strongest beliefs about the role of the psychological professional in the interview process? a. the interviewer should let the patient control the process; b. the interviewer should stay out of the process, just ask questions and record answers; c. the interviewer should take charge of the situation and do most of the talking; d. the interviewer should be a participant observer   6.72
136-7

All except one of the following are among the four stages of the interview that Sullivan identified. Which is NOT one of those four stages? a. detailed inquiry; b. inception; c. intense encounter; d. interruption   6.73
141-142

During the critically important third phase of the interview, what typically characterizes the patient, according to Sullivan.
a. walking around the obvious; b. sexual talk; c. over-disclosure; d. transference   6.74
                                                                                                141

Security operations are a. skills that allow avoidance of forbidding gestures; b. the patient's evasive interview strategy
c. the interviewer's subtle attempts to "bring the patient out"; d. attempts to hide true feelings   6.75
                                                                                                141

Foresight is a. a future orientation as opposed to Freud's orientation to the past; b. looking back in order to see forward better; c. the uncanny ability to predict the future; d. the capacity to look ahead for good experiences and to avoid bad ones
                                                                                                6.76
                                                                                                142

"Notice changes in the body" refers to a. therapists perceptions of the physiological changes in the patient's body; b. the patient's learned ability to detect increases/decreases in the tension of anxiety; c. the therapists perceptions of the patient's changes in body posture; d. the mutual inspection by therapist and patient of each other's body posture   6.77
                                                                                                142

"Notice marginal thoughts" involves a. the thoughts of the therapist; b. thoughts that are of little significance but are presented as if they are important; c. the two critics, I_1 and I_2
d. the thoughts the therapists makes in the margins of her or his notes   6.78
                                                                                                142

Which of the following refers to the "rather intelligent creature" (critic) who appears during the interview process? a. the one-way mirror that permits the therapist to see the patient, but not vise versa; b. the mirror that reflects the impressions we are making on others back to us; c. the one-way mirror that permits the patient to see the therapist, but visa versa; d. the mirror that distorts the perceptions we have of other people   6.79
                                                                                                142

"Make prompt statements of all that comes to mind" involves which of the following? a. just mentioning everything that comes to mind; b. promptly mentioning thoughts, especially those with emotional content; c. talking rapidly because it prevent self-censureship of thoughts; d. trusting the situation to the extent of expressing the thoughts that it provokes   6.80
                                                                                                142-143

All except one of the following best characterize the limitations of Sullivan and his work? Which does NOT characterize those limitations? a. because of the obscurity of his thought, there are no organizations pursuing Sullivanianism today; b. Sullivan was no scientist; c. there has been little direct research on Sullivan ideas; d. some of Sullivan's concepts border on the trivial

6.81

143-144

All except one of the following comments about Sullivan and his work highlight reasons why he, his ideas, and methods are worth considering by modern psychological thinkers. Which is NOT something about Sullivan worth considering? a. some of his concepts are nearly profound and still in use; b. his eccentric nature may be a sign of his as yet untapped genius; c. his brilliant writings, noted for their clarity, contain many concrete ideas that have been overlooked; d. much of his thinking was highly original

Extra Items

6.82

126

Which of the following is most true with regard to whether Sullivan was gay? a. close friends and colleagues indicate that he was definitely gay; b. in his day, people who were not "straight" did not say so in public; c. he was actually bisexual: both men and women reported affairs with him; d. the many women with whom he had affairs confirm that he was heterosexual

6.83

128

All of the following were possible aspects of Sullivan's personal diversity, except one. Which was NOT an aspect of Sullivan's diversity? a. ethnicity (national origin of his family); b. sexual orientation; c. mental health status; d. physical disability

6.84

128

What new personification category did Blechner propose? a. the not any longer me; b. the unimagined people me; c. the maybe me; d. the supernatural me

6.85

129

All of the following, except one, represent our relationships with significant others. Which is NOT a representation of our relationships with significant others? a. imaginary playmates; b. extraterrestrial creatures; c. literary figures; d. idealized public figures

6.86

128

Sullivan's identity was related to all of the following diversity dimensions, except one. Which dimension was his identity NOT related to? a. race; b. religion; c. mental health; d. sexual orientation

6.87

130-131

Which of the following represents the "magic" characteristic of the parataxic thinking mode? a. fairy tales seem to come true; b. animals are believed to think; c. things "just happen"; d. airplanes seem to fall from the sky

6.88

132

The "nipple to lips" experience relates to all of the following, except one. To which does "nipple to lips" NOT relate?

a. breast; b. bottle; c. oral stage; d. syntaxic mode   6.89
                                                               132

All of the following are examples of forbidding gestures, except one. Which is NOT an example of forbidding gestures?
a. spanking; b. cold voice tone; c. a wrinkled brow; d. a too tight grasp   6.90
                                                               132-133

All of the following are kinds of reactions that the child may learn during interactions with parents that lead to development of the self-system, except one. Which is NOT one of those reactions? a. distemperament; b. anger; c. disgust; d. shame   6.91
                                                               134

Which of the following is one of the "main avenues to acquiring new, useful information" which was borrowed by Sullivan from others who preceded him? a. trial and error; b. rewards and punishments; c. anxiety gradient; d. learn by anxiety   6.92
                                                               135

Which of the following is a kind of person who is critical to the development of the child during the juvenile era? a. peer; b. chum; c. compeer; d. confidant   6.93
                                                               137

Which of the following involves taking on a sexual role that is different from one's usual role? a. isophilic; b. katasexual; c. amphigenital; d. paragenital   6.94
                                                               138

Establishing "relationships of love for some other person" is central to which Sullivanian stage? a. pre-adolescence; b. infancy; c. childhood; d. late adolescence   6.95
                                                               139-140

Who did the famous monkey studies relating to Sullivan's attachment to and contact with the mothering one? a. Harlow b. Shaver; c. Bowlby; d. Maslow   6.96
                                                               140

Harlow and Suomi showed that young monkeys can serve as
a. sort of social engineers; b. sexual surrogates; c. therapists d. colony leaders   6.97
                                                               140

According to Sullivan, what intrudes upon the assessment of a patient's personality? a. the Oedipus Complex; b. the assessor's personality; c. the patient's personality; d. the atmosphere in the assessment room   6.98
                                                               141

During the Sullivanian interview process, what does the patient need from the interviewer? a. to be told what to do ; b. to allowed to do all the talking; c. indications that he/she is doing fine and is "approved"; d. assurances that the session won't last too long
                                                               6.99
                                                               143

The computer search of literature citations naming the theorists covered in this text, found that Sullivan a. was cited almost as much as Freud; b. was cited more than average; c. was never cited; d. was rarely cited

6.100
143-144

Who may have been heavily influenced by Sullivan? a. Freud b. Maslow; c. Horney; d. Jung

6.1,c	6.27,d	6.53,b	6.79,d
6.2,d	6.28,a	6.54,a	6.80,a
6.3,b	6.29,b	6.55,d	6.81,c
6.4,c	6.30,d	6.56,a	*Extra*
6.5,d	6.31,a	6.57,c	*Items*
6.6,b	6.32,b	6.58,d	6.82, b
6.7,c	6.33,d	6.59,c	6.83, d
6.8,b	6.34,a	6.60,d	6.84, c
6.9,d	6.35,b	6.61,b	6.85, b
6.10,d	6.36,b	6.62,b	6.86, a
6.11,b	6.37,c	6.63,c	6.87, c
6.12,c	6.38,d	6.64,a	6.88, d
6.13,a	6.39,d	6.65,d	6.89, a
6.14,b	6.40,a	6.66,c	6.90, a
6.15,d	6.41,c	6.67,d	6.91, b
6.16,a	6.42,c	6.68,d	6.92, c
6.17,c	6.43,d	6.69,c	6.93, c
6.18,d	6.44,d	6.70,b	6.94, d
6.19,d	6.45,a	6.71,d	6.95, a
6.20,b	6.46,d	6.72,c	6.96, c
6.21,c	6.47,b	6.73,a	6.97, b
6.22,b	6.48,b	6.74,a	6.98, c
6.23,d	6.49,b	6.75,d	6.99, d
6.24,b	6.50,b	6.76,b	6.100, c
6.25,c	6.51,b	6.77,c	
6.26,b	6.52,d	6.78,b	

Chapter 7

Multiple Choice Items for the Chapter on Erikson

7.1
148-149

All except one of the following are true of Erikson and his contributions. Which is NOT true of Erikson and his contributions? a. he only finished high school; b. he was denied a position at Harvard because he lacked proper academic credentials; c. he is famous for the "identity crisis" d. he popularized the idea that personality development does not end at adolescence

7.2
149

Erikson's real father a. was unknown even to his mother; b. was a famous German scientist; c. was a Danish man he never met; d. was actually named Homburger

7.3
149

Erikson's was harassed at the synagogue and at school because a. he was Jewish; b. he was a Jewish child in an Aryan family; c. his adopted father was Jewish; he was not, but was sometimes regarded as Jewish; d. he and his family was Jewish but split: his mother and the children were devout, but his father wasn't

7.4
149

How did Erikson describe himself during his childhood? a. morbidly sensitive; b. happy, but not content; c. sad, but fulfilled; d. moody

7.5
149-151

All except one of the following were true of Erikson as a young man. Which was NOT true of him as a young man?; a. he was a painter; b. he was a substitute teacher, replacing his friend, a heir to the Tiffany fortune; c. he became a confidant of Freud, often talking with the master, deep into the night; d. he was invited to undergo training as a child analyst under Anna Freud

7.6
149-151

All except one of the following was true of Erikson as a young man. Which was NOT true of him as a young man? a. he was trained in the Montessori method; b. he was rejected as an analyst in training by Freud, because he lacked credentials c. he was Freud's chauffeur; d. he felt stifled by the overprotectiveness of the woman analyst

7.7
149-151

All except one of the following were true of Erikson as he underwent training as a analyst. Which was NOT true of his time in training? a. he was put off by the conservatism and dogmatism of the Vienna group; b. he and his Canadian born, U.S. student wife fled to the U.S. when Hitler took power; c. he became the first child analyst in Boston; d. he became a star in the graduate psychology program at Harvard   7.8
150-151

Erikson's time with the Sioux and Yurok convinced him that a. Native Americans were the only people not subject to developmental crises; b. Freud's sexual ideas were not universal; c. Jung's archetypes were manifested in Native American artifacts; d. Native Americans were nothing like European Americans   7.9
151

Upon his death, one of Erikson's colleagues likened him to a. Freud; b. Gandhi; c. Murray; d. Jung   7.10
151

Which of the following of Erikson's books was a Pultizer Prize winner? a. Childhood and Society; b. Young Man Luther; c. Gandhi's Truth; d. Life Cycle Completed   7.11
151

Late in his life, Erikson became concerned about the rights of a. the elderly; b. people of color; c. Hindus; d. the disabled
7.12
152

About Freud's emphasis on childhood trauma, Erikson declared, "If everything 'goes back' into childhood, then a. it will be nearly impossible to trace"; b. everything is someone else's fault"; c. why even consider the present?" d. the future has no meaning"   7.13
153

All of the following were true of Erikson's reactions to women, except one. Which was NOT true of Erikson regarding women? a. he rather universally used masculine pronouns; b. girls, he said, were dominated by attractiveness and motherliness themes; c. he changed, matured, and listened to the founders of the women's movement; d. he like Freud could never accept that refined women could have passion and sexual wishes
7.14
152

Maturity to Erikson was a. an all-or-none phenomenon b. a never ending process; c. inevitably achieved only by the very elderly; d. never even approximated by anyone
7.15
154

To Erikson, conquest of the tasks associated with a stage was cast in terms of a. psychic libidinal conflict; b. sexual orientation; c. Oedipal resolution; d. poles   7.16

153

Resolution of the dilemmas associated with each stage is in terms of a. insights; b. strengths; c. weaknesses; d. psychic upheaval   7.17

153

Psychosocial refers to a. sociological analysis of psychic factors; b. psychological analysis of social factors; c. the union of physical yearnings and cultural forces; d. the opposition of Freud's instincts (id) and cultural forces (superego)   7.18

153

In "eipgenesis" a. stages emerge one on top of another b. the superego unfolds; c. sexual maturity is reached d. resolution of each stages emerges from the insights at each stage   7.19

153

Erikson was influenced by philosophical idea a. thesis and antithesis; b. categories of the mind; c. neoassociationism d. nihilism   7.20

154

Erikson's "favorable ratio" refers to a. the ratio of superego to id forces; b. the ratio of strengths to weaknesses; c. the ratio of identity to anti-identity forces; d. the ratio of pull to the positive pole relative to pull to the negative pole   7.21

154

During Erikson's infancy stage, satisfaction leads to a. joy; b. striving for superiority; c. basic trust; d. exaltation

7.22

154

Basic mistrust is a. the feeling that one has been abandoned and the need to find new significant others; b. the feeling of abandonment and helpless rage accompanying uncertainty of satisfaction; c. the feeling that the world is not to be trusted anymore than disappointing parents; d. the feeling that one can trust only a few significant others, and no one else   7.23

151

The strength of the infancy stage is a. love; b. kindness; c. hope; d. power   7.24

155

An institutional safeguard is a. a means to protect institutions b. a process by which institutions, such as marriage, are protected from destruction; c. a way that institutions guard against encroachment by other institutions; d. a cultural unit that protects and promotes products of crisis resolution

7.25

155

During Erikson's early childhood stage a. the child resolves the trust issue; b. the child becomes able to exercise its will c. still has trouble grasping things; d. can now do more for itself that others can do for it   7.26

155

The poles of Erikson's early childhood stage are a. trust versus mistrust; b. love versus malice; c. industry versus inferiority d. autonomy versus shame and doubt   7.27

155

The strength of Erikson's early childhood stage a. hope; b. love; c. will power; d. care   7.28

156

Which of the following of Freud's ideas is applied by Erikson to his early childhood stage? a. anal stage; b. Narcissistic stage c. oral receptive type; d. rationalization   7.29

156

During Erikson's play stage a. girls and boys enjoy equality; b. sexual feelings are absent for both genders; c. boys are as interested in domestic games as girls; d. boys develop sexual feelings and girls orient to pursuing the attention of their fathers
7.30

156

Which of the following appears during Erikson's play age? a. parataxic functioning; b. conscience; c. prototaxic functioning; d. basic anxiety   7.31

15156

Initiative is a. the ability to restrain pursuits of desires and urges; b. acting on one's desires, urges, and potentials c. taking charge of one's life at the expense of possible alienation of the mothering one; d. advancing cognitively to the point of making rational judgments about one's life   7.32

156

How did Erikson part company with Freud on the issues of the boy's "falling for his mother?" a. he felt that the boy actually "falls for" his father; b. he believed that the boy "falls for" a females sibling, or, lacking one, for a female relative such as an aunt; c. he believed that the boy never "falls for" his mother at all, in the possessive sense; d. the main reason the boy "falls for" and has fantasies about his mother is that she is crucial to his survival and prosperity   7.33

156

The strength of the play age is a. fidelity; b. hope; c. care; d. purpose   7.32

156

Failure to resolve the crisis of the play age can a. psychopathic acting out; b. exhibitionism; c. manic depressive psychosis (bipolar); d. depression   7.35

157

During Erikson's school age a. boys' sexual awareness first appears; b. children begin to lay the groundwork for becoming adults; c. girls first pursue attractiveness and nurturance d. both genders renounce their "immature" need to be playing most of the time   7.36

Which of Freud's ideas did Erikson apply to the school age period? a. Oedipal Complex; b. Latency period; c. oral receptive-aggressive; d. intellectualization   7.37
15157

To Erikson, inferiority is a. an outcome that occurs if children perceive their skills or status among peers to be inadequate b. children's tendency to be sexually interested for the first time but unable to perform sexually; c. feeling lost and helpless in an adult world; d. feeling overwhelmed by the standards and demands placed on oneself by one's society   7.38
157

Competence, the strength of Erikson's school age is a. overcoming inherent inferiority; b. striving for superiority through compensation for weaknesses; c. the free exercise of dexterity and intelligence in the completion of serious tasks d. the humility to recognize one's weaknesses and deficiencies and to address them   7.39
157

The poles of Erikson's crisis at the adolescent stage are a. identity versus identity confusion; b. intimacy versus isolation; c. generativity versus stagnation; d. integrity versus despair   7.40
158

According to Erikson, identity issues for teens may be reflected in a. genital maturity in the Freudian sense; b. cognitive maturity that allows teens to make mature decisions; c. identity confusion that may be manifested in being punk one month and preppy the next; d. resolutions of the conflicts of the past stages   7.41
15158

What identity dilemma might the boy face during Erikson's adolescence stage?; a. whether to begin sexual exploration or repress it; b. whether to remain a child or become an adult; c. whether to leave the nest or remain a while longer; d. whether to become the macho figure represented by his father or a more gender neutral person   7.42
159

According to Erikson, what do adolescents do in response to the question "Who am I?"? a. respond with the label for the career they hope to pursue; b. respond with their gender identity; c. form cliques for mutual defense against enemies d. withdraw from social relations with peers in order to hone and refine their own uniqueness   7.43
158-159

How did Erikson view adolescent rebellion? a. he thought that it should be more disciplined as in his day; b. with the assumption that is was not all bad; c. with some chagrin because his theory fails to address the formation of youth

gangs today; d. with ambivalence as he felt that rebellion was a necessary evil, but an evil never-the-less 7.44
158

Erikson viewed unrest among youth as a sign of a. a healthy, open society, ready for needed change; b. a general upheaval that would threaten society's existence; c. a positive signal that a society exercised the proper level of control over its youth; d. a warning that a society is sick 7.45
158

The strength of the adolescent period (Erikson) is a. trust; b. care; c. fidelity; d. creativity 7.46
158

Of fidelity, Erikson believed a. it is a sign of immaturity; b. it is the cornerstone of identity; c. it is the essential means of resolving autonomy versus shame and doubt ; d. it is the most important accomplishment of young adults 7.47
158

According to Erikson, to what are might adolescents most likely fall prey? a. sexual permissiveness; b. religious fanaticism c. apathy; d. totalitarian ideology 7.48
159

Traditionally, parents have been the standard used by their children to develop their identities. Why is that less so today? a. parents are, in many cases, not available enough to have impact on their children; b. urban living has made parents indifferent to childrearing; c. drugs have made children unmanageable; d. parents and their children are not able to communicate any more 7.49
159

During Erikson's young adult stage, males and females differ a. in the quest for love and procreation; b. in their world philosophies; c. in their attention to social norms; d. in their orientation to work 7.50
159-160

What are the poles of Erikson's crisis at the young adulthood stage? a. love versus malice; b. hope versus hopelessness c. intimacy versus isolation; d. integrity versus despair
7.51
160

Isolation (Erikson) means a. the failure to develop peer cliques; b. the failure to establish meaningful relationships with caregivers; c. the failure for individuation to develop; d. the failure to secure close and cooperative relationships with the same and opposite gender 7.52
160

The strength of the young adult period is; a. love; b. care; c. fidelity; d. hope 7.53
161

Generativity is a. hoping for the best and doing the best for hope; b. not asking why, but asking why not; c. replacing rearing children with other pursuits; d. establishing and guiding the next generation   7.54
160

The strength of the middle adulthood stage is; a. contentment; b. fidelity; c. love; d. contentment   7.55
162

Stagnation is a. the end of hope; b. the beginning of the end c. the arrest of the ripening process; d. the termination of serious relationships   7.56
162

Care is a. the broadening concern for what has been generated by love, necessity, or accident; b. the end of the longing for deep and meaningful relationships and the beginning of building those relationships; c. universal concern d. moral rectitude   7.57
162

According to Erikson, old age is a. submission to mortality b. the conquest of mortality; c. a time for reaping the harvest of one's heavily laden fields; d. wit in full bloom   7.58
162

The poles of the dilemma of old age are a. trust versus distrust; b. intimacy versus isolation; c. integrity versus despair; d. identity versus identity confusion   7.59
162-163

What is Erikson's problem with his concept "wisdom?" a. it implies only academic knowledge; b. it is too religious in nature c. it is too strenuous an achievement; d. it is a stereotype of the elderly   7.60
161

Which is an example of how, during the school age, the "adult rules of work" that children learn and the role-teaching games they play are different for different cultures? a. Eskimo children play in the snow; b. Chinese children play a stick ball game; c. Masai children care for livestock; d. Maori children practice an early form of the "bunji jump"   7.61
163-164

What happens at the mid-life transition, according to Levinson? a. repression of feelings of mortality; b. heightened awareness of mortality; c. promotion of feelings of immortality; d. a feeling of renewal or despair, depending on one's gender   7.62
164

De-illusionment means a. the same thing as disillusionment b. the eye-opening experience of realizing that ones has disillusioned others; c. the tendency for middle-aged people to debunk the illusions of their peers; d. a recognition that assumptions and beliefs about self and the world are not true
7.63

Which is a likely event at the mid-life crisis, according to Levinson a. hostile attacks on family and friends; b. manic depressive episodes; c. schizophrenic-like reactions d. family and career may be replaced and a new life style adopted   7.64

What occurs during Levinson's "individuation" process? a. the person begins to become an in-dividual; b. a person is changed so that there is a clearer separation between self and world; c. the person abandons her or his former self in favor of an entirely new individual; d. the middle-aged person's personality becomes individuated or fragmented   7.65

Levinson's individuation relates to which of Erikson's concepts? a. integrity; b. absolution; c. generativity d. epigenesis   7.66

What proportion of Levinson's sample suffered the mid-life crisis? a. nearly 100%; b. 54%; c. 33%; d. 80%   7.67

According to Levinson, what causes us to consider our own mortality? a. pressure from friends and family who remind us of our approach to old age; b. stereotypes that apply to middle-aged persons; c. declines in function; d. the end of the repression that we were able to maintain before the wrinkles opened out eyes   7.68

According to Levinson, what is the solution to our crisis of mortality? a. a legacy; b. a pledge; c. resignation; d. defiance   7.69

According to Sheehy, age 35 begins a. a time of despair for men; b. a period of resolute soul searching for men; c. a dangerous period for women; d. a time of regression for both sexes   7.70

What do women begin to fear at about age 35, according to Sheehy? a. an empty nest; b. a husband with a wandering eye; c. a biological ticking clock that signals diminished chances of passing along her genes; d. leaving home to go to work and thereby withdrawing from her role as wife into a role of "provider"   7.71

What might women suffer from as they reenter the work force, according to Sheehy? a. fear of success and desire for it; b. reluctance to leave the children at home during the day; c. concern that her husband will feel deserted; d. frustration that competitors for advancement are way ahead of them

7.72
164-165

All except one of the following are possibilities for women at the mid-life crisis (Sheehy) except one. Which HAS LOW PROBABILITY for them at this time? a. an affair; b. joyful anticipation; c. divorce; d. running away

7.73
165-166

All except one of the following are among the outcomes of Ochse's and Plug's (1986) investigations of poles associated with Erikson's stages. Which was NOT among their outcomes? a. the more the positive poles were represented in subjects, the higher their senses of well-being; b. black and white South African subjects showed almost identical responses c. intercorrelations among poles tended to be high regardless of whether subjects had yet passed crises; d. intimacy versus isolation and generativity versus stagnation emerged from factor analysis

7.74
165-166

All except one of the following are among the outcomes of Ochse's and Plug's (1986) investigations of poles associated with Erikson's stages. Which was NOT among their outcomes? a. there were contradictions to the epigenesis notion that earlier crises are resolved before later; b. over all subject categories, intimacy was higher for men than for women c. factor analysis yielded an "identity" factor; d. there were declines in the potency of poles associated with earlier stages, but increases for poles associated with later stages

7.75
167

In their study of generativity and authoritarianism, Peterson, Smirles, and Wentworth (1997) found all of the following except one. Which was NOT one of their findings? a. parents generativity was positively related to openness; but negatively related to authoritarianism; b. extraversion was negatively related to generativity but positively related to authoritarianism; c. high authoritarian parents conflicted with their children; d. conscientiousness and generativity were positively related

7.76
166

Which of the following was a finding of Kowaz's and Marcia's (1991) study of industry? a. the correlations among the measures of industry were low; b. the cognitive component of industry was poorly correlated with achievement; c. "level of reasoning" was positively related to industry; d. for teachers' judgments, being "on" versus "off" task was negatively related to industry scores

7.77
166

What did McAdams, Ruetzel, and Foley find (1986) in their investigation of generativity? a. TAT scores were unrelated to generativity; b. Rorschach scores were positively associated

with a measure of generativity; c. power and intimacy were inversely related; d. power and intimacy were positively related to generativity 7.78
167

What did Franz, McClelland and Weinberger (1991) find in their follow-up of research done in the 1950s a. having close friends at mid-life, a long, happy marriage, and children was positively related to generativity; b. having a mid-life crisis was negatively related to generativity; c. integrity and despair were positively related; d. having children predicted unresolved dilemmas from previous periods 7.79
16167

For women, "achievement motive" was related to what kind of expression in the study by Peterson and Steward (1993)? a. generativity expression outside the home; b. care expressed inside the home; c. parenting; d. personal productivity 7.80
166

All of the following were found by McAdams and Mansfield (1996) and this team plus de St. Aubin and Diamond (1997), except one. Which was NOT a finding of this research team? a. communion (self-sacrificing and being one with others) was positively related with generativity; b. the high generativity group was higher on moral steadfastness than a low generativity group; c. the high generativity group was higher on prosocial future goals than the low generativity group; d. there was no difference between the high and low generativity groups on early family advantage 7.81
168-169

All except one of the following are limitations of Erikson's thought and work. Which is NOT a limitation a. some of his concept-labels seem chosen without reason or logic; b. none of his concepts have received research support; c. some of his concepts are murky at best; d. his concept epigenesis has been weakened by research results 7.82
168

What may we conclude about Erikson's contributions? a. the support for Erikson's childhood poles is especially strong; b. he is the father of the powerful notion "mid-life crisis"; c. he proved that personality does not change much after adolescence; d. he was responsible for the idea of opposites
Extra Items 7.83
149

In appearance, Erikson was a. short with a dark complexion; b. tall with brown hair and eyes; c. tall and blond; d. pale with dark hair and eyes 7.84
149

Instead of going to college, Erikson a. began a trek around the world; b. got married and began a large family; c. signed on as a merchant marine; d. took up painting; 7.85

Working with the Sioux and the Yurok, Erikson discovered
a. that Jung's archetypes were not valid; b. evidence for
Freud's psychosexual stages; c. that passing through stages of
identity acquisition was universal; d. evidence for the strength
"power"   7.85
What of Erikson's early "sexism" orientation to females?
a. he never abandoned it; b. he changed; c. he became a male
feminist; d. he became even more anti-female   7.86
With regard to "mistrust" during the infancy period, Erikson
thought it important to a. learn mistrust; b. reject mistrust even
at this early stage of life; c. disregard mistrust; it is inevitable but
undesirable; d. put the consideration of mistrust until
adolescence   7.87
After becoming trusting, the child at the second of Erikson's
stages must become a. patient; b. self-willed; c. caring; d. artful
                                                                 7.88
A child who suffers from "shame and doubt" is likely to be
a. mean and stubborn; b. tentative and self-effacing
c. reserved and bombastic (manic-depressive like); d. spiritual
and lofty   7.89
One source of "guilt" during the play age is a. is lack of sexual
interest at a time when it is expected; b. inability to relate to the
parent of the same sex; c. failure to demonstrate capability
when the initiative is taken; d. the conflict between love and
hate   7.90
How is "learning adult rules of work" seen in children's play?
a. games of tag; b. kick ball games; c. hide and seek; d. playing
"house" or "doctor"   7.91
Condemnation of those who are "different" can lead to
a. a "sick soul"; b. "resolute mind"; c. delinquency; d. passivity
                                                                 7.92
What crisis does middle adulthood involve? a. integrity versus
despair; b. productivity versus futility; c. industry versus
inferiority; d. intimacy versus isolation   7.93
A danger of embracing "ideology" during the teen years is that
a. it is likely to be religious cult ideology; b. almost all
ideologies are "bad"; c. ideologies tend to be weak; d. an
ideology can become a basis of identity   7.94

Who or what may be providing a substitute for the parental standard of children's identity? a. fads such as piercing the skin with various objects; b. the media; c. religion; d. cults

7.95
162

What is the constant companion of stagnation a. elation-depression; b. heart-break ;c. love lost; d. boredom   7.96
162

Despair can result in a. loss of sensory abilities; b. a Pollyannaish disposition; c. psychological death
d. obstinateness   7.97
161

What word might Erikson have used in place of generativity?
a. genuineness b. creativity; c. spirituality; d. optimism

7.98
161

Which is a manifestation of "generativity"? a. the "advice" that middle aged people offer younger people; b. the continual talk about "my generation" that middle-aged people are apt to display; c. the work on the part of middle-aged people to generate more work for younger peopl; d. middle aged people's love of generating dilemmas for young people to resolve   7.99
163-164

A mid-life crisis can result in an entirely new lifestyle, or appear a. as one psychotic break after another; b. as a creative act, such as painting a single, grand picture; c. as a simple coming to terms with loss of dreams; d. as a tendency to cry   7.100
164

Divorce of a 35 year old women often means a. taking on a new husband; b. a nervous breakdown; c. an hysterical disorder; d. a tendency toward conservatism   7.101
167

Adams (2000) thought that generativity was similar to which of the following? a. adolescent romantic love; b. mature adult integrity; c. adulthood contentment; d. care expressed by parents to children   7.102
161

Erikson knew that trust is imparted differently in other societies where a. infants are strapped on their mothers' backs facing away from her; b. infants are isolated from parents for the first several months; c. children are reared exclusively by their parents; d. children are severely punished

7.1,b	7.49,a	7.95, d
7.2,c	7.50,c	7.96, c
7.3,c	7.51,d	7.97, b
7.4,a	7.52,a	7.98, a
7.5,c	7.53,d	7.99, c
7.6,b	7.54,d	7.100, a
7.7,d	7.55,c	7.101, d
7.8,b	7.56,a	7.102, a
7.9,b	7.57,d	
7.10,c	7.58,c	
7.11,a	7.59,c	
7.12,b	7.60,d	
7.13.d	7.61,b	
7.14,b	7.62,d	
7.15,d	7.63,d	
7.16,b	7.64,b	
7.17,c	7.65.c	
7.18,a	7.66,d	
7.19,a	7.67,c	
7.20,d	7.68,a	
7.21,c	7.69,c	
7.22,b	7.70,c	
7.23,c	7.71,d	
7.24,d	7.72,b	
7.25,b	7.73,b	
7.26,d	7.74,b	
7.27,c	7.75,b	
7.28,a	7.76,c	
7.29,d	7.77,d	
7.30,b	7.78,a	
7.31,b	7.79,a	
7.32,d	7.80,b	
7.33,d	7.81,b	
7.34,b	7.82,b	
7.35,b	*Extra*	
7.36,b	*Items*	
7.37,a	7.83, c	
7.38,c	7.84, d	
7.39,a	7.85, b	
7.40,c	7.86, a	
7.41,d	7.87, b	
7.42,c	7.88, b	
7.43,b	7.89, c	
7.44,d	7.90, d	
7.45,c	7.91, c	
7.46,b	7.92, b	
7.47,d	7.93, d	
7.48,a	7.94, b	

Chapter 8

Multiple Choice Items for the Chapter on Fromm

8.1
174

Fromm's lengthy criticism of Freud centered on a. Freud's treatment of women; b. the claim that "psychoanalysis can define man scientifically" ; c. Freud's assertion that Thanatos is the ultimate goal of life; d. Freud's treatment of childhood neuroses

8.2
174

Who did Fromm consider to be more important a thinker than Freud? a. Einstein; b. Churchill; c. Marx; d. Hegel

8.3
175

What makes Fromm stand out from most of the theorists covered so far? a. he was the only priest among them; b. he had a organ defect; c. he was the only one with a degree in chemistry and physics; d. he had a Ph.D.

8.4
175

Sociopsychological refers to a. the sociological side of people that sheds light on the psychological side; b. the same thing as social psychology; c. the psychological study of groups d. the sociological study of the individual

8.5
175

Fromm was a. Catholic; b. Muslin; c. Jewish; d. Methodist

8.6
175

Fromm characterized his father as a. brilliant; b. sadistic c. a religious fanatic; d. highly neurotic

8.7
175-178

All of the following were true of Fromm regarding his beliefs, except one. Which was NOT true of Fromm's a. he was strongly influenced by existentialism; b. he was clearly an orthodox follower of Freud; c. he, like Horney, was trained at the Berlin Institute; d. he said that each society has its own personality

8.8
177

Fromm flirted with ; a. communism b. capitalism; c. totalitarianism; d. utopianism

9.8
175

Fromm was greatly affected by what event during his young adulthood? a. the suicide of a young woman after the death of her father; b. the carnage of the Spanish Civil War c. the poverty he saw when he visited China d. the speeches of Haig, a Rumanian philosopher

8.10
175

Fromm's credibility during his training as an analyst was undermined by a. the fact that he was Aryan; b. the coincidence of his birth date and Hitler's; c. the observation that he was lacked a commanding stature; d. the fact that he did not have medical training   8.11
                                                                                          176

Among the titles of Fromm's books was a. The Coming of Christ; b. Truths of the Old Testament; c. Freud and Monotheism; d. Escape from Freedom   8.12
                                                                                          176

Fromm quarreled with what popular notion of his day? a. every dog has its day; b. what goes around comes around; c. armaments preserve peace; d. there is a thin line between good and evil   8.13
                                                                                    176-177

What horrified Fromm during World War II a. the carnage in his own country; b. the observation that Germany's young men were buying their country's propaganda and paying with their lives; c. that each country thought that God was on their side, when in fact, God opposes all war; d. the futility of politics by other means   8.14
                                                                                          177

Fromm spent among his most productive years a. at the University of Berlin; b. in Mexico; c. vacationing in the Orient d. working as a trainee in Vienna under Freud   8.15
                                                                                          178

Which of the following is crucial to the existential position? a. personal responsibility; b. coming to grips with the unconscious; c. ending exploitation; d. building warm and satisfying human relationships   8.16
                                                                                          177

That Fromm was a lifetime socialists was reflected a. the fact that he ran for office in Vienna as a socialist; b. the fact that he was expelled from the U.S. because he was a communist; c. his concept "humanistic communitarian socialism"; d. his love of Stalin   8.17
                                                                                          178

Fromm's basic concept "humanistic psychoanalyst" refers to a. a blend of existentialism and Hegelian philosophy; b. the humanitarian training of analysts that he promoted in the Freudian camp; c. the phenomenal approach that emphasizes people before all else; d. the belief in the essential worth and dignity of each person   8.18
                                                                                          178

Existential refers to a. a philosophy that has not be translated into other disciplines; b. people's most immediate experience, the conditions of their existence, and the necessity of exercising freedom amid chaos; c. the belief that all entities, whether animal, vegetable or mineral, are living beings,

invested with meaning and purpose; d. a religious position that has scientific applications
9.19
179

Frame of orientation refers to a. a goal that gives meaning to people's existence and position in the world; b. the frame of reference that allows persons to rise above their squalid existence; c. a cognitive "map" of people's natural and social worlds; d. a kind of orientation that takes into account both the spiritual and the natural world
8.20
179

Object of devotion refers to a. a goal that gives meaning to people's existence and position in the world; b. the frame of reference that allows the person to rise above their squalid existence; c. a cognitive "map" of people's natural and social worlds; d. a kind of orientation that takes into account both the spiritual and the natural world
8.21
179

Relatedness refers to a. relating to the norms of one's society b. the necessity to unite with other human beings; c. the need to relate different aspects of the personality; d. relating the self to the selves of significant others, most especially the mothering one
8.22
179

Which is a symbiotic union? a. a homosexual marriage b. the union of opposites; c. the crocodile and the birds that feed on its pests; d. the deer and the prairie dog that warns it of danger
8.23
179

Symbiotic union can take which of the following forms a. prey and predator; b. parallel; c. in sync; d. passive
8.24
180

Automaton conformity refers to a. automatic conformity to family norms; b. a mindless conformity to peers; c. giving up freedom for union with society; d. allowing no deviation from strict conformity
8.25
180

The active symbiotic form can be summed up in which of the following words?; a. equity; b. sadism; c. ambivalence d. cooperativeness
8.26
180

Mature love refers to a. union under the condition of preserving one's integrity; b. self-sacrifice; c. being able to rather totally submit to the needs of a loved one; d. love that matures with time, like a fine wine
8.27
180-181

Rootedness refers to a. is a deep craving to maintain one's natural ties; b. is laying down roots in a particular geographical locale; c. is becoming rooted in the soil of a fertile career; d. is the kind of stubbornness that ensures that one will not give up one's individuality 8.28

180

The need to form new roots is analogous to a. the desire for sexual contact; b. the need for physical contact with a mothering one; c. the desire for freedom from the demands that one roam the psychological realm; d. joining the brotherhood of man 8.29

181

According to Fromm, identity is a. the need to be aware of oneself as a separate entity; b. the acceptance of others beliefs about who one is; c. the event that occurs when a person unites with a loved one and they merge identities; d. learning to identify with the roles that one has been assigned by society

8.30

181

Fromm's ideas about medieval roles reminds one
a. Horney's tyranny of the shoulds
b. Jung's personas
c. Freud's "totem and taboo"
d. Sullivan's forbidding gestures 8.31

181

Unity refers to a. uniting with the spirit of one's ancestral past b. uniting with the social unit, in ancient times, the tribe; c. forming a union of trust and dependency, such as a marriage; d. a sense of inner oneness within one's self and with the natural world outside 8.32

181

Failure to achieve unity is associated with which of the following?
a. a lonely and shy disposition
b. substance abuse
c. a hollow existence and aimless wandering
d. the need to submit to whoever will take one in 8.33

182

Transcendence is a. the act of transforming one's passive role of creature into that of an active creator; b. rising above the squalor of one's hopeless existence to the heights of self-sufficiency; c. leaving the concrete realm for the spiritual realm d. the transmittal of self into an altered state, not unlike that experienced with use of psychoactive drugs 8.34

182

Which of the following is the alternative to creation, according to Fromm? a. despair; b. intellectual devastation; c. a spiritual vacuum; d. destructiveness 8.35

180

Effectiveness refers to a. the child's illusion of personal causation; b. proficiency in social relations; c. compensating for being in an overpowering world by developing a sense of

"making a dent"; d. the ability to cause outcomes to occur in the lives of important others
8.36
1182

According to Fromm, which of the following signals a hallmark development in the child's expanding world? a. "No!"; b. "Please?"; c. "Can I...can I?"; d. "I do...I do!"
8.37
183

Excitation and stimulation refer to a. creating excitation and stimulation for significant others; b. exercising the nervous system; c. thrill seeking by another name; d. generating reservoirs of excitation for future use
8.38
183

In relation to Fromm's theory, which of the following is "brain food." a. varied sensory stimulation; b. internal thoughts and feelings; c. dopamine; d. acetylcholine
8.39
183

During REM dreaming a. our muscles are wide awake; b. the brain displays slow waves; c. we could talk out loud and walk if need be; c. the brain acts as if it is receiving sensory input
8.40
183

Famous Canadian psychologist D.O. Hebb performed what kinds of experiments in order to show that the brain needs constant input in order to function properly? a. classical conditioning experiments; b. experiments in which subjects were blasted with loud and bright sounds and sights; c. cognitive and affective insulation experiments; d. experiments where variation in visual, auditory, and tactile stimulation was eliminated
8.41
183

Which of the following falls into the category "simple stimuli"? a. accidents; b. reading a novel; c. painting (art); d. being with loved ones
8.42
183&185

All of the following are activating stimuli, except one. Which does NOT fit into the category of "activating stimuli"?; a. sex-related movies; b. reading a novel; c. painting (art); d. being with loved ones
8.43
185

Fromm defines personality as a. the traits that one has; b. the complex of intra- and inter- psychic forces that, as a unit, represent the totality of the individual; c. the interconnection of the psychological structures that constitute what we call "mentality"; c. the inherited and acquired psychic qualities characterizing one individual, making her/him unique
8.44
185

Which are the two levels upon which character develops? a. conscious and unconscious; b. active and passive;

c. individual and social; d. external and internal   8.45
                                                                      185

Individual character refers to a. an automatic action sequence
governed by the unconscious; b. the pattern of behavior
characteristic of a given person; c. the soul of the person, as
opposed to the psyche of that person; d. the moral fiber of a
person, or the lack of it   8.46
                                                                      185

Social character refers to a. the set of norms that characterize
a society; b. individual behavior under the influence of cultural
nuances; c. the core of a character structure common to most
people of a given culture; d. the moral fiber of a society, or the
lack of it   8.47
                                                                      185

What did Fromm believe can be inferred from an analysis of a
single individual? a. the relation between that person's
conscious and unconscious processes; b. the totality of the
social structure in which the person lives; c. whether that
person is the product of a sane or insane child rearing process;
d. the relationship of that person to significant other person's in
her or his life   8.48
                                                                      186

Which of the following is one of the two types of social
character that Fromm identified? a. absolute; b. resolute;
c. applicable; d. nonproductive   8.49
                                                                      186

Each type of social character is cast in terms of which of the
following a. assimilation/socialization; b. active/passive; c.
sadistic/masochistic; d. fruitful/fruitless   8.50
                                                                      186

Persons of the receptive orientation a. hoard material goods;
b. take things by force or cunning; c. exchange goods for
money; d. experience the source of goods as outside
themselves   8.51
                                                                      186

If receptive people are religious (Fromm) a. they are
demanding of God; b. they expect everything from God and
nothing from their own efforts; c. they seek to match gifts from
God with good works of their own; d. they tend to blame God for
whatever happens to them   8.52
                                                                      186

Persons of the exploitive orientation a. hoard material goods
b. take things by force or cunning; c. exchange goods for
money; d. experience the source of goods as outside
themselves   8.53
                                                                    186-186

All of the following are true of the exploitive orientation, except
one. Which is NOT true of that orientation? a. cynical;
b. jealous; c. hostile; d. psychotic   8.54

How did Hitler exploit Europe's Jews?   a. he taught the German people to hate them; b. he used them as the van guard of his early military adventures; c. he used their vast resources to fuel his war machine; d. he convinced the German people that losing WW I was not their fault, the Jews betrayed them
8.55
188

Which kind of society reflects the exploitive orientation? a. today's American society; b. the communes of 1930's England; c. the ancient Aztecs; d. Stalinist Soviet society
8.56
187

How does the hoarding orientation differ from the receptive and exploitive a. the goods come from inside, not outside; b. the goods come from outside, not inside; c. people, not materials, are the object of concern; d. there is a desire to relate benevolently to others
8.57
182

Fromm, like Horney, was concerned about; a. animal rights b. the exploitive potential of humans; c. the power of the Oedipal complex; d. political relations between the U.S. and Europe
8.58
187

Which kind of society represents the hoarding orientation? a. feudal lords and barons; b. stratified societies; c. societies adopting the Puritan ethic; d. societies ruled by blood thirsty dictators
8.59
188

Which of the following relates most closely to the marketing orientation? a. retaining objects and materials for future use b. exploiting others for self-gain; c. "purchasing" other nations through warfare; d. supply and demand
8.60
189

In a marketing society a. people battle to look like "one of a kind"; b. relationships are based on one-way exploitation c. people buy relationships by sacrificing themselves in the exchange; d. there are no goods as valuable as those one has hidden away
8.61
189

Which kind of society represents the marketing orientation? a. feudal lords and barons; b. stratified societies; c. societies adopting the Puritan ethic; d. capitalistic societies
8.62
189-190

Which of the following is true of the necrophilous character? a. a keen ability to use others; b. a fascination with death; c. a need to give and to receive; d. a submission to a "magic helper"
8.63
190

Necrophilous character is related to which of Freud's concepts?; a. receptive type; b. anal expulsive; c. Eros; d. Thanatos

8.64
190

Which of the following represents Speer's Hitler dream? a. Hitler places wreath after wreath on a war memorial; b. Hitler and Stalin duel; c. Speer lies prostrate before Hitler; d. Hitler comes into possession of a powerful bomb, unlike any known to humans

8.65
190

Which of the following was among the necrophilous dreams presented in the text?
a. Hitler and Stalin duel
b. dream of the "superdestroyer"
c. woman disappears and is replaced by a man
d. children dance around corpses

8.66
191

Which of the following represents the necrophilous character? a. feudal lords and barons; b. stratified societies; c. societies adopting the Puritan ethic; d. societies ruled by blood thirsty dictators

8.67
191

In the productive orientation a. producing the most goods possible with one's capabilities is of paramount importance; b. producing more than others is the goal; c. being a productive citizen, as that is defined in a society, is the aspiration; d. developing an attitude of relatedness to the world and oneself is the chief motive

8.68
191

All except one of the following are human capacities that characterize the productive orientation. Which is NOT one of those capacities? a. productive reasoning; b. productive love c. productive work; d. productive spirituality

8.69
191

Assimilation and socialization modes associated with the productive orientation are _____ and _____, respectively. a. producing, consuming; b. giving, receiving; c. creating, integrity; d. hoping, realizing

8.70
192-194

All of the following are among Fromm's contributions, except one. Which is NOT among his contributions a. development of widely used personality tests; b. introduced the positive orientation, biophilia; c. laid the groundwork for the humanists d. author of interesting books on popular issues

8.71
192

Which of the following fits best with biophilia? a. marketing; b. productive; c. conservation; d. loyalty

8.72
192

When Fromm and Maccoby (1970) investigated social character in a Mexican village, which orientation was strongest?; a. marketing; b. exploitative; c. receptive d. necrophilous

8.73
193

In Fromm and Maccoby (1970), what kind of crop did the productive-hoarding Mexican villagers plant? a. corn; b. cotton; c. sugarcane; d. rice

8.74
179

Existential needs refer to a. needs that must be met if one's existence is to be meaningful; b. needs that transcend the realm of the natural and encroach on the supernatural; c. needs that can be met only through self-actualization; d. needs that Fromm came to appreciate as he studied the ancient Aztec culture

8.75
194-195

All of the following were limitations of Fromm's thought and work, except one. Which was not a limitation? a. he neglected the humanitarian perspective; b. he condemned melting into the collective; c. his theory collapses sources of variation, such as gender, ethnicity, and religion; d. generalizing a character type to an entire society is very difficult to support

8.76
194-195

Which of the following was probably Fromm's greatest contribution? a. his socialistic perspective; b. his realistic, but pessimistic perspective; c. his needs; d. his influence on current humanistic thought
Extra Items

8.77
195

Burston counted all of the following as reasons that psychologists and psychiatrists have rejected Fromm, except one. Which did he NOT count as a reason they rejected Fromm? a. Fromm had no training in medicine; b. Fromm was too qualitative; c. Fromm to applied his political/social views to psychology; d. Fromm wrote about ethics

8.78
179

Frame of orientation and object of devotion a. are basically unrelated; b. are related through their connection to "rootedness"; c. provide a synthesis of one's self and one's life circumstances; d. offer the hope that all other needs will be met if these two are met

8.79
177

Declaring the "other side" in a war to be evil a. makes sense according to Fromm: fulfilling the object of devotion need dictates it b. is reciprocated: when one looks at the "other," one sees what the other sees when looking at oneself, evil; c. is regrettable, but human nature, according to Fromm; d. is actually beneficial, according to Fromm: the two sides tend to eventually see the contradiction in each seeing the other as evil

8.80
180

Fromm's notions about mature love are most reminiscent of a. Freud's latency period; b. Horney's self-assessment; c. Erikson's identity resolution at the young adult stage; d. Sullivan's emphasis on interactions with significant others

8.81
180-181

What can detach us from our roots? a. any act of unkindness b. too much emphasis on the needs of others; c. any interaction with members of another ethnic group beyond what is practically necessary; d. not knowing the language or traditions associated with our culture

8.82
181

Where is the true and certain path to unity (Fromm)? a. at the "top of the mountain"; b. it lies in developing human reason and love; c. it is found in the pursuit of happiness; d. at the heart of evil one will find the soul of goodness;

8.83
182

By creative acts, humans can (Fromm) a. bring out the hidden artist in oneself; b. serve the greater good to the greatest degree; c. rise above the "creature" in them and ascend to new heights; d. obtain the ultimate spiritual experience, akin to Maslow's peak experience

8.84
182

All of the following are ways to be effective (Fromm), except one. Which is NOT a way to be effective?; a. eliciting a smile; b. destroying property; c. making a noisy clatter; d. permitting others to do for oneself

8.85
178

Existentialists value a. being resolved to one's fate; b. consciousness; c. cleanliness; d. devotion to others

8.86
183

What happened when D. O. Hebb's collaborators had students live two to four days under conditions of no sensory variation? a. tragically, two of them died; b. tragically, five of them became permanently psychotic; c. they subsequently were able to learn whatever they studied much more efficiently; d. their brains malfunctioned

8.87
183

What happened when D. O. Hebb's collaborators had students live two to four days under conditions of no sensory variation? a. all of them were thereafter unable to endure "white noise"; b. one of them reported that a tiny spaceship was firing pellets at his arm; c. most of them expressed a very trusting attitude toward experimenters; d. several of them pleaded with the experimenters to allow them to continue with the experiment

Simple stimuli (Fromm) can be characterized by all of the following, except one. Which is NOT a legitimate characterization of simple stimuli?   a. knee-jerk; b. automatic; c. gut reaction; d. require great effort

Compared to simple stimuli, activating stimuli are a. knee-jerk b. automatic; c. gut reaction; d. require great effort

Which of the following is a key word in Fromm's definition of personality? a. spiritual; b. unique; c. unconscious d. mystical

Character (Fromm) develops at which two levels a. conscious and unconscious; b. biological and environmental; c. individual and social; d. inward and outward

All of the following are among Fromm's social characters, except one. Which is NOT among the social characters? a. extra-sensory; b. receptive; c. exploitive; d. hoarding

"Being" involves a. a condition that is unique to each entity, human or rock; b. the burdensomeness of total responsibility for oneself; c. Fromm's more pessimistic view, relative to other humanists; d. denial of death

Computer game-players who favor games that involve mutilation and dismemberment of humanoid figures fit which of Fromm social character types best? a. hoarding; b. exploitive; c. receptive; d. necrophilous

Biophilia refers to a. love of all creatures; b. a person who prefers plants to people; c. love of life; d. a defender of the biosphere

All of the following refer to "Existential needs" except one. Which does NOT refer to "existential needs"? a. needs for certain satisfactions that are sought by all humans; b. needs that must be met if one's existence is to be meaningful; c. needs for the development of one's inner being; d. needs that must be met if one's talents are to be exploited

Fromm's Mexican villagers showed all of the following, except one. Which did they NOT show to an appreciable degree?
a. alcoholic; b. exploitative; c. productive-hoarding;
d. receptive

8.1,b
8.2,c
8.3,d
8.4,a
8.5,c
8.6,d
8.7,b
8.8,a
8.9,a
8.10,d
8.11,d
8.12,c
8.13,b
8.14,b
8.15,a
8.16,c
8.17,d
8.18,b
8.19,c
8.20,a
8.21,b
8.22,c
8.23,d
8.24,c
8.25,b
8.26,a
8.27,a
8.28,d
8.29,a
8.30,b
8.31,d
8.32,b
8.33,a
8.34,d
8.35,c
8.36,d
8.37,b
8.38,a
8.39,d
8.40,d
8.41,a
8.42,a
8.43,d
8.44,c
8.45,b
8.46,c
8.47,b
8.48,d

8.49,a
8.50,d
8.51,b
8.52,b
8.53,d
8.54,d
8.55,d
8.56,a
8.57,b
8.58,c
8.59,d
8.60,a
8.61,d
8.62,b
8.63,d
8.64,a
8.65,b
8.66,d
8.67,d
8.68,d
8.69,c
8.70,a
8.71,b
8.72,c
8.73,d
8.74,a
8.75,a
8.76,d
Extra Items
8.77, a
8.78, c
8.79, b
8.80, c
8.81, d
8.82, b
8.83, c
8.84, d
8.85, b
8.86, d
8.87, b
8.88, c
8.89, d
8.90, b
8.91, c
8.92, a
8.93, a
8.94,d

8.95, c
8.96, a
8.97, b

Chapter 9

Multiple Choice Items for the Chapter on Rogers

9.1
200

How does Rogers compare to other humanistic theorists? a. his impact is in the cognitive realm, not the humanistic; b. he is more of a philosopher that the; c. he applied science to understanding people rather than to validating his therapy, showing the biological side of humans, and rendering his concepts testable; d. his ideas has been validated by systematic research more than the ideas of other humanistic theorists

9.2
201

Rogers' family life was characterized by fundamentalist religion. However, later he had trouble with; a. the concept of original sin ; b. guilt over abandoning his religion
c. churches wishing to train ministers in Rogerian therapy
d. people who regarded themselves as fundamentalists

9.3
201

Which of the following was among Rogers' favorite books as a youth? a. the old testament; b. Freud's Interpretation of Dreams c. Feeds and Feeding; d. Fromm's Art of Loving
9.4
201

What enlightening experience did Rogers have during his youth? a. a trip to China; b. a peak experience
c. a drug experience; d. a couple of years in a monastery

9.5
202

Who probably influenced Rogers the most? a. Freud; b. Jung
c. Rank; d. Jung
9.6
202

What model for addressing psychological problems was rejected by Rogers? a. the Jungian model; b. the psychiatric model; c. the clinical psychology model; d. the medical model

9.7
202

Which is most consistent with Rogers' growth model?
a. psychological patients are sick and need some kind of treatment; b. disturbed people need a structured kind of therapy; c. obstructions in people's paths are to be removed so they can move beyond being normal; d. patients need love and understanding in order to be cured of their psychological sicknesses

9.8
203

Which of the following characterized Rogers when he was in his eighties, in the years before he died? a. convalescence; b. "The days are not long enough to accomplish my purposes."; c. "I spend my time these days enjoying relaxing, playing with my grandchildren, and playing an occasional round of golf."; d. training new converts to Rogerian methods
9.9
204-205

All except one of the following are stereotypes of Rogers. Which is NOT one of those stereotypes? a. he never became angry; b. he regarded himself as a counselor; c. he often became impatient with clients; d. he believed that empathy was a passive process
9.10
204

What was Rogers' reaction to a white psychologist who claimed that a black, South African revolutionary was just trying to get attention? a. he brought the two together for a private conference; b. he consoled the black revolutionary; c. he became angry at the white psychologist; d. in characteristic style, he let the two of them work it out on their own
9.11
204

During his sessions in South Africa, what happened when a key black participant left the group? a. ran after him and attempted to persuade him to return; b. began to cry; c. scolded the person whose remarks led to the exodus; d. talked quietly to the group to console them on their loss
9.12
205

Why did Rogers include "counseling" in the title of one of his books a. in fact, counseling was his primary identity; b. he and his students thought the inclusion would recruit counselors to the Rogerian approach; c. he thought "counseling" to be a more worthy discipline than psychology; d. he was a member of the Counseling Division of the American Psychological Association
9.13
207

Which of the following is most consistent with humanistic psychology? a. exercising freedom of choice in a chaotic world; b. a need to absorb the patient's pain; c. a respect for the concept "cure"; d. emphasis on the whole person
9.14
205-206

Which of the following was NOT one of Rollo May's six basic existential issues? a. the existing person is centered in her or his self; b. the courage to be; c. the extension of life; d. anxiety
9.15
206

What hypothesis did Rogers deduce from May's six existential issues? a. all human are created equal; b. the more the self is threatened, the more the neurotic behavior; c. life and death are related in a complex matrix that can be deciphered only during extended therapy; d. existential therapy will work better if it is brief

9.16
206

What did Rollo May call "animal level of awareness" that we share with other creatures? a. primate consciousness; b. vigilance; c. anticipation; d. subduction

9.17
207

Phenomenology involves a. experiencing the phenomenon of moral rectitude; b. people sharing common experiences; c. the belief that one person can never appreciate the experience of another person; d. a desire to grasp reality as each person uniquely perceives it

9.18
207

Which of the following statements best characterized the phenomenological (humanistic) approach? a. clear one's mind of presuppositions; b. do unto others as they do unto you c. render to Caesar what is Caesar's and to God what is God's; d. what does not overwhelm me makes me stronger

9.19
207

Empathy, according to Rogers, is a. the emotional linkage between the infant and significant other people; b. sensing and participating in the emotions of other people; c. offering one's own emotions as a taste of one's own inner self; d. guiding the emotions of another person from sick to well

9.20
202

All of the following are approaches or views of the humanistic psychologists, except one. Which is NOT an approach or view of humanistic psychologists?; a. helping people find the kind of insight that will allow them to return to normalcy; b. the human organism is a total being whose physical, psychological, and spiritual aspects cannot be separated; c. idiographic d. person centered

9.21
206

According to May, which distinguishes humans for others creatures? a. consciousness; b. feelings; c. concern about threats to our existence; d. self-consciousness

9.22
207

Rogers believes; a. in the idiographic approach to understanding individuals; b. the client and the therapist should be equal in the psychotherapy setting; c. therapists should let the client do all the talking; d. therapists should never show strong emotional reactions during therapy

9.23
208

What sort of college classroom procedure did Rogers pioneer? a. students running the entire class; b. student active participation as a partial replacement of the traditional lecture; c. the Rogerian tendency to reflect student's questions back to them, rather than provide any answers to questions;

d. transforming the classroom into a "be all you can be" arena
9.24
208-209

All except one of the following are characteristic of the actualizing tendency. Which is NOT one of those characteristics? a. organismic; b. active; c. opportunistic d. selective
9.25
209

Which of the following is Rogers' example, recalled from his youth, of the actualizing tendency? a. the behavior of fighting fish; b. the growing of potatoes in the basement; c. the struggles of worker ants; d. the clinging of the tomato vines
9.26
209

Which of the following is Rogers' conception of self-actualizing person(s)? a. a person who engages in a lifelong process of realizing his or her potentialities to become a fully functioning person; b. persons who do the best they are capable of doing, and who develop themselves to the most complete stature possible for them; c. persons who strive from a felt minus to a felt plus situation by engaging all the inner strength they can muster; d. a person who must excel at whatever she or he attempts whether in the realm of work, love, or art
9.27
209

Which of the following captures the difference between experience and awareness (Rogers)? a. experience is based in the past, awareness in the present ; b. experience encompasses emotions, awareness encompasses cognitions; c. experience is more concrete than awareness; d. experience involves emotions and perceptions, while awareness is appreciation of experience
9.28
209

According to Rogers, which is a characteristic of the self-actualizing person? a. time competency; b. high quantitative skills; c. unusual modes of verbal expression; d. a tendency to devote oneself to others to the exclusion of reserving time for oneself
9.29
210

Which of the following is a distinguishing mark of humanistic Rogerian psychology? a. self-sacrifice; b. duty to others; c. belief in the importance of the self; d. belief that all problems have solutions
9.30
210

Which of the following is most related to Rogers' conception of the ; ? a. the balance point between conscious and unconscious processes; b. the composite of all of the other personality structures; c. the culmination of all the person's hopes, dreams, and aspirations; in other words the mature

personality; d. the organized, conceptual whole composed of perceptions of characteristics of "I" and "me"
9.31
210

To Rogers the self is functionally equivalent to a. the personality; b. the self-concept; c. the junction of conscious and unconscious processes; d. emotions, cognitions, and perceptions occurring at a given moment
9.32
204

According to Rogers, the self is a. static after adolescence; b. unable to understand itself; c. personality manifested; d. a continuing process, not a fixed end-point
9.33
210

The ideal self is a. almost always an unobtainable self; b. an aspiration without bounds; c. the self a person most values and desires to be; d. how one should be, as defined by one's culture
9.34
210

Congruency refers to a. behavioral consistency; b. consistency between the self-concept and experiences relating to the self c. being what one is supposed to be; d. the coincidence of conscious and unconscious desires
9.35
210

According to Rogers, denial is a. refusal to think about or address whatever is too hard to bear; b. refusal to accept who we are; c. a reinterpretation of an experience so as to make it consistent with how one wants things to be; d. the inability to recognize or accept the existence of an experience that has occurred
9.36
210

According to Rogers, distortion is a. refusal to think about or address whatever is too hard to bear; b. refusal to accept who we are; c. a reinterpretation of an experience so as to make it consistent with how one wants things to be; d. the inability to recognize or accept the existence of an experience that has occurred
9.37
210-211

Which is Rogers' example of incongruence? a. the young woman who was beautiful but outwardly claimed she was plain; b. the boy who lifted girls skirts; c. the man who was a voyeur; d. the woman who had a good sexual experience, but told her friends it was bad
9.38
211

Defensiveness is illustrated by a. reaction aimed at maintaining the self in the face of contradictory information b. one of those several Freudian mechanisms that Rogers put to good use; c. the same as "denial"; d. the same as "distortion"
9.39
202

How did Rogers describe Adler's manner of relating to a child?\

a. a little rough, but with an undercurrent of kindness; b. very direct and employing a deceptively simple manner; c. rather authoritarian, in an ironically Freudian manner; d. very scientific; he addressed the child only after administering a battery of tests

9.40
212

What will be the result of continued defensiveness?
a. psychosis; b. restructuring of the personality; c. new insights; d. maladjustment

9.41
206

Which of the following was a hypothesis that Rogers deduced from May's six existential issues? a. the more people struggle with their demons the more depressed they become; b. the higher the level of material attainment, the more false is one's self-perceptions; c. the more the self is free from threat, the more one will exhibit self-affirming behaviors; d. the shorter the therapy, the greater the self-concept development

9.42
208-209

According to Rogers, what sort of interaction is important to personality development? a. between environments and actualization tendencies; b. between the here and now and the past; c. between infant and siblings; d. between conscious and unconscious

9.43
212

Which of the following is the best definition of positive regard?
a. regarding relations with other people in a positive light;
b. other people communicating to oneself that one is accepted, valued, worthwhile and trusted simply for being who one is;
c. regarding other people as one might hope they will regard oneself: positively; d. the experience of oneself as making a positive difference in others' lives and receiving warmth, liking, respect, and caring from others

9.44
212

Which of the following is the best definition of unconditional positive regard? a. regarding relations with other people in a positive light; b. other people communicating to oneself that one is accepted, valued, worthwhile and trusted simply for being who one is; c. regarding other people as one might hope they will regard oneself: positively; d. the experience of oneself as making a positive difference in others' lives and as receiving warmth, liking, respect, and caring from others

9.45
212-213

Which of the following is the antithesis of being prized, valued, and accepted? a. reciprocating those feelings; b. accepting conditions of worth set up by other people; c. trying to be more than one is; d. being concerned that in being all one can be, one may end up more than someone else

9.46

Which of the following allows the person to pursue self-actualization? a. release from the tyranny of the shoulds b. developing insight during therapy; c. welding archetypes to consciousness; d. overcoming inferiority   9.47

213

Which is a common misconception of unconditional positive regard? a. few therapist use it; b. a child's behavior is approved no matter what its nature; c. it usually backfires: the child will ignore it; d. it is naive: the child will see through it and exploit it   9.48

213

Accurate empathy is a. empathy, but with evaluation of self by others standards; b. understanding a person's thinking rather than emotions;213 c. accurately perceiving a person's inner world non-evaluatively; d. empathy that comes with practice at perceiving one's own inner world   9.49

213

Congruence in the interpersonal sense refers to a. two people being highly similar on an ideological level; b. two people sharing the same critical beliefs; c. two people being concerned about the same emotional issues; d. people who feel the same level of comfort with the issue they are considering   9.50

214

Positive self-regard refers to a. an ability that some people have and others do not have; b. accepting one's behavior no matter what its nature; c. regarding oneself positively when one's behavior warrants it; d. a favorable attitude toward oneself   9.51

214

"Locus of evaluation" involves what problem? a. locating one's processes of evaluation only within oneself; b. the source of evidence about oneself, inside one's self or outside; c. the ambiguity of locating the sources of evidence about one's self. d. how to get rid of all forms of self-evaluation   9.52

212-214

All of the following are necessary conditions for productive therapy, except one? Which is NOT a necessary condition? a. accurate empathic understanding; b. congruence; c. initial, mutual liking on the part of client and therapist; d. positive regard   9.53

215

All except one of the following are stages in Rogerian therapy. Which is NOT a stage? a. client communicates about externals, not about self; b. client finally breaks down and laughs or cries or otherwise displays emotional apoplexy;

c. client accepts own feelings in all their immediacy and richness; d. client trusts new experiences and relates to others openly and freely
9.54
215

In therapy example, during the initial session, what problem did the lawyer-client express? a. he was not making enough money; b. his marriage was going badly owing to the long hours he spent working; c. his children were materialistic d. he was actually unaware of any problem, and, thus was evasive
9.55
215

What life discrepancy does the lawyer-client uncover in an early session? a. he and his wife disagree on how to rear their children; b. the children want everything but want to contribute nothing; c. some of his partners are behaving ethically and some are not; d. someone he knows is doing well in his career, but his interests are elsewhere
9.56
215

What does the lawyer-client really want to do with his life? a. be sole owner of his company; b. be an artist; c. be a "mountain man"; d. enter the priesthood
9.57
216

In a late session, what direction does the lawyer-client's expressions take? a. he relates how foolish he had been in thinking of giving up law; b. he talks almost exclusively about his paintings and current feelings; c. he begins to avoid talking about conflicts in his life and talks about past successes; d. he mentions his children no more; instead he focuses on aspirations for his firm
9.58
216-218

Which of the following is a contribution of Rogers? a. he has had great impact on personality assessment; b. he pioneered long-term therapy; c. he has had great impact on personality psychology; d. he has shown that science has no place in assessing therapy
9.59
216-218

Which of the following is a contribution of Rogers a. he was a self-proclaimed pioneer in counseling; b. he correctly recognized that therapy, humanism, and classroom procedures don't mix; c. he showed the importance of the phenomenological perspective; d. he convinced other humanists they have no business dealing in issues of international conflict
9.60
216-218

Which of the following is a contribution of Rogers? a. he recognized that therapeutic methods have no place in the classroom; b. he showed that it is pointless to attempt to validate therapeutic techniques; c. he guided professionals away from concern about what a person should be; d. he, like Skinner, found "freedom" a misguided concept

9.61

216-218

All except one of the following are contributions of Rogers. Which is NOT a contribution?   a. development of the Adjective Check List; b. an understanding of persons; c. appreciation of the role of caring interpersonal relations in personality growth; d. demonstrations of scientific openness and theoretical flexibility

9.62

217

Regarding the scientific method for understanding people, Rogers a. made it the backbone of his therapeutic technique; b. fully rejected it, especially in regard to evaluation of the effectiveness of his therapy techniques; c. felt that science could begin anywhere, even outside the lab; d. remained puzzled regarding the scientific approach and never quite grasped how it related to his techniques

9.63

212

Which was an original idea of Rogers? a. existentialism; b. unconditional positive regard; c. phenomenology; d. character structure

9.64

216

Regarding people, what did Rogers emphasize? a. trust in them; b. respect for their urges; c. individual differences in their traits; d. conflicts between them

9.65

216

Like Sullivan, Rogers emphasized a. movement orientations toward others; b. generativity; c. methodology; d. interpersonal relations

9.66

215-216

What is most true of Rogers?   a. he often blurted out his opinion of what was wrong with a client on the first session; b. he often developed strong feelings toward his clients c. he never offered advice to clients;; d. he violated protocol by scolding clients

9.67

217

What "first" did Rogers score way back in 1942?   a. he became the first psychologist to win the Nobel prize; b. he recorded and transcribed therapy session; c. he wrote President Roosevelt and, in his letter, correctly predicted the current explosion in mental health problems; d. he resigned from the American Psychological Association because they would not accept his ground-breaking "Ethical Principles for Psychologists"

9.68

217

About science, Rogers believed
a. it belongs only in the laboratory
b. it has no application in the realm of psychotherapy
c. scientific theory and procedures should be flexible

d. it should be abandoned by psychologists whose phenomena are too elusive to accommodate scientific criteria

9.69

217-218

Which of the following Rogerian ideas did Harrington, Block, and Block (1987) translate into scientifically testable variables? a. empathy; b. the relationship between child rearing practices and creativity; c. the relationship between therapist's level of accurate empathy and the level of therapeutic outcomes; d. self-actualization

9.70

218

All except one of the following were items given to parents in Harrington's, Block's, and Block's (1987) study of Rogers' ideas regarding child rearing. Which was NOT among those items? a. "I respect my child's opinions and encourage him to express them."; b. "I believe that children should be seen and not heard"; c. "I encourage my child to be curious, and to explore and question things."; d. "I reward my child when he does well in school and punish him when he does poorly."

9.71

218

Harrington, Block, and Block (1987) related measures of Creativity Fostering Environment (CFE), derived from Rogers writings, to measures of creativity. What did they find? a. few relationship, except between CFE and spontaneity; b. over-all, positive relationships between CFE instruments and instruments that measure creativity; c. a high correlation between CFE and parental indulgence of children's disruptive but curious behavior; d. a negative relationship between CFE and logo creativity

9.72

219

To what did Rogers devote many of his last years? a. improving his therapeutic style; b. setting up programs around the country to teach his methods ; c. visiting universities around the world to promote client centered therapy; d. travel around the world to engage in conflict resolution

9.73

219

What did Dennis, a Protestant, say about Becky, a Catholic, during Rogers' sessions in Northern Ireland? a. "I can never relate to her." ; b. "That she is Catholic never made a difference to me; we've been friends since we were wee children."; c. "If Becky is Catholic, you just put her in a wee box and that is the end of it."; d. "Ours is a tragic romance. We can't tell our parents that were are lovers."

9.74

219

By the end of Rogers' sessions in Northern Ireland, what was the state of the relationship between Dennis, a Protestant, and Becky, a Catholic? a. they remained enemies, but, at least, were willing to continue meeting under the auspices of the local Catholic Charities; b. they agreed to "bury the hatchet" and chair further sessions after Rogers left; c. they agree to tell their parents about their long-standing romance; d. as Becky put it: "Words couldn't describe what I feel towards Dennis...I felt that here I got a friend and that was it."

9.75
219

Which of the following was one of Rogers' passions late in his life? a. an end to animal abuse; b. shelters for battered women c. nuclear disarmament; d. homes for street children

9.76
218-221

All except one of the following are limitations of Rogers' thinking and approach. Which is NOT a limitation? a. Rogers saw no need to evaluate his therapeutic techniques; b. in therapy he adamantly refuses to be confrontational; c. he accepted self-reports despite problems with them; d. his non-directive approach is not for everyone, especially for clients who need direction

9.77
218

All except one of the following Rogerian concepts is difficult to translate into testable terms. Which is NOT difficult to test? a. creativity promoting child rearing practices; b. genuineness in interpersonal relationships; c. the essential goodness of people; d. empathy

9.78
221

What was probably Rogers' strongest point? a. his willingness to submit his methods to scientific scrutiny; b. the person he was; c. his willingness to travel to conflict "hotspots" d. his devotion to his student

Extra Items

9.79
204

How did Rogers approach doing therapy with an African-American client? a. he approached him or her just like he did any other client; b. he was a bit more authoritarian with her or him; c. he became the client's student in a "course" on African-American experience, before he began his usual procedures d. he worked especially hard at understanding him or her, so that, should he fail in gaining an understanding, he could terminate therapy early, thus protecting the client

9.80
204&219

All except one of the following were among Rogers' experiences with diversity. Which of the following was NOT among Rogers' diversity experiences? a. he visited South Africa for sessions on conflict resolution; b. he visited Ireland for sessions on conflict resolution; c. his theory had influence on those who deal with interracial and intercultural relationships; d. he became accomplished in doing therapy with Latino people

9.81
207

To Rogers, an experience is a. valid only if objectively verified; b. in the eye of those involved who are targets of the experience; c. real to the experiencer at the time of the experience; d. has no reality in the usual sense of the word
9.82
207

Which of the following did Rogers try to avoid a. revealing himself to his clients; b. talking during therapy; c. showing any emotion during therapy; d. scientific detachment   9.83
207-208

The organismic propensity for actualization is true of all of the follow except one. For which of the following is the propensity for actualization NOT true? a. glaciers; b. protozoa; c. potatoes; d. rabbits   9.84
209

Which of the following is a characteristic unique to the self-actualizing person? a. irritability; b. thoughtfulness c. time competency; d. argumentativeness   9.85
210

Which is true of the "self" in relation to Rogers' theory? a. he was the first to deal with the self; b. he, late in his career, abandoned the self; c. the self is between the conscious and the unconscious; d. the self is clearly central to his point of view
9.86
210

Successfully pursuing the ideal self is (Rogers) a. hopeless b. a major pre-condition to feelings of worth; c. possible only for the elderly; d. possible only after having attained self-actualization   9.87
211-212

What did Rogers share with Freud and Horney a. a belief in the primary importance of the unconscious; b. an intense interest in neurosis; c. a belief that people construct defenses against threat; d. a commitment to dream analysis   9.88
204

While Rogers may not have been so committed to "equality" between himself and his clients, he did a. reject any authoritarian posture on the part of the therapist; b. embrace equal participation on the part of client and therapist in terms of amount of time spent talking; c. reject attempts on the part of clients to take charge of their own therapy; d. embrace the idea that the therapist was subordinate to the client in the sense of human worth   9.89
212-213

All of the following are pre-conditions necessary for growth and change, except one. Which is NOT a pre-condition for growth and change? a. establishing a symbiotic relationship with another person; b. developing accurate empathy; c. achieving

congruence in personal relations; d. developing positive self-regard
9.90
214

Apart from positive regard, accurate empathic understanding, and congruence, which did Rogers think to be important for the realization of change during therapy? a. excellent verbal skills b. motivation to change; c. social support at home; d. lack of conflict in personal relations
9.91
216-218

Which of the following is properly listed among Rogers' contributions? a. rejection of the scientific method; b. invention of the "talking" therapy; c. recognition that theory if fallible d. taking notes during therapy
9.92
219

What Gilda, a Protestant, tell Rogers she would do if she saw an IRA man lying on the ground? a. I would help him up. b. I would ignore him; I wouldn't want to get involved. c. I would prey for him. d. I would step on him.
9.93
219-220

Rogers the therapist has been criticized for a. his stoic silence during therapy; b. his unwillingness to offer clients advice c. being authoritarian during therapy; d. forcing clients to continue in therapy for years
9.94
220

If you are a well-known person, which can you most likely expect? a. nothing but praise; b. making a fortunate c. to be criticized; d. harassment from the government
9.95
220

To the charge of Rogers' alleged lack of genuineness during filmed therapy sessions, Graf replied a. the short filmed-sessions were too preliminary to reveal Rogers' genuineness b. Rogers actually showed genuineness by being confrontational; c. Rogers' repeated crying in response to client's statements of misery showed his genuineness; d. the sessions revealed genuineness, but it was too subtle to be noticed by other than the trained eye
9.96
218-221

For which has Rogers been criticized? a. substance abuse; b. having an affair with a client; c. repudiating his humanistic educational philosophy; d. abandoning his family
9.97
221

Kirschenbaum, regarding Rogers' humanistic educational philosophy, indicated; a. agreement with Coulson that Rogers had abandoned the philosophy; b. that Rogers became even more radical regarding humanistic education as he got older c. that there is insufficient evidence to determine where Rogers finally stood on humanistic education; d. that Rogers had good reasons for abandoning humanistic educational philosophy

9.98
214

In so far as Rogers defined "personality" he equated it to
a. traits; b. behavior; c. feelings of worth; d. self

9.99
203

Which of the following is among Rogers' most basic
assumptions?; a. people are resistant to change; b. people are
inherently good; c. personality is based on consistent traits
d. sexuality is never an important factor in a person's well
being

9.100
221

Rogers exemplified a. persistence; b. the "pull yourself up by
your boot straps" credo; c. the best of the human spirit
d. infallibility

9.101
202

All of the following were Rank's notions that greatly influenced
Rogers, except one. Which was NOT one of Rank's notions that
influenced Rogers? a. patient's self-acceptance is learned in
protective therapy; b. the person's unconscious is of primary
importance; c. patients should freely express emotions during
therapy; d. the emphasis is on the patient's immediate,
emotional experience

9.1,d
9.2,a
9.3,c
9.4,a
9.5,c
9.6,d
9.7,c
9.8,b
9.9,c
9.10,d
9.11,b
9.12,b
9.13,d
9.14,c
9.15,b
9.16,b
9.17,d
9.18,a
9.19,b
9.20,a
9.21,d
9.22,a
9.23,b
9.24,c
9.25,b
9.26,a
9.27,d
9.28,a
9.29,c
9.30,d
9.31,b
9.32,d
9.33,c
9.34,b
9.35,d
9.36,c
9.37,b
9.38,a
9.39,b
9.40,d
9.41,c
9.42,a
9.43,d
9.44,b
9.45,b
9.46,a
9.47,b
9.48,c

9.49,d
9.50,d
9.51,b
9.52,c
9.53,b
9.54,c
9.55,d
9.56,b
9.57,b
9.58,c
9.59,c
9.60,c
9.61,a
9.62,c
9.63,b
9.64,a
9.65,d
9.66,c
9.67,b
9.68,c
9.69,b
9.70,d
9.71,b
9.72,d
9.73,c
9.74,d
9.75,c
9.76,a
9.77,a
9.78,b
Extra
Items
9.79, c
9.80, d
9.81, c
9.82, d
9.83, a
9.84, c
9.85, d
9.86, b
9.87, c
9.88, a
9.89, a
9.90, b
9.91, c
9.92, d
9.93, b
9.94, c

9.95, a
9.96. c
9.97, b
9.98, d
9.99, b
9.100,c
9.101, b

Chapter 10

Multiple Choice Items for the Chapter on Maslow

10.1
225

Which of the following was within the grasp of everyone according to Rogers, but reserved for only a few, according to Maslow? a. self; b. positive regard; c. self-actualization d. unconditional positive regard

10.2
225

Which was a difference between Rogers and Maslow? a. they had different sexual orientations; b. their family backgrounds were different; c. only one of them was a humanis; d. their assumptions about people were very different

10.3
226

Maslow's father married a. into wealth; b. because he had to; c. when he was 57 years old; d. his first cousin, Rose

10.4
226

What claim did Maslow make about his mother? a. she was the kindest person he ever know; b. she was the brightest person he ever knew; c. she was cold and vicious; d. she was a sickly person

10.5
226

All except one of the following were among Maslow's mother's alleged cruelties? Which was NOT among those cruelties? a. she broke his prized 78 RPM records; b. she subjected him to "religious harassment"; c. she killed his kitten; d. she stole the money he had carefully saved

10.6
226

The best way to describe Maslow's father in relations to him was a. cruel; b. warm; c. absent; d. violent

10.7
227

What menace did Maslow face during his youth? a. gangs; b. polio; c. the draft; d. starvation

10.8
227

What obstacle did Maslow face during his youth? a. dyslexia; b. anti-Semitism; c. teachers thought he was retarded; d. being born in Europe, he had to learn English

10.9
227

What problem did Maslow share with Horney during their youth? a. they were both subject to anti-Semitism; b. they both came from poverty; c. they both felt unattractive; d. they were both dyslexic

10.10

What problem did Maslow face when he began to select a college? a. low college entrance scores; b. no money and no ability to get a loan; c. poor high school preparation; d. anti-semitism

227

10.11

227-228

What characterized Maslow's undergraduate years?
a. miserable grades; b. several failed romances; c. repeated illnesses; d. changing schools

10.12

228

What dinosaur-among-professors turned Maslow off to psychology? a. Wundt; b. Titchener; c. Harlow; d. Koffka 10.13

228

Which of the following was one of the reasons that Maslow left Cornell?; a. Bertha; b. he was accused of criminal activity; c. he wanted to go to an all-Jewish school; d. he wanted to study with Wundt

10.14

228

Who was the reason that Maslow finally transferred to University of Wisconsin? a. Wundt; b. Titchener; c. Harlow; d. Koffka

10.15

228

To whose monkey laboratory did Maslow migrate while at the University of Wisconsin? a. Wundt; b. Titchener; c. Harlow d. Koffka

10.16

229

Which was a limitation that Alderfer (1989) noted in Maslow as a person? a. he was unable to act in ways consistent with his own theory; b. he smoked so much that he offended most of his graduate assistants; c. it was rumored that he was a sexual harasser; d. he was so shy that he could not even stand up and talk to a class;

10.17

229-230

Why did Maslow stick with his early monkey research as long as he did? a. greed; b. success; c. he did not want to leave Wisconsin; d. Bertha had several babies in a row, making a move impossible

10.18

229-230

When Maslow returned to New York City to take a position at Columbia, all except one of the following luminaries were available to him. Who was NOT in New York at the time?
a. Thorndike; b. Horney; c. Harlow; d. Adler

10.19

230

Classic Gestalt psychology held that a. therapy ought to be confrontational; b. elements of perception could be discovered through introspection; c. the secret to dealing with abnormal behaviors is cognitive therapy; d. simple perceptions are wholes made up of integrated parts

10.20

230

All of the following are Gestalt laws of organization, except one. Which is NOT a Gestalt law? a. grouping similar objects together to form a whole; b. figure and ground--face/vase--can be seen at the same time; c. grouping proximal objects together; d. incomplete objects are closed perceptually

10.21
230

What Gestalt-like principle was basic as far as Maslow was concerned? a. people are equally worthy; b. similarities among people out-weigh differences; ; c. the person is an integrated, organized whole; d. closure is the most important part of therapy

10.22
231

In discussing existentialism as presented by May, Maslow credited that movement with emphasizing what "human predicament"? a. life in the face of death; b. the gap between human aspiration and human limitations; c. reincarnation d. good and evil as part and parcel of each person's constitution

10.23
231

Needs, according to Maslow, are a. opposite to motives; b. motion-propelling organization directed toward goals; c. simple tensions that demand to be satisfied; d. satisfactions that are sought by all humans

10.24
232

What is unique about Maslow's point of view?; a. he considered needs; b. he considered multiple motives; c. he considered self-actualization; c. he has used the experimental method

10.25
232-233

According to Maslow, while the needs a person experiences are universal, a. the order they are experienced varies from person to person; b. some people have more needs due to bigger body size; c. methods used to satisfy needs may be specific to peoples' culture; d. the number of needs in the hierarchy of needs varies around the world

10.26
222-233

Maslow thought that environments are a. critically important for understanding human behavior; b. important mainly during childhood; c. difficult or impossible to specify; d. what we make of them

10.27
233

Maslow believed a. a particular motivation cannot be considered in isolation from other motivations; b. all people are created psychologically equal; c. the "drive" concept is highly useful; d. Gestalt psychology contributed nothing to his point of view

10.28
233

"Do people live by bread alone?" (Maslow)   a. yes, always;

b. yes, except when bread is prohibited by culture; c. no, all people can always deny the needs of the flesh; d. no, when bread is plentiful other needs emerge

10.29
233

The physiological need level is often experienced by a. psychotic people; b. homeless people; c. immigrants of all kinds; d. priests

10.30
233

Safety needs are a. met only after esteem needs; b. aroused in only a small minority of the world's people; c. include the security that comes with having enough to eat and drink; d. include security, protection, stability, law and order, and freedom from fear and chaos

10.31
233

Belongingness and love needs a. are met after esteem needs b. are the most important needs; c. include security and freedom from physiological want; d. include a sense of place in family and groups

10.32
234

Esteem needs a. include being cared for by a mothering one b. are the highest in the hierarchy; c. include personal desires for adequacy; d. include affectionate relations with people

10.33
234

Need for self-actualization a. is the second highest need on the hierarchy; b. includes the desire for self-fulfillment c. includes personal desires for adequacy; d. includes desires for respect from other people

10.34
234-238

All of the following are true of self-actualization, according to Maslow, except one. Which is NOT true of self-actualization? a. potentially, everyone can become self-actualized; b. it is becoming what one potentially is; c. it is not a deficiency need d. it is becoming everything that one is capable of being

10.35
238

Deficiency needs refers to a. the meta-needs; b. a category of needs that includes self-actualization; c. the first four needs d. all the needs except meta-needs

10.36
234-235

Who among the following is most likely to continually experience D-needs?   a. psychotic people; b. religious fanatics; c. people on medication; d. impoverished people

10.37
236-238

Which is sufficient for attaining self-actualization? a. satisfaction of D-needs; b. sufficient conditions for attaining self-actualization would be difficult of impossible to state; c. all physiological needs must be met; d. safety needs must be met

Self-actualization is a. a D-need; b. a growth need
c. a meta-need; d. a transcendental need

10.38
238

In Maslow's scheme, prepotent means a. the same as
impotentl; b. omnipotent; c. stronger and more immediately
demanding than higher-order needs; d. stronger and more
immediately demanding than lower-order needs

10.39
235

Hierarchical needs are a. only part of the biological needs that
humans seek to satisfy; b. arranged in a shifting pattern; c. only
effective during childhood; d. not met in all-or-none fashion

10.40
235

All except one of the following are exceptions to the rule that
lower-order needs must be met before higher-order needs.
Which does NOT represent one of those exceptions? a. Jesus
Christ; b. Ghandi; c. former President Clinton; d. anyone who
can gradually deny lower order needs

10.41
235

The most typical reversal to the usual order of need
satisfactions is (Maslow) a. security needs before physiological
needs; b. esteem needs before belongingness needsc. self-
actualization needs before esteem needs; d. esteem needs
before physiological needs

10.42
235-236

Who is most likely never to get beyond the first two levels?
a. homeless people; b. priests; c. war veterans; d. rich people

10.43
236

What was Maslow's view of human nature?   a. there is no such
thing; b. nurture is more important than nature; c. same as
Rogers': all humans are equal; d. it is inborn

10.44
236

An instinctoid is a. an object of Maslow's scorn; b. the same
thing as an instinct; c. instinct-like; d. like an instinct, but never
biological

10.45
236

Maslow's instinctoid a. includes both needs and values;
b. includes only lower order needs; c. includes only higher
order needs; d. included everything but meta-needs

10.46
236

According to a view that Maslow rejects, how does the infant
learn love? Through a. classical conditioning; b. instrumental
conditioning; c. associative learning; d. emotive learning

10.47
236

10.48
236

Maslow believed a. all people are equal; b. most people are not worthy; c. some people are good choosers and some bad choosers; d. some people are more equal than others

10.49
237

Self-actualizers a. could be anyone; b. are not everybody, but number in the millions; c. are people who are nearly perfect: for practical purposes: they have no faults; d. fulfill themselves by making complete use of their potentialities

10.50
237

With Maslow as the selector, all of the following would be self-actualizers, except one. Who would NOT likely be considered a self-actualizer by Maslow? a. President Ronald Reagan b. Thomas Jefferson; c. Einstein; d. Martin Luther King

10.51
238

What percent of college students are self-actualizers, according to Maslow a. 15%; b. <1%; c. 5%; d. 75%

10.52
238

Meta-needs include a. esteem needs; b. love and belongingness needs; c. cognitive needs; d. transcendental needs

10.53
238

Meta-needs are a. lower in the hierarchy than self-actualization; b. more immediate and prepotent than D-needs; c. relatively easy to satisfy; d. growth needs

10.54
238

Which best characterizes the example self-actualized person? a. well rounded; b. deeply turned inward; c. a citizen of the world; d. he is his ethnicity

10.55
238

All except one of the following are B-values. Which is NOT a B-value? a. wholeness; b. completion; c. playfulness; d. self-sacrifice

10.56
238

Peak experience refers to a. the top of the experience hierarchy; b. the experiences one has at her or his peak of life c. intense, mystical experiences associated with wonder and awe; d. the equivalent to drug experiences

10.52
238

All except one of the following are peak experiences, except one. Which is LEAST likely to qualify as a peak experience? a. a roller coaster ride; b. space walk; c. religious conversion d. making it to the top of Mount McKinley

10.58
239

Which of the following are among Maslow's emphases? a. all humans are basically equal; b. the biological origin of human needs and values; c. the contention that self-actualization is

difficult to attain, but possible for everyone; d. the primacy of brotherly love
10.59
239

What is Maslow's problem with the scientific approach to understanding people? a. it relies too heavily on maladjusted subjects; b. laboratories are no place to study humans' behavior; c. the results of experimental animal studies are generalized to people; d. experimental controls are too difficult to institute
10.60
239

What is Maslow's problem with clinical approaches to understanding people? a. they rely too heavily on maladjusted subjects; b. clinical setting are no place to study humans' behavior; c. the results of clinical animal studies are generalized to people; d. clinical controls are too difficult to institute
10.61
239-240

An environment that would foster self-actualization would include all except one of the following. Which would NOT foster self-actualization? a. assurances that all individuals get necessary raw materials; b. getting out of the way whenever possible; c. accepting delays and abandonment of choices; d. placing a few chosen, psychologically healthy people in leadership positions
10.62
239

Eupsychia refers to a. a place where differences between people would melt away; b. a utopian society characterized by psychological health among all members; c. a kind of therapy in which the client is the therapist; d. a condition of transcendental exultation
10.63
239-240

What would Eupsychia be like? a. like any other commune, but without authoritarian leadership; b. prone to valuing what is simple, loving, and unselfish; c. a paradise in which each person has what she or he wants out of life; d. a new form of life style in which people are permitted to pursue whatever they want
10.64
240

Which of the following is a Maslow idea that has been very valuable in applied settings? a. instinctoids; b. multiple motivations; c. biology as a base for everything d. the hierarchy of needs;
10.65
240

All of the following, except one, are applications of Maslow's ideas. Which is NOT an application? a. management: recognition of employees' need satisfaction pursuits; b. speech-pathologists: select a need to be the focus of a conference; c. clergy: establishing the need level of congregation members; d. self-actualization in athletes

10.66
240

What did Sherrill and colleagues (1990) find when they administered the Personality Orientation Inventory (POI) to blind and sighted athletes? a. blind athletes scored lower on the Existentiality and Self-acceptance scales; b. blind athletes scored high on the Existentiality and Self-acceptance scales; c. sighted athletes had higher POI scores, overall; d. blind athletes had higher POI scores, overall

10.67
241

What problem did Wicker and colleagues (1993) find earlier with studies of Maslow's hierarchy? a. subject samples were too small; b. there was a tendency to use only rare self-actualized persons as subjects; c. there was a tendency to ignore meta-needs; d. these studies tended to use a measure of "importance" of need satisfaction

10.68
240

Kasser and Ryan (1996) found that all of the following were aspirations that were negatively associated with self-actualization, except one. Which was NOT among those that these researchers found to be inversely related to self-actualization? a. for great power; b. for financial success c. for an appealing appearance; d. for social recognition

10.69
240

Graham and Balloun (1973) found; a. no correlations between level of satisfaction and desire for satisfaction, as expected b. no correlations between level of satisfaction and desire for satisfaction, contrary to expectations; c. a positive correlation between level of satisfaction and desire for satisfaction, as expected; d. a negative correlation between level of satisfaction and desire for satisfaction, as expected

10.70
241

All except one of the following were findings of Williams' and Pages' (1989) study of safety, belongingness and esteem needs. Which is NOT among their findings?; a. student subjects were, on average, functioning at the esteem level; b. needs at lower levels were rated "important" but not "salient" (on the mind); c. a substantial minority of student subjects, 30%, were deemed either functioning at the self-actualization level or about to move to that level; d. need satisfaction was high for all levels, but was lowest for the esteem level

10.71
241

What did Wicker's and Wiehe's (1999) subjects who wrote about success at being close with another person show that subjects who wrote about lack of success did'nt show? a. attainment of the esteem level; b. attainment of the belongingness and love level; c. attainment of the safety and security level; d. attainment of self-actualization

10.72

What did Mathes, Zevon, Roter, and Joerger (1982) find that was peculiar to people who reported peak experiences? a. intense happiness; b. a feeling of being special and entitled c. being drawn to religion; d. having a feeling of uncontrollable power over others

10.73

All except one of the following are criticisms lodged against Maslow's conceptions of self-actualization? Which is NOT a criticism? a. Maslow arrived at self-actualization by proclaiming "super personalities" as experts on self-actualizing; b. Maslow's sample of "super personalities" was small and arbitrarily selected; c. Maslow ignored abundance motivation in favor of deficiency motivation; d. Maslow's used myself as a standard for judging whether a candidate "super personality" was worthy of being included in his sample

10.74

All except one of the following are criticisms lodged against Maslow's conceptions of self-actualization? Which is NOT a criticism? a. Maslow placed the broadest needs at the narrow apex of the pyramid; b. research showed that Maslow's self-actualization and Frankl's self-transcendence were not highly similar; c. Maslow falsely saw self-actualizers as selfish; d. Maslow's self-actualization is neither universal or necessarily the best rendition of human fulfillment

10.75

Why is self-realization, extracted from Buddhism, possibly a more meaningful and productive self-fulfillment entity than self-actualization? a. there is more hard evidence to support it b. it is based on a superior religion; c. it is a more active process; d. it is even more selective than self-actualization: even fewer people are self-realized

10.76

All except one of the following are elements of Buddha path to Nirvana. Which is NOT among those elements? a. suffering is abolished only by eliminating cravings; b. self-sacrifice and devotion to others is a sign of inner spiritual weakness; c. adhere to moral conduct; d. maintain mental discipline

10.77

All of the following, except one, are flaws in self-actualization as Maslow conceived of it. Which is NOT a flaw? a. self-actualizers tend to be such self-absorbed people that they rarely make contributions to society; b. "self-actualization" is an inherently ambiguous term; c. self-actualization in Maslow's theory is not the same as self-actualization as manifested in the super-personalities; d. self-actualizers tend to have a limited number of close, personal relationships

10.78

Which of the following is a problem with "peak experiences?"
a. there are almost no reports of them; b. only people who are
self-actualizers have them; c. non-self-actualizers report them
d. most peak experiences are not profound or noteworthy

10.79
245

Which of the following is a limitation of Maslow's hierarchy of
needs? a. fields outside of psychology have had no use for the
hierarchy; b. there is no evidence that the needs are ordered
as Maslow's claimed; c. there are no viable measures of any of
the hierarchy's needs; d. Maslow never explained how self-
actualization could be different from the other needs in that it is
not quelled by satisfaction

10.80
245-246

All except one of the following are reasons why Maslow should
be considered one of the great psychologists. Which is NOT a
reason for his greatness? a. the evidence supporting self-
actualization is accumulating so fast, criticism of the notion may
someday be deemed trivial; b. Maslow's idea that entities may
be arranged in hierarchies is original with him and has spread
to all other branches of science; c. better and better measures
of the basic needs are being developed, thus, ensuring the
longevity of the hierarchy; d. Maslow is a model for us all in that
he overcame a distressing childhood and anti-semitism to
become a fine person and major contributor

Extra Items

10.81
227

An example of the anti-Semitism that Maslow faced during
childhood; a. children teased him because of the cap he wore;
b. children teased him because of his braids; c. a teacher
repeatedly referred to him in class as the "Hymie"; d. a teacher
made spell words until he misspelled one

10.82
227-228

Cornell University a. among the few major Eastern universities
admitting Jews when Maslow applied to college; b. displayed
not even a hint of anti-Semitism; c. was where Maslow did all of
his undergraduate work; d. was well known as the most anti-
Jewish university in the Eastern U.S.

10.83
231

Drives are a. opposite to motives; b. motion-propelling
organization directed toward goals; c. simple tensions that
demand to be satisfied; d. satisfactions that are sought by all
humans

10.84
229

During the protest era of the 60s, Maslow a. Maslow shunned
the protesters; b. Maslow was a natural for the role of Guru
c. Maslow was in the forefront of the protest movement;
d. Maslow was a secret informer for the FBI

10.85
229

Young Maslow had an interest in a. film; b. collecting moths; c. fencing; d. dominance in monkeys

10.86
230

What does a person see in the face and vase figure? a. either the face of the vase; b. both the face and the vase; c. neither the face nor the vase; d. a mixture of the face and the vase

10.87
232

Only the rarest thought, behavior, or feeling is likely to a. have any important meaning; b. be repeated; c. have only motive behind it; d. be practical

10.88
234

Which one of the following is least likely to be a way to bolster self-esteem? a. be a good hunter; b. be an outstanding pottery maker; c. be a feared "witch doctor"; d. be a loyal assembly line worker

10.89
235

Impoverished people operate at what need level on Maslow's hierarchy? a. self-esteem; b. safety and security; c. D-needs d. belongingness and love

10.90
234

Related to Maslow's theory, success in school and in sports leads children to a. self-efficacy; b. esteem; c. arrogance d. self-regulation

10.91
235

Who may suffer a permanent loss of love (Maslow)? a. the elderly; b. psychopaths; c. brain damaged people; d. motherless women

10.92
237

All of the following are properly considered "self-actualizers" except one. Who is NOT properly considered a self-actualizer?; a. Elizabeth Taylor; b. Harriet Tubman; c. Malcolm X; d. Mother Teresa

10.93
238

Which is more likely to be possessed by self-actualizers than others? a. selflessness; b. mathematical ability; c. B-Values d. Q-needs

10.94
233

Taoistic philosophy values all of the following except one. Which does it NOT value? a. material; b. simple; c. loving d. unselfish

10.95
240

If high-level management does not attempt to approximate self-actualization, a. the business will fail; b. creativity will be locked out of the executive board room; c. employees will be show a marked lowering of achievement; d. work loads are likely to increase

10.96
242

According to Kiel, how should Maslow's hierarchy be changed? a. make it broad where the broadest needs are found; b. make it square to equate the needs; c. make it round so that all needs are connected to all other needs; d. make it rectangular with the most important needs to the left   10.97
241

What measure did Wicker and colleagues (1993) find to be an improvement on the usual index of hierarchy need satisfaction? a. importance; b. intensity; c. intention
d. salience   10.98
231

Maslow quarreled with which existential positions? a. "what is so essential to humans they can't do without it?"; b. they see the self as emerging from the choices that people make
c. that, as people transcend themselves, they become more members of their species and less members of their culture; d. their belief that free will is not possible with taking responsibility   10.99
245

What did Neher (1991) find to border on the absurd regarding Maslow theory? a. his refusal to ever even consider that needs might be fulfilled in other than the order represented by the hierarchyb. his insistence that self-actualization belongs at the top of the hierarch; c. his refusal to use any other standard but himself when deciding who is self-actualized; d. his view of culture as opposing organismic need fulfillment   10.100
243

About Maslow's self-actualization, Mittleman (1991) wondered a. whether it is better thought of as "openness" ; b. about the theory's remarkable similarity to Freud's; c. whether the theory can beimproved; d. whose theory is more important

10.101
244

What is the problem with Maslow's call to "transcend culture"? a. nothing, it is something we must all do; b. those who abandon their cultures may still be treated badly because of their cultures; c. being identified with people everywhere is not psychological sound; d. almost no one ever tries to transcend his/her culture

10.1,c	10.49,d	10.95,b
10.2,b	10.50,a	10.96,a
10.3,d	10.51,b	10.97,c
10.4,c	10.52,c	10.98,a
10.5,d	10.53,d	10.99,d
10.6,c	10.54,c	10.100,a
10.7,a	10.55,d	10.101, b
10.8,b	10.56,c	
10.9,c	10.57,a	
10.10,d	10.58,b	
10.11,d	10.59,c	
10.12,b	10.60,a	
10.13,a	10.61,d	
10.14,d	10.62,b	
10.15,c	10.63,b	
10.16,a	10.64,d	
10.17,b	10.65,c	
10.18,c	10.66,a	
10.19,d	10.67,d	
10.20,b	10.68,b	
10.21,c	10.69,d	
10.22,c	10.70,c	
10.23,d	10.71,a	
10.24,b	10.72,b	
10.25,c	10.73,d	
10.26,d	10.74,c	
10.27,a	10.75,c	
10.28,d	10.76,b	
10.29,b	10.77,a	
10.30,d	10.78,c	
10.31,d	10.79,d	
10.32,c	10.80,b	
10.33,b	*Extra*	
10.34,a	*Items*	
10.35,c	10.81,d	
10.36,d	10.82,a	
10.37,b	10.83,c	
10.38,b	10.84,b	
10.39,c	10.85,d	
10.40,d	10.86,a	
10.41,b	10.87,c	
10.42,c	10.88,d	
10.43,a	10.89,c	
10.44,d	10.90,b	
10.45,c	10.91,b	
10.46,a	10.92,a	
10.47,c	10.93,c	
10.48,c	10.94,a	

Chapter 11

Multiple Choice Items for the Chapter on Kelly

11.1
250

Kelly's approach may be designated a. behavioral; b. psychodynamic; c. cognitive; d. transcendental

11.2
250

Which best describes Kelly's background? a. son of a preacher; b. big city boy; c. wealthy upper crust; d. child of professors

11.3
251

Which best characterizes Kelly's first experience in a psychology class? a. he was disappointed by it; b. he formed no impression about it; c. he developed very negative feelings about the professor; d. he liked it so much he went into psychology

11.4
251

What was Kelly's reaction upon first reading Freud? a. joy; b. confusion; c. incredulity; d. laughter

11.5
251

Kelly was prone to all of the following, except one. Which was he not prone to? a. sarcasm; b. anger; c. skepticism; d. humor

11.6
251

Concerning Pavlov, famous Russian discoverer of classical conditioning, Kelly; a. was filled with admiration; b. he was not quite sure why we should be grateful to him; c. he thought that Pavlov made about as much sense as Freud, a lot of sense d. he was openly incensed

11.7
252

How did Kelly's former students regard him? a. with affection b. with suspicion; c. with fear and admiration; d. as a major put-down artist

11.8
252

All of the following are ways that colleagues regarded Kelly, except one. Which was NOT one of the ways he was regarded? a. scholar; b. warm friend; c. teacher; d. counselor

11.9
251

Which of the following was among Kelly's early careers? a. engineer; b. school teacher; c. traveling salesman d. physics teacher

11.10
252

Which of the following beliefs was attributed to Kelly?

a. all people are academically equal; b. attention to the external environment is the most reasonable approach to understanding people; c. in psychology, as in other sciences, there are only theories, no truths; d. biological determinism

11.11
253

To Kelly, the forces that determine behavior are a. external; b. internal; c. mostly external, partly internal; d. extrapsychic

11.12
253

What governs people, according to Kelly?   a. hedonic forces b. consequences of behavior; c. the way they construe events in their worlds; d. past reinforcement schedules

11.13
253

Like Adler, Kelly believed that people are   a. afflicted with feelings of inferiority; b. future oriented; c. always striving for superiority; d. subject to shock

11.14
253

What may have contributed to Kelly's pragmatic approach? a. he was the son of professors; b. his background in law dictated pragmatism; c. he learned from his politician father d. he was an engineer during the great depression

11.15
253

Kelly saw himself as   a. a bit above others; b. no different from those he studied and helped in therapy; c. not well respected by other psychologists; d. a person with am antagonistic point of view

11.16
253

A program to deal with personal problems was like a. a fishing expedition; b. a wild game hunt; c. a well-organized party d. a scientific experiment

11.17
254

According to Kelly, in order to address a personal problem, a person must do all of the following, except one. Which is NOT one of Kelly's recommendations? a. pinpoint the issues b. become intimate with the problem; c. exercise controls and make observations; d. generalize observations to related situations

11.18
254

A construct is a. a concept by another name; b. a cognitive structure that is a hidden organizer of experience, both internal and external; c. a personality entity that is analogous to Freud's ego, but without implications for instinctual satisfactions; d. a way of construing events so that the future is anticipated

11.19
254

According to Kelly, personality is a. a collection of traits each guiding a different sphere of life; b. an organized system of constructs that may be ranked in importance; c. a framework of

personal dispositions that, together, operate in the real world in order to secure satisfactions; d. traits organized according to similarity   11.20
                                                                                        254

A postulate is a. an elaborate hypothesis; b. another name for "theory"; c. a basic assumption; d. a fundamental principle
                                                                                        11.21
                                                                                        254

Kelly's fundamental postulate is; a. the assumption that a person's psychological processes are routed through various channels by the way the person anticipates events
b. humans can solve their problems if they are provided with another person to act as a sounding board off which they can bounce their emotions; c. the important events for understanding humans are internal; d. people are able to accurately predict their outcomes in the future, provided they record past rewards   11.22
                                                                                        254-255

What is Jim's problem as he sees it on a superficial level?
a. Professor Martinson's stubbornness and inconsistency
b. his friend Joan's unwillingness to appreciate his predicament and offer any sympathy; c. his own stupidity for missing so much class; d. Joan's unwillingness to consider any relationship with him, but friendship   11.23
                                                                                        255

What is Jim's real problem, related to his construct system?
a. he really can't stand Professor Martinson; b. he is overwhelmed with self-loathing; c. he wants Professor Martinson to trust him; d. he wants Joan to be closer to him
                                                                                        11.24
                                                                                        255-256

All except one of the following are among Joan's characterization of Jim or advice to him. Which was NOT among those characterizations or bits of advice?
a. "go tell Professor Martinson off; you shouldn't let anyone push you around"; b. "you (Jim) don't learn from experience"; c. "let Professor Martinson know he is one of the good guys"; d. "you (Jim) are too stiff and formal"   11.25
                                                                                        256

All of the following are Joan's constructs revealed in her conversation with Jim, except one. Which is NOT her construct? a. admire-not admire; b. intelligent-stupid; c. good-bad; d. like me-not like me   11.26
                                                                                        255

All of the following are among Jim's constructs, except one. Which is NOT among his constructs?; a. educated-uneducated
b. trust-distrust; c. intelligent-stupid; d. admire-not admire
                                                                                        11.27
                                                                                        257

A construction system is   a. a system of tightly organized traits
b. an organization of constructs with the more important at the
top and the less important at the bottom; c. the system of intra-
and inter- psychic entities in a relationship that allows the
organism to function at maximum efficiency; d. personality
structures working in unison   11.28
                                                                257

Constructs at the top of a construct system are called
a. superior; b. anterior; c. superordinate; d. elevated
                                                                11.29
                                                                257

The emergent pole is   a. the contrasting end; b. the primary
and principle end; c. the highest pole; d. the more dense pole
                                                                11.30
                                                                257

The implicit pole is; a. the contrasting end; b. the primary and
principle end; c. the highest pole; d. the more dense pole
                                                                11.31
                                                                257

Which of the following is true of the relationship between the
emergent and implicit poles? a. the implicit pole is present,
even if never expressed; b. the implicit pole is the primary pole;
c. the implicit pole appears first, then the emergent pole;
d. the implicit pole is never present and expressed   11.32
                                                                257

According to Kelly, and similar to Jung, people see the world in
terms of   a. significant others; b. unsatisfied needs; c. one's
ancestral past; d. contrasts   11.33
                                                                257

Adopting the construct "tolerant" almost always   a. fails to affect
the adopter; b. lowers the adopter's prejudice level; c. brings
"intolerant" with it; d. includes adoption of the construct
"thoughtful"   11.34
                                                                258

The range of convenience refers to   a. the events to which a
construct is most readily applied; b. the extent and breadth of
the event-category to which a construct applies; c. the range of
constructs that a particular person has developed during
maturation; d. the level of development of the person's
construct system   11.35
                                                                258

The range of focus refers to   a. the events to which a construct
is most readily applied; b. the extent and breadth of the event-
category to which a construct applies; c. the range of constructs
that a particular person has developed during maturation;
d. the level of development of the person's construct system
                                                                11.36
                                                                258

"Impermeable" refers to; a. the level of rigidity of a person's construct system; b. the degree to which a person's construct system is inpenetrable, and, therefore, not subject to change c. the hardness of the surface of a person's construct system d. the tendency for some constructs not to change in terms of range of convenience and place in the construct system

11.37
258

"Commonality" refers to   a. the common ground of two or more constructs with a single construct system; b. the sharing of constructs of two or more people with similar experience c. the sharing of construct systems by two or more people with similar experience; d. the near identity of the emergent and implicit poles for some constructs   11.38
258

"Individuality" refers to   a. the uniqueness of a construct: it is shared with no other construct system, although some approximations to it may exist in other systems; b. differences between construct systems in terms of the constructs contained in each and in how they are organized; c. the degree to which constructs are individual: that is, unconnected to other constructs; d. differences among individuals who share the same construct system   11.39
258

To Kelly, anxiety is   a. what people experience when their construct systems do not apply to critical events; b. what people experience when a new construct appears to be entering the system and may be dominant; c. what people experience when their construct system appears to be fusing with that of another person; d. people's realization that their entire construct system will be over-hauled   11.40
258

To Kelly, fear is   a. what people experience when their construct systems do not apply to critical events; b. what people experience when a new construct appears to be entering the system and may be dominant; c. what people experience when their construct system appears to be fusing with that of another person; d. people's realization that their entire construct system will be over-hauled   11.41
258

To Kelly, threat is a. what people experience when their construct systems do not apply to critical events; b. what people experience when a new construct appears to be entering the system and may be dominant; c. what people experience when their construct system appears to be fusing with that of another person; d. people's realization that their entire construct system will be over-hauled   11.42
259

Joan the scientific psychotherapist made which of the following recommendations to Jim?; a. apologize to Professor Martinson b. suck-up to Professor Martinson, like everyone else; c. try admiration on Professor Martinson and then replicate: do it again in hopes the result will be the same; d. control for extraneous variables when dealing with Professor Martinson: be sure to be neat and well groomed when talking to the Professor   11.43
259

If Jim carries out Joan's suggestions he will be a. making a big mistake: she wants him to tell Professor Martinson off; b. creating greater commonality with Professor Martinson's construct system; c. displaying constructive alternativism: adopting the assumption that his present interpretations of his life situation are subject to change; d. assuming constructive chaos: his constructs will become disorganized and neither resemble the system he currently has or the one that is ideal for him   11.44
260

All except one of the following are coincidences of Kelly's thought with that of other theorists. Which is NOT one of those coincidences? a. like Skinner, he believed in change via human intervention; b. like Maslow, he believed that something like instincts lie behind behavior; c. Like Rogers he did not believe that one and only one set of procedures is effective in therapy; d. like Skinner and Rogers, Kelly was concerned about creativity   11.45
259

Jim's construction system, is organized by "extension of the cleavage line," which means a. constructs are arranged in a concentric pattern; b. whole constructs fall under superordinate emergent and under superordinate implicit poles; c. constructs bear adversarial relationship to one another such that each opposes and complements the other; d. subordinate constructs fall directly under the corresponding emergent and implicit poles of the superordinate constructs   11.46
259

Joan's construct system is organized by "abstracting across the cleavage line," which means a. constructs are arranged in a concentric pattern; b. whole constructs fall under superordinate emergent and under superordinate implicit poles; c. constructs bear adversarial relationship to one another such that each opposes and complements the other; d. subordinate constructs fall directly under the corresponding emergent and implicit poles of the superordinate constructs   11.47
259

Elements are a. entities that can be thought of as the atoms that make-up constructs; b. objects, beings, or events

c. all those entities to which the construct applies; d. one of those entities to which a construct applies that may be used as its name   11.48
                                                                259

Context (Kelly) refers to   a. entities that can be thought of as the atoms that make-up constructs; b. objects, beings, or events c. all those entities to which the construct applies; d. one of those entities to which a construct applies that may be used as its name   11.49
                                                                259

"Symbol" (Kelly) refers to   a. entities that can be thought of as the atoms that make-up constructs; b. objects, beings, or events c. all those entities to which the construct applies; d. one of those entities to which a construct applies that may be used as its name   11.50
                                                                260

Predictability refers to (Kelly)   a. the ability to predict the future b. the child's ability to predict what its parent are going to do with regard to it; c. parents' ability to predict what their children will do with regard to parent/child exchanges; d. the ability to predict the outcome of social interactions   11.51
                                                                261

How did Johnny, in the text's sample case, ensure that his parents were predictable? a. he behaves exactly as they want him to; b. he suppresses behavior as well as he can in their presence; c. he misbehaves; d. he waits until they behave and then mimics what they do   11.52
                                                                261

Dependency constructs are a. more rare, according to Kelly, than Freud would predict; b. a reference to the level of interdependency among the constructs of a system; c. a reference to the level of dependency of one's constructs on those of another person; d. special constructs that revolve around the child's survival needs   11.53
                                                                261

Tight constructs yield _____ predicitability while loose constructs yield _____ predictability. a. good; poor b. unvarying; varying; c. weak; strong; d. definite; indefinite
                                                                11.54
                                                                262

A role involves   a. behaving in ways that meet the expectations of important other people; b. the social equivalent of a cognition; c. acting out a part without actual becoming the person implied by the part; d. a commitment to a certain social order   11.55
                                                                262

According to Kelly, guilt is a. feeling badly about violating some social norm; b. feeling badly about violating the requirements of some role; c. the result of the perception that

one is being dislodged from an important role; d. the result of the perception that one has failed the people who have prescribed one's roles   11.56
262

Elaborative choice refers to   a. selecting an alternative aligned to one construct dimension which appears to provide greater opportunity for elaboration; b. a period of trying on for size the various constructs available in one's repertory; c. attempting to expand a construct dimension so that it applies to more situations; d. working with constructs to bring out implicit poles
11.57
262

Circumspection phase refers to   a. a period during which one construct is allowed to appropriate the situation and define a pair of alternatives from which to choose; b. a period of trying on for size the various constructs available in one's repertory c. a period during which choice is delayed until the individual is able to size up the situation; d. a decision time in which the person selects one of the alternatives provided by the construct that has preempted the situation   11.58
262

Preemption phase refers to   a. a period during which one construct is allowed to appropriate the situation and define a pair of alternatives from which to choose; b. a period of trying on for size the various constructs available in one's repertory c. a period during which choice is delayed until the individual is able to size up the situation; d. a decision time in which the person selects one of the alternatives provided by the construct that has preempted the situation   11.59
263

The choice phase is   a. a period during which one construct is allowed to appropriate the situation and define a pair of alternatives from which to choose; b. a period of trying on for size the various constructs available in one's repertory; c. a period during which choice is delayed until the individual is able to size up the situation; d. a decision time in which the person selects one of the alternatives provided by the construct that has preempted the situation   11.60
271

Which is a problem with supporting Kelly's Personal Construct Theory? a. he has not defined his terms consistently; b. each person's construct system is different; c. his concepts are too nebulous and abstract; c. he has failed to even attempt to define some of his concepts   11.61
263

Kelly thought that a critical testable aspect of his theory is that people cast their worlds in terms of opposites. Lyle tested that assumption and found   a. subjects were able to cast words into the same categories as had pilot subjects; b. factor analysis

showed that there was little correspondence between word classifications by the two sets of subjects; c. subjects in the main study tended to classify words in categories diametrically opposed to those used by previous subjects; d. as Kelly would expect, subjects tended to favor abstracting across the cleavage line to extension of the cleavage line   11.62
263-264

Benesch and Page (1988) investigated the circumstances under which individuals are able to appreciate the important constructs of other people. Under what conditions did they find that peers were able to accurately perceive the constructs of targets? a. when peers and targets had known each other for at least three years; b. when there was little commonality between the construct systems of peers and targets; c. when peers' and targets' construct systems were organized alike; d. when the constructs in question reflected high meaningfulness and stability   11.63
264

What did Viney, Benjamin, and Preston (1989) find when they investigated elderly people who had suffered the loss of a spouse? a. remarkably, these people showed little change in their construct systems: their systems still fit their; b. the elderly showed clear signs of threat: their whole systems were in danger of being overhauled; c. the elderly showed guilt: they were concerned about being dislodged from important roles d. the elderly showed fear: new constructs were entering their construct systems and could dominate   11.64
264

A cognitively complex person is   a. a person with very complex constructs; b. a person who is intelligent by virtue of having a highly unique construct system; c. a person who has a construct system with many well differentiated constructs d. a person who has a construct system that is characterized by constructs that are well related to one another   11.65
264

A cognitively simple person   a. a person with very simplex constructs; b. a person who lacks intelligent by virtue of having a construct system that is unlike others'; c. a person who has a construct system with many constructs that are highly distinct from one another; d. a person who has a construct system that is characterized by blurred distinctions among constructs
11.66
264-266

All except one of the following are research findings regarding cognitively complex and simple people and differences between the cognitive conditions they represent. Which is NOT a complex-simple research finding? a. complex persons are better at predicting the behavior of others; b. simple people are, on average, unable to maintain social relations for long periods of time; c. people are more complex when describing their in-group, compared to an out-group; d. college students showed more complexity in their descriptions of their own age group

11.67

264-266

All except one of the following are research findings regarding cognitively complex and simple people and differences between the cognitive conditions they represent. Which is NOT a complex-simple research finding? a. complex business-administration masters-degree candidates were higher on all the highly valued traits investigated; b. young males gave older males more extreme evaluations than they gave to members of their own age group; c. when arousal was moderate or high, high complex subjects were more discriminating of non-verbal behaviors than low complex subjects; d. politicians who showed some tolerance for slavery were more complex than either extreme slavery supporters or abolitionists   11.68

266

The Role Construct Repertory (REP) Test is   a. variation of the Personality Orientation Inventory that assesses the relations among a person's; b. a device for determining whether one's construct system is organized by extension of the cleavage line or abstracting across the cleavage line; c. an assessment device designed to reveal a person's construct system d. a measurement instrument to ascertain individual differences in the constructs people have in their systems

11.69

267

How have researchers revised the Role Repertory Test (REP) so that it is applicable to a variety of settings? a. they have replaced the fixed role titles (mother, sister, etc.) with titles appropriate for the circumstances being studied; b. they have abandoned the requirement that subjects cast constructs into emergent and implicit poles ; c. that have added many role titles to those that Kelly used; d. they have changed the procedure so that subjects no longer have to use role titles: they specify constructs directly   11.70

267

All except one of the following is an application of the Role Repertory Test (REP) to business and industry. Which is NOT an actual use? a. soft drink companies are experimenting with using the REP to differentiate between varieties of their products (Pepsi versus Diet Pepsi) b. product names were used in the place of usual role titles to discover the constructs used by home testers of perfumes and cosmetics; c. the REP procedure was used to discover the beliefs, values, and items-of-interest used by senior managers; d. the constructs of effective and ineffective loan officers were ascertained by use of REP procedures   11.71

268-269
All except one of the following are steps in fixed role therapy. Which is NOT one of those steps? a. the client describes himself in terms of central and troublesome constructs; b. the client decides which of his troublesome constructs should be the focus of therapy; c. the therapist writes a fixed role for an imaginary character and the client acts out the part of that character using the new role; d. the client tries out the role and he and the therapist discuss reactions of others   11.72

270-271
Which is a criticism that hits at the heart of Kelly's theory? a. he has failed to relate his concepts one to the other; b. his notion of the construct system defies available neurological evidence; c. his ideas about developmental psychology conflict with those of several other theories; d. for some constructs the implicit pole is not a true opposite of the emergent pole, but its negation   11.73

270
What is the strength of PCT with regard to its applicability to diverse cultures? a. the theory has no real underlying assumptions, so it cannot conflict with cultural norms; b. the REP instructions would not have to be translated into other languages; c. constructs are not restricted to internal entities with specific content, such as that associated with "extravert" d. the same role persons usable with applications of the REP in this culture will be usable for other cultures   11.74

270-271
What question may be posed about the poles used in examples by Kelly and Lyle? a. why do so many people share the same poles?; b. do real people's constructs have poles that are so extremely different in favorability?; c. are the poles that have been used in research representative of normal people's poles?; d. is it reasonable to expect that the same people will have the same constructs at different points in time   11.75

270-272
All except one of the following are criticisms lodged against Kelly and his theory. Which is NOT one of those criticisms? a. some emergent poles do not have true opposites; b. Kelly has not been able to explain just why his theory qualifies as "cognitive"; c. REP test results for one person do not readily generalize to other persons; d. some of Kelly's concepts have not been verified   11.76

271-272
Which of the following is a short-coming of the Role Construct Repertory (REP) Test? a. it has seldom proven useful in real world; b. it is virtually uncorrelated with other personality tests

c. the assumptions behind it are alien to the most popular orientation in the U.S.; d. the REP test does not measure what it claims to measure   11.77
272

Which is a major contribution of Kelly? a. he has developed a theory that illuminates the subtle nuances of the parent-child relationship; b. he has been one of the few psychologists to highlight the importance of the cognitive approach; c. he has been responsible for one of the most thorough research programs on record; d. he has been among the relatively few psychologists who has promoted the "one subject, one client at a time" approach   11.78
265-266

Greenfeld and Preston (2000) examined Supreme Court Justices' decisions and found; a. the more they agreed, the more complex they were; b. they showed more complexity in defense of legal precedents; c. they showed simplicity in defense of legal precedents; d. they were more complex if they were liberal than if they were conservative
Extra Items   11.79
251

Regarding Kelly's sarcasm a. it was less prominent than his warmth; b. it was always harsh; c. it was rarely evident; d. it was always subtle   11.80
251

Kelly was quite sarcastic about Pavlov's famous research involving a. cats trying to get out of a puzzle box; b. rats running a maze; c. bears raiding a bees' nest; d. dogs salivating to a bell   11.81
252

Clearly, Kelly was a. sometimes downright mean; b. versatile c. into mysticism; d. a noted stage hypnotists before going into psychology   11.82
252

Kelly spent most of his years as a professor at a. Fort State College; b. Iowa State University; c. Brandeis University d. Ohio State   11.83
252

Kelly wrote a. many volumes; b. relatively little; c. a memoir that tells of his development as a psychologist; d. mostly in journals, not books   11.84
253

Most psychologists view themselves as objective. They view their clients and research subjects as a. incapable of objectivity; b. also objective; c. somewhat subjective d. semi-objective   11.85
251

Kelly opposed the conception of people as a. mentalism; b. present centered psychology; c. humanism

d. understandable by reference to "Ss" and "Rs"   11.86
                                                               258

Jim's superordinate construct "trust-distrust" can be said to have a. really only one pole; b. only a few elements associated with it; c. a wide range of convenience; d. an flavor of simplicity to it   11.87
                                                               258

When an individual discovers that her of his constructs do not apply to critical events anymore, he or she experiences
a. threat; b. distortion; c. anxiety; d. fear   11.88
                                                               258

Joan pleads with Jim to   a. make his constructs more permeable; b. kiss up to Professor Martinson; c. to consider the C-P-C cycle; d. go out with her so they can talk things over
                                                               11.89
                                                               260

Despite Kelly's protests to the contrary, his position has been viewed as basically; a. behavioristic; b. Freudian; c. Adlerian
d. phenomenological   11.90
                                                               257

Venus Williams, the tennis star, symbolizes which of Joan's constructs? a. male-female; b. like me-not like me; c. admire-don't admire; d. trust-distrust   11.91
                                                               261

Dependency constructs tend to be   a. complex; b. easy to change; c. global; d. free flowing   11.92
                                                               264-266

Which characterizes the "cognitively simple" interviewee?
a. many constructs; b. few constructs, but good differentiation among them; c. a tendency to see self and others as different
d. the belief that people are the same in different contexts
                                                               11.93
                                                               267

In fixed role therapy, the client   a. opposes whatever the therapist does; b. gives up an important role; c. plays an imaginary character; d. rapidly switches roles   11.94
                                                               265

Park and her colleagues (1992) found which of the following when they investigated constructs describing in-group and out-group? a. no differences in descriptions; b. more complexity in descriptions of the in-group; c. fewer sub-groups in the in-group; d. more simplicity in the in-group   11.95
                                                               265

Park and her colleagues (1992) found which of the following when they investigated constructs describing in-group and out-group?; a. more complex descriptions of the out-group;
b. fewer constructs were used in describing the in-group;
c. more sub-groups were seen in the out-group; d. more sub-groups were seen in the in-group   11.96

Tetlock, Armor, and Peterson (1993) found that abolitionists were a. actually strongly in favor of slavery, but rejected it for political reasons; b. were relatively cognitively simple
c. were relatively cognitively complex; d. fought for their construct "all people are equal", though they expected to lose
11.97
270

Which of the following is true of PCT-REP when it is applied to non-Western cultures? a. it fits only Western cultures; b. it actually fits Eastern cultures best; c. it can be easily adapted to any culture ; d. it requires major alteration to apply to any other culture
11.98
270

All of the following are reasons why PCT is applicable to a broad spectrum of cultures, except one. Which is NOT a reason why PCT is broadly applicable to diverse cultures? a. its one-person-at-a-time; b. its open-ended; c. its flexible; d. its content-specific
11.99
270

Which of the following makes PCT broadly applicable to diverse cultures?   a. it is short and thus easy to reinterpret for different cultures; b. different role-persons can be used for different cultures; c. its content is specific, making translation to other languages easy; d. it was actually developed for used in Asia and Africa
11.100
272

Kelly a. is rather unknown outside the U.S.; b. has produced so much literature it is difficult to mine his concepts from his writings; c. is well-known among British psychologists
d. is of declining interest in the U.S.

11.1.c	11.49,d	11.95,d
11.2,a	11.50,a	11.96,b
11.3,a	11.51,c	11.97,c
11.4,c	11.52,d	11.98,d
11.5,b	11.53,b	11.99,b
11.6,b	11.54,a	11.100,c
11.7,a	11.55,c	
11.8,d	11.56,d	
11.9,a	11.57,b	
11.10,c	11.58,a	
11.11,b	11.59,d	
11.12,c	11.60,b	
11.13,b	11.61,a	
11.14,d	11.62,d	
11.15,b	11.63,c	
11.16,d	11.64,c	
11.17,d	11.65,d	
11.18,d	11.66,b	
11.19,b	11.67,a	
11.20,c	11.68,c	
11.21,a	11.69,a	
11.22,a	11.70,d	
11.23,c	11.71,b	
11.24,a	11.72,d	
11.25,b	11.73,c	
11.26,d	11.74,b	
11.27,b	11.75,b	
11.28,c	11.76,c	
11.29,b	11.77,d	
11.30,a	11.78,b	
11.31,a	*Extra*	
11.32,d	*Items*	
11.33,c	11.79,a	
11.34,b	11.80,d	
11.35,a	11.81,b	
11.36,d	11.82,d	
11.37,b	11.84,a	
11.38,b	11.84,b	
11.39,a	11.85,d	
11.40,b	11.86,c	
11.41,d	11.87,c	
11.42,c	11.88,a	
11.43,c	11.89,d	
11.44,b	11.90,b	
11.45,d	11.91,c	
11.46,b	11.92,d	
11.47,b	11.93,c	
11.48,c	11.94,b	

Chapter 12

Multiple Choice Items for the Chapter on Rotter and Mischel

12.1
276

A concept in common to Mischel and Rotter is
a. expectancies; b. drive; c. anticipations; d. constructs

12.2
276

Social learning is a. learning the social rules of one's society
b. the variety of learning that relies on one's social ability;
c. acquiring useful information through interacting with people
and other elements of the environment; d. obtaining a level of
sophistication in terms of relations with others that will allow a
person to relate successfully to others 12.3
277

How did Mischel expand on Rotter's social learning theory?
a. he totally redefined learning; b. he made social learning
theory broader and deeper so that it became applicable to
other areas of psychology, such as perception; c. he backed off
from Rotter's denunciation of traits; d. he inserted cognitive and
affective factors as the controllers of behavior 12.4
277

The interaction point of view holds that a. the interaction of the
parent and the child is critical to the child's development; b. the
interplay of cognitive and emotional processes determine
behavior; c. interactions with people's peers shape their social
behavior; d. the interplay between internal entities or person
factors and social situations should be emphasized 12.5
277

Social cognitive learning theory a. holds that personality traits
and social situations interact; b. involves acquiring useful
information through interacting (relating) to people and other
elements of the environment; c. proposes that important factors
are cognitive facilities, not traits; d. involves subordinating
social factors to cognitive factors in attempts to understand
human behavior 12.6
277

Personal factors a. are memories of previous experiences,
that determine what skills, strategies, and affects produce
current behavior; b. are points along various behavioral
dimensions each corresponding to a personal disposition; c.
are factor dimensions with points through which one's
personality profile line is drawn; d. are reasoning factors that

allow the person to contrive ways to cope with distressing
environmental factors   12.7
                                                                   277
Mischel was born near the professional residence of which of
the following? a. Freud; b. Adler; c. Allport; d. Jung   12.8
                                                                   277
Like Rotter and Maslow, Mischel was reared in   a. Vienna;
b. Prague; c. Chicago; d. Brooklyn   12.9
                                                                   278
All except one of the following were interests of Mischel during
his undergraduate years. Which was NOT an interest?
a. psychology; b. painting; c. ESP (Extrasensory Perception)
d. sculpture   12.10
                                                                   278
Who does Mischel credit with being his mentor? a. Rotter; b.
Kelly; c. Skinner; d. he was a Rotter student, but Kelly
influenced him   12.11
                                                                   278
Interest in which of the following was stimulated when Mischel
spent time in Trinidad studying religious cults? a. competency;
b. characterizing events; c. delay of gratification; d. internal
locus of control   12.12
                                                                   278
Which of the following is one of Mischel's beliefs? a. different
people are essentially cognitively identical; b. people know
themselves better than psychologists can come to know them
c. cognitive psychology does not deserve to be as neglected as
it has been in the last decade; d. childhood and adulthood
should be studied separately because they involve different
processes   12.13
                                                                   279
In Mischel's 1968 book Personality Assessment, he brought
forth what famous thesis? a. cognitive factors are important to
understanding human social behavior; b. sociobiology; c.
functional autonomy; d. cross-situational behavioral
consistency, the basic notion underlying traits, is suspect
                                                                   12.14
                                                                   279
According to Mischel, is there behavioral stability in any way?
a. no; it is generally poor; b. it exists for genetically determined
traits only; c. there is temporal stability for prototypical
behaviors; d. it exists for traits that began to develop early in life
                                                                   12.15
                                                                   280
Which of the following does NOT belong to the "Cognitive,
Affective Personality System" (CAPS) sequence that ends in
behavior? a. detection of aspects of the situation that activate
cognitive-affective encoding units; b. the situation is
transformed into affective units; c. encoding units stimulate

cognitive-affective mediating units that influence the strength of behavioral units; d. behavioral units determine behavioral outcomes   12.16
                                                                    280-281

Mischel's) CAPS a. is a series of closely interconnected traits; b. is characterized by available cognitive and affective units; c. is a collection of points along behavioral; d. is a social unit composed of all the important interpersonal relationships a person has experienced   12.17
                                                                    280

Competency refers to   a. embracing both the cognitive ability to size-up a situation so that one understands how to operate in it effectively and the ability to perform behaviors that will lead to success; b. the cognitive ability to discriminate between relevant and irrelevant situations and the emotional control to delay acts; c. ability to operate efficiently in a situation; d. aptitude in social relations   12.18
                                                                    281

The feature(s) of a situation   a. are the physical factors that one must take into account in pursuing the reinforcements that a situation has to offer; b. is some part of the total situation, such as factors associated with people who are present when the situation is unfolding; c. refer to the range of elements of a situation compared to another situation; d. refer to the specific elements associated with a situation   12.19
                                                                    284

What did Ayduk et al. (2000) discover about "rejection sensitive" (RS) people? a. all were unable to delay gratification (DG); b. they were reluctant to respond to incidences of perceived rejection; c. DG buffered RS people against interpersonal difficulties; d. when provoked, they were "cool responders"   12.20
                                                                    281

Characterizing events   a. is like characterizing other people; we attribute events to them; b. assessing the "personality of events"; c. is placing events in meaningful categories d. is ascertaining the character of those events   12.21
                                                                    298

According to Mischel, who will be successful in a situation? a. whoever is most successful in "reading" the dominant components of the situation; b. the person with the highest level of social intelligence; c. whoever is most familiar with the peculiarities that differentiate the situation from other situations; d. the person who is most familiar with the personalities of the other persons operating in the situation   12.22
                                                                    281

Shoda and Mischel (1993) found which factor to be important in determining individual differences in categorizing situations?

a. people's images of reinforcement; b. the closeness of people's situational relationships with others; c. the complexity of people's thinking about the situations; d. people's goals relevant to the situations   12.23

281-282

What must we remember about a situation's events, according to Mischel?   a. all of those events are outside oneself b. one's own behaviors are important events, because they can change the situation; c. events associated with a situation are stable over time; d. for practical purposes, all of the events associated with a situation are invested in people   12.24

282

To Mischel, a stimulus   a. is a very definite, well defined component of a situation; b. is any impetus for behavior; c. is always physical, like the classroom temperature; d. is always a person, like the classroom professor   12.25

282

For Mischel, expectancy is   a. a belief based on past experience that provides a prediction of future outcomes b. the probability held by the person that reinforcement will occur as a function of a behavior in a specific situation; c. anticipation of future reinforcement values; d. the hopes one has regarding the likelihood of reinforcement in the future
                              12.26

282

A value of an outcome a. is Rotter's method of calculating the payoff for a behavior; b. is how much one prizes results of behavioral or stimulus occurrences in a situation; c. is Mischel's method of calculating the intensity of reactions to a behavior in a situation; d. is an abstract form of qualifying what one wants, behaviorally speaking, from a situation   12.27

282-283

Which of the following shows the importance of values of outcomes? a. people react more rapidly to obtain valued outcomes; b. people react more intensely to obtain valued outcomes; c. some clients will value the therapist's approval and some won't; d. almost all party-goers will value the outcomes associated with small talk at a party   12.28

282

According to Mischel, success   a. is in the eye of other beholders; b. is relative to effort; c. is recasting a situation so that one is able to experience smooth social interactions in it d. is effectively performing the behaviors which yield valued outcomes   12.29

283

Self-regulatory plans are   a. plans to regulate behavior to the satisfaction of others; b. rules established in advance of behavioral performance that guide determining what behavior would be appropriate under particular conditions; c. rules that

determine whether it will be profitable to behave in a specific ways in the presence of particular persons; d. a special form of expectancy   12.30
283

Which of the following is an example of a self-regulatory plan?
a. deciding what to do if, at a party, things are dragging a little
b. planning how to deal with a past behavioral transgression;
c. deciding on how to behave at the time one must behave;
d. working out what to do after an invited speaker doesn't show
12.31
283

Delay of gratification refers to   a. putting off gratification until a more desirable source of gratification is available; b. post-poning future gratifications until the present one have been "consumed"; c. halting pleasureful activity when it is in progress so that one can reconsider long term implications of continued gratification; d. postponing some pleasure so that it can be enjoyed to the maximum degree or in the most optimal way
12.32
283-284

Which of the following is a component of the procedure used by Mischel and his colleagues in investigating delay of gratification? a. a child is placed in a distraction free room and asked whether she or he would prefer a little or much of a desired object; b. children ring a bell to signify that they have succeeded in delaying gratification; c. children rate the desirability of objects, and it is determined whether or not they actually "consume" the highest rated object; d. children are given their least preferred object and allowed to bargain with others for a more desired object   12.33
284

All of the following except one are among the strategies that children adopt to delay gratification. Which is NOT one of their strategies? a. children attempt to bargain with other children present for a more desirable object as a means of delaying "consumption" of the object that they currently possess
b. covering up the preferred objects (M&Ms) or leaving them in the open; c. thinking of the preferred object abstractly (M&Ms are buttons not "yummy") or concretely; d. thinking of the task at hand or the future enjoyability of the preferred object   12.34
284

What important factor did Mischel and colleagues find was significantly correlated with delay of gratification? a. marital happiness; b. number of close friends; c. adolescent cognitive/academic competence; d. attractiveness to the opposite sex   12.35
286

All of the following are problems with trait theory (Big 5) but not with Cognitive Social theory according to Cervone and

colleagues, except one. Which is NOT one of those problems?
a. traits are defined in circular fashion; b. the trait position is
descriptive, rather than explanatory; c. trait theory relies heavily
on context (situations) in it's explanation of trait-behavior
relations; d. trait theory fails to recognize that a person's beliefs
about when it is appropriate to be extraverted determine when
she is extraverted.   12.36
                                                                  284
How did Shoda, Mischel and Wright (1989) show that people
are interactionists?   a. subjects were asked to choose the most
plausible explanations of behavior from definitions of several
such explanations; b. with situations specified, impressions
were more accurate in predicting differences among children in
over-all, actual aggression; c. when people are not allowed to
use qualifiers or conditional statements they were better able to
predict aggression in children; d. people were asked how
another person typically behaves and then how that person
behaves in a specific situation   12.37
                                                                  285
When Wright and Mischel (1988) took a closer look at the "trait"
statements used by subjects to explain behavior, they found
a. a lack of confidence in those statements on the part subjects;
b. that a tentative tone of voice was being used by subjects;
c. qualifiers of statements were being used by subjects
d. subjects often wanted to "take back" their statements;
                                                                 12.38
                                                                  285
What kind of language have Mischel and colleagues come to
use in describing the behavior-situation relations that are
peculiar to particular individuals?   a. logistic; b. probabilistic; c.
inferential; d. if-then   12.39
                                                              286-287
Shoda, Mischel and Wright (1993) scored all of the following
behaviors of summer-camp-children except one. Which one
did they NOT score? a. physical aggression; b. passive
aggression; c. pro-social behavior; d. compliant behavior
                                                                 12.40
                                                                278-9
Shoda, Mischel and Wright (1994) considered all of the
following situations confronting summer-camp-children except
one. Which one did they NOT consider?; a. peer teased,
provoked, or threatened target child; b. adult praised target
child; c. peer tattled on target child; d. adult warned target child
                                                                 12.41
                                                              286-287
Shoda, Mischel and Wright (1993) graphed a child's reactions
to the various situations confronting it on two different
occasions. What did the figure show?   a. a different behavioral
pattern across situations at time 2 compared to time 1; b.

exactly the same behavioral pattern across situations at time 2 that was shown at time 1; c. a behavioral pattern across situations at time 2 that was the opposite of that shown at time 1; d. a behavioral pattern across situations at time 2 that was very similar to the pattern shown at time 1   12.42
288

All of the following are contributions of Mischel, except one. Which is not one of his contributions?   a. he had developed one of the most used personal attribute measures in psychology; b. he challenged the assumption of behavioral stability; c. he has successfully championed the interactionist point of view; d. he caused trait theorists to sharpen their definitions and hone their research procedures   12.43
289

Shoda and Mischel (1993) cite evidence that when Japanese people describe themselves they a. they use trait labels; b. they mix trait labels with behavioral labels; c. they refer to social roles; d. they refer to professional roles   12.44
289

What may an African-American mean when sh/e says to a group of European-Americans, "Whites are racists."? a. literally, all whites are racists; b. most whites are racists; c. actually, few whites are racists and none of those present; d. the white who "yelps" the loudest at the racist charge is suspected of being a racist   12.45
289

What did Menon et al. (1999) find when they compared East Asians with North Americans on the causal attributions for behavior each group makes? a. both attributed cause for behavior to dispositions; b. East Asians made causal attribution for behavior to collectives; c. North Americans made causal attribution for behavior to collectives; d. for only North Americans, to what they attributed behavior depended on circumstances   12.46
289-290

Which is a reason that Mischel will be remembered in the history of personality psychology? He showed   a. that personality tests predict behavior well; b. that delay of gratification is unrelated to most traits; c. that we can conceive of personality free of trait assumptions; d. that children are behaviorally more than we thought   12.47
290

As a youth, Rotter visited "Maslow's library" in Brooklyn and read   a. Mischel; b. Jung; c. Sullivan; d. Freud   12.48
283

Rotter's undergraduate major was   a. psychology; b. literature; c. chemistry; d. sociology   12.49
290

Social psychologist's Solomon Asch got Rotter interested in the work of Gestalt psychologist   a. Lewin; b. Wertheimer; c. Koffka; d. Kohler   12.50
290

What person who also influenced Rogers and Maslow had impact on Rotter? a. Horney; b. Sullivan; c. Adler; d. Jung
12.51
291

What was Rotter's problem when he arrived at the University of Iowa? a. shyness; b. inadequate preparation; c. homesickness d. poverty   12.52
291

Rotter's Ph.D. degree was in   a. experimental psychology; b. clinical psychology; c. developmental psychology; d. biological psychology   12.53
291

Who was counted among Rotter's colleagues at Ohio State University? a. Sullivan; b. Kelly; c. Skinner; d. Murray
12.54
292

Rotter believes   a. people gripped by the forces of a powerful situation show a general trend in behavior; b. people gripped by the forces of powerful internal factors show a general trend in behavior; c. most people are controlled by external factors d. most people are controlled by their unconscious processes
12.55
292

In Phares' (1962) "chance" and "skill"   a. subjects in the chance condition were told to take a chance each trial; b. subjects in the chance condition were told that different buttons would stop the shock on different trials; c. subjects in the skill condition were told that different buttons would stop the shock on different trials; d. subjects in the skill condition were asked to exercise their skills on each trial   12.56
292

In the Gambler's Fallacy a. people believe that in the long run they will win; b. people believe that in the short run they will win; c. people expect that a failure on one attempt means that failure on a subsequent attempt becomes more likely; d. people expect that a failure on one attempt means that success on a subsequent attempt becomes more likely
12.57
292

People in the "chance condition" of Phares' (1962) experiment behaved differently than people in the "skill condition" a. without qualification; b. only in the case of male subjects; c. but there were considerable individual differences within each condition; d. and there were few individual differences within each condition   12.58

All except one of the following are among the basic assumptions of Rotter's theory. Which is NOT one if his basic assumptions?; a. the unit of study of personality is the interaction between the person and her or his environment and physiology; b. personality constructs are not dependent for explanation on constructs in any other field; c. in order to understand personality it is only necessary to study the environment in which people are embedded; d. not all behavior of an organism may be usefully described with personality constructs   12.59
292

Who performed best in the skill and chance condition?
a. females; b. skill condition subjects; c. chance conditions subjects; d. reinforcement condition subjects   12.60
285

Reinforcement refers to   a. anything that has an influence on the occurrence, direction or kind of behavior; b. rewards for performing behavior; c. aversive stimulation delivered after the performance of behavior; d. the degree of preference for any reinforcement to occur if the possibilities of different reinforcements are equal   12.61
292

Reinforcement value refers to   a. anything that has an influence on the occurrence, direction or kind of behavior; b. rewards for performing behavior; c. aversive stimulation delivered after the performance of behavior; d. the degree of preference for any reinforcement to occur if the possibilities of different reinforcements are equal   12.62
292

A psychological situation is   a. the physical circumstance in which the person behaves; b. characterized in a way peculiar to a person, allowing her to categorize it with or differentiate it from other situations; c. social circumstance in which the person must decide how to behave vis a vis other persons in the setting; d. the social circumstanceof the person's behavior
12.63
293

To Rotter, situations   a. are more physical than psychological b. more social than psychological; c. in the eye of the beholderd. without an analog in the psychological realm 12.64
293

According to Rotter, expectancy is   a. the probability held by a person that a particular reinforcement will occur as a function of a specific behavior in a specific situation; b. the likelihood that whatever one does will result in a reinforcement, provided only that she or he is attentive to magnitude and value of the reinforcement; c. looking ahead; d. eyes on the top of the head
12.65

A generalized expectancy is a. an expectancy that generalizes from one person to another person; b. an expectancy that generalizes from one situation to another situation; c. an expectancy that holds for a number of situations that are dissimilar to one another to some degree; d. an expectancy that holds for a number of situations that are similar to one another to some degree   12.66

When are generalized expectancies likely to operate? a. in most situations; b. in familiar situations; c. in new or ambiguous situations; d. in all situations   12.67

Locus of control refers to a. the degree to which people expect that reinforcement is dependent on their conscious processes versus the degree they expect it is due to unconscious processes; b. whether control is impossible, probable, or highly likely; c. whether the possibilities for control are stable, internal, and global, or unstable, external, and specific; d. the degree to which people expect that reinforcement is dependent on their characteristics versus the degree they expect it is due to luck, fate, chance, or powerful others   12.68

External control refers to   a. the perception that reinforcement is dependent on one's behavior or characteristics; b. the perception that reinforcement is dependent on luck, chance, fate, or powerful others; c. whether control is impossible, probable, or highly likely; d. whether the possibilities for control are stable, internal, and global, or unstable, external, and specific   12.69

Internal control refers to a. the perception that reinforcement is dependent on one's behavior or characteristics; b. the perception that reinforcement is dependent on luck, chance, fate, or powerful others; c. whether control is impossible, probable, or highly likely; d. whether the possibilities for control are stable, internal, and global, or unstable, external, and specific   12.70

Rotter points out that external and internal locus of control are NOT equivalent to a. classical conditioning orientation b. instrumental conditioning orientation; c. traits; d. levels of consciousness;   12.71

All except one of the following are alternatives for items on the I-E scale. Which is NOT an alternative on the scale? a. I'm a pretty confident person. I can make things happen; b. I live my life one day at a time; c. My voice is heard above the crowd d. I'm pretty much indifferent.;   12.72

All of the following are characteristics of externals, relative to internals, except one. Which is NOT a characteristic? a. conformist and compliant; b. maladjusted; c. worn out and uptight; d. low anxiety 12.73

Who is most likely to abuse substances? a. internals; b. externals; c. internals or externals, depending on gender d. internals, but a firm conclusion awaits an I-E measure specifically referring to alcohol use situations 12.74

What did Mamlin, Harris and Case (2001) find when they studied the belief that people with learning disabilities (LD) feel a lack of control of their destinies? a. there was no evidence bearing on the subject; b. actually they tend to feel in control of their destinies; c. they found serious fault with the sources of evidence for this belief; d. they confirmed this belief 12.75

All except one of the following are true of the relationship between locus of control and divorce. Which is NOT true of that relationship? a. married people are more internal than either single of divorced people; b. internals showed less post-divorce distress than externals; c. people who are internal for marital satisfaction are more active and direct in problem solving than externals; d. externals are less likely to have a divorce 12.76

All the following are true of recent research on locus of control (LC) and computer use/mastery and LC and health issues. Which is NOT true of that research? a. internals have positive attitudes toward computers; b. LC played no role in the relationship between computer attitudes and experience with computers; c. identical twins were alike on LC scores; d. a genetic/environmental factor was related to a "Powerful Other's" scale 12.77

Which of the following is a correct description of results of studies designed to change externals? a. teachers who were more origins than pawns after some training they received, experienced greater professional advancement ; b. the less origin the classroom environment, the greater was children's self-worth, cognitive competence, and mastery motivation; c. origin-like behavior was related to high aggression; d. students became more external after four half-hour sessions centering on "personal growth experiences" 12.78

Which is NOT an item on the I-E scale? a. My voice is heard above the crowd.; b. I steer clear of everything from bingo to

poker.; c. I don't care very much about anything.; d. Me, I stick with the winners.
12.79
295-296

Which is NOT an item on the I-E scale? a. I plan my day, my week, my month, and my year. b. I rely on neither luck or effort. c. People just seem to drown me out. d. If you are lucky, you're rich; if not, join the crowd.
12.80
295-296

Which was not an item on the I-E scale? a. I think life is partly a gamble, and partly due to our efforts? b. Sometimes I feel powerless, the victim of mysterious forces. c. I like to compete because if I win, I can say "I did it." d. It's really quite simple: if you're good and work hard, you succeed.
12.81
298-299

Rotter was a pioneer   a. in promoting the existence and viability of personality traits; b. in considering multiple determinants of behavior and the advantages that control over circumstances provide people; c. in considering social factors; d. in renouncing the Oedipal Complex and Penis Envy without going so far as to reject the unconscious
12.82
300

Social desirability (SD)--the need to please others by displaying the characteristics that are valued in out society--is a problem for Rotter, because   a. externals are more prone to SD than internals; b. internals are more prone to SD than externals; c. in so far as SD contaminates the I-E Scale, it may measure response distortion rather than a personality factor d. his research have been especially prone to SD because he tells subjects which end of the scale is the "good" end
12.83
300

Defensive externals   a. believe that they are controlled by fate or luck; b. are competitive, do well on tests, and endorse external items, but only to blame others for their failures; c. are no problem for Rotter's theory; d. are really the only kind of external because passive externals are so rare they are practically non-existent
12.84
300-301

All except one of the following are reasons why Rotter will be remembered in the future. Which is NOT a reason he will be remembered? a. he is the founder and only proponent of the social learning point of view; b. his I-E scale; c. his recognition that the stability of personal attributes is limited; d. his belief in the importance of considering the interplay of personal attributes and environmental factors
Extra Items
12.85
278

Young Walter Mischel preferred _____ to S-R psychology when he selected reading material. (fill the blank from below)

a. Jung; b. existentialism; c. Marx; d. romanticism   12.86
279

Mischel reflected on the observation that people perceive cross-situational consistency in their own and other people's behavior   a. but scientific observations do not support consistency; b. and they are basically perceiving correctly; c. but they are incorrect in regard to other's people behavior; d. but they are incorrect in regard to their own behavior
12.87
279

Why are we, in Western Society, obsessed with "consistency"? a. the reasons are buried in the past; b. there is a brain mechanism in people of European heritage that dictates consistency; c. consistency means such valued characteristics as "being reliable"; d. it is a habit we learn as children in order to stay out of trouble   12.88
282

Should you loudly proclaim that what one or your professors is saying in class is nonsense, which Mischelian concept would immediately come into play? a. locus of control; b. self-efficacy c. personality system; d. expectancy   12.89
285

"Discriminative facility" is   a. sensitivity to subtle cues of a situation that affect behavior; b. negatively correlated with social intelligence; c. common among very young children; d. unrelated to being good at "if...then" relations   12.90
280

Which of the following happens to each of us when someone slaps a label on us? a. we have been understood; b. we have been exploited; c. we have been offered encouragement d. we have been stereotyped   12.91
287

The children in Mischel's summer camp   a. showed remarkably high behavioral consistency, but their circumstances were unusual; b. showed not even a hint that they might repeat behaviors over time; c. showed patterns of behavior across situations that they repeated when they encountered the same situations again; d. showed consistency across some sets of situations, but inconsistency across other sets   12.92
288

What ensures that "interactionism" will one day actually reign supreme in the area of personality? a. it is a natural replacement for the notion "trait"; b. it is the only reasonable point of view; c. it is gaining strength among graduate students in psychology; d. it is now being given considerable "lip service" by personality psychologists   12.93
289

Why is it important to consider "language" when studying personality cross-culturally? a. because it is essential to get good translations of tests from English to native languages; b. language can shape cognitive processes; c. it is necessary to find out the ways in which a native language resembles the language of a personality theory; d. language as the medium of communication is "culture free"   12.94
                                                                  289

When asked to explain others' behavior, Indian Hindus mention   a. the context of others' behavior; b. social roles of the behavioral performers; c. traits; d. religious figures who behave similarly to those others   12.95
                                                                  289

Which of the following relates to a charge of "racist" seemingly hurled at "all whites"? a. you can teach old dogs new tricks which they can't unlearn; b. what comes around goes around c. throw a stone into a pack of dogs and the one that yelps is the one that was hit; d. what will be be will be   12.96
                                                                  281

Mischel has been accused of over-stating his case for   a. trait-like cognitions; b. the rejection of trait-like consistency c. variation of cognition with variation of culture; d. the stability of behavior in a situation from one occasion to occasion
                                                             12.97
                                                                  290

Which is Mischel's greatest contribution? a. demonstrating that therapy does not work; b. showing that behavior is temporally consistent; c. arguing that it takes at least 100 traits to account for personality; d. showing that there is consistency in the pattern of behaviors a person displays across situations
                                                             12.98
                                                                  299

Which did the external profiled in the text say about himself? a. I'm the smartest man I know.; b. I've tried to help people plan for their future.; c. It's better to be lucky than good.; d. People who try too hard irritate others.   12.99
                                                                  291

Why did Rotter leave Ohio State for the U. of Connecticut? a. his family was back East; b. he was no longer able to work with George Kelly; c. he found the experimental emphasis at Ohio State too oppressive; d. he found the fascist spirit of Communist-baiting Senator Joe McCarthy to be less significant in the East   12.100
                                                                  299

When did the did the external profiled in the text change jobs? a. after going to school to acquire technical skills; b. when his daughter married and moved near a factory that was hiring; c. when he sold himself to a prospective employer; d. when he saw a circled ad in a newspaper's classified section   12.101

As to behavioral consistency, it follows from Rotter's view that a. there is no observable behavioral consistency; b. a person may show some consistency across situations he/she sees as highly similar; c. some people are very consistent, while others are very inconsistent; d. consistency is in the "eye of the beholder"
12.102

According to Rotter, all of the following are ways that a person may categorize classical music, except one. Which is NOT a way that classical music is likely to be classified   a. a peculiar kind of vibration in the air; b. entertainment; c. a scholarly endeavor not unlike reading classic literature; d. a waste of time
12.103

Which would Rotter never say about locus of control? a. it has two extremes "internal" and "external" with many points between them; b. the two extremes are like skill vs. luck c. either extreme is like a "trait"; d. people would to score in and around the mid-point between the two extremes
12.104

All of the following are advantages of Cognitive Social Theory (CST) over trait theory (Big 5), according to Cervone's group, except one. Which is NOT one of those advantages? a. CST requires little information to predict behavior; b. CST recognizes that a trait "conscientiousness" doesn't mean the same thing even to the same person operating in different situations; d. CST refers to cognitive-affective processes that operate in sync in response to situational stimulation

12.1,a	12.49,a	12.96,b
12.2,c	12.50,c	12.97,d
12.3,d	12.51,d	12.98,c
12.4,d	12.52,b	12.99,d
12.5,c	12.53,b	12.100,d
12.6,a	12.54,a	12.101,b
12.7,a	12.55,b	12.102,a
12.8,d	12.56,d	12.103,c
12.9,c	12.57,c	12.104,a
12.10,d	12.58,c	
12.11,c	12.59,b	
12.12,b	12.60,a	
12.13,d	12.61,d	
12.14,c	12.62,b	
12.15,b	12.63,c	
12.16,b	12.64,a	
12.17,a	12.65,d	
12.18,b	12.66,c	
12.19,c	12.67,d	
12.20,c	12.68,b	
12.21,a	12.69,a	
12.22,d	12.70,c	
12.23,b	12.71,d	
12.24,a	12.72,d	
12.25,a	12.73,d	
12.26,b	12.74,c	
12.27,c	12.75,d	
12.28,d	12.76,b	
12.29,b	12.77,a	
12.30,a	12.78,c	
12.31,d	12.79,b	
12.32,a	12.80,a	
12.33,a	12.81,b	
12.34,c	12.82,c	
12.35,d	12.83,b	
12.36,b	12.84,a	
12.37,c	*Extra Items*	
12.38,d	12.85,b	
12.39,b	12.86,a	
12.40,c	12.87,c	
12.41,d	12.88,d	
12.42,a	12.89,a	
12.43,c	12.90,d	
12.44,d	12.91,c	
12.45,b	12.92,d	
12.46,c	12.93,b	
12.47,d	12.94,a	
12.48,c	12.95,c	

Chapter 13

Multiple Choice Items for the Chapter on Bandura

13.1
304

Bandura's theory, relative to that of Rotter and Mischel is
a. more focussed; b. less extensive; c. broader; d. more tuned

13.2
305

The still made by fellow Yukon highway workers may have
stirred Bandura's interest in   a. brewing; b. mechanics;
c. constructionism; d. innovation;

13.3
305

What was remarkable about Bandura's early schooling? a. he
went to private schools; b. he went to a school for
disadvantaged children; c. his school was rated one of the best
in his country; d. he went to a school so small, he was forced to
learn on his own

13.4
305

What was all the rage during Bandura's time at the University
of Iowa? a. learning theories; b. Freudian theory; c. the new
cognitive movement; d. existentialism

13.5
305-306

All except one of the following show how chance played a role
in Bandura's life. Which does NOT illustrate the role of chance
in his life?; a. early arrival at the University narrowed his
choices to taking a psychology class; he became hooked on
psychology; b. had he not been playing golf on a certain day,
he would not have met his wife-to-be; c. during a conditioning
experiment, the automatic equipment broke, but the monkeys
learned anyway by observing each other; d. his wife happened
to be working in a hospital where the "Great Imposter" played
doctor

13.6
306

Which of the following is an indication of Bandura's warmth
and humanity? a. he and his wife have many children; b. he is
very religious; c. he loves poetry; d. on his 70th birthday,
students at St. Edwards University, who were studying his
theory, sent him a birthday card

13.7
309

Observational learning is   a. learning how people and animals
make observations; b. learning by observing models as they
perform useful behavior; c. making observations about the
learning processes; d. a special form of operant learning in
which cognition plays a role

13.8

306-308
Bandura's theory focuses on a. the consistency of behavior
b. both the variability and stability of behavior; c. the variability
of behavior; d. the magnitude of behavior in proportion to
environmental influence; 13.9
306-308
In social cognitive theory a. people function as contributors to
their own motivation, behavior, and development within a
network of reciprocally interacting influences; b. the balance
and counterbalance of internal and external forces operate to
influence both the emotional and cognitive processes as the
individual attempts to adapt to her or his environment; c. the
order of importance of factors is indicated in the label: social
first, cognition second; c. human functioning is emphasized
because "cognition" precludes the consideration of animal
functioning 13.10
306
Person factors, behavior, and the environment are a. engaged
in an adversarial relationship; b. are independent entities
c. are locked into a reciprocal relationship; d. are enveloped in
"two at a time relationships": behavior-environment;
environment-person factors, etc. 13.11
307
In terms of behavior and neurobiological functions
a. causation is one way: neurobiology affects behavior; b. by
the time behavior emerges, it has "lost touch" with
neurobiology; c. to paraphrase Freud, "behavior knows nothing
of neurons" (nerve cells); d. behavior influences neurobiology:
frequent exposure to something can reshape the brain
13.12
307
In terms of environment and neurobiology a. causation is one
way: environment affects neurobiology; b. causation is one
way: neurobiology affects environment; c. environment can
affect neurobiology: women living together find that their
menstrual cycles become synchronized; d. neurobiology can
affect environment: "figments of people's imaginations" such as
UFOs have been know to literally make an imprint on the
environment 13.13
308
Personal agency refers to a. a person acting as an agent on
her or his behalf; b. coming to believe that one can make things
happen that will benefit oneself and others; c. the ability of
certain people to affect their environment in a way that benefits
others; d. the aspiration of most people regarding their ability to
change their environment 13.14
308
"Proxy agency" means" a. the same thing as "collective
agency"; b. an approximation to agency; c. an agent who is

proximal to oneself; d. enlisting others to help control
circumstances affecting one's life   13.15
                                                       309

Forethought refers to   a. anticipation of likely consequences of
future actions; b. eyes in the back of the head as opposed to
eyes up front; c. learning that thinking ahead is the best way to
understand the past; c. the observation that learning is a matter
of far-reaching concentration   13.16
                                                       309

Why is a child's copying of her parents behavior not mere
mimicry? a. she always makes major changes in it; b. she is
not conscious that she is copying, she just goes thoughtlessly
through the motions of copying behavior; c. she is always
coached in the behavior by her parents; d. she has awareness
of what parents have done and thoughtfulness about the
implications of what's done   13.17
                                                       310

"Model" (Bandura) refers to   a. a framework of ideas, as
opposed to a full-blown theory; b. ways to framing an idea or
thought; c. a person who performs a behavior for an audience,
showing how to do it and why it is beneficial; d. a sort of
prototypical behavior that stands as an exemplar for others to
adopt   13.18
                                                       310

"Modeling" refers to   a. displaying a framework of ideas, as
opposed to relating a full-blown theory; b. defining ways to
frame an idea or thought; c. the act of performing a behavior
before one or more observers; d. offering a sort of prototypical
behavior that stands as an exemplar for others to adopt
                                                       13.19
                                                       310-311

How do people react to a model's behavior? a. they turn it over
in their heads, relating it to information they already have; b.
they passively soak it up; c. they absorb it, as in osmosis
d. they mimic it, and in the process, learn it, integrate it, and
prepare to use it   13.20
                                                       310

In "symbolic modeling,"   a. an object comes to symbolize a
model; b. verbal and pictorial means are used to convey
information necessary for the adoption of behavior; c. a
behavior is presented in symbolic form instead of the usual
concrete form; d. models symbolize other models   13.21
                                                       310-311

What happens when an observer adopts a behavior from a
model? a. the behavior is simply recorded in the motor systems
of the brain; b. the behavior is immediately and compulsively
practiced; c. the behavior is immediately assimilated to other
previously possessed behaviors so that it loses its former

identity; d. a internal representation of the behavior is created and that representation is honed and refined   13.22
311

What kind of model is a person likely to observe? a. anyone in a relevant setting performing relevant behavior; b. successful models: those who have done well generally and on specific tasks; c. anyone who is performing attractive behavior d. persons who are similar to oneself or share one's life situation, regardless of their behavioral effectiveness
13.23
311

An incentive is   a. any thing, concrete or abstract, that creates anticipation of a positive outcome following behavioral performance; b. a payoff following successful performance of behavior or sequence of behaviors; c. a feeling of anticipation, however vague, regarding a up-coming, significant event in the life of the person; d. roughly the same thing as reinforcement
13.24
312

What may be more important than rewards from others? a. rewards from institutions, such as the government; b. rewards that are symbolic rather than actual: the perception of others' approval; c. the knowledge that rewards would have been forthcoming had others witnessed one's performance; d. self-reward   13.25
312

Goals (Bandura) are   a. essential to a firm sense of self; b. illusions that must be eliminated, if people are to succeed; c. all that one needs to succeed; d. anticipated achievements that are in line with current personal standards   13.26
312

Self-regulatory processes are (Bandura)   a. restricted to delay of gratification; b. internal, cognitive/affective functions that guide and govern efforts toward goal attainment; c. are the external forces and pressures that ensure the individual will adhere to her/his goals; d. are a sub-category of incentives
13.27
312

Self-efficacy is   a. a more general kind of self-esteem b. a means of becoming more efficient; c. beliefs about one's ability to perform behaviors yielding expected outcomes d. feelings that one can perform adequately as long as one experiences support for important others   13.28
313

Participant modeling   a. is participating in research as a model b. is when a person with low self-efficacy imitates a model's efficacious behavior; c. is when several models perform the same behavior for a single observer; d. is when an observer

takes on the role of model and models a behavior for the
benefit of the person who was previously the model   13.29
314

All except one of the following were used as examples
Bandura used to illustrate resilience in the face of set-backs.
Which is NOT one of Bandura's examples of people who have
persisted in the face of failure? a. Steve Forbes; b. Robert
Goddard; c. Van Gogh; d. e. e. cummings   13.30
313

In vicarious expectancy learning   a. one learns a behavior by
observing another person; b. one learns to expect what a
model is likely to do in a particular situation; c. people adopt
other persons' expectancies concerning future events
d. people expect to learn from a model because of verbal
promises of future performances on the part of the model
13.31
313

Response facilitation refers to; a. processes that make a
response easier to perform; b. facilitating the responses of
others as they perform those responses; c. old responses
being disinhibited as a result of watching a model's
performance; d. people facilitating the responses of other
people in a reciprocating process
13.32
315

Diffusion of innovation   a. occurs when prestigious models try
something new, displaying its benefits for others; b. is defusing
a new behavior before it catches on; c. is advertising an old
behavior as if it were a new one; d. is the random spread of
new and old behavior so that the origin of each is obscured
13.33
315

According to Bandura, which is a limit on adopting a novel
behavior? a. even simple behavior may be obsolete by the
time one learns it; b. one may lack the skills to perform the new
behavior; c. people tend to adopt "what's new" whether it has
any benefits to it; d. by the time one adopts a behavior it is no
longer novel   13.34
315

Extrinsic rewards refer to   a. rewards from within the individual
b. rewards originating outside the individual; c. rewards at the
top of the hierarchy of rewards; c. rewards with especially great
longevity   13.35
315-316

Intrinsic rewards refer to a. rewards from within the individual
b. rewards originating outside the individual; c. rewards at the
top of the hierarchy of rewards; c. rewards with especially great
longevity   13.36
315

According to Bandura, longterm maintenance of a behavior depends largely on   a. repeated practice of the behavior; b. how long ago the behavior was adopted; c. how complex the behavior happens to be; d. developing intrinsic rewards for the behavior   13.37
                                                                                      315

Intrinsic motivation refers to   a. desire for intrinsic rewards b. motivation originating outside the individual; c. motivation at the top of the hierarchy of motivations; c. motivations with especially great longevity   13.38
                                                                                      315-316

How do we know that intrinsic motivation is at work? a. behavior is persistent in the absence of obvious external rewards; b. one must observe the persistence of a behavior in the absence of external rewards and behavioral alternatives c. one must observe that the strength of the behavior grows as a function of the amount of time devoted to the behavior; d. the behavior must be unusual and unique to the performer
                                                                                      13.39
                                                                                      316

Self-evaluation refer to   a. roughly the same thing as "self-esteem"; b. adopting and applying other's evaluations of oneself; c. setting up a set of criteria for determining how well one is doing relative to comparable others; d. evaluating one's performance at various points along the way to task completion and issuing a judgment of its value   13.40
                                                                                      314

Who said to Hadley Cantril that he "learned many years ago never to waste time trying to convince my colleagues"? a. Robert Goddard; b. James Joyce; c. Auguste Rodin; d. Albert Einstein   13.41
                                                                                      316

Vicarious reinforcement refers to   a. "middle-man" reinforcement; b. reinforcement that is secondary to primary reinforcement; c. when one observes another person being rewarded for performing a behavior; c. when one observes oneself being rewarded for performing a behavior   13.42
                                                                                      316

Social comparison refers to a. comparing one's behavior to the social norms of one's society relevant to that behavior; b. comparing the social norms of different societies that are relevant to a particular behavior; c. determining how well one is doing in life by comparing oneself to others sharing one's life situation; d. determining how well someone is doing by comparing that person with others sharing her or his life situation   13.43
                                                                                      316

Which is most likely to increase the impact of a model's behavior on observers? a. the degree to which the behavioral

performance is emphatic; b. whether the model is rewarded for the behavioral performance; c. how long it takes the model to perform the behavior; d. the magnitude of the model's behavior
13.44
316

Defensive behaviors are (Bandura) a. adopted in order to cope with unpleasant events that are anticipated on future occasions; b. the behavioral manifestation of Freud's defense mechanisms; c. employed to ward off unwanted behaviors of others; d. employed in order to protect the individual's self-esteem from change
13.45
316

What is associated with defensive behavior (Bandura)? a. anxiety, initially; b. anxiety, continually; c. displacement d. rationalizations
13.46
316-317

Defensive behavior (Bandura) is difficult to change because a. it has such a long reinforcement history; b. it is usually such ingrained behavior; c. it allows avoidance of unpleasant events in the future; d. it ensures that unpleasant feelings from the past will not return
13.47
317

Why take a stuffed bear to bed? a. it increases the child's self-efficacy; b. it substitutes for the absent parental figure c. it keeps the wolves away; d. it it is an effective self-exonerative process
13.48
317

Self-efficacy is a. another name for "self-confidence"; b. useful in dealing with negative, but not positive, behaviors; c. a process for becoming very efficient; d. a self-regulatory mechanism
13.49
317

A phobia is a. a fear of something scary; b. a problem for most people; c. a very minor psychological disorder; d. an irrational fear
13.50
317

Self-efficacy is a. rarely researched; b. heavily researched c. little supported by research; d. aimed at negative behaviors only
13.51
310

People who are spider phobics a. have a trivial problem; b. have a problem that cannot be dealt with in a few hours of work with a model; c. may have an incapacitating problem d. need long-term psychotherapy
13.52
317-318

All except one of the following are behaviors of spider phobics in the Bandura, Reese, and Adams (1982) study of means to change phobics. Which is NOT one of those behaviors? a. one phobic nearly destroyed her house trying to bash spiders;

b. one phobic could not take a bath for fear of spiders in the tub; c. one phobic would vomit for hours at exposure even to a picture of a spider; d. one phobic leaped out of the car she was driving upon noticing a spider in the car   13.53
317

What was the first step in the Bandura et al spider phobic study?   a. show subjects photos of spiders; b. assure subjects that they will not have to touch a spider during the course of the study; c. have subjects touch a spider right away so that the worse part is over quickly; d. give subjects a behavioral avoidance test to determine their initial level of self-efficacy
13.54
318

Which of the following was an item found on the behavioral avoidance test the Bandura et al spider phobic study?
a. stepping on a spider; b. allowing a spider to crawl on subjects' laps; c. subjects imagined that a spider was eating them; d. pretending that a spider was not present   13.55
318

Which of the following was a result of the Bandura et al spider phobics study? a. several subjects failed to ever even approach a spider; b. regardless of efficacy level, subjects' observations of the model allowed them to finally interact with the spider; c. a few subjects immediately were able to handle a spider; d. self-efficacy predicted performance almost perfectly
13.56
322

Bandura, and the Italian team plus Carnillo Regalia (2001) studied the relationship between transgressive behavior (e.g., lying) and several other factors. What did they find? a. prosocialness was unrelated to transgressive behavior; b. self-regulatory efficacy was directly, positively related to trangressive behavior; c. academic efficacy was positively related to transiveness behavior; d. social efficacy was negatively related to transgressive behavior through prosocialness   13.57
318

All of the following are among the findings of the Bandura et al spider phobics study, except one. Which is NOT among those findings? a. by the end of the experiment, only subjects in the high efficacy condition showed high self-efficacy; b. there was a very direct relationship between subjects' assigned level of self-efficacy and their behavior performance after treatment; c. if a subject indicated that she felt she could at most place her hands on the inverted bowl containing the spider, she could not go beyond that behavior; d. phobics were, by the end of the experiment, able to touch a creature that had terrorized them for a lifetime   13.58
312

All except one of the following were findings in the Wiedenfeld, O'Leary, Bandura, Brown, Levene, and Raska (1990) study of snake phobics that was patterned after the earlier study. Which was NOT a finding? a. self-efficacy stayed at rock bottom during the pre-test phase; b. slow growth of perceived self-efficacy was associated with sluggish immune-system functioning; c. high heart acceleration was associated with lower immunological status; d. the slower the growth of self-efficacy, the lower were cortisol levels   13.59
319

Rather than promoting the view of addicts as powerless drug abuser, what does Bandura suggest? a. empower them
b. teach them delay tactics; c. get them away from enablers
d. give them some new incentives   13.60
319-320

What did Epel, Bandura and Zimbardo (1999c) find out about homeless people? a. they were all oriented to the past; b. those with high self-efficacy searched more for housing; c. those high in present orientation searched for housing for a shorter time; d. those with low self-efficacy stayed in temporary housing for a shorter time   13.61
320

All of the following were included in Schwarzer's (2001) model for changing health-related behavior, except one. Which was NOT included in the model? a. perceived health self-efficacy; b. outcome expectancy; c. time orientation; d. recovery from set-backs   13.62
321

Bandura and his Italian colleagues (2001) found all except one of the following to fall along the path to children's careers in the medical professions. Which was NOT found along that path? a. children's academic aspirations; b. parental social efficacy; c. children's social efficacy; d. children's educational/medical efficacy   13.63
321

All except one of the following was a finding of the study by the Italian team, Bandura, and Zimbardo (2000) on pro-socialness and aggressiveness? Which was NOT a finding of that study? a. aggressiveness had no effects on academic achievement; b. prosocialness had a direct, positive effect on academic achievement; c. early academic achievement was unrelated to later academic achievement; d. prosocialness was unrelated to popularity
13.64
320-321

The Bandura et al (1996a) study in Itlay that investigated what contributes to academic achievement included all of the following variables, except one. Which was NOT included?;

a. socioeconomic status; b. physical maturity; c. children's academic efficacy; d. parents academic aspirations for their children   13.65
                                                                        321

In the Bandura et al Italian study aimed at finding out what relates to depression in children, which was NOT an overall finding for boys? a. boys interpersonal relations were importantly related to depression; b. boys with low academic efficacy had low academic achievement; c. boys who were low in cooperativeness with peers tended to be depressed; d. boys wih high problem behavior tended to be depressed   13.66
                                                                        323

What does dehumanization allow people to do? a. ignore the consequences of others' actions; b. be indifferent to others c. kill, torture, and unjustly imprison; d. go about our business
                                                                        13.67
                                                                        324

Which of the following is an advantageous comparison? a. comparing oneself to people of great wealth; b. comparing what certain people do to what other people do; c. comparing oneself to similar others in the hope that one does a little bit better than them; d. excusing deplorable behavior by declaring that others do it also   13.68
                                                                        324

Which of the following is an example of euphemistic labeling? a. anti-personnel device; b. European American; c. loaded gun; d. Kodak moment   13.69
                                                                        324

Saying that gays and lesbians brought persecution on themselves is an example of   a. euphemistic labeling; b. gradualistic moral disengagement; c. moral justification; d. blaming the victim   13.70
                                                                        324

Which one of the following is a definition of displacement or a definition of diffusion of responsibility? a. spreading the responsibility among actors for having been forced to perform an act; b. displacing, for example, aggression onto other than the person who attacked oneself; c. spreading the responsibility for taking some action to other persons present d. displacing oneself from the scene of a reprehensible act
                                                                        13.71
                                                                        324

Which of the following amounts to moral justification? a. saying that victims of AIDS are at fault for their condition; b. using phrases like "body count"; c. placing the blame for one's deplorable acts onto others; d. seeking support for one's deplorable acts in the Bible   13.72
                                                                        325

In symbolic modeling   a. models are always humans
b. models may be non-human; c. a model symbolizes a need of
the observer; d. primitive cognitive processes are involved
13.90
311
An incentive is   a. food presented after "proper behavior" has
been performed; b. money paid following work performed; c.
praise following a kind deed; d. an offer of money to be paid
after a subsequent favor has been performed
13.91
312
What leads to effortful performance? (Bandura)   a. setting
goals and getting feedback on progress toward them
b. being promised relief from some aversive condition;
c. having had a history of effortful performance; d. cooperating
with others   13.92
312
All of the following are attempts at self-influence, except one.
Which is NOT an attempt at self-influence? a. bribing others to
praise oneself; b. self-praise; c. acceptance of challenge
d. valuation of personal standards   13.93
313
The most efficient method for boosting self-efficacy is
a. concrete reinforcements following performances;
b. performance accomplishment; c. classical conditioning
d. systematic desensitization   13.94
314
What do many famous and acclaimed writers have in common
(Bandura)? a. almost all became rich during their lifetimes
b. many of them were repeatedly rejected by publishers before
their writings were finally writings published; c. most were
scorned in their own lifetimes; d. many of them were neurotic or
psychotic, conditions that made the creative artists they
became   13.95
314
Resilience is   a. roughly the same thing as persistence;
b. mental toughness analogous to physical toughness;
c. the ability to absorb rejection and failure, but still maintain
the belief that one can accomplish what one desires to do
d. the continuation of important pursuits with just as much vigor
after success as before succeeding   13.96
323
Self-exonerative processes refer to   a. rationalization in a
social form; b. seeking to induce others to exonerate oneself
from blame for inhumane acts; c. cognitive activities that allow
people to dissociate themselves from the outcomes of their
acts; d. public attempts to persuade others that one should be
exonerated for inhumane acts because they were done at the
behest of authority   13.97

Why do some people spend so much time watching TV (Bandura)? a. they lack alternatives; b. it is intrinsically motivating; c. TV has been proven more educational than books; d. they got the habit as children and cannot shake it
13.98

319

What did Epel, Bandura, and Zimbardo (1999c) find to be related to likelihood to enroll in school among homeless people? a. high self-efficacy; b. future orientation; c. academic efficacy; d. prosocialness
13.99

320

How is self-efficacy related to health? a. people who are generally efficacious are more resistant to disease than others; b. it isn't: research by Bandura and colleagues failed to show any such relationship, just as they predicted; c. one study showed that rapid acquisition of self-efficacy was associated with relatively high immunological status; d. self-efficacy affects health by acting through the self: a resilient self was associated with higher health status
13.100

323-324

What did an experimenter in Bandura, Underwood, and Fromson (1975) call would-be recipients of electric shock that got them shocked more than others? a. perceptive; b. animalistic; c. understanding; d. insensitive
13.101

323

Why do some people steal and commit other crimes (Bandura)? a. such behavior may be among the few alternatives open to them; b. their self-efficacy is low because of ineffective parenting; c. they are reacting against the coercion that they feel is being used against them; d. relative to other outcomes, the incentives are low and the likelihood of negative future outcomes is high;
13.102

323

Rather than "character flaws" what explains humans inhumanity to humans (Bandura)? a. inherent pessimism; b. religious radicalism; c. a game of mental gymnastics; d. a moral blunting coming with witnessing brutal acts
13.103

326

Men beat women because a. of too much testosterone; b. brutality is natural to them; c. women allow them to do it; d. of self-exonerative processes

13.1,c	13.49,d	13.95,c
13.2,d	13.50,b	13.96,c
13.3,d	13.51,c	13.97,a
13.4,a	13.52,a	13.98,b
13.5,c	13.53,d	13.99,c
13.6,d	13.54,b	13.100,b
13.7,b	13.55,d	13.101,a
13.8,b	13.56,d	13.102,c
13.9,a	13.57,a	13.103,d
13.10,c	13.58,d	
13.11,d	13.59,b	
13.12.c	13.60,b	
13.13,b	13.61,c	
13.14,d	13.62,b	
13.15,a	13.63,d	
13.16,d	13.64,a	
13.17,c	13.65,a	
13.18,c	13.66,c	
13.19,a	13.67,d	
13.20,b	13.68,a	
13.21,d	13.69,d	
13.22,b	13.70,c	
13.23,a	13.71,d	
13.24,d	13.72,b	
13.25,d	13.73,a	
13.26,b	13.74,c	
13.27,c	13.75,b	
13.28,b	13.76,c	
13.29,a	13.77,a	
13.30,c	13.78,c	
13.31,c	13.79,d	
13.32,a	13.80,a	
13.33,b	13.81,d	
13.34,b	13.82,c	
13.35,a	13.83,b	
13.36,d	13.84,d	
13.37,a	13.85,b	
13.38,b	*Extra*	
13.39,d	*Items*	
13.40,d	13.86,c	
13.41,c	13.87,b	
13.42,c	13.88,d	
13.43,b	13.89,b	
13.44,a	13.90,d	
13.45,a	13.91,a	
13.46,c	13.92,a	
13.47,c	13.93,b	
13.48,d	13.94,b	

Chapter 14

Multiple Choice Items for the Chapter on Skinner

14.1
331

Behaviorism is a. a school of thought that is centered around the affective implications of behavior; b. concerned with the cognitive implications of behavior; c. a school of thought founded by William James; d. a school of psychology for which the basic subject matter is overt behavior   14.2
331

Radical behaviorism   a. is a new name for behaviorism, Skinner being dissatisfied with the old one; b. a form of behaviorism that eliminates classical conditioning from consideration; c. considers currently observable events and also potential, future events that can be observed and measured; d. considers only present events that have behavioral manifestations detectable either by the senses or by modern electronics;   14.3
332

Walden II (1948) described; a. a laboratory of the future in which people were the subjects of experiments and animals are the experimenters; b. a story of the demise of mentalism c. a autobiographical novel by Skinner, disclosing his contempt for non-behaviorists; d. a book about a utopian society in which punishment is shunned and rewards guide people to full exploitation of their skills   14.4
332

Skinner first became intrigued with psychology   a. at age 40; b. at an early age; c. during graduate training; d. during his mid-twenties   14.5
332

All except one of the following were among the famous people who influenced Skinner early in his life. Which was NOT one of those famous people?   a. Bertrand Russell; b. Robert Frost; c. Hermann Von Helmholtz; d. H. G. Wells   14.6
332

Among Skinner's adventures during early adult-hood was a. living with a woman in Greenwich village; b. sky diving c. underwater exploration; d. exploring the jungles of South America   14.7
333

Regarding Skinner's personality, as it can be understood from his own descriptions,   a. it is difficult to pin down; b. it is

definitely on the fringe of normalcy; c. it is rather uninteresting; d. it evidences cognitive simplicity 14.8
333

Throughout his career Skinner liked to a. praise his critics: it confused them; b. tweak the nose of the psychological establishment; c. experience the adventures that characterized his youth; d. avoid controversy 14.9
334

Which of the following is true of Skinner? a. he was an S-R psychologist; b. he was something of an environmentalist c. he begrudgingly believed in the unconscious, but gave it little role in his theory; c. he emphasized thoughts with emotional content 14.10
334

According to Skinner, a consequence is a. the same thing as a response; b. anything that happens after something else has occurred; c. an event that is initiated by the organism but is maintained by the experimenter; d. an event that occurs after a response and changes its probability 14.11
334

Which of the following is an example of "natural selection?" a. humming birds with beaks that, through mutation, happen to be ideal for dipping into the flowers found in their habitat b. coyotes rummaging among the ruins of ghost towns for items useful in lair building; c. the birds that live on the rhinos; d. the fishes that take up residence in the depths of the ocean in natural caves, relative to their cousins that attempt to survive in the open at shallow levels 14.12
335

According to Skinner, genetic endowment; a. has nothing to do with behavior; b. absolutely explains behavior at a reductionistic level; c. explains behavior for some individuals, but not others; d. predisposes people to certain behaviors rather than others 14.13
335

According to Skinner, by "freedom" we mean a. that we can choose from various behaviors rather than having our actions controlled by environment; b. that we are free to choose behaviors, except that we cannot arrange reinforcement contingencies; c. that we are not naturally prone to accepting dictatorships; d. that we naturally reject control by other people
14.14
335-336

Malignant environmental circumstances may continue to control people, because a. people are inherently masochists b. they may bring immediate positive consequences c. there is no way to arrange environmental circumstances to produce desired consequences; d. malignant consequences are more powerful than positive ones 14.15

When we demand freedom, what do we really mean, according to Skinner?   a. freedom from institutional oppression; b. freedom to ward off the influences of others; c. freedom from negative or aversive consequences; d. freedom to do what we will to others   14.16

Skinner was wrongly charged with   a. being an environ- mentalist; b. believing in the importance of consequences c. advocating coercive control of behavior; d. proposing a utopian society based on operant principles   14.17

According to Skinner, by "dignity" we mean   a. self-respect b. growing old gracefully; c. giving people credit for what they do; d. making sure that everyone is respected   14.18

Skinner credited one of his speeches to   a. himself; b. his genetic endowment and his particular environment; c. his speech writer; d. to happenstance: he thought it impossible to cite the multiple factors that contributed to his speech

14.19

Mentalism is (Skinner)   a. the ancient notion "mind over matter"; b. the belief that thought and feelings determine behavior, not external consequences; c. the belief that, through the will, one can ultimately and absolutely control behavior; d. Jung's idea that something like archetypes ultimately determine behavior   14.20

Skinner believed that mentalistic terms of today   a. were contrived purposefully by past linguists to promote mentalism; b. have evolved from those of the early language users; c. originally referred to behavior; d. are fading in use by ordinary people   14.21

According to Skinner, the observation that feelings and thoughts occur at about the same time as behaviors indicates a. absolutely nothing to anyone: it is happenstance; b. that they cause behavior; c. that they are caused by the forces that also cause behavior; d. why they are mistaken for causes of behavior   14.22

All except one of the following are words that Skinner has identified as one-time references to behavior. Which is NOT a word that was at one time identified with behavior? a. congratulate; b. experience; c. intention; d. image

14.23

Operant conditioning is   a. an automatic reaction to a stimulus

b. conditioning responses such as salivation; c. operating on the environment with consequences that influence repetition d. acting without regard to consequences 14.24
330

According to Skinner, contingent means a. independence of events; b. whether events are separated in time or occur together; c. inhibition of one event by another; d. dependence of an event on the prior occurrence of another event338 14.25
330

Reinforcement occurs when a. two events occur simultaneously, one a stimulus event and the other a response event; b. some event is contingent on the prior performance of some response; c. three or more events occur in synchrony d. there is present consumable objects such as food, water, etc.
14.26
338

Positive reinforcement refers to a. any event having a "+" valence; b. an event that increases the likelihood of a response upon which the event is contingent; c. an event that decreases the likelihood of a response upon which the event is contingent; d. a response contingent on a previous stimulus
14.27
338

The Skinner Box a. is what Skinner facetiously called his office; b. is where Skinner raised his daughter; c. is where Skinner keep notes on his experiments; d. is a cage for conditioning animal's responses 14.28
338

Which of the following is an operantly conditioned response? a. a dog's salivating when presented with food; b. a baby's startle response when a loud sound is sounded; c. a cat's hissing when confronted with a dog; d. a baby's crying responses followed by the appearance of a parent with food in hand 14.29
339

Rate of responding a. when it is stable, indicates that conditioning has been completed and a new response acquired; b. when it is variable, indicates that conditioning has been completed and a new response acquired; c. is a index of extinction: the more variable the rate the greater the extinction; d. is an index of magnitude of conditioning; magnitude is high when the response rate is variable 14.30
339

During extinction procedures a. there are no responses; b. a response is not followed by a reinforcer; c. a response is followed by a reinforcer; d. the animal is sacrificed for neurological examination 14.31
339

Shaping is   a. a process by which natural variability in behavior is exploited so that a new behavior is acquired by reinforcing successive approximation to it; b. a process by which the environment of an animal is resculptured to fit the genetic propensities of the animal (e.g., panel is presented to a pigeon rather than a lever); c. restructuring a stimulus until it is a useful reinforcer; d. restructuring the experimental set-up until the conditions for successful conditioning prevail   14.32
339-340

All except one of the following are instances of positive reinforcement in the life of a student. Which is NOT an instance of positive reinforcement?; a. presenting an id card at a cafeteria followed by food presentation; b. the observation of an attractive person is followed by an increase in heart rate c. class attendance is reinforced by a stimulating lecture; d. activities in the library are followed by "the joy of learning"
14.33
340

In negative reinforcement, a response increases in likelihood when it is followed by   a. presentation of a stimulus; b. the termination of a stimulus; c. the intermittent presence of a stimulus; d. the increase in strength of a stimulus   14.34
341

Avoidance refers to   a. jumping away from shock after it has been delivered; b. waiting until the shock is terminated and then jumping away from the area where the shock occurred c. jumping away from the shock-area in reaction to a warning light just as the shock is being delivered; d. jumping away from the shock-area in reaction to a warning light just before the shock is delivered   14.35
341

In punishment, responses that are followed by the presentation of a stimulus   a. increase in likelihood; b. maintain the same likelihood; c. increase or decrease in likelihood, depending on the species of subjects; d. decrease in likelihood   14.36
341

Which of the following is an example of negative reinforcement? a. a child watches her bratty little brother, so she will not have to do her boring homework; b. a child is given praise for having been gentle instead of aggressive with his little sister; c. a man is presented with an award for outstanding service; d. a women is shocked each time she lights up a cigarette   14.37
341

About punishment, Skinner believed; a. it is the most effective way to control behavior; b. while it is the most effective way to control behavior, its use is unethical; c. it only has temporary effects; d. it is counterproductive: resistance to coercion causes

organisms to respond at higher rates in the presence of
punishment   14.38
341

All except one of the following are unfortunate side effects of
punishment. Which is NOT such an effects? a. loss of self-
esteem; b. fear that others might attack oneself; c. failure to
respond aggessively to an attack; d. failure to perform
beneficial responses   14.39
342

As a fairly typical parent, how does Aliza respond to her son
hitting her? a. she reasons with him; b. she tries to ignore his
attack; c. she scolds him; d. she hits him back   14.40
342

As a fairly typical mother, how does Aliza respond to Rudy's
attacks on his sister? a. she tells him, "Now Rudy, you know
that is naughty." b. she hits him; c. she says, "Wait 'til your
father gets home!"; d. she spanks the sister for provoking Rudy
                                                                14.41
342

Rudy has learned from his mother that physical punishment is
a way to control people. How does it show up in his behavior?
a. he has become very good at verbally persuading his sister to
give him his way; b. he uses physical violence and threats of
violence to control his sister. he displaces his aggression onto
the little boy next door; d. he turns his aggression inward by
mutilating himself   342
342-343

Rudy has learned from his mother that physical punishment is
a way to control people. How does it show up in his behavior?
a. he shows cruelty to animals; b. he shows high risk taking
behavior: he has been hurt several times doing dare-devil
tricks on his bicycle; c. he shows aggression at school
d. he shows low self-esteem and self-hatred   14.43
342-343

If one is angry because someone has aggressed against him
or her, how will one's subsequent aggression against a third
party affect future aggressiveness? a. it will have no effect on
future aggression; b. it will "blow off some steam" making future
aggression less likely; c. it will suppress future aggression
because of fear of retaliation; d. it will follows the adage
"aggression begets aggression": aggression gives rise to more
aggression   14.44
342

When Aliza hits Rudy in retaliation for his attack on her, what
has she become? a. a "bad mother"; b. a fool: she should
have hit him BEFORE he hit her; c. a model who teaches
aggressiveness to Rudy; d. a hostile/aggressive personality
type   14.45
342

What subtle lesson does Rudy learn when his mother hits him back harder when he hits her? a. parents are basically mean b. there is no justice; c. he should be in a position to escape if he is planning to hit his mother; d. one can get away with aggression if one is big and strong enough   14.46
342-343

What did Skinner know about the aversive stimulation (physical punishment) as a way to control behavior?; a. under specifiable conditions, it can work very well; b. it will never work; c. there has been no research to address whether it will work or not; d. research results all points in just one direction: punishment always make its victims more aggressive
14.47
343

Which is chief among the conditions that must hold if punishment is to effectively control behavior? a. it must not be too severe; b. it must be very severe; c. the target of punishment must not know when it is coming; d. it must be administered by an authority figure   14.48
343

Which of the following must be true of the threat of punishment if it is to deter future aggression? a. it must not be too severe; b. it must be very severe; c. the target of punishment must not know when it is coming; d. it must be administered by an authority figure   14.49
343

Which of the following must be true of the threat of punishment is to deter future aggression? a. the occurrence of the punishment must be of uncertain likelihood; b. the threatened potential aggressor 336must be very angry; c. the potential aggressor who is threatened must have much to gain from future aggression; d. the person who is threatened must know that any future aggression will be followed immediately by punishment   14.50
343

In Rudy's case, which of the following represents the degree to which the conditions that must hold if threat of punishment is to effectively deter future aggression are actually in force?; a. in Rudy's case, all the conditions that must be met to deter future aggression are in force; b. in Rudy's case, none of the conditions that must be met to deter future aggression are in force; c. in Rudy's case, only the condition "punishment must be severe" is in force; d. in Rudy's case, only the condition "the potential aggressor must not be very angry" is in force
14.51
343

Given the condition for threat of punishment to reliably deter criminal assault are met, what then becomes the problem? a. no problem: our judicial system can now meet these conditions;

b. it is never possible to meet any of these conditions; c. these conditions have actually been met by our system and we now know that they do not work to deter aggression; d. meeting these conditions would threaten our democratic system

14.52
343

What is Skinner's attitude toward the notion of "personality"? a. he rejected it; b. he thought it was harmless but useless; c. he embraced it; d. he ignored it

14.53
343

What happened when Skinner declared that "the verbal community" reinforces correct speech and that is how children learn to speak? a. linguistic scientists readily agreed; b. the entire linguistic community rose up against him declaring that "parental training" plays no significant role in language development; c. linguist Noam Chomsky rejected Skinner's account of language development in favor of his innate "language faculty"d. for the first time, linguists began to debate about the degree to which lessons from adults influence language development

14.54
345

Skinner reared his daughter in a   a. typical nursery by atypical procedures; b. in a box featuring temperature and humidity control; c. in an apparatus not unlike a Skinner box in terms of reinforcement delivery; d. in a special, contingency controlled, outdoor area

14.55
345

In her special environment, Skinner's daughter was   a. lonely; b. unhappy; c. the center of attention; d. able to roam over a wide area

14.56
345

What were some of the advantages of the special environment Skinner arranged for his daughter? a. she was isolated so she would not be a bother to her parents; b. lack of exposure to other children prevented quarreling; c. several health problems were prevented; d. she learned not to cry, because it did no good

14.57
346

What was wrong with calling Debs "aircrib" a "box"? a. it is too impersonal;. b. it was more round than square; c. it actually had only three sides; d. "box" meant coffin at the time the aircrib was used.

14.58
346

Which happened to Skinner after Deb's "aircrib" was written up in Ladies Home Journal? a. it was suggested that his own university sue him; b. he was granted Psychology's highest award; c. he was fired by Indiana University; d. Child and Family Services threatened to take Debs away

14.59
344

In Skinner's <u>Walden Two</u> Fraizer, the leader, describes himself
a. only at others' insistence; b. with reference to traits; c. by
analogy; d. with a long string of trait labels   14.60
                                                          346

When Skinner "revisits" Walden II years later, Burris and
Frazier appear to be their same old selves. What are the
implications of their remaining much the same? a. Skinner was
not very creative as a writer; b. reinforcement should have
made them different after a time; c. this stability is not surprising
due to the "protected" and invariability circumstances at
Walden II; d. in this show of invariance over time, Skinner
provides testimony to the stability of personality   14.61
                                                             346

According to Skinner, what kind of objects predominate in
paintings? a. uninterpretable images; b. abstractions; c. food
d. nonhuman forms   14.62
                                                          346

According to Skinner, successful artists; a. merely copy other
artists; b. have ideas that originate in their own minds;
c. avoid displaying objects with survival value (hands);
d. copy from their own experience   14.63
                                                          346

In describing artists and their art, Skinner begins to sound
somewhat like   a. Jung; b. Murray; c. Cattell; d. Sullivan
                                                           14.64
                                                           347

How was the economy of <u>Walden Two</u> different from that of
Western society? a. it wasn't and that was the point;
b. everyone was "paid" the same; c. manual labor yielded the
highest "pay"; d. some people did not have to work at all
                                                           14.65
                                                           347

In <u>Walden II</u> people   a. chose a job or profession and stuck
with it; b. tried a wide variety of pursuits, but eventually
migrated to what they were genetically disposed to perform
well; c. tried a wide variety of pursuits, but eventually ended up
doing whatever provided the greatest range of reinforcers for
the greatest number people; d. rotated from job to job
continually   14.66
                                                          348

Skinner thought that cultures develop according to
a. S-R principles; b. principles of classical conditioning
(respondent conditioning); c. principles of operant
conditioning; d. principles of observational learning
                                                           14.67
                                                           348

Africans brought to the U.S. carried certain cultural traditions
with them that survived because the environment here selected
them. Which may represent one of those traditions?

a. preferences for certain African foods; b. African housing traditions; c. African religious traditions; d. African communication via drums   14.68
348

What was the constitution of the Board of Governors at Walden II?; a. half were women; b. two-thirds were professors; c. 80% were white males; d. half were people of color
14.69
349

In Gromly's (1982) study of genetic endowment and reinforcement   a. fraternity men were isolated in a cave for a month; b. fraternity men kept a log of experiences; c. instances of aggression were recorded by an observer; d. anti-social behaviors were investigated   14.70
349

In Gromly's (1982) study involving fraternity men, what supposedly genetic characteristic was under investigation? a. sociable-extraverted; b. conscientiousness c. sexual behavior; d. trustworthiness   14.71
349

The Skinnerian point to Gromly's (1982) study was a. environment determines energetic behavior regardless of the genes; b. environment selected energetic behaviors for those people who were genetically inclined to be energetic c. an interaction of environment and the genes determines energetic behavior, with the strongest winning out; d. in this case, the genes are solely responsible of determining energetic behavior, the environment played no role
14.72
349

Behavior therapy   a. is, ironically, a form of psychotherapy that relies on ignoring behavior rather than reinforcing it; b. was a term introduced by Wolpe; c. was a late in the life interest of Skinner; d. is psychological therapy employing behavioral techniques   14.73
350

In the example of behavior modification involving a shy child a. a stranger talked to the child; b. the child's behavior, talking to a stranger, was reinforced; c. the child's behavior, approaching a stranger, was reinforced; d. the child's refusal to talk was punished   14.74
350

Which of the following is an example of a secondary reinforcer? a. food; b. oxygen; c. water; d. money   14.75
351

According to J. Jung (1978) the behavior-emotion sequence that Skinner endorses   a. is not amenable to testing via experiments and has been subjected to severe criticism

b. is undoubtedly the most sound point of view; c. may be the best point of view, but, while readily testable, has yet to be tested; d. is certainly the inferior point of view, according to much experimental work
14.76
351-352

What will save the Skinnerian position in the future?
a. sticking with Skinnerian principles, no matter what;
b. uniting with the cognitive movement; c. leaning a little in the "mentalistic" direction; d. paying more attention to classical (respondent) conditioning
14.77
351

What is the point of the 60 Minutes-Laurence Olivier episode involving Shakespeare's Othello? a. Olivier was outstanding because his genetic disposition was properly exploited by his environment; b. Olivier's purely private suffering was enormously important to him, even though it had no external manifestations; c. Olivier was shown reinforcing a young actor playing Othello, thus, he demonstrated positive reinforcement d. Olivier was shown screaming at a younger actor who was playing Othello badly, thus, he demonstrated negative reinforcement
14.78
351

With a little flexibility, what area might Skinnerians begin to consider that they have not considered before? a. behavior therapy; b. perception; c. language; d. eliminating undesirable behaviors
14.79
352

After this death, commentators on Skinner indicated which of the following have much in common with Skinnerianism?
a. quantum physics; b. metaphysics; c. existentialism
d. psychoanalysis
14.80
352

Which of the following support the claim that Skinner is now more important that Freud? a. citations in the psychological literature; b. the all-time list of contributors compiled by historians of psychology; c. a survey by Time magazine
d. his ideas appear in many different kinds of psychology texts
14.81
352

For which of the following productive ideas is Skinner responsible? a. deprogramming of people just out of;
b. sounding the alarm about international relations, pointing out the need to emphasize positive rather than negative reinforcement; c. time out; d. backward conditioning
14.82
351-352

To which of the following has Skinner NOT made important contributions? a. developmental psychology; b. sensation and perception; c. psychotherapy; d. personality

14.83
332

About his childhood, Skinner remembers a. his Boy Scout troop helping wounded World War I soldiers; b. his adventures in the deserts of the Southwest; c. not being close to his parents and their Protestant traditions; d. getting particularly strong affection and support from his grandparents

14.84
333

What discovery did Skinner make that caused him to guard his life lest the important find be lost? a. what is now called classical conditioning; b. the empirical law of effect; c. the effects of aversive stimuli; d. the extinction graph

14.85
333

To what scientists' Hall of Fame was Skinner elected? a. The American Psychological Society; b. The National Academy of Sciences; c. The Royal Academy of Natural Science; d. The National Science Foundation

14.86
334

That there are certain European peoples who have among them men with very stout thighs and calves illustrates what? a. racial differences; b. that some people are superior in some ways; c. that irrelevant traits can become ingrained in a group d. that the men may represent selection for pushing a primitive plow

14.87
335

What is the way we recognize Skiiner's view of freedom, that is not fully recogniaed? a. the freedom to determine our own behaviors in an absolute sense; b. the freedom to think any thought we wish and have it determine our behaviors; c. the attribution of our own behaviors to our enviroment d. the freedom to determine the consequences of our responses without arranging contingencies in our environments

14.88
336

The fundamental attribution error is a. attributing another person's behavior to a personality trait, while ignoring environmental determinants; b. attributing our own behavior to environmental determinants, while ignoring trait causation; c. deciding that the determinant of a behavior is a certain stimulus; d. deciding that a behavior is determined by one stimulus as opposed to another stimulus

14.89
337

"Comprehend" originally meant (Skinner) a. to understand b. to grasp; c. to phantom; d. to aspire

14.90
338

The name of a stimulus that is presented (event) as a consequence of a response is a. reward; b. reinforcer c. tribute; d. outcome

14.91

What did Palmer and Hollin (2001) report regarding the relationship between delinquency and parental behavior? a. it was nil; b. it was positive: the more the parental warmth the more the delinquency; c. it was positive: the more the punishment meted out by parents, the more the delinquency; d. it was curvilinear: the less the punishment the more the delinquency to a moderate level of punishment; at very low punishment levels, delinquency increased   14.92

337

Regarding Skinner's alleged opposition to theory a. he actually looked forward to a behavioral theory based on careful observation; b. he opposed all theory because he felt all theories would have mentalistic elements; c. his opposition to all theory was real; d. he actually softened near the end of his life and began supporting a bit of mentalism in behaviorism   14.93

352

Which of the following is one of Skinner's ideas? a. psycho-therapy; b. reverse psychology; c. common sense applied to science; d. time out   14.94

345

How did Rudy respond to the physical punishment he received? a. he became very submissive; b. he was controlling and aggressive toward his sister; c. he cried excessively; d. he cowered in a corner while assuming a fetal position   14.95

346

Which of the following is a condition that must be met if threat of punishment is to deter future aggression? a. the threatened punished must not be severe; b. there must be a long time between the to-be-punished act and the actual punishment ; c. the threatened person must not be very angry; d. the threatened person must have little to gain from future aggression   14.96

344

Chomsky's "language faculty" has been analogized to a. a microcomputer in the brain; b. a microchip in the brain; c. a spirit in the nervous system; d. a homunculus (little person) in the brain   14.97

337

What somewhat mentalistic terminology will modern behavior-ists have to consider adopting if radical behaviorism is to survive?; a. language faculty; b. self-serving bias c. expectations; d. response variations   14.98

346

What attribute of art, scorned by Skinner, is often thought by others to be its reinforcing aspect? a. its intrinsically rewarding

qualities; b. its extrinsically rewarding qualities; c. its timeless nature; d. its genuine spontaneity   14.99
                                                                347

Who does some menial work at Walden II? a. a leader ; b. a physician; c. a professor; d. all do at least some menial work
                                                                14.100
                                                                347-348

In Walden II, people tended to migrate to jobs that fit their genotypes and reinforcement histories; a. still, they performed all the job types at least occasionally; b. and, then, they never performed other jobs; c. but often they migrated back to previous jobs; d. nevertheless, many never found a job niche
                                                                14.101
                                                                349

Skinner coined the term   a. psychosis; b. classical conditioning c. instrumental conditioning; d. behavior therapy   14.102
                                                                350

Which of the following was a secondary reinforcer in the demonstration of a shy child learning to communicate with an adult stranger? a. the stranger's reply to the child's remark b. the child's reply to the stranger's remark; c. the stranger's smile; d. the child's arm movements   14.103
                                                                351

Solving a never-before-encountered math problem in the head is an example of   a. primary reinforcement; b. extinction; c. relearning after operant conditioning; d. the importance of thoughts unrelated to behavior   14.104
                                                                352

Whose ideas have influenced more different fields of psychology? a. Skinner; b. Adler; c. Jung; d. Eysenck   14.105
                                                                351

Kimble (2000) would add all the following to Skinnerian terminology, except one. Which would he NOT add? a. cognition; b. affect; c. fortitude; d. coping   14.106
                                                                351

Which of the following is the sequence that DeGrandpre (2000) would introduce instead of Skinner's response/reinforcement sequence (R=response; C=consequence; S=stimulus) a. RC = SR; b. SRC→RS; c. S-R=R-C; d. R-C→[S-R]

14.1,d	14.49,d	14.95,d
14.2,c	14.50,b	14.96,d
14.3,d	14.51,d	14.97,c
14.4,b	14.52,a	14.98,a
14.5,c	14.53,c	14.99,d
14.6,a	14.54,b	14.100,a
14.7,a	14.55,c	14.101,d
14.8,b	14.56.c	14.102,a
14.9.b	14.57,d	14.103,d
14.10,d	14.58,a	14.104,a
14.11,a	14.59,d	14.105, c
14.12,d	14.60,d	14.106, d
14.13,a	14.61,c	
14.14,b	14.62,d	
14.15,c	14.63,a	
14.16,c	14.64,c	
14.17,c	14.65,b	
14.18,b	14.66,c	
14.19,b	14.67,d	
14.20,c	14.68,a	
14.21,d	14.69,b	
14.22,a	14.70,a	
14.23,c	14.71,b	
14.24,d	14.72,d	
14.25,b	14.73,b	
14.26,b	14.74,d	
14.27,d	14.75,a	
14.28,d	14.76,c	
14.29.a	14.77,b	
14.30.b	14.78,b	
14.31,a	14.79,c	
14.32,b	14.80,d	
14.33,b	14.81,c	
14.34,d	14.82,b	
14.35,d	*Extra*	
14.36,a	*Items*	
14.37,c	14.83,c	
14.38,c	14.84,d	
14.39,d	14.85,b	
14.40,c	14.86,d	
14.41,b	14.87,c	
14.42,c	14.88,a	
14.43,d	14.89,b	
14.44,c	14.90,b	
14.45,d	14.91,c	
14.46,a	14.92,a	
14.47,b	14.93,d	
14.48,b	14.94,b	

Chapter 15

Multiple Choice Items for the Chapter on Murray

15.1
356

Murray's point of view provides a bridge from the cognitive approaches and radical behaviorism to   a. radical cognitivism; b. psychodynamics; c. personality traits; d. social-personality psychology
15.2
357

How is Murray valuable at this point in the text? a. he reminds us of the social-personality theorists; b. he, in one way or another, resembles most of the theorists previously covered c. his ideas are very different from those of other covered theorists; d. he illustrates, in his own work, all of the weaknesses of the other theorists
15.3
357

Murray was born on   a. a voyage to America from England; b. the fourth of July; c. the arctic circle in Canada; d. what is now Rockefeller Center, in New York City
15.4
357

About his mother, Murray felt   a. exactly as did Maslow about his mother; b. that she favored his siblings; c. that she favored him over his siblings; d. that she was not very bright
15.5
357

Murray's "organ defect" as Adler would have called it was a. he stuttered up into the 1930s; b. he had a withered arm; c. he was decidedly ugly; d. he was dyslexic
15.6
358

Regarding his father, Murray held all of the following opinions, except one. Which was NOT among his opinions of his father? a. he was mean and ornery; b. he was a nice guy; c. he lacked ambition; d. he was predictable
15.7
358

What problem did Murray have throughout his life?   a. he stuttered until the day he died; b. he was unable to maintain the level of admiration he initially felt for anyone; c. he could not overcome feeling inferior because of his withered arm; d. he knew he could have amounted to more had he tried harder
15.8
357

What problem did Murray have throughout his life? a. he was, as Horney would say, excessively and morbidly modest; b. he acquiesced too easily when others opposed him; c. he felt ashamed about his lack of academic credentials; d. he suffered from a "marrow of misery and melancholy"   15.9
358

Which person, who had provided his own mistress with accommodations, attempted to discourage Murray from providing his mistress with accommodations? a. Jung b. Adler; c. Fromm; d. Allport   15.10
358

Christiana Morgan and Murray built   a. a warm, loving, and untroubled relationship; b. a professional counseling practice together; c. a personality laboratory together for which they shared the credit equally and in which they both worked throughout their lives; d. a tower as a monument to their love   15.11
375

Christiana Morgan produced how many original drawings that became TAT cards? a. 2; b. 0; c. 1; d. 5   15.12
357-359

Murray was something of an expert on all of the following, except one. On which was he NOT expert? a. biochemistry; b. experimental psychology; c. medical science; d. Moby Dick   15.13
358

Murray was all of the following, except one. Which does NOT apply to him? a. narcissistic; b. a leader; c. high in need for achievement motivation; d. totally lacking in loyalty for people who served him well   15.14
360

Which psychologist turned Murray off to psychology during his undergraduate days? a. Titchener; b. Allport; c. Musterberg d. William James   15.15
360

When Murray consulted a neurologist about Freud's theory, he was told   a. that Freud was respected for his early work in neurology ; b. that Freud was the only psychiatrist that the neurologist trusted; c. that Freud's work was interesting, but had nothing to do with neurology; d. that Freud's ideas were the greatest phallusy of the age   15.16
360

Which characterized Murray's initial impression of Jung? a. I thought he was rather dull. b. He was the first full-blooded, all encompassing, spherical human being I had ever met. c. He wasn't good with his concepts...he'd believe anything I told him that was along the lines that he liked. d. He was mediocre for such a famous person.   15.17

Among the first psychology classes that Murray regularly attended was   a. one that he taught; b. a class taught by Gestaltist K. Wertheimer; c. a class taught by Allport; d. one where he assisted Floyd Allport   15.18

What stereotype did Murray fit?   a. the pointy headed college professor; b. the absent-minded professor; c. the psychologist who is always trying to figure out other people; d. the student who goes into psychology to solve his own personal problems   15.19

What theorist's ideas did Murray follow fairly closely early in his psychological career? a. Freud; b. Horney; c. Adler; d. John B. Watson   15.20

All of the following, except one, was true of Murray's own experience of undergoing psychoanalysis. Which was NOT true of his experience in psychoanalysis?; a. he thought the analyst was a nice guy; b. he laughed his way through it; c. he had an affair with the analyst's wife; d. he became disillusioned with psychoanalysis   15.21

What belief did Murray and Maslow share? a. a belief in the essential worth of every person; b. humans are dynamic wholes, not meaningfully dividable into parts and pieces c. self-actualization is open only to a chosen few; d. it is best to conceive of human emotion, cognition, and behavior in terms of wholly conscious processes   15.22

All of the following characterized Murray's years at Harvard, except one. Which did NOT characterize his years there? a. Chairperson E.G. Boring warned him that he would be ostracized from the American Psychological Association for his outspoken comments about colleagues; b. attempts by famed neuropsychologist Karl Lashley to oust him; c. a sense of belonging and support from department members; d. founding of a personality laboratory that eventually produced research resulting in a famous book   15.23

Murray condemned all except one of the following. Which did he NOT condemn? a. John B. Watson; b. a strong emphasis on the unconscious; c. scientism; d. experimental psychology   15.24

One of Murray's most basic assumptions was   a. the personality is a series of fragmentations; b. humans are essentially worthy; c. the experimental approach is more

effective than the clinical approach; d. one should study individual organisms, not aggregates of organisms
15.25
363
The "long unit" refers to   a. the organism's life cycle; b. the unit of measure that best approximates the depth of the organisms consciousness; c. the unit of measure that best approximates an interval rather than an ordinal level of measurement; d. the scale used to measure personality
15.26
354
A "unitary trend" is   a. an assumption that activity is organized and directional, not willy nilly; b. a pattern of bodily movements per se, divorced from its effect; c. a tendency toward unity in the numerical sense; d. a kind of behavior that occurs only once
15.27
363
An actone is   a. an assumption that activity is organized and directional, not willy nilly; b. a pattern of bodily movements in and of itself, divorced from its effect; c. a tendency toward unity in the numerical sense; d. a kind of behavior that occurs only once
15.28
363-364
Like Mischel, Murray recognized that   a. cognitive analysis is preferable to trait analysis; b. traits' existence is not supported by the evidence; c. delay of gratification should be a central concept in anyone's research program; d. temporal consistencies exist
15.29
364
Regnant refers to   a. the royal road to the unconscious; b. dominant configurations in the brain; c. the observation that the personality is like a King's court, a hierarchy of needs; d. the totality of brain processes occurring during a single moment
15.30
373
On which of the following defense mechanisms did whites and Asians score differently, according to Hibbard et al. (2000)? a. sublimation; b. projection; c. denial; d. rationalization
15.31
373&375
According to Ackerman et al. (1999) and Porcerelli et. al. (2001), which of the following represented the different symptoms of borderline personality patients and a serial-rapist-murderer, respectively? a. overly optimistic; confident; b. hallucinatory; delusional; c. vague identity; sadistic; d. suppresses aggression; anxious
15.32
364
According to Murray, "need" means   a. desires for certain satisfactions that are sought by all humans; b. the drive to overcome inferiority; c. the tendency to structure one's life so as

to optimize the probability of overcoming basic anxiety and the aftermath of suffering at the hands of "forbidding gestures";
d. a construct which stands for a force in the brain that organizes perception, intellection, and action toward transformation of an unsatisfying situation into a satisfying one
15.33
364

How did Maslow and Murray differ greatly regarding the concept "need?" a. only Murray equated need to drive
b. only Maslow equated need to drive; c. only Maslow held that needs dwell in unconsciousness; d. only Murray arranged needs into a hierarchy
15.34
364

To Murray, a need could be thought of as a. purely psychological phenomenon; b. equivalent to an ego element c. a more or less consistent trait of personality; d. an entity that is more related to the environment than to brain processes
15.35
364

All except one of the following was true of Murray's "need." Which was NOT true of his "need?" a. needs are subordinated to personality traits; b. needs are drive-like; c. needs arise to transform an unsatisfactory situation into a satisfactory one d. needs ready the organism to respond to a push from the rear
15.36
365

Viscerogenic needs a. involve basic physiological drives, and, as such are relatively self-explanatory ; b. are forces with directional properties; c. refer to the positive-need-promoting vectors that describe movement toward objects and people d. refer to the negative-need-promoting vectors that describe movement away from objects and people
15.37
364

Psychogenic needs; a. refer to the negative-need-promoting vectors that describe movement away from objects and people; b. are forces with directional properties; c. refer to the positive-need-promoting vectors that describe movement toward objects and people; d. have viscerogenic needs as their foundation
15.38
365

Vector(s) a. refer to the negative-need-promoting pointers that describe movement away from objects and people; b. refers to forces with directional properties; c. refer to the positive-need-promoting pointers that describe movement toward objects and people; d. are secondary to viscerogenic needs and may be derived from them
15.39
365

Adience a. refers to the negative-need-promoting vectors that describe movement away from objects and people; b. refers to forces with directional properties; c. refers to the positive-need-promoting vectors that describe movement toward objects and people; d. is secondary to viscerogenic needs and may be derived from them   15.40
                                                                              365

All except one of the following are examples of needs in the adience category. Which is NOT a need in the adience category? a. n Achievement; b. n Succorance; c. n Order; d. n Noxavoidance   15.41
                                                                              365

Abience a. refers to the negative-need-promoting vectors that describe movement away from objects and people; b. is a force with directional properties; c. refers to the positive-need-promoting vectors that describe movement toward objects and people; d. is secondary to viscerogenic needs and may be derived from them   15.42
                                                                              365

All except one of the following are needs in the abience category. Which is NOT a need in the abience category? a. n Aggression; b. n Inviolacy; c. n Infavoidance; d. n Contarience   15.43
                                                                              356

Which of the following is the need to avoid failure, shame, humiliation, or ridicule by concealing disfigurement and refraining from attempts at anything beyond one's powers?; a. n Inviolacy; b. n Contrarience; c. n Infavoidance; d. n Abasement   15.44
                                                                              365

According to Murray, strength refers to a. rhythms of activity and rest; b. when no incentive will arouse a need; c. when a need is inactive but susceptible to excitation by appropriate stimulation; d. a property of a need that is measured in terms of it frequency, intensity, and duration   15.45
                                                                              365

A need is strong if it is a. persistent; b. insistent; c. submerged (unconscious); d. durable   15.46
                                                                              367

During a typical day, a person is likely to (Murray) a. experience needs one at a time; b. take a particular course of action designed to satisfy several needs; c. arrange needs into a hierarchy; d. consider more simplex needs first

                                                                              15.47
                                                                              367

Which of the following is refers to a fusion of needs? a. an image of a bird floating free in the air; b. a phase of dominance succeeded by a phase of deference; c. being paid to sing solo

in public; d. sexual needs felt by a person whose parents would condemn her for sexual expression 15.48
367

Fusion of needs refers to (Murray) a. cases where needs are related to their opposites in alternating phases; b. when needs oppose each other within the personality, giving rise to harassing spiritual dilemmas; c. when one or more needs are activated in the service of one or more other needs; d. a single action pattern that satisfies two or more needs at the same time
15.49
367

Subsidiation of needs refers to (Murray) a. cases where needs are related to their opposites in alternating phases b. when needs oppose each other within the personality, giving rise to harassing spiritual dilemmas; c. when one or more needs are activated in the service of one or more other needs d. a single action pattern that satisfies two or more needs at the same time 15.50
367

Contrafactions of needs refers to (Murray) a. cases where needs are related to their opposites in alternating phases b. when needs oppose each other within the personality, giving rise to harassing spiritual dilemmas; c. when one or more needs are activated in the service of one or more other needs; d. a single action pattern that satisfies two or more needs at the same time 15.51
367

Conflicts of needs refers to (Murray) a. cases where needs are related to their opposites in alternating phases; b. when needs oppose each other within the personality, giving rise to harassing spiritual dilemmas; c. when one or more needs are activated in the service of one or more other needs; d. a single action pattern that satisfies two or more needs at the same time
15.52
367

Cathexis (Murray) refers to a. investments or attachments of the personality's libidinous energy either to real objects in the external world or to fantasized images in the inner world; b. a process by which an object evokes a need; c. attraction to an object because of its sexual connotations; d. objects that determine what other objects we are attracted to 15.53
368

A need integrate or complex (Murray) a. refers to mental contents in the psyche that agglutinate or stick together like the climbing of red blood cells and eventually take up residence in the personal unconscious; b. is a constellation of needs revolving around a central theme (mother); c. is formed when

312

images of cathected objects become integrated in the mind with the needs and emotions they customary excite
d. is a variation on the theme of the Phallic stage in which objects associated with the opposite sex parent (mustache and painted lips) become attractive   15.54
367

Regarding a need integrate or complex (Murray), a bird soaring in the air may be cathected by the need to be free (n Autonomy). As such, whose concept does Murray's complex resemble most? a. complex (Freud); b. complex (Jung) c. Archetype (Jung); d. frame of orientation (Fromm)
15.55
369

What famous case did Murray used to examine the possibility that dreams are clairvoyant? a. the Hersch kidnapping b. the Clutter murders; c. the flight of Bonnie and Clyde d. the Lindbergh kidnapping   15.56
369

Murray collected some 1300 dreams sent to him in response to a newspaper ad. All except one of the following are facts related to those dream descriptions. Which is NOT a fact relating to the dream descriptions? a. the ad was placed before details about the relevant crime were known to the public; b. the actual facts of the case included that the victim died of skull fractures and its naked body was found in a shallow grave in some woods near a road; c. the actual facts of the case included that the victim was strangled and transported to Germany where its decomposed remains were found in the crawl-space of a deserted house; d. in about 5% of the dreams the victim of the crime appeared to be dead
15.57
369

All except one of the following are facts about or interpretations of the 1300 dreams collected by Murray. Which is NOT a fact or interpretation? a. an ex-convict of German extraction was convicted of the crime; b. only ten dreams were at all accurate in predicting the details of the crime; c. in three of the partially accurate dreams, dreamers claimed that they had the dreams before the crime had actually happened; d. Murray concluded that, indeed, dreams are clairvoyant
15.58
368

Press refers to   a. the tension of anxiety and its aftermath b. a directional tendency in the object or situation c. internal forces or energy that fuels the Psyche; d. the encroachment of the id into the realm of the superego, according to Murray   15.59
368

The contrast between cathexis and press is summed up in which of the following statements? a. only in cathexis is there any influence on the person; b. only in press is there any influence on the person; c. in both cases the person is made to do something or other; d. only in the case of press is something done to the person   15.60
368

Which of the following is the time orientation of press? a. mostly future; b. mostly present; c. equally present and past; d. mostly past   15.61
370

All except one of the following are examples of press. Which is NOT a good example of a press? a. p Affiliation; b. p Abstention; c. p Aggression; d. p Rival   15.62
370

All except one of the following are examples of press. Which is NOT a good example of a press? a. p Affiliation; c. p Regnant d. p Rival   15.63
368

Very often aspects of the present situation excite   a. images of past pressive situations; b. other objects in the present situation; c. primitive urges; d. the operation of complex/press interactions   15.64
370

Which of the following is a good example of a press?
 a. a dominant person in an individual's life who restricts and strains the individual; b. an image of a smoggy atmosphere; c. exhibitionistic behavior followed by modest behavior; d. n Noxavoidance S n Infavoidance   15.65
369-370

Thema   a. are cases where needs are related to their opposites in alternating phases; b. refer to a process by which an object evokes a need; c. are formed when traces (images) of cathected objects in familiar settings become integrated in the mind with the needs and emotions they customary excite d. refer to a combination of a particular need and a particular press or pressive object   15.66
370

To which personality test did Murray's needs contribute directly? a. Personality Orientation Inventory; b. Personality Research Form; d. Minnesota Multiphasic Personality Inventory; d. Rorschach   15.67
370

What is the value of the Paunonen, Jackson and Keinonen (1990) stick figure test that is based on Murray's needs? a. it is more enjoyable to clients and subjects who are high in verbal skills; b. it is useful for administration to sophisticated clients and subjects, such as psychologists; c. it is useful for

cross-cultural research; d. it is more challenging for most
people who take it, relative to the original form   15.68
                                                          370
Singer's (1990) reconception of Murray's needs took which
form? a. needs were cast as temperaments; b. needs became ,
life goals; c. needs were reinterpreted as attitudes;
d. needs were seen to be unconscious wishes   15.69
                                                          370-372
The Thematic Apperception Test (TAT) is   a. a test that
assesses unconscious motivation via the use of ambiguous
ink-blots onto which clients or subjects project their own
motivations; b. a paper an pencil test that assesses various
dimensions of abnormal behavior in a multiple choice format;
c. an instrument for assessing the person's self-reflective
perceptions revealing thema that are evoked by some
ambiguous pictures; d. a projective test in which respondents
are asked to draw a picture of some neutral entity, such as a
house, that is then analyzed for information concerning needs
                                                          15.70
                                                          371
Which of the following is an advantage of the TAT?
a. because the pictures are ambiguous, it is assumed that
whatever the subject/client says about them comes from her or
his own mind; b. because of the structured format of the test,
validity is higher than for unstructured tests; c. because the
subject/client is drawing a picture about a neutral entity, he or
she is expected to project his or own motivations onto the
picture; d. because the subject/client is responding to items that
are associated with, but do not mention, abnormal behavior
categories, she or he has no idea that abnormal behavior is
being assessed   15.71
                                                          372
All except one of the following are major problems with the
TAT. Which is NOT a major problem? a. total cards are what is
considered, even though each card contains two figures; b.
adding objective methods to TAT scoring reduces the
projective nature of the test; c. it used pictures that date to a
previous era; d. when objective methods of scoring the TAT
have been used, only a few concepts have been involved
                                                          15.72
                                                          372
All except one of the following are ways that Potkay and
colleagues solved some of the problems of the TAT in a
research project they did. Which is NOT one of their solutions?
a. they had subjects respond to some new cards that were
assembled using the same criteria used by Murray in coming
up with the original cards; b. single figures were considered

c. use of the Adjective Generation Technique avoided scaling problems; d. subjects were allowed to use any concepts contained in their repertoires of words   15.73
372

All except one of the following are findings of Potkay and colleagues in their study of the TAT using the Adjective Generation Technique (AGT) Which is NOT a finding? a. agreement on descriptions of TAT figures was remarkable, considering each subject could use any of hundreds of words available to her or him; b. if figures were male, they tended to be described as old and sad; c. if the figures were female they tended to be described as loving and nurturing; d. female figures were favorably described, relative to male figures
15.74
374

Which of the following is the most accurate description of the person Murray and Morgan (1981) used in their study of TAT clinical analysis and interpretation? a. she was lower-middle class, the daughter of a machinist, who had a permanent look of tearfulness about her; b. an elderly man of some prominence (politician) who smiled so much it structured his wrinkles and molded his lips; c. a teenage girl with such a blank look on her face, it appeared that her facial muscles were paralyzed d. a college music student from a Southern Methodist family who squinted his eyes to such an extreme it looked as if a flash bulb had just gone off in his presence   15.75
374-375

All except one of the following were among the bits of background information on the Murray-Morgan client who responded to the TAT. Which was NOT among those pieces of information? a. the boy witnessed the castration of a bull and, thereafter, insisted on wearing an athletic supporter on all occasions; b. the client shied away from water and animals c. the client played with dolls and was effeminate; d. the client did not masturbate until age 18   15.76
372-373

All except one of the following were among the TAT findings in modern times. Which is NOT among those findings? a. sexually abused child and adolescent females showed more primitive and simple characterization of people; b. men who had been sexual predators tended to see bloody women in the TAT cards; c. abused girls showed sexual preoccupation; d. TAT picture descriptions revealed causal explanations for "bad events"   15.77
373&375

Which of the following is correct regarding validity research on the TAT? a. the comparison of whites and Asians on TAT scores was all good news for the TAT; b. TAT scores did well

predicting American Psychiatric Association criteria for personality disorders; c. TAT scores did well predicting Minnesota Multi-Phasic Personality Inventory scores for personality disorders; d. TAT SCORS scores did show some predictive validity for some purposes   15.78
                                                                                                    376
Which of the following is one of the of diversity principles?
a. all people are created equal; b. diversity includes everyone
c. one must be a member of a minority group to be a part of diversity; d. only minorities and women have a right to claim they are oppressed   15.79
                                                                                              376-377
All except one of the following are limitations of Murray point of view or work. Which is NOT a limitation? a. as soon as ideas occurred to him they became fact; b. he was confused about whether his needs were actually drives or traits of personality
c. there are no research results consistent with his ideas
d. Murray more or less guided his colleagues in selecting the TAT pictures   15.80
                                                                                                    378
Which of the following is true of Murray and his contributions?
a. Murray's narcissism left him with no friends; b. no one can deny the historical significance of the TAT; c. Murray was popular wherever he went, especially among colleagues at Harvard; d. Murray took most of his ideas from others' theories
                                                                                                    15.81
                                                                                                    378
Which of the following is true of Murray and his contributions?
a. he never talked or wrote about others' theories or ideas, much less tried to reconcile them with his own concepts;
b. he had no associations or interactions with famous psychologists of his day; c. he was responsible for developing the most used objective personality test available today
d. he was a warm and kind person who inspired the love and admiration of countless psychologists
Extra Items   15.82
                                                                                              358-360
Which was true of the relationship between Murray and Christiana Morgan? a. they never even considered getting married; b. they were very discreet: his wife and her husband never knew about their affair; c. they became living reflections of anima and animus; d. they finally got married when Murray divorced his wife Jo   15.83
                                                                                                    359
Murray's first meaningful relationship with a; a. was with a prostitute dying of syphilis; b. was with Christiana; c. was with Jo; d. was with a graduate student who worked in his lab as an assistant   15.84

360

Which describes an experience that Murray had when he visited Jung? a. Jung encouraged him to set up his lover Christiana in an apartment; b. Murray had several Extrasensory Perceptual experiences; c. in the few days with Jung, "the great flood-gates of the wonder-world [unconscious] swung open" d. during psychoanalysis with Jung, "I at last gained insight into the bottomless pit of my depression"   15.85

362

Regarding Murray's psychoanalyst's wife a. she was rather rotund and plain; b. he immediately fell in love with her; c. Christiana became jealous of her; d. Murray imagined that she was attracted to him   15.86

362

Which is the most accurate description of Murray's relationship with his colleagues at Harvard? a. warm and close; b. cordial, but not familiar; c. they were proud to call him colleague, because he had a M.D. and a Ph.D.; d. they fought like dragonflies   15.87

362

What was it about Murray that made Harvard Psychology Chair Boring quake with fear? a. Murray's reputation as a "put-down artist"; b. that Murray was about to puncture psychology's soft underbelly; c. that Murray's criticisms of his colleagues would cost Boring his job, because the two were considered a clique d. Murray's threat to leave Harvard if he was not treated with more respect   15.88

364

An image of food aroused by smells from the environment is a a. complex; b. pressive object; c. thema; d. regnant response   15.89

365

All of the following are Viscerogenic needs, except one. Which is NOT a viscerogenic need?; a. n Inviolacy; b. n Harmavoidance; c. n Coldavoidance; d. n Expiration

15.90
365

Which represents "avoidance/withdrawal" (Murray)? a. adience; b. n Abasement; c. abience; d. n Order   15.91

367

Contrafactions of needs a. are needs served at the same time; b. are opposing needs; c. are reminiscent of Jung's equivalence; d. are reminiscent of Freud's complexes

15.92
367

Cathexis, in its original Freudian form, meant a. the investment of psychic energy in some object; b. to fuse some object to some other similar object; c. to implode an object in

318

the act of eliminating its influence; d. the extrication of an
energy form from an object   15.93
                                                        368
Complexes   a. do something to us or for us; b. are the same in
Murray thought as they were in Freud; c. are very similar to
Jung's archetypes; d. make us do something   15.94
                                                        370
"p Affiliation>n Affiliation" refers to   a. contrafactions of needs;
b. thema; c. fusion of needs; d. complexes   15.95
                                                        371
With new more objective scoring, introduced around 1949, the
TAT   a. became as reliable and valid as any objective
instrument; b. became the most reliable and valid of projective
instruments; c. ironically, became less reliable and valid,
leading to the return of original methods; d. still was scored in a
somewhat haphazard and unsystematic manner   15.96
                                                        372
Contrary to expectations, Potkay and colleagues found
a. evidence contrary to the usual sexism: females were
described more favorably than males; b. evidence that males
were described more favorably, a surprise in view of the nature
of the card/pictures; c. little variation in the descriptions of the
figures in the card/pictures; d. a tendency for the figures in the
card/pictures to be described in a rather uniformly positive
manner   15.97
                                                      374-375
The client in the Murray/Morgan TAT study dreamed of
a. being lifted into the stratosphere on the wings of turtle doves;
b. being repeatedly pierced by the horn of a unicorn; c. being
chased by a bull; d. being the object of the affections of two
beautiful women   15.98
                                                      372-373
Who tends to describe TAT figures in fewer words (Johnson,
1994)   a. abused adolescents; b. Alzheimer's patients
c. manic depressives; d. paranoids   15.99
                                                        375
Recent disclosures indicate that Christiana Morgan (Morgan,
1995) was   a. a minor figures in the original TAT research;
b. the person most responsible for the TAT research and the
TAT pictures; c. a major figure in the TAT research, but only in
the 1950s when Murray turned the TAT lab over to her; d. was
a major figure in the early TAT research, and the senior author
of several early TAT articles   15.100
                                                        376
For whom among the poor are there no government program
specifically targeting them? a. African American women; b.
legal immigrants; c. young European American males
d. Vietnamese   15.101

All of the following are conclusions drawn by Lilienfeld et al., (2000) regarding the TAT, except one. Which is NOT one of their conclusions? a. results support contradictory expectations regarding correlations of TAT scores with personality test scores; b. some results contradict intuition: depressives have more positive affect than normals; c. anti-social people didn't differ from others on TAT moral standards scores; d. over-all the TAT showed poorer validity than the Rorschach   15.102

What is the irony of Murray's use of the derisive term "scientism"? a. he was never really a scientist; b. some of his own concepts have the flavor of superficial science c. he actually loved science, if you read between the lines of his research reports; d. he really could care less about science
15.103

All except one of the following are possibilities regarding where Murray got the idea for the TAT picture-method. Which Is NOT one of those possibilities? a. a student in one of his classes suggested the method to him; b. he got the idea from the book "Look Homeward Angel"; c. he and Christiana got the idea from prior work by psychiatrist Louis Schwartz; d. he got the idea from the archives of a colleague who died before publishing it

15.1,c	15.48,d	15.93,d
15.2,b	15.49,c	15.94,b
15.3,d	15.50,a	15.95,d
15.4,b	15.51,b	15.96,a
15.5,a	15.52,b	15.97,c
15.6,a	15.53,c	15.98,b
15.7,b	15.54,c	15.99,d
15.8,d	15.55,d	15.100,c
15.9,a	15.56,c	15.101,d
15.10,d	15.57,d	15.102,b
15.11,c	15.58,b	15.103,d
15.12,b	15.59,d	
15.13,d	15.60,a	
15.14,c	15.61,b	
15.15,d	15.62,c	
15.16,b	15.63,a	
15.17,a	15.64,a	
15.18,d	15.65,d	
15.19,a	15.66,b	
15.20,c	15.67,c	
15.21,b	15.68,b	
15.22,c	15.69,c	
15.23,b	15.70,a	
15.24.d	15.71,c	
15.25,a	15.72,a	
15.26,a	15.73,b	
15.27,b	15.74,d	
15.28,d	15.75,a	
15.29,b	15.76,b	
15.30,c	15.77,d	
15.31,c	15.78, b	
15.32,d	15.79,c	
15.33,a	15.80,b	
15.34,c	15.81,d	
15.35,a	*Extra*	
15.36,a	Items	
15.37,d	15.82,c	
15.38,b	15.83,a	
15.39,c	15.84,c	
15.40,d	15.85,d	
15.41,a	15.86,d	
15.42,a	15.87,b	
15.43,c	15.88,d	
15.44,d	15.89,a	
15.45,a	15.90,c	
15.46,b	15.91,c	
15.47,c	15.92,a	

Chapter 16

Multiple Choice Items for the Chapter on Cattell and Eysenck

16.1
382

What is in common between Cattell and Eysenck? a. both are decidedly Freudia; b. both conceive of personality in trait terms; c. both emphasize cognitive facilities rather than traits d. neither is a researcher; they are more philosophers than scientists

16.2
383

All of the following are true of Cattell's background, except one. Which is NOT true of Cattell's background? a. he is middle-class English; b. he described his parents and teachers as exacting; c. he hints that his own high intelligence comes from his father; d. he claimed to have quite a happy childhood

16.3
383-385

All except one of the following is true of Cattell as a youngster. Which is NOT true of Cattell's youth? a. he enjoyed an idyllic childhood on the English coast; b. he, as a Scout, tended wounded World War I soldiers; c. he had affection, but little respect, for his school headmaster; d. he admitted to sibling rivalry involving his brother

16.4
384-385

All except one of the following was true of Cattell's early career. Which was NOT true of his early career?; a. he became involved in the eugenics movement; b. he had a stomach disorder; c. his first wife died; d. he was hired at Columbus University, New York City, by Edward Thorndike

16.5
383

What were his impressions of World War I? a. he was too young to be conscious of it; b. he was impressed with the destructiveness of modern warfare; c. he secretly favored the Germans; d. he repeatedly wept when he saw wounded troops

16.6
385

As an empiricist, Cattell believed a. theory first, data second; b. doing experiments provides the best approach to understanding people; c. the best approach to getting the facts about personality is a series of seemingly unrelated studies: attack personality from all sides at once; d. one collects data

first then filters and sifts it through various statistical techniques until the facts emerge 16.7
385

The inductive-hypothetico-deductive spiral refers to
a. detecting regularities in data leading to a hypothesis from which consequences are deduced, leading to further data from which new regularities are induced, and so forth ; b. that which tells what a person will do when placed in a particular situation; c. a framework that integrates environmental situations with characteristics of the person in attempts to understand the person; d. a procedure for determining the number and nature of factors underlying larger numbers of measures 16.8
386

Personality   a. involves detecting regularities in data leading to a hypothesis from which consequences are deduced, leading to further data from which new regularities are induced, and so forth; b. is that which tells what a person will do when placed in a particular situation; c. is a framework that integrates environmental situations with characteristics of the person in attempts to understand the person; d. is a procedure for determining the number and nature of factors underlying larger numbers of measures 16.9
386

Where does Cattell stand in the nature-nurture debate? a. on the nature side; b. on the nurture side; c. he leans to the nurture side; d. he prefers a blend of the two, rather than either one or interactions between them 16.10
386

"Econetic model" refers to   a. detecting regularities in data leading to a hypothesis from which consequences are deduced, leading to further data from which new regularities are induced, and so forth; b. that which tells what a person will do when placed in a particular situation; c. a framework that integrates environmental situations with characteristics of the person in attempts to understand the person; d. a procedure for determining the number and nature of factors underlying larger numbers of measures 16.11
386

Factor analysis   a. involves detecting regularities in data leading to a hypothesis from which consequences are deduced, leading to further data from which new regularities are induced, and so forth; b. is a method which tells what a person will do when placed in a particular situation c. involves a framework that integrates environmental situations with characteristics of the person in attempts to understand the person; d. is a procedure for determining the

323

number and nature of factors underlying larger numbers of measures   16.12
                                                                    387

Factor (Cattell) refers to   a. an internal entity that stands between types and traits and mediates their relationship b. a global unit that subsumes behavior, cognition (including traits) and feelings; c. a manifestation of a personality trait, rather than the trait itself; d. a hypothetical construct that is applied to a data cluster (set of items) and suggests what it is measuring   16.13
                                                                    387

The "analysis" in factor analysis refers to   a. the process of exploring a raw data set using the "eyeball technique" in search of regularities; b. the "talking process" that is used with the client; c. a series of statistical procedures involving intercorrelations among items and correlations of items with item-clusters, ending in a factor; d. a method that specifies a theory, derives a hypothesis from that theory, tests the hypothesis, draws conclusions, and projects those conclusions back onto the theory   16.14
                                                                    387

"Loadings" refers to   a. factors that are neither at the top or the bottom of the hierarchy of personality components, but can shift about the middle; b. factors that encompass several primary factors and are called superfactors; c. factors that are relatively pure and narrow in scope; it can be arranged that they are statistically independent; d. correlations of particular items with a given factor   16.15
                                                                    387

"Primary" refers to (Cattell)   a. factors that are neither at the top or the bottom of the hierarchy of personality components, but can shift about the middle; b. factors that encompass several more restricted factors and are called superfactors; c. factors that are relatively pure and narrow in scope; it can be arranged that they are statistically independent; d. correlations of particular items with a given factor   16.16
                                                                    387

"Secondary" refers to (Cattell)   a. factors that are neither at the top or the bottom of the hierarchy of personality components, but can shift about the middle; b. factors that encompass several primary factors and are called superfactors; c. factors that are relatively pure and narrow in scope; it can be arranged that they are statistically independent; d. correlations of particular items with a given factor   16.17
                                                                386-387

The basic assumption behind factor analysis is   a. each measure is unrelated to each other measure; b. all measures relate to a significant degree to all other measures; c. certain simple responses intercorrelate or vary together and thus are grouped togetherd. certain simple responses are entirely independent of each other and cannot be related to each other
16.18
394

Which of the following did Cattell believe to be genetically determined? a. super-ego-strength; b. self-sentimentc. resilience; d. comeuppance
16.19
386

What does it mean when a group of subjects endorse an item and also endorse other items? a. the items are relatedb. the items are unrelated; c. the items are negatively correlated; d. the items are uncorrelated
16.20
387

What determines the assignment of a label for a factor? a. chance; b. the analysis alone determines the assignment; c. the researcher's best judgmentd. a new analysis especially designed to name labels
16.21
387-388

A primary factor is to a secondary as   a. statistical analysis is to an intuitive analysis; b. luck is to chance; c. hope is to despair; d. source traits are to second-order traits
16.22
386

What is the starting point of Cattell's personality investigations? a. very complex behavior; b. projective test results; c. insights gained in psychoanalysis; d. simple responses
16.23
387

"A common trait" is   a. so specific to an individual that no one else could be scored on its dimension; b. that which can be measured for all people by the same battery of tests and on which the people differ in degree rather than in form; c. a permanent entity that does not fade in and out; it is inborn or develops during the life course and regularly directs behavior; d. a psychological entity that fades in and out
16.24
387

"Trait" is   a. so specific to an individual that no one else could be scored on its dimension; b. that which can be measured for all people by the same battery of tests and on which the people differ in degree rather than in form; c. a permanent entity that does not fade in and out; it is inborn or develops during the life course and regularly directs behavior; d. a psychological entity that fluctuates or varies over time and thus is transitory 16.25
387

Which of the following doesn't fit any of Cattell's kinds of traits? a. so specific to an individual that no one else could be scored on its dimension; b. that which can be measured for all people by the same battery of tests and on which the people differ in degree rather than in form; c. a permanent entity that does not fade in and out; it is inborn or develops during the life course and regularly directs behavior; d. a psychological entity that fluctuates or varies over time and thus is transitory   16.26
387

"Unique trait" is   a. so specific to an individual that no one else could be scored on its dimension; b. that which can be measured for all people by the same battery of tests and on which the people differ in degree rather than in form; c. a permanent entity that does not fade in and out; it is inborn or develops during the life course and regularly directs behavior; d. a psychological entity that fluctuates or varies over time and thus is transitory   16.27
387-388

All of the following is true of "second order traits," except one. Which is NOT true of second order traits? a. subsumes others traits; b. called superfactors; c. pure and narrow in scope; d. called secondary factors   16.28
387

Exvia-invia is synonymous with   a. envious-not envious; b. extraversion-introversion; c. exogenous-endogenous d. external-internal   16.29
388

To Cattell, anxiety is   a. the feelings of tension and upset, the source of which may be difficult to identify; b. a state of extremely unpleasant emotional discomfort; c. what a person experiences when his or her construction system does not apply to critical events; d. what happens to a person when she or he experiences the symptoms of fear, but is unable to identify the source of threat   16.30
388

All except one of the following are true of source traits. Which is untrue of source traits? a. pure and narrow in scope; b. a primary factor dimension; c. a single unitary influence; d. occupies the highest rank among traits (most broad and general)   16.31
388

An ability trait is   a. exclusively related to the motor skills; b. refers to motivations and interests; c. a general personality trait that is usually stylistic, in the sense that it deals with such as tempo and persistence; d. reflected in the manner of response to the complexity of a situation, selected after the

individual is clear on what goals he or she wants to achieve in that situation   16.32
                                                                                                                        388

A temperament trait is   a. exclusively related to the motor skills. b. refers to motivations and interests; c. a general personality trait that is usually stylistic, in the sense that it deals with such as tempo and persistence; d. reflected in the manner of response to the complexity of a situation, selected after the individual is clear on what goals he or she wants to achieve in that situation   16.33
                                                                                                                        388

A dynamic trait is   a. exclusively related to the motor skills b. refers to motivations and interests; c. a general personality trait that is usually stylistic, in the sense that it deals with such as tempo and persistence; d. reflected in the manner of response to the complexity of a situation, selected after the individual is clear on what goals he or she wants to achieve in that situation   16.34
                                                                                                                        388

An erg is   a. an innate source of reactivity (drive) directed to a certain goal and accompanied by a certain quality; b. a motivational entity that is oriented to turning an unsatisfactory situation into a satisfactory one; c. an emotional unit that is expressed in anxiety, joy, sadness and so forth; d. an instinctual structure that is bent on satisfaction of physiological urges   16.35
                                                                                                                        388

An attitude is (Cattell)   a. cognition, affect, and conation directed to some object; b. a cognitive representative of a social motive: prejudice is an attitude; c. an expression of an ergic goal that is generally subsidiated to an erg(s); d. an orientation or inclination in a particular direction: vector
                                                                                                                        16.36
                                                                                                                        388

A sentiment is   a. an emotional unit that is expressed in anxiety, joy, sadness and so forth; b. an instinctual structure that is bent on satisfaction of physiological urges c. a motivational entity that is oriented to turning an unsatisfactory situation into a satisfactory one; d. a set of attitudes the strength of which has become correlated through their being all learned by contact with a particular social institution such as school, home, country   16.37
                                                                                                                        388

"Dynamic lattice" refers to   a. a network of cognitive, affective, and conative orientations bounded by the social realm at the bottom and by the intellectual realm at the top; b. the tracing of

327

the subsidiation of attitudes, one to another ending in the satisfaction of a number of primary ergic goals; c. a complex of interrelated psychic entities, each observable and measurable d. the intricate interrelation among aspects the physiological, the intellectual, and the external world, including the social realm   16.38
388-398

Which of the following is true of Cattell's personality classification system? a. the system is laid out horizontally, left to right, so that the different kinds of traits have equal rank; b. the system includes unique traits, but these are basically ignored by Cattell; c. second order traits can be subsidiated under source traits; d. source traits can be subsidiated under states   13.39
388

Which of the following refers to a source trait?; a. emotionality b. traits which are correlated but do not form a factor, hence, determined by more than influence; c. a tendency to wink upon completing a question; d. "I like to scuba diving"   16.40
389

Which of the following refers to a surface trait? a. emotionality; b. traits which are correlated but do not form a factor, hence, determined by more than influence; c. a tendency to wink upon completing the expression of a question; d. "I like to scuba diving"   16.41
387

Which of the following refers to a unique trait? a. emotionality; b. traits which are correlated but do not form a factor, hence, determined by more than influence; c. a tendency to wink upon completing the expression of a question; d. "I like to scuba diving"   16.42
389

Cattell got the idea of "g" from   a. Jensen; b. Eysenck; c. Spearman; d. Burt   16.43
389-390

All of the following relate to Cattell's notions about intelligence, except one. Which does NOT relate to intelligence? a. intelligence is primarily a result of the individuals' assimilation of the lessons taught by their solutions to puzzles provided them by their environment; b. "g" subsumes the primary mental abilities; c. one form of general intelligence is largely innate and adapts itself to all kinds of material, regardless of previous experience; d. one form of intelligence is largely abilities learned at school, representing the application of the other form, and is a function of the amount and intensity of schooling   16.44

328

All of the following are contributions of Cattell, except one. Which is NOT a contribution of Cattell? ; a. developed the 16 PF; b. identified developmental trends; c. an innovator in the area of factor analysis; d. integrated Freudian theory, cognitive theory, and behaviorism bringing scientific respectability to them 16.45

391
All except one of the following are dimensions of Cattell's 16PF. Which is NOT a dimension of the 16PF a. reserved-outgoing; b. vulnerable-invulnerable; c. sober-happy-go-lucky d. relaxed-tense 16.46

392-395
All except one of the following are limitations of Cattell's thinking or work. Which is NOT a limitation? a. there are several factor analytic methods and it is not possible to say which is "right"; b. deciding on how many factors to isolate is a somewhat arbitrary process; c. deciding what name to assign factors is a somewhat arbitrary process; d. like Murray and others, Cattell has conjured up personality factors "off the top of the head," without benefit of research input 16.47

393
Heritability a. is simply another name for the nature-nurture debate; b. assumes that all of a trait is determined by the genes, then attempts to assess which of several candidate genes is most important to the trait; c. popularly refers to the proportion of the variability in a trait that is accounted for by the genes; d. refers to a research design for discovering which is more important for the determination of personality traits, nature or nurture 16.48

393
Multiple Abstract Variance Analysis (MAVA) a. is simply another name for the nature-nurture debate; b. assumes that all of a trait is determined by the genes, then attempts to assess which of several candidate genes is most important to the trait; c. popularly refers to the proportion of the variability in a trait that is accounted for by the genes; d. refers to a research design for discovering relative proportions of environmental vs. heredity determination for personality traits 16.49

394
Across two studies investigating the heritability of factors such as ego-strength, super-ego strength and self-sentiment, Cattell and his colleagues found a. estimates across the two studies were later judged by Cattell to be incorrect; b. results of one study were not entirely in line with those of the other study

c. heritability was equal and high for all the factors across the studies; d. heritability was equal and low for all the factors across the studies   16.50
393-395

All of the following are true about heritability estimates, except one. Which is NOT true of heritability estimates? a. if high heritability is the case for a characteristic, it is impossible for any imaginable environmental intervention to affect its expression; b. heritability estimates are good only for the population used, at the time it is used; c. heritability is an average statistic and population measure and provides no information about how a given individual might have developed under different conditions; d. heritability estimates made with the use of "whites" are meaningless when applied to "blacks"   16.51
393-395

All of the following are true of "heritability" or Cattell's use of it, except one? Which is NOT true of heritability or Cattell's use of it? a. it was originally developed to estimate how successful animal breeders would be in their efforts to breed for certain desirable traits; b. the very act of dividing up variation in a trait is suspect from a genetic point of view; c. Cattell's methods have been criticized on statistical grounds ; d. if the criticisms of heritability and its use are correct, it is certain that the genes have nothing to do with factors like intelligence   16.52
396

All except one of the following are among Sternberg's broad categories of intelligences. Which is NOT among his categories?; a. g_c; b. g; c. creativity; d. street smarts
16.53
397

Which of the following is an alternative to usual assumptions about intelligence? a. the genes almost certainly play some role in intelligence; b. intelligence may be relative rather than absolute; c. the environment plays at least some role in intelligence; d. intelligence is the same the world over 16.54
396

Which newly defined ability involves monitoring and controlling one's feelings? a. State Control; b. Amygdaloid Constraint; c. Ambivalence Moderation; d. Emotional Intelligence 16.55
396

Daniel Goleman popularized a new intelligence that involves all of the following except one. Which is not involved? a. self-lessness; b. mood control; c. self-motivation; d. people skills
16.56
395-400

Which of the following represents a "disaster at the end of Cattell's career"? a. his promotion of eugenics cost him a prestigious award; b. he died of cancer at an early age; c. he suffered a third and final divorce; d. his children condemned him   16.57
                                                                          398
Which has Cattell consistently condemned during his life? a. prejudice; b. race mixing; c. any hint of environment influence on behavior; d. the empiricist's approach to research
                                                                          16.58
                                                                          399
Which of the following charges have been lodged against Cattell?; a. he faked date (made it up); b. he was a poor mathematician; c. he habitually avoided peer review of his publications; d. he failed to cite other's research   16.59
                                                                          403
"Trait," according to Eysenck, is a. a permanent entity that does not fade in and out like a state; b. a neuropsychic structure having the capacity to render many stimuli functionally equivalent; c. defined as a theoretical construct based on observed intercorrelations between a number of habitual responses; d. a second-order dimension made up of statistically intercorrelated primary traits   16.60
                                                                          403
Type, according to Eysenck, is a. a permanent entity that does not fade in and out like a state; it is inborn or develops early b. a neuropsychic structure having the capacity to render many stimuli functionally equivalent; c. defined as a theoretical construct based on observed intercorrelations between a number of habitual responses; d. a second-order dimension made up of statistically intercorrelated primary traits
                                                                          16.61
                                                                          403
Which is true of Eysenck's beliefs about the three factors he emphasized? a. he believes that there other factors that have yet to be discovered; b. he does not believe that each person belongs either to one end of each dimension, or the other, as he acknowledged in the concept "ambivert"; c. his rank ordering of the importance of the factors is 1) Neuroticism, 2) Psychoticism, 3) Extraversion-introversion; d. he believes that the reason that Psychoticism has received more research attention than the other two is because of its stronger implications for disturbed behavior   16.62
                                                                          403
Which of the following statements is an actual quote of Eysenck? a. The genes play an important role in the

determination of personality ... but environment puts strict limits on their influence. b. My attempts to add conscientiousness and agreeableness to the other three factors has been met with indifference. c. There is reason to believe that people's personalities are [importantly] influenced by the order of their birth into their families. d. Personality is determined ... by a person's genes; ... environment('s) influence is severely limited.   16.63
404

Eysenck and others have produced evidence to support the claim that extraversion has been linked to   a. the ascending reticular activating system; b. the limbic system; c. the endocrine glands; d. the amygdala   16.64
404

Eysenck links Neuroticism to   a. the ascending reticular activating system; b. the limbic system; c. the endocrine glands; d. the amygdala   16.65
404

Eysenck links Psychoticism to   a. the ascending reticular activating system; b. the limbic system; c. the endocrine glands; d. the amygdala   16.66
404

All except one of the following are believed by Eysenck to be more similar among identical twins pairs than among fraternal twins pairs. Which is NOT one of the phenomena for which he claims there is greater similarity among identical twins?; a. personality; b. criminality; c. neurotic behavior; d. altruistic behavior   16.67
404

Which of the following relates to Eysenck's "scientific model for studying personality"? a. factor analysis is the method of choice to be used exclusively in the study of personalit; b. observe first, hypothesize later; c. in terms of explanation, one seeks to answer questions about "why" personality is the way it is d. pure genetic research -- laboratory experiments involving a search for gene products -- investigating populations rather than traits is the proper approach   16.68
405

"Specific responses" refers to (Eysenck) a. responses at a micro-level; b. responses that are often too subtle to be detected with the naked eye; c. everyday behaviors or experiences that may or may not be characteristic of an individual; d. specific responses that recur under similar circumstances, such as regularly saying "hi" to a neighbor
16.69
405

"Habitual responses" refers to (Eysenck); a. responses at a micro-level; b. responses that are often too subtle to be detected with the naked eye; c. everyday behaviors or experiences that may or may not be characteristic of an individual; d. specific responses that recur under similar circumstances, such as regularly saying "hi" to a neighbor
16.70
405

Which of the following is the order with which Eysenck and colleagues extracted the three main factors from their questionnaire development research? a. N,P,E; b. P,E,N; c. N,E,P; d. E,P,N
16.71
405

All of the following are descriptions of high Ns, except one (Eysenck). Which does NOT describe high Ns? a. restless; b. practical jokers; c. moody; d. touchy
16.72
405

All of the following are descriptions of high Es, except one (Eysenck). Which does NOT describe high Es? a. short-tempered; b. on the move; c. optimistic; d. sexually impersonal
16.73
405

All of the following are descriptions of high Ps, except one (Eysenck). Which does NOT describe high Ps?; a. liking of odd things; b. imperturbable; c. undervaluing people d. socially withdrawn
16.74
406-408

All except one of the following are research results that support Eysenck's theory. Which is NOT a supportive result? a. extraverts react more strongly to negative than to positive stimuli; b. introverts were more likely to salivate to lemon juice; c. extraverts are better than introverts at pursuing multiple goals at the same time; d. only extraverts favored commercials played at a louder volume
16.75
406-408

All except one of the following are research findings, or relate to findings, in support of Eysenck's ideas. Which is NOT a research finding in support of Eysenck? a. the detrimental effect of alcohol was significantly worse for extraverts; b. a stimulant improved the performance efficiency of introverts, but not extraverts; c. lemon juice affected the responses of extraverts; d. children showing the symptoms of "mass hysteria" displayed a combination of high extraversion and high neuroticism scores
16.76
409

All of the following are limitations or criticisms of Eysenck's ideas or work, except one. Which is NOT a limitation/criticism? a. Gray's and others' points of view may have more explanatory power than Eysenck's for some purposes; b. he felt that theory should not enter the scientific process until after a phenomenon is repeatedly confirmed by research; c. some evidence suggests that brain mechanisms other than the reticular activating system are behind the observation of greater sensitivity to stimulation shown by introverts; d. extraverts positivity bias stems from their attraction to positively valenced stimuli   16.77
                                                                           410

Which of the following may represent a way to finesse the debate on whether intelligence is "genetically determined"? a. begin with the assumption that environmental causation is the whole story, and go from there; b. early enrichment may actually shape the nervous system, and, thereby, change the expression of a gene; c. concede the importance of the genes for intelligence, and deal with other important factors, such as emotional development; d. end the debate by making the assumption that the genes and the environment are equally important   16.78
                                                                     410-411

Which of the following has proved to be a serious challenge to Eysenck's belief in the primary importance of E,N, & P? a. research supporting Allport's conception of traits; b. research suggesting that only two dimensions are needed to account for personality; c. The Big Five; d. research that show E,N, & P are all actually environmentally determined   16.79
                                                                           411

Which of the following represents Eysenck's greatest contribution? a. his thesis that the genes determine personality; b. he has help make extraversion-introversion the king of personality concepts; c. his insistence that there are only three second-order factors; d. his development of measures of Neuroticism and Psychoticism
Extra Items   16.80
                                                                   384-395-398

Which of the following did Cattell endorse throughout his life that he later related to "genthanasia"? a. invia-exvia; b. a theoretic approach to personality; c. environmentalism d. eugenics   16.81
                                                                           384

Among the first jobs that Cattell held was a. Professor at the University of London; b. reader at Cambridge University

c. psychologist in the schools; d. Director of Research at the Maudsley Hospital 16.82
385
Which was a sign of stress shown by Cattell early in life and continuing into later life? a. a functional stomach disorder b. multiple divorces; c. many, many jobs during his career d. a tendency to stutter when under pressure 16.83
386
Which of the following is Cattell's formula for personality? a. $P = (g + e)^2$; b. $R = f(S.P)$; c. $R = h - e/2$; d. $P = H \times E$
16.84
394
Self-sentiment refers to a. feelings about the self that amount to self-esteem; b. the sentiment structure centered upon maintenance of the self-concept and believed to be genetically determined; c. learning consisting of a re-arrangement of satisfactions among a number of conflicting, independent drives; d. the feelings a person has toward her or himself that originates in perceptions of him or her on the part of other people
16.85
295-398
Cattell stands accused of which of the following? a. praising Hitler; b. publishing "data" that he made up; c. being entirely wrong about the contribution of the genes; d. being a communist 16.86
387
Which is true of second-order traits (Cattell) a. second-order traits are subsumed under primary factors; b. each secondary trait may be thought of as composed of lower order traits c. second order traits are lowest in Cattell's hierarchy of traits; d. Cattell thought that second order traits provided the best understanding of personality 16.87
389
In the figure depicting the erg-sentiment-attitude relationship, for the protection erg, the sentiment is "country" and the related attitude set includes a. both "armed forces" and "President of the U.S."; b. only "armed forces"; c. both Catholic church and Knights of Columbus; d. only Catholic church 16.88
390
g_f refers to a. general intelligence; b. a general factor composed largely of abilities learned at school; c. spatial ability d. an ability that is largely inherited 16.89
390

335

g_c refers to a. general intelligence; b. a general factor composed largely of abilities learned at school; c. spatial ability; d. an ability that is largely inherited   16.90
400

With what controversial figure did Eysenck work even as an undergraduate? a. Arthur Jensen; b. Edward L. Thorndike; c. Raymond Cattell; d. Sir Cyril Burt   16.91
390&395

All of the following are true of the 16PF except one. Which is NOT true of it? a. "John Skyman" is a composite profile of airline pilots; b. relaxed-tense is one if its dimensions; c. it has been used to diagnose a variety of psychological problems; d. it is the most widely used personality measure in research and clinical settings   16.92
384

Eugenics is a. now dead and gone; b. still an issue in Canada and in German universities; c. very much alive and well in the U.S. where it is still applied to severely retarded people; d. died with the Nazis   16.93
402

How do Cattell and Eysenck differ in their approach to research? a. only Eysenck uses factor analysis; b. Cattell starts with hypotheses drawn from data; Eysenck starts with theory; c. only Cattell uses factor analysis; d. Cattell emphasizes the experimental approach while Eysenck emphasizes the factor analytic approach   16.94
402

Eysenck charged that Cattell's 16 primary factors are, contrary to Cattell's own claims regarding them,; a. actual pure: unrelated to each; b. really secondary factors; c. actually impure: correlated with each other; d. probably independent of each, as only secondary factors should be   16.95
392-393

All of the following are sources of bias involved in the practice of factor analysis, except one. Which is NOT a source of bias?; a. the selection of items for factor analysis is based on the analyst's biases, rather than on previous research; b. certain factor analytic solutions are promoted, rather than others; c. naming factors is an entirely subjective process; d. the correlational statistics used in factor analysis are arbitrarily chosen   16.96
396

All of the following are categories of intelligence proposed by Howard Gardner, except one. Which is NOT one of Gardner's categories? a. crystallized intelligence; b. musical ability

c. kinesthetic ability; d. knowing oneself and knowing others
16.97
397
What do Australian Aboriginal children show more of than
Australian children of European heritage? a. quantitative
ability; b. verbal ability; c. spatial-visual ability
d. abstract thinking ability
16.98
399
Cattell has tended to publish his research in a. the most
respected and most rigorous journals; b. edited and strictly
peer reviewed books; c. in journals noted for their lenient
reviews; d. in popular magazines
16.99
395
All of the following CANNOT be accounted for Cattell's
"genetic" point view except one. Which CAN Cattell's "genetic"
view account for? a. the rapid, worldwide increase in IQ; b. the
observation that g^f is changing faster than g^c; c. that the black-
white IQ gap is closing; d. that the IQs of identical twins are
strongly, positively correlated
16.100
401-402
All except one of the following were either accusations hurled
at Eysenck or controversial positions he has adopted in some
form. Which is NOT one of those accusations or controversial
positions?. a. he was anti-Germanic; b. he was a fascist
c. he seemed to espouse "heredity is everything"; d. he
advocated and emphasized just three personality dimensions
16.101
405
A person who is carefree, even-tempered, stable and reliable
would score at an extreme on which personality dimension?
a. E; b. P; c. I; d. N
16.102
407-408
Of the personality dimensions mentioned in this book, which
has received the most research attention? a. ego-strength;
b. internal-external; c. delay of gratification; d. extraversion
16.103
407-408
All of the following have been related to extraversion in recent
research, except one. Which has NOT been related to
extraversion? a. unconscious motivation; b. positive and
negative mood; c. positive life events; d. optimism   16.104
410
Which of the following is a bogus question?; a. How many
factors underlie personality? b. Is the "black-white" I.Q. gap
inherited? c. Are personality and intelligence related?

337

d. Do psychologists need to study early personality development? 16.105

410

All of the following are true of research into the effects of early environmental enrichment, except one? Which is NOT true of research into enrichment effects? a. classic studies showed that rats reared in enriched environments scored very high on a rat I.Q. test, regardless of their genetic endowment; b. William Greenough and colleagues have demonstrated that early exposure to enriched environments increases the complexity of nerve cell branching; c. CT, PET, and MIR research has shown that children reared in enriched environments have larger brains and more nerve cells than children reared in other environmentsd. Craig Ramey and colleagues have shown that children for whom the genetic prediction would be low intelligence have shown sustained high intelligence following exposure to early enrichment 16.106

408

According to Eysenck in his last article, research study results may disagree a. only if the theory behind the research is wrong; b. because researchers have failed to understand each other; c. because different extraneous conditions hold for the studies; d. because different statistical methods are used by the researchers

16.1,b	16.46,d	16.89,b
16.2,c	16.47,c	16.90,d
16.3,d	16.48,d	16.91,d
16.4,b	16.49,b	16.92,b
16.5,b	16.50,a	16.93,b
16.6,d	16.51,d	16.94,c
16.7,a	16.52,a	16.95,d
16.8,b	16.53,b	16.96,a
16.9,a	16.54,d	16.97,c
16.10,c	16.55,b	16.98,c
16.11,d	16.56,a	16.99,d
16.12,d	16.57,b	16.100,a
16.13,c	16.58,c	16.101,d
16.14,d	16.59,c	16.102,d
16.15,c	16.60,d	16.103,a
16.16,b	16.61,b	16.104,b
16.17,c	16.62,d	16.105,c
16.18,b	16.63,a	16.106,c
16.19,a	16.64,b	
16.20,c	16.65,c	
16.21,d	16.66,d	
16.22,d	16.67,c	
16.23,b	16.68,c	
16.24,c	16.69,d	
16.25,d	16.70,c	
16.26,a	16.71,b	
16.27,c	16.72,d	
16.28,b	16.73,b	
16.29,a	16.74,a	
16.30,d	16.75,b	
16.31,d	16.76,b	
16.32,c	16.77,b	
16.33,b	16.78,c	
16.34,a	16.79,b	
16.35,c	*Extra*	
16.36,d	*Items*	
16.37,b	16.80,d	
16.38,b	16.81,c	
16.39,a	16.82,a	
16.40,d	16.83,b	
16.41,c	16.84,b	
16.42,c	16.85,d	
16.43,a	16.86,b	
16.44,d	16.87,a	
16.45,b	16.88,d	

Chapter 17

Multiple Choice Items for the Chapter On Allport

17.1
415
Which is a big difference between Allport and the other trait theorists, Murray, Cattell, and Eysenck? a. Allport was the only one to come from poverty; b. Allport was only one to rely on research; c. Allport was humble; c. Allport was the only one not to have a schema for classifying traits 17.2
416
Allport's father was all except one of the following. Which was NOT true of Allport's father?; a. a physician; b. a politician c. a humanitarian; d. a businessman 17.3
416
Whose home life was Allport's most like? a. Maslow; b. Murray; c. Horney; d. Rogers 17.4
416
Which was the Allport's family outlook? a. broadly humanitarian ; b. radically religious; c. atheist; d. agnostic 17.5
416
In whose footsteps was young Allport destined to tread? a. Murray; b. Thorndike; c. Titchener; d. Floyd Allport 17.6
417
Jenny, the mother of young Allport's friend Ross; a. aroused Allport's sympathy because she was retarded; b. practically adopted Allport and later his wife Ada; c. often flirted with Allport; d. was uneasy around Allport 17.7
406
Allport, like Maslow, had a bad experience with a. Lashley; b. Burt; c. Titchener; d. Rainey 17.8
417
When Allport visited Freud in Vienna, and related a story about his ride to Freud's house, how did Freud react? a. he laughed, much to Allport's embarrassment; b. he immediately offered an elaborate interpretation; c. he asked whether the little boy in the story was Allport; d. he related a story of his own 17.9
417
Allport's dissertation a. was justly criticized by Titchener; b. was one of the first on record about personality; c. was at first rejected, but finally accepted; d. was on a topic in visual perception 17.10
417-418

All except one of the following were true of Allport's career. Which was NOT true about his career? a. before graduate school, he taught chemistry at Simpson College; b. he was a president of the American Psychological Association; c. he consistently condemned oppression and praised social consciousness; d. he participated in successful efforts to establish a multi-disciplinary department at Harvard   17.11
419

All except one of the following was true of Allport's view of humanism and existentialism. Which was NOT true? a. he took a dim view of dark and dismal outlook of Europe's existentialists; b. he was more concerned about the self than about self-actualism; c. he accepted some aspects of both points of view; d. he found nothing worthy about existentialists' concerns about death   17.12
420

Nomothetic theorists   a. are inclined to derive general laws concerning how a relatively few traits apply to all people b. emphasize the experimental rather than the factor analytic approach; c. are inclined to study each individual's unique traits without attempting to find a place for each along a relative few trait dimensions; d. emphasize the discovery of the maximum number of trait dimensions needed to account for personality   17.13
420

Idiographic theorists   a. are inclined to derive general laws concerning how a relatively few traits apply to all people; b. emphasize the experimental rather than the factor analytic approach; c. are inclined to study each individual's unique traits without attempting to find a place for each along a relatively few trait dimensions; d. emphasize the discovery of the maximum number of trait dimensions needed to account for personality   17.14
420

How did Allport feel about the importance of cross-situational consistency in relation to traits? a. he felt it to be very important, just as do other trait theorists; b. unlike other trait theorists, he felt it to be very important; c. like Mischel, he saw the evidence as not supporting cross-situational consistency; d. he found it to be of less concern than other trait theorists   17.15
420

Allport was a pioneer   a. factor analyst; b. nomothetic theorist c. interactionist; d. chaos theory researcher   17.16
420

How did Allport feel about the unconscious? a. he agreed with Murray on its importance; b. he dismissed it entirely; c. he considered it to be of primary importance; d. he felt that depth psychology may plunge too deep   17.17
420

What has been the fate of the idiographic approach, since Allport's time? a. it has faded into oblivion; b. although still a minority orientation, it is gaining advocates among contemporary psychologists; c. it is now the orientation of choice among most personality psychologists; d. it has the same status as in Allport's time: it is being rather completely ignored   17.18
421

How did Allport contribute to the development of the Adjective Generation Technique (AGT)? a. he was the first to attach values to generated words; b. he did a classroom demonstration that suggested it; c. he launched a research program using a form of the AGT, but eventually abandoned it; d. he used a version of the technique in a famous study that attracted a lot of attention   17.19
420

To Allport, personality is   a. a pattern of traits that interact to produce behavior; b. that which predicts what a person will do in a situation; c. the dynamic organization within the individual of those psychophysical systems that determine his characteristic behavior and thought; d. the relatively enduring pattern of recurrent interpersonal situations which characterize a human life   17.20
420

Dynamic organization refers to (Allport) a. the interplay of forces within an integrated system of tightly connected components; b. the neo-Freudian instinctoids that guide the personality of the individual in directions that will yield satisfactions; c. unconscious motivations; d. the observation that personality is neither exclusively mental nor neural (physical)   17.21
420

Psychophysical refers to (Allport)   a. the interplay of forces within an integrated system of tightly connected components; b. the neo-Freudian instinctoids that guide the personality of the individual in direction that will yield satisfactions; c. unconscious motivations; d. the observation that personality is neither exclusively mental nor neural (physical)   17.22
422-423

According to Allport, different people are hostile   a. in a complex combination of ways; b. in exactly the same ways c. in different ways; d. in ways that differ only according to physical size and gender   17.23
422

Trait (Allport)   a. is a permanent entity that does not fade in and out like state; it is inborn or develops during the life course and regularly directs behavior; b. is represented as a statistical factor and defined as a theoretical construct based on observed intercorrelations between a number of different

habitual responses; c. is a construct referring to processes that convert an unsatisfying situation into a satisfying one though activations of appropriate actones; d. is a neuropsychic structure having the capacity to render many stimuli functionally equivalent, and to initiate and guide equivalent (meaningfully consistent) forms of adaptive and expressive behavior   17.24
                                                                    422

Allport recognized that   a. traits cause people to behave in much the same manner in many different situations; b. a different environmental context would call forth a different response to functionally equivalent stimuli; c. each person occupies a certain position on a trait dimension, and, while all other persons may be located on the same dimension, some will occupy different positions; d. in terms of traits "all people are created equal"   17.25
                                                                422-423

All of the following are among Allport's characteristics of traits, except one. Which is NOT one of his characteristics of traits? a. they can be established empirically; b. they are less generalized than a habit; c. they are not synonymous with moral or social judgment ; d. acts that are inconsistent with a trait are not proof of the nonexistence of the trait   17.26
                                                                    422

Why would a "kind" person be inconsistently kind? a. because the person really does not have the kindness trait; she or he just behaves in a kind fashion sometimes; b. because some settings in which the individual acts do not call forth the kindness trait; c. because the individual consciously sometimes turns kindness off so as to not look like "goodie two shoes"; d. because the individual consciously sometimes turns kindness off so as not to violate the norm "don't be too consistent" 17.27
                                                                    422

Common traits (Allport) a. are traits that a group of people who all have something in common (same ethnic background) share with one another; b. can be measured for all people by the same battery of tests on which the people differ in degree rather than in form; c. are those aspects of personality in respect to which most people within a given culture can be profitably compared; d. are traits that are so common that they have been of little interest to personologists   17.28
                                                                    422

A personal disposition is   a. a trait that is unique to a particular individual; b. is a trait that, while held in common with other people, is manifested only similarly, not identically, in each person; c. is a propensity to behave in a certain way toward some social stimulus; d. is an internal entity that guides social behavior directed toward entire groups of people   17.29
                                                                    423

How did Allport handle the dilemma created by using the same labels for both common and unique traits?; a. unfortunately, he didn't; apparently he was never aware of the problem; b. he suggested that a label for a trait be redefined for each person; c. he indicated that a trait label has a different flavor when referring to particular person than when the reference is to people in general; d. he was aware of the problem but ignored it, claiming that it rarely caused interpretative problems

17.30
423

A cardinal p.d. is   a. a personal disposition that, like the cardinal (bird), can alight anywhere in the hierarchy of personality factors; b. a disposition that is less conspicuous, less generalized, less consistent, less often called into play, and more peripheral; c. is one of the entries on the relatively large list of traits we use to summarize an individual's personality; d. is pervasive and outstanding in the life of a person

17.31
422

A central p.d. is   a. a personal disposition that, like the cardinal (bird), can alight anywhere in the hierarchy of personality factors; b. a disposition that is less conspicuous, less generalized, less consistent, less often called into play, and more peripheral; c. is one of the entries on the relatively large list of traits we use to summarize an individual's personality d. is pervasive and outstanding in the life of a person

17.32
422

A secondary p.d. is   a. a personal disposition that, like the cardinal (bird), can alight anywhere in the hierarchy of personality factors; b. a disposition that is less conspicuous, less generalized, and less consistent; c. one of the entries on the relatively large list of traits we use to summarize an individual's personality; d. pervasive and outstanding in the life of a person

17.33
423

Why did Allport create a theory of personality development? a. to correct all the problems of other such theories; b. to show how the self evolves during development; c. to show how the unconscious evolves during development; d. to address the "critical periods" during which traits must develop of they will not appear

17.34
423

"Proprium" refers to   a. me as felt and known the self as "object" of knowledge and feeling; b. the center or fulcrum of the personality; c. the organized, consistent, conceptual whole composed of perceptions of the characteristics of the "I" or "me"; d. is the total personality, the unifying core of the psyche that ensures a balance of conscious and unconscious forces

17.35
424
During early infancy, Allport's first stage,   a. a self develops
that is fused with the mothering one's self ; b. a self that is
dominated by what Freud would call id forces develops;
c. there no sense of self; d. a self develops that is vague,
nebulous, and generally ill-defined   17.36
424
Allport's bodily self is   a. a self that is confined to the central
core of the body; b. developing during Allport's fourth stage
c. of little value in structuring the child's world; d. a set of
sensations that emanate from the muscles, joints, tendons,
eyes, ears, and so on   17.37
424
Self-identity (Allport) refers to   a. expanding oneself to include
all those significant aspects of one's environment, including
people; b. the continuity of self over, past, present, and future
that results from the operation of memory; c. pride in one's
pursuits and accomplishments; d. hopes and aspirations that
develop from the perceptions and expectations that others
have of oneself   17.38
424
Self-esteem (Allport) refers to   a. expanding oneself to include
all those significant aspects of one's environment, including
people; b. the continuity of self over, past, present, and future
that results from the operation of memory; c. pride in one's
pursuits and accomplishments; d. hopes and aspirations that
develop from self-perceptions   17.39
425
Extension of self refers to   a. expanding oneself to include all
those significant aspects of one's environment, including
people; b. the continuity of self over, past, present, and future
that results from the operation of memory; c. pride in one's
pursuits and accomplishments; d. hopes and aspirations that
develop from self-perceptions   17.40
425
Self-image refers to   a. expanding oneself to include all those
significant aspects of one's environment, including people;
b. the continuity of self over, past, present, and future that
results from the operation of memory; c. pride in one's pursuits
and accomplishments; d. hopes and aspirations that develop
from the perceptions and expectations that others have of
oneself   17.41
425
Rational coper refers to   a. the sense of selfhood that is not
merely able to solve problems, but also can reason them
through "in the head"; b. a late in childhood mechanism that
arises in response to environment stress; its job is to reduce
stress; c. a personality trait equivalent to Freud's

intellectualization; d. planning for the future by setting long-range goals   17.42
426

Which is NOT likely to occur during adolescence? a. an identity crisis; b. teens try to cast off the conscience of the parents; c. teens inevitably perform some anti-social behavior, such as breaking a minor law; d. conscience shifts from outside the self to within   17.44
426

According to Allport, what happens when the individual leaps the gap between adolescence and adulthood? a. the individual waxes and wanes with regard to having a sense of identity, sometimes looking like a three year old; b. the boundaries of the self become contracted; c. withdrawal from relations with others occurs; d. the individual does not know what experiences and roles to grasp for the self and which to cast aside   17.45
427

Functional autonomy refers to   a. a process by which a new system of motivation evolves from an older one, but stems from tensions different from those of the original; b. when the functions of the body become autonomous from those of the personality; c. the person's intention to remake the personality in a unique image, separate from the images of significant others; d. when the cognitive functions of the person separate from those of the emotions   17.46
427

Which of the following is an example of functional autonomy? a. a person does something over and over; finally that person is compelled to do whatever is done repeatedly; b. a person becomes a physician because her mother wants her to be, but during her residency she becomes intensely interested in research, and devotes her life to medical discovery; c. a person becomes a nurse because he wants to help people heal and as he progresses in his profession he becomes more and more involved with his patients, experiencing more and more fulfillment; d. a person decides to do something for some reason and continues to do it for that same reason during the rest of her or his life   17.47
427

According to Allport, what is the "problem of maturity"? a. to forget the past; b. to orient to the future c. to continually re-evaluate oneself according to consistent criteria; d. to extend oneself into the spheres of ones' life
17.48
427

All except one of the following are ways of extending oneself in the process of maturing. Which is NOT one of those ways of extending oneself? a. plan a spiritual excursion (it does not

have to be to Mecca, but it could be to the top of a moderate
mountain); b. cultivate warm relating of self to others;
c. develop emotional security or self-acceptance; d. develop
realistic perceptions of self and skills (intelligence helps to
achieve maturity, but it does not guarantee it)   17.49
                                                                                    427
Frustration tolerance refers to (Allport) a. helping others to
deal with the inevitable frustrations in their lives; b. being
tolerant of other groups (ethnic, religious, etc.) regardless of
how frustrating they may be; c. when things go wrong, not
pitching a tantrum, blaming others, or wallowing in self-pity
d. tolerating frustrations, even if it would be reasonable to
become upset   17.50
                                                                                    428
Which is a problem that most people have, according to
Allport? a. we all spend much of our time wallowing in self-pity
b. we think that we have insight into ourselves, but we do not
c. we tend to believe that we have others figured out, but we do
not; d. we talk of being more tolerant of other people, but the
more we talk, the less tolerant be become   17.51
                                                                                    428
"A genuine sense of humor" is   a. being able to laugh at other
people's jokes, even when we think they are not funny;
b. being open enough to laugh at jokes about sexual and
aggressive matter; c. being able to laugh along with others,
even if we do not feel like it; d. being able to laugh at the things
we love, including ourselves and all that pertains to us, and still
to love them   17.52
                                                                                    428
Why are people who are able to laugh at themselves generally
liked? a. they can tolerate self-humiliation; b. a person with a
good sense of humor communicates a match between
perceptions of self by self and by others; c. people who laugh
at themselves are regarded as clever, because we know that
they have chosen only their trivial foibles to laugh at; d. they
are versatile and flexible   17.53
                                                                                    428
Directedness (Allport) refers to   a. having a goal or goals in life
toward which one strives; b. being adept at directing the lives of
others with whom we are intimate; c. looking to the future, not
the past; d. looking to the future, not the present   17.54
                                                                                    428-429
Allport believed that some value orientation is necessary for a
unifying philosophy to take shape. All except one of the
following are among the six types that express value options
best. Which is NOT among those types? a. the theoretical;
b. the economic; c. the skeptical; d. the esthetic   17.55
                                                                                    429-430

All of the following are characteristics of intrinsically religious people, except one. Which is NOT characteristic of intrinsically religious people? a. optimistic; b. self-deceptive; c. tend to manipulate the impressions they make on others; d. tend to be prejudice   17.56
                                                                      429-430
All except one of the following are among Allport's conceptions of religion and religious experience. Which is NOT one of those conceptions? a. he was fascinated with the possibility of a higher power that is the center of human experience; b. religious sentiment can be immature: a deity is adopted who favors the person's immediate interests; c. although there are exceptions to the rule, few people have achieved true religious fulfillment outside organized religion; d. religious motivation can be extrinsic--in the interest of self-esteem maintenance--or intrinsic--an end in itself, something that one surrenders to, not something to use   17.57
                                                                      430
All except one of the following are true concerning generic conscience. Which is NOT true? a. it is different from the must sayer of childhood; b. it basically is "there" to tell us when we do wrong that we should feel bad; c. it is not troubled by a knee-jerk need to avoid any transgression; d. minor slips and sins are not its concern   17.58
                                                                      431
According to Allport, prejudice is a. rejecting another group because members of your own group expect you to do so; b. felt or expressed antipathy based upon a faulty and inflexible generalization and may be directed toward a group as a whole, or toward an individual because he is a member of the group c. a negative sentiment reserved for those who do not fit the image one has of "acceptable persons"; this image is in a continual state of flux so that new "unacceptable persons" can periodically be taken in under its umbrella; d. an intolerant attitude toward anyone other than oneself   17.59
                                                                      431-432
All except one of the one of the following are levels on the Social Distance Scale. Which is NOT one of those levels? I would admit (members of this group): a. to kin by marriage b. to my country; c. to my club; d. to my religious denomination
                                                                      17.60
                                                                      438
Towbs-Schwen and Fazio (2001) found which of the following to be the type of motivation for controlling prejudice that was related to parents being prejudice and lack of contact with blacks? a. to look like a "good person"; b. to be concerned about acting prejudice; c. to fool black people with a liberal façade; d. to avoid disputes
                                                                      17.61

What did Allen (1975) find when he had white subjects who were classified as prejudiced, ambivalent, or unprejudiced react to African-American targets using items on the Social Distance Scale? a. only prejudiced subjects discriminated against targets; b. both prejudiced and ambivalent subjects discriminated against targets; c. all categories of subjects, even those who claimed not to discriminate against targets, did discriminate; d. contrary to predictions, none of the three categories of subjects discriminated against targets

17.62
432

The reverse discrimination effect is   a. reversing one's discriminations from time to time; b. discriminating against groups that discriminate against your own group; c. vacillating between accepting and rejecting a group; d. showing more positivity toward some other group than toward your own group

17.63
433

Racism is   a. the orientation of extremist, like members of the Klan, not other people; b. widespread negative negative sentiment directed toward African-Americans and other people of color; c. a propensity to reject people who are not "white" d. a reference to the behavior of people who are full of hate and intolerance, and openly express those feelings   17.64
433

When or under what circumstances is racism likely to show itself? a. in just about any circumstance; b. when "whites" or people of color happen to be near one another; c. when choices of others for intimate, committed, permanent relations are made; d. whenever there are social cues in the environment that suggest that racial rejection is appropriate

17.65
433

Regarding the relationship between prejudice and racism, Figure 17.1 (separate graphs for prejudice and racism) shows all except one of the following. Which does it not show? a. there are large individual differences in prejudice; b. individual differences in the incorporation of racism are quite small c. racism shows up even in the choice/reactions of people who claim to harbor little of no prejudice; d. racism shows up only in the choice-reactions of high prejudiced people   17.66
434

After examining the polls assessing antagonisms toward various group, what did Allport conclude? a. four-fifths of the American population harbors enough antagonism toward minority groups to influence their daily conduct; b. one-fifth of the American population harbors enough antagonism toward minority groups to influence their daily conduct; c. there is a

lunatic fringe in America who harbor vicious dispositions toward members of certain groups; d. few Americans are affected by racism, but many Americans are prejudiced
17.67
434
Besides choices for intimate, committed, permanent relations, where does racism show up? a. in beliefs of most religions; b. in the behaviors of children as young as age two and a half c. in subtle behaviors; d. in the behaviors we very regularly display when we deal with strangers
17.68
424
Allport was a pioneer   a. in the use of the term "altruism" b. in using factor analysis; c. in doing longitudinal research (each subject's responses are measured repeatedly); d. in challenging the concept "race"
17.69
437
All except one of the following are criteria that may have to be met before "race" is reasonably applicable to humans? Which is NOT one of those criteria? a. consensually accepted criteria for differentiating among races must be developed and shown to erect boundaries between "races"; b. variability within "races" must be adequately reconciled with assumptions of intraracial uniformity; c. it must be shown that there is absolutely no overlap between any "racial" group one may define, and any other "racial" group; d. overlap among races must be reconciled with the assumption that "races" are meaningfully distinct
17.70
437
A stereotype is   a. the same as prejudice, except that it is in the realm of emotion, rather than cognition; b. an exaggerated belief that members of a group possess a certain trait; c. an exaggerated belief that members of a group are all evil; d. the orientation of a person who is said to be "racist"
17.71
437
Though there may be a grain of truth to a stereotype, what is always false about them? a. there are no traits that are more common among one group than another; b. only large groups will have members who all share a trait; c. stereotypes come in contradictory pairs: for each stereotype of a group (they are all religious fanatics) there is a contradictory stereotype (they are all superficially religious); d. it is almost always false to assume that most of any large group possess any trait one can conjure up, except traits that define the group
17.72
437
Over the years, what has happened to the stereotype of the Japanese held by people in the United States? a. it has remained remarkably positive; b. it has remained remarkably

negative; c. it has varied greatly in positivity; d. it was non-existent until the recent Japanese "economic miracle"   17.73
425

All except one of the following were among the stereotypes of African-Americans held by white individuals according to a list taken from Allport's (1954) book? Which was NOT on that list? a. gamblers; b. happy-go-lucky; c. athletic; d. lazy   17.74 .
437-438

All except one of the following are stereotypes of African-Americans held by European Americans as revealed in the study by Allen (1996)? Which is NOT one of those stereotypes? a. arrogant; b. friendly; c. loud; d. lazy   17.75
437-438

All except one of the following are stereotypes of European Americans held by African-Americans as revealed in the study by Allen (1996). Which is NOT one of those stereotypes? a. friendly; b. prejudiced; c. smart; d. corrupt   17.76
438

According to Allport, the traits of highly prejudiced people can be summarized in which of the following terms? a. selfish; b. ignorant; c. threat oriented; d. mean spirited   17.77
439-440

All of the following are characteristics of prejudiced people, except one (Allport). Which is not one of those characteristics? a. ambivalent about parents; b. moralistic; c. tending to dichotomize; d. superficially friendly   17.78
439-440

All except one of the following are characteristics Allport attributed to prejudiced persons. Which is NOT one of those characteristics? a. high in need for definiteness; b. tending to externalize; c. tending to find safety in institutional memberships; d. tending to prefer abstractness to concreteness   17.79
439

Low tolerance for ambiguity is related to which of the following?; a. intrinsic religiosity; b. a tendency to see others as falling into many categories; c. seeing illusory movement to be highly variable trial to trial both in terms of direction and in terms of extent; d. seeing illusory movement to be constant in extent trial to trial, and constant in direction trial to trial   17.80
440

All except one of the following accurately describes authoritarians. Which is NOT an accurate description of authoritarians? a. tending to have low grade point averages if they majored in the liberal arts; b. tending to admire dictators; c. tending to be conservative and anti-gay; d. preferring a disorderly, weak society so they can exert their "superiority"   17.81

441

All of the following are important contributions of Allport, except one. Which is NOT one of his important contributions? a. he was the voice of moderation on the issue of behavioral consistency; b. he was one of only one or two theorists to look at personality development in stages; c. his idiographic approach recognized a neglected point: each person is very different from each other person, and each is very complex; d. his book on prejudice, though published in 1954, is still having impact today   17.82

441-442

All of the following are limitations of Allport's ideas or work, except one. Which is NOT a limitation? a. his "theory" is really a series of mini-theories; b. his insistence on the extreme uniqueness of each person makes the task of understanding humans look very daunting; c. the boundaries between some of his concepts are so indistinct as to be exceedingly hazy; d. he vacillated concerning what he meant by nearly all of his terms: publications a year or two apart contained changes in definitions that were left unacknowledged   17.83

442

Allport viewed "black" experience as simply a variant of "white" experience. By contrast, DuBois referred   a. the duality of "white" experience; b. the duality of "black" experience c. "black" experience as being the reverse of "white experience"; d. "white" experience as being tainted by privilege   17.84

442

One of DuBois' dualities was   a. extropunitive-intropunitive; b. internal-external; c. collectivism-individualism; d. private-public   17.85

442-443

All of the following are reasons why Allport and his works are worth remembering? Which is NOT one of those reasons? a. Allport's ideas are unique because he insisted on never using anyone else's ideas; b. he is one of a few psychologists who are so unusually warm and genuine that they are models for us all; c. that he developed mini-theories rather than a global theory may be a direction for other psychologists to take; d. his trait classification system was perhaps the only one based on the centrality of traits to the individual
Extra Items   17.86

416

Allport's life of social consciousness began   a. late in his life; b. during his childhood; c. at mid-life; d. during pre-graduate school travels abroad   17.87

417

Allport did all except one of the following during his undergraduate days. Which did he NOT do? a. became

interested in social ethics courses; b. spent a brief period in a seminary; c. worked in the Student's Army Training Corps d. worked for the Humane Society   17.88
419

Allport's book partially entitled Becoming did NOT include which of the following? a. any allusion to "traits"; b. coverage of anything related to social issues; c. mention of developmental issues; d. mention of self-actualization, empathy, or peak experiences   17.89
420

Allport was most critical of which of the following? a. social psychology; b. self-actualization; c. common sense; d. psychoanalysis   17.90
417

Allport portrayed Rinehart a. an evil person; b. as a projection of his own benevolence; c. as dull and uninteresting; d. as too much the apple of his mother's eye   17.91
429

Which is true of the "mature person I have known"? a. he didn't show maturity until old age; b. he is satisfied with where he is in life and is not trying to change; c. he is still dealing with loss in his life; d. he is learning more and more every day
17.92
417

How did Allport come to regard Jenny's family?; a. a typical stable, well-adjusted family; b. a typical unstable, ill-adjusted family; c. a puzzle he was never able to solve; d. an exception to the rule that families function well   17.93
424

Which of the following best serves to provide the child with continuity of identity? a. parental attention; b. sibling rivalry c. his/her name; d. expectation of him/her on the part of others
17.94
427

Yin, who works at a factory has a maturity problem, because a. he is so traditional; b. he is too money oriented; c. he has no close friends and no spouse; d. he is task involved rather than ego-involved   17.95
429-430

Extrinsic religious orientation is characterized by   a. religion as an end in itself; b. utilitarianism: use of one's religion; c. few friends outside the church; d. large donations to the church
17.96
429

Intrinsic religious orientation is characterized by; a. religion as an end in itself ; b. utilitarianism: use of one's religion; c. many friends outside the church; d. prejudice   17.97
430

Research has shown that extrinsically religious persons

a. tend to be altruistic; b. tend not to be depressed; c. tend to be optimistic; d. tend to be prejudiced   17.98
430
All of the following are true of the research on intrinsic-extrinsic religiosity, except one. Which is NOT true of that research? a. "intrinsic" and "extrinsic" (E/I) are opposite ends of the same continuum; b. hypercompetitive people tended to be high on the E scale and prejudiced; c. for the entire range of E/I scores, the relationships of E to I is at best slightly negative: r = - .20; d. some research has uncovered two kinds of Es   17.99
419
Allport was a humanistic   a. all levels; b. only at a theoretical level; c. at no level; d. at a personal level   17.100
433
Who is most properly called "racist" according to the text? a. all European Americans; b. highly prejudiced people c. anyone who displays any kind of discrimination according to race; d. people who are not minorities   17.101
433
According to the text, "racism"   a. and "racist" have exactly the same meaning; b. is dying rapidly in the U.S.; c. is incorporated by almost all majority people; d. is a greatly overblown concept   17.102
434
Among people who are low in prejudice, "racism"   a. is non-existent; b. is extremely rare; c. varies greatly from person to person; d. shows up only in choices/reactions that involve intimacy, commitment, and permanency and in subtle ways
17.103
438
What are the implications of the observation that most European Americans incorporate racism, yet only a relative few are racists? a. most lie about their level of discrimination; b. most ought to be considered racists; c. certain childhood experiences and child rearing practices may be among the factors that cause some to become racists; d. just as criminal behavior may be caused by the genes, racist behavior may be largely determined by the genes   17.104
436-436
All of the following are finding of early studies on the subtle manifestations of prejudice, except one. Which is NOT a finding of the early studies? a. younger liberals more frequently hung up on black than white callers; b. whites helped blacks less than whites when failure to help could be attributed to non-racial attributes of blacks; c. the more positive was white subjects' attitudes toward blacks in a mock experiment where whites read instructions to blacks, the more negative was their voice tone; d. in a mock jury study, white jurors showed

discrimination against blacks in conviction rate and sentencing only if race was an issue in the trial   17.105
435
When Wittenbrink, Judd, and Park (1997) primed subjects with the word "black" and then presented them with a stereotype of blacks, what did they find? a. whites responded faster to negative stereotypes of blacks than to positive stereotypes; b. whites responded faster to positive stereotypes of blacks than to negative stereotypes; c. whites responded with the same speed to positive stereotypes of blacks and of whites; d. whites responded with the same speed to negative stereotypes of blacks and of whites   17.106
436
When Lepore and Brown (1997) presented white subjects with both stereotypes ("athletic") and racial labels ("blacks") as primes, what did they find? a. high but not low prejudiced whites displayed racism's effects when the prime was a stereotype; b. low but not high prejudiced whites displayed racism's effects when the prime was a stereotype; c. both high and low prejudice subjects showed racism's effects equally if they were primed with a racial label; d. only high prejudiced subjects showed signs of racism when all subjects were primed with a racial label

17.1,c	17.49,c	17.95,b
17.2,b	17.50,b	17.96,a
17.3,d	17.51,d	17.97,d
17.4,a	17.52,b	17.98,a
17.5,d	17.53,a	17.99,c
17.6,b	17.54,c	17.100,b
17.7,c	17.55,d	17.101,c
17.8,c	17.56,c	17.102,d
17.9,b	17.57,b	17.103,c
17.10,a	17.58,b	17.104,d
17.11,d	17.59,d	17.105,a
17.12,a	17.60,d	17.106,d
17.13,c	17.61,c	
17.14,d	17.62,d	
17.15,c	17.63.b	
17.16,d	17.64,c	
17.17,b	17.65,d	
17.18,b	17.66,a	
17.19,c	17.67,c	
17.20,a	17.68,d	
17.21,d	17.69,c	
17.22,c	17.70,b	
17.23,d	17.71,d	
17.24,b	17.72,c	
17.25,b	17.73,c	
17.26,b	17.74,d	
17.27,c	17.75,a	
17.28,a	17.76,c	
17.29,c	17.77,d	
17.30,d	17.78,d	
17.31,c	17.79,d	
17.32,b	17.80,d	
17.33,b	17.81,b	
17.34,a	17.82.d	
17.35,c	17.83,b	
17.36,d	17.84,c	
17.37,b	17.85,a	
17.38,c	*Extra*	
17.39,a	*Items*	
17.40,d	17.86,b	
17.41,a	17.87,b	
17.42,d	17.88,d	
17.43,c	17,89,d	
17.44,d	17.90,b	
17.45,a	17.91,d	
17.46,b	17.92,d	
17.47,d	17.93,c	
17.48,a	17.94,d	

Appendix: Film List

Film List for Personality Theories

Sigmund Freud
Hosted by Edward de Bono, this program, for "The Greatest Thinkers Series," profiles the founder of psychoanalysis. In a dramatized interview with de Bono, Freud explains his theories about the human unconscious, which have brought about a revolution in "thinking about thinking." Live action video. 30 mins.
. [Insight Media, 2162 Broadway, NY, NY 10024-0621; 1-800-233-9910]

Freud: The Hidden Nature of Man
Using dramatized interviews with Sigmund Freud, this video examines the psychologist's theories of psychoanalysis, the Oedipus complex, the unconscious, infantile sexuality, and the relationship of the id, ego, and superego. It uncovers Freud's ideas in the same way the psychologist himself uncovered them -- through the analysis of dreams. 29 mins.
. [Insight Media, 2162 Broadway, NY, NY 10024-0621; 1-800-233-9910]

Sigmund Freud: His offices and Home
Using documentary photographs, this program takes viewers to Freud's home in Vienna to see the environment in which he worked. Narrated by Eli Wallach, it provides a rare view of Freud's personal world. It shows his collection of antiquities and points out the parallels between his interest in archeology and his own explorations in the past. 17 mins.
[Insight Media, 2162 Broadway, NY, NY 10024-0621; 1-800-233-9910]

C. G. Jung: A Matter of Heart
This in-depth biography of Carl Gustav Jung uses rarely seen ome movies, archival footage and interviews with family, ends, colleagues and students to provide a revealing rtrait of this inspiring man and his contributions to the field o psychiatry. Live action video. 107 mins.
. nsight Media, 2162 Broadway, NY, NY 10024-0621; 1-800-2 -9910]

The Wisdom of the Dreams: The World of C. G. Jung
Viewers follow Jung's life from childhood to his work with
Freud and then to their professional break. Jung's conception
of archetypes is explored. The Program includes interviews
with former pupils and advocates of his theory. Rare footage
of Jung and his travels to Africa, Britain, and New Mexico is
included. Live action. 3 vols. 60 mins. each
. [Insight Media, 2162 Broadway, NY, NY 10024-0621; 1-800-
233-9910]

Jung on Film
This interview with Carl Jung provides a glimpse into his life
and motivations. Jung discusses his collaboration with Freud,
the insights he gained from his patients' dreams, the
evolution of his work, and the fascinating turns taken by his
own life. 77 mins.
   [Insight Media, 2162 Broadway, NY, NY 10024-0621; 1-800-
233-9910]

For Videos on Alfred Adler:
write Librarian, Alfred Adler School, 65 Wacker Place, Suite
2100, Chicago, Il 60601-7203 or call the librarian at 312-
201-5900.

For Videos on Harry S. Sullivan:
write the William Alanson White Institute of Psychiatry,
Attention: Sandra Wilk, 20 W. 74th St. New York, NY 10023

Erik Erikson
In part one, Erikson talks about the background of his
involvement with psychoanalysis and his theory of the eight
stages of psychosocial development. In part two he discusses
libido theory, ego identity and identity crisis, positive and
negative identity, existentialism, cross-cultural research,
fixation, and the values of psychotherapy. 50 mins. each.
[University Film and Video, 1313 Fifth st. S.E., suite 108,
Minneapolis, MN 55414, Minnesota: 800-542-0013; out-of-
state: 800-847-8251]

Erik H. Erikson: A Life's Work
This video combines biographical information about Erikson
with his theoretical proposals. It includes archival materials

and new live action footage with commentary by Erikson's colleague Brenman-Gibson, offering a sense of the relationship between the life experience of a theorist and the work that resulted. 38 mins.
[University Film and Video, 1313 Fifth st. S.E., suite 108, Minneapolis, MN 55414, Minnesota: 800-542-0013; out-of-state: 800-847-8251]

Journey in Self: Humanism
This award-winning video is a dramatic, moving documentary of an intensive basic encounter group. Eight participants from various parts of the country meet for the first time in front of cameras to share some of the most intimate aspects of their lives. The film focuses on four group members and contains highlights of the most emotional moments of their interaction. Film maker Stanley Kramer does the introduction. 47 mins.
[Psychological & Educational Films, 3334 E. Coast Hwy., Suite 252, Corona Del Mar, CA 92625, 714-494-5079]

A Conversation with Carl Rogers
In this two-part series, Rogers is interviewed by Keith Berwick. Rogers comments on a variety of subjects including his thinking on client-centered therapy, on humanistic psychology and his close affinity for a phenomenological approach to human beings. He also talks about the relevance of the education we are offering our students and the dilemma of our educational institutions. Two parts, 30 mins. each.
[Psychological & Educational Films, 3334 E. Coast Hwy., Suite 252, Corona Del Mar, CA 92625, 714-494-5079]

Reflections
In response to interviewer Bennis' explorations, Rogers unfolds his theories and how they were formed. He speaks of his childhood and how his upbringing on a farm influenced his tenacity and resourcefulness...how sibling rivalry spawned a shrewd sense of strategy...how the support from his wife, Helen, contributed to his freedom to develop. Two parts, 30 mins. each.
[Psychological & Educational Films, 3334 E. Coast Hwy., Suite 252, Corona Del Mar, CA 92625, 714-494-5079]

Maslow and Self-actualization
In the first part of this interview, Maslow addresses the dimensions of honesty, humor, social interest, love, awareness, efficient perception, freshness of appreciation, the peak experience, and ethical awareness. In the second part he talks about the dimensions of freedom, detachment, creativity, spontaneity, trust, life mission, autonomy, and acceptance. Two parts, 30 mins. each.
[Psychological & Educational Films, 3334 E. Coast Hwy., Suite 252, Corona Del Mar, CA 92625, 714-494-5079]

Albert Bandura
In part one of two parts, Bandura reviews the influences on his theoretical and research development, and discusses cognitive and social behavior modification, social learning, modeling, and aggression. In the second part, he recalls his classic Bobo Doll experiment, and discusses the effects of aggression and violence in the media, morality and moral disengagement, self-efficacy, reactions to criticism, and plans for the future.
Part one: 29 mins., part two: 28 mins.
[University Film and Video, 1313 Fifth st. S.E., suite 108, Minneapolis, MN 55414, Minnesota: 800-542-0013; out-of-state: 800-847-8251]

B. F. Skinner on Behaviorism
Skinner discusses behavior modification, behavioral technology, and the uses of positive reinforcement in shaping human behavior. He also addresses programmed instruction, the application of behaviorism to a wide variety of social concerns, and the concept of utopia. 28 mins.
. [Insight Media, 2162 Broadway, NY, NY 10024-0621; 1-800-233-9910]

Token Economy: Behaviorism Applied
B. F. Skinner explains operant conditioning and differentiates between positive reinforcement and punishment. Taking viewers to two institutions that have applied the principles of behavior modification, the program examines the use of "tokens" in behavior modification and reinforcement therapy. 23 mins.

[Insight Media, 1-800-233-9910, 2162 Broadway, NY, NY 10024-0621]

Hans Eysenck
Richard I. Evans interviews Eysenck about the controversies surrounding his professional life and about his view of Freud, psychotherapy, aesthetics, behavior therapy, and intelligence. As usual, Eysenck pulls no punches about anything. 60 mins.
[Penn State, Audiovisual Services, Special Services Building, University Park, PA 16802; 1-814-865-6314]

Insight Media
Here is a great "one-stop" shopping center for personality videos (P. O. Box 621, N Y, NY 10024-0621; 800-233-9910). Aside from films about Rollo May, Skinner, Bandura and Eysenck, their "Theories of Personality," "Personality," and "Discovering Who You Are: Theories of Personality" cover theorists neglected elsewhere: Adler, Horney, Cattell, and Kelly

Rollo May on Existential Psychology
Rollo May explores existentialistic notions such as will, freedom, being, anxiety, intentionality, loneliness, intimacy and ways to give meaning to experience. 30 mins. [Insight Media, 2162 Broadway, NY, NY 10024-0621; 1-800-233-9910]

The Case of Estella Monroe: A Personality Viewed From Multiple Perspectives

At 35, Estella Monroe is a raven-haired beauty with a troubled past. Outwardly she is the bright and bubbly single mother of five year old Sammy. The struggle within her is submerged in the fathomless depth of her dark eyes. Though her marriage failed her career is booming. The manager of a thriving law office, she looks forward to a salary that approaches six figures, despite the handicap of having only an undergraduate degree from a little known college in Arizona. Starting as a rank and file secretary, her obvious intelligence and organizational skills allowed her to rise to the lofty position of manager in only a few years.

Balancing an expanding career and motherhood has been difficult. Since the end of her ill-fated marriage, Estella has grown increasingly close to her young son. Sammy cries when she leaves him at pre-school and demands to sleep with her at night. She grants his every wish, a propensity that carries over into her social life. Friends can always count on Estella. Still her current boyfriend Rudi feels neglected. He is not allowed to stay over because of Sammy and is frequently put off on the weekend since Estella brings home office work.

Estella's parents disapproved of her marriage. Her husband Bob was "not one of us." But the failure of the marriage had little to do with his ethnicity. Bob was arrogant and dominating. He opposed Estella's pursuit of a college degree. Yet he could not control her. Her need to excel was evident early in her life. She thought it was the only thing her mother admired about her. Married at eighteen and declared unable to bear children, Estella insisted on working outside the home, a source of perpetual conflict with her husband. Having only a high school education at the time, the "glass ceiling" was very low for Estella, but she always reached it quickly. Frustrated at having to change jobs when she reached the limit of advancement, Estella was determined to enter college. Taking mostly night classes so she could work, she graduated with honors in five years.

363

Estella Monroe

At this point she was 27 and worried that Bob might accept a promotion. If he did, they would have to move to Chicago. Estella did not want to leave her friends and parents. For the first time she thought of divorce. When she expressed her feelings to her parents, they were appalled. Although they never accepted Bob, divorce was a sin. She relented and made the move when Bob was promoted.

Two years later she was working in the law office, advancing nicely, and rather content for the first time in years. Then she got what she had always wanted, just when she had decided she no longer wanted it. Estella became pregnant. Her physician guessed that Bob had low a sperm count, but, by chance, conception had happened anyway, against the odds. Estella even thought of abortion, though her parents would have disowned her. It was the thoughtfulness of her bosses that made up her mind. She could have leave with partial pay and return to work in six months with no damage to her seniority.

As soon as she saw Sammy, Estella knew her life had changed. He would always be at the center of her universe. Sammy was not, however, a boon to her marriage. Bob was concerned about his career and usually found a job-related reason for failure to participate in child rearing. Estella had tolerated a lot from him over the years, but this was too much. With good legal advice readily available, she soon had a favorable divorce settlement. The alimony and her attractive salary were more than enough to allow her to continue working and provide good day-care for Sammy.

Estella was determined that things would be different for Sammy. Her mother had been rather cold, showing little affection. It almost seemed that her mother had held her at arms length. If Estella attempted to cuddle up, she was pushed away. Her mother's reluctance was written on her face. Estella rarely saw smiles meant for her. Instead her mother's physiognomy was regularly twisted into a grimace whenever Estella attempted to communicate some need.

Despite estrangement from her mother, Estella cannot rid herself of all the "musts" and "shoulds" her mother had drummed into her head. She still feels compelled to attend church at least three times a week. If left to her own devices, she would still attend church, but not so regularly. Her mother's admonition "family first" also continues to ring in

Estalla Monroe
her ears. When she brings home office work she feels
guilty. Satisfying the feelings of obligation left over from her
childhood is a major source of stress in her life.

Estella is determined that Sammy not be subjected to the
treatment that she received from her mother. She constantly
communicates affection to Sammy, but clearly separates
her reactions to his behavior from her feeling about him as
a person. If he misbehaves, she ignores what he has done,
even if he continues the bad behavior and it lapses into a
tantrum. Sammy has gotten the message: it is he she cares
about, not what he does. He has also abandoned much of
his undesirable behavior.

The treatment that Sammy receives has made him very
dependent. He is jealous of any attention Estella pays any
one else. That is not a great problem with boyfriend Rudi.
He genuinely likes Sammy and has been able to gain the
child's confidence. He often reads to Sammy and plays
video games with him. The only times they have had
problems was when Rudi was receiving Estella's attention
and Sammy wanted it. Estella is usually able to manage
those situations without difficulty. She is patient with both of
"her boys" except when she feels that Rudi is intruding too
much into her relationship with Sammy.

Rudi does not think it proper that she sleeps with Sammy.
Estella told him that it had been a tradition in her family for
the children to sleep with their parents until they were
approaching pubescence. Nevertheless, Rudi does not
understand. "Sammy will never grow up," he exclaimed in
an exasperated tone, "You'll keep him a baby forever." She
told him to "butt out" and that was the end of that. Later
when she casually remarked that she frequently bathes with
Sammy, Rudi could not muster the nerve to even make a
comment.

Despite these problems, Sammy was developing normally.
He is intelligent and cooperates with the caretakers and
children in his class. However, Sammy is peculiar in some
ways. For example, he is terribly frightened of insects.
Apparently he acquired this irrational fear from Estella.
Since childhood, upon encountering any kind of insect,
Estella would shriek and frantically clamber to the highest
point in the room. A few observations of this frenzied
behavior was sufficient to make Sammy eternally frightened

365

of insects.

Fear of insects is not the only irrational feelings that Sammy has adopted from his mother. As a child and continuing into adulthood, Estella has harbored an extraordinary fear of death. The problem dates to an incident that occurred when she was only eight years old. Her grandmother, to whom she was strongly attached, died suddenly and little Estella was confronted with much weeping and wailing. To make matters worse, at the funeral she was required to "kiss Grandmother good-bye." Hoisted into the coffin, Estella's was pushed toward her grandmother's face and her lips smeared across the dead woman's cheek. She has been unable to get the taste of the chalky make-up out of her memory. Whenever something she is eating reminds her of that taste, the whole scene comes back to her. Nightmares and incessant questions about death ensured that her fear grew stronger with time.

As an adult, Estella constantly talks about death and reads books on the subject. Of the vast repertoire of topics about which she is knowledgeable, it is the only one that causes her friends to scurry for cover. When a favorite aunt died shortly after Sammy's fourth birthday, Estella went on a crying binge and made many unfortunate comments in front of Sammy. Already distressed by his mother's tears, Sammy had no resources to deal with remarks such as "she's gone forever .. we'll never see her again." Even more upsetting was Estella's references to her own demise. Constantly she cried that she was bound to die soon herself. She would hug Sammy and say, "Will you miss me?" Soon Sammy was having his own nightmares.

Among Estella's other eccentricities is a penchant for superstitious behavior. If she spills some salt, she must throw some over her shoulder. Once when she broke a mirror, her friends laughed uproariously at her feverish antics designed to ward off seven years of bad luck. In fact, they often tease her about her superstitions. Her typical reaction to this good natured ribbing is one of the reasons they are so fond of her. Estella can not only tolerate other people laughing at her foibles, she frequently laughs at herself. Once while giving a talk she committed a Spoonerism or word reversal. When the audience laughed, she continued with several intentional faux pas, including, "The best way to handle long lines waiting to use the max

Estalla Monroe
fachine is a sheet-up sign" for "The best way to handle long
lines waiting to use the fax machine is a sign-up sheet."

Estella is also a collector. She rarely throws anything away.
While storing something, she is frequently heard to say
"You'll never know when you might need this stuff." Laying
aside something for the future is not confined to trivial
objects. She invests and saves her money rather than
satisfy an immediate impulse. Occasionally she drains off
some of the interest and dividends from her financial
interests to buy something special. Living frugally is not
difficult because she has an absolute genius for finding
items on sale. As a result of these farsighted measures she
and Sammy dress well, live in a fashionable apartment and
drive a late-model automobile, but there is still plenty left
over for a "rainy day."

Aside from her career and "her boys," friends are also a
central part of Estella's life. At work she is closest to Peter, a
happily married young lawyer who was hired about the
same time as she was, and Maria a matronly secretary who
had taken Estella "under her wing." Peter confided in
Estella about his marital problems, which tend to be rather
minor, and about his aspirations for his family. To her he is
the kind of confident that her husband never was, nor her
father, for that matter. She views Peter as the big brother
she never had, even though he is actually a year younger
than she. Maria, by contrast is more the mother she felt she
never had. Estella feels free to interrupt Maria's work with a
request for advice about a personal problem whenever one
arises. This is despite the fact that Estella is Maria's boss.
Estella can also call Maria at home at any hour of the day or
night if she's having difficulties with Sammy or has had a
spat with Rudi. Other friends include the elderly priest at the
church she attends and the woman who owns the shop
where Estella buys most of her clothes. The priest will drop
by unannounced periodically, usually about dinner time. He
is always welcome. She feels that she benefits from his
wisdom. The shop owner is a frequent lunch companion.

The last quadrant in Estella's sphere is her obsession with
becoming a singer. As a pre-teen she sang in the church
choir and was often complimented on her voice. She has
not, however, gotten up the courage to sing solo, even as
an adult. Irrationally, she says "I'm good, but other people
won't think so." No one has been able to coax her into

singing even in front of an audience of one. The closest she has come to a public performance is allowing Rudi to listen to a tape she had recorded in private. Even in this exceptional case, she refused to stay in the room while he listened. Rudi's lavish and sincere praise for her haunting rendition of "Wildfire" was received with much blushing and many "you-don't-really-mean-its." Still Rudi could not persuade her to sing live.

Estella's major concern these days is "growing old." Now, it is even more true than ten years earlier that when she enters a room eyes flit in her direction like humming birds irresistibly drawn to flowers. "Stunning," "elegant," and "magnificent," not to mention "beautiful," are among the glowing terms recently used by strangers upon first encountering her. Still she worries about wrinkles and sags. Constantly she laments becoming 40 "in only five years." She does not believe she can survive it. Friends laugh at her complaints, pointing out that she is becoming ever more breath-taking with each passing year. But all this praise is the problem. Unconsciously she has grown to crave these remarks about her appearance. Deep down she believes that people will not care for her any more when her looks fade. She fails to understand that her many other fine qualities are the reasons why others continue to support and love her.

Basically Estella feels that she is at the cross-roads of her life. She likes the way her career as law-office manager is going, but she sees her dream of being a singer slipping away. Although she likes managerial work, she wonders, "is that the real me?" Continuation in the law office could use up the few years she feels she has left to launch a singing career. Also her relation with Rudi is in limbo. She worries that he is only infatuated with her appearance. If she waits too long, her looks may fade and he may abandon her. On the other hand, does she want another marriage? The bitter taste of her union with Bob still lingers. If she marries Rudi, he may want children, but does she? If she does, she should marry soon; her child bearing years are numbered. These unresolved issues dominate her thinking.

Theorists' View of Estella Monroe

Freud would obviously rather immediately focus on Estella's relationship with Sammy. Because sleeping with Sammy continued a family tradition, he would probably assume that Estella also slept with her parents. This practice along with Estella's conflict with her mother would lead him to assume that Estella's Electra complex was full blown but not entirely resolved. Freud, however, might be puzzled by the lack of reference to her father, except to reveal that they do not communicate well. Perhaps Estella has repressed her attraction to her father. In any case, she has assembled all the makings for a powerful Oedipal situation for Sammy, except for the absence of a father figure.

Freud might also see her collecting behavior as consistent with an anal retentive disposition. Fromm would undoubtedly disagree. He would see the collecting as evidence of a hoarding orientation. When retaining objects lapses into delay of gratification, in the form of Estella's saving and investing behavior, Mischel would see it as a favorable development. He would view her ability to delay gratification to be consistent with her high intelligence. Further, he would undoubtedly see her as possessing numerous competencies.

Cattell would concede that Estella is bright, but would probably see her as manifesting crystalized general ability rather than fluid general ability, because he would know of her college education, but be ignorant of her genetic background. He might note that she has been able to successfully satisfy conflicting drives or ergs. Finally, he might see her as possessing an active self-sentiment that, nevertheless, is not characterized by entirely satisfactory maintenance of her self-concept.

Estella's preoccupation with death would surely make Freud think that Thanatos had grabbed more than its share of libidinal energy. Here again Fromm would likely disagree. He would see her obsession with death as evidence for a necrophilous character. Because of her ethnic background, Fromm would want to investigate the social character of Estella's culture for clues concerning her personality. He would also see the reluctance to pursue the object of devotion, singing, as a failure of transcendence.

Further, he would probably declare her deficient in mature love.

Jung would probably dub Estella an extravert, because of her gregariousness and outgoing nature. Eysenck, however, might not concur. To him it is a rare person whose behavior is extreme enough to fit one of the other ends of the introversion-extraversion scale. Instead he might consider her an ambivert who leans to the extravert end of the continuum. He would also likely see her as low on the P (Psychoticism) scale, but not so low on the N (Neuroticism) scale.

Jung would also likely refer to Estella's many personas. She is working hard at playing the role of mother, while at the same time being a good employee and a true friend. Despite her age, individuation is still in its earlier stages. Disturbances such as her fear of death and superstitious behavior might lead him to believe that she has not yet achieved the proper balance between conscious and unconscious forces that signifies a healthy self. Lastly, he might see reticence to unite with a man and her conflict with her mother as evidence for struggles involving the archetypes animus and anima.

Skinner would note with approval that Estella has appropriately dealt with Sammy's undesirable behavior by instituting extinction procedures rather than with the use of punishment or negative reinforcement. In addition, he might also assume that Estella is genetically predisposed to be a singer, but has not developed her vocal skills because her environment does not afford the proper consequences for singing behavior. He might suggest that she could immerse herself in a different environment where the needed consequences are available.

In regard to the frustrated singing career, Rogers would certainly notice the incongruence between Estella's self-concept, which is highly invested in being a singer, and her actual experience, which barely includes singing. There is likely to be a gap between her ideal self and her real self. Rogers would find it to be critically important that she express her need to sing. He would also undoubtedly notice the unconditional positive regard she affords Sammy. Due to the fact that she has several confidants, he would probably attribute empathy to her. However, while

Estalla Monroe
she has positive regard for others, she apparently does not
have fully developed positive self-regard.

Maslow would almost certainly rule out self-actualization as
a possibility for Estella in the near future. He would
probably notice that she had dwelled at the lower levels of
the hierarchy of needs (Deficiency Needs) during her
childhood and even during part of her adulthood. Presently
she might be seen as reaching no higher than the esteem
level. If she is to obtain self-actualization, she will have to
seriously address her desire to become a singer. Until then
peak experiences are unlikely for her. Likewise, cognitive
needs and esthetic needs are unlikely to arise. In fact,
Estella will probably still be addressing belongingness and
love needs in the future.

Bandura would advise that Estella work on her self-efficacy
for singing. In a way she had begun this effort by allowing
Rudi to listen to her sing on tape. The next step might be to
solicit the cooperation of a singer who would model singing
in front of a small group for Estella. After this vicarious
experience, Estella might manage to sing in front of Rudi,
then before some other trusted people, and finally, with
more help from the singing model, in front of some
strangers. With her self-efficacy thus boosted through
performance accomplishment, she might be ready for a true
public performance. Bandura would notice that Estella had
modeled fear of insects for Sammy. He would suggest that
she also work on her self-efficacy for encountering insects
so that, eventually, she can model interactions with insects
for Sammy in order to eliminate his fear.

Allport would see the desire to sing as functionally
autonomous. Its probable origin was joining the church
choir to satisfy a need to belong or to accommodate
parental pressure to be active in the church. In time,
however, singing became an end in itself. A further sign of
Estella's maturing personality is her genuine sense of
humor, including a willingness to poke fun at herself. As a
child and continuing into adulthood, he would likely see her
as developing propriate striving and rational coping. In
addition, he would find her personality to be that of an
unprejudiced person, partly because she openly, rather
than covertly, criticizes her parents.

Kelly would have little difficulty specifying several strong constructs applicable to Estella, even without giving her the REP test. These include "loyal," "trustworthy," "compassionate," "outgoing," "hard-working," "ambitious," and "conscientious." While her construction system would be relatively easy to specify, its structure would be more difficult to conceive. He might opt for extension of the cleavage line--subordinate constructs fall directly under the corresponding emergent and implicit poles of her superordinate constructs. The rationale would be that this is a more common arrangement and fits cases like Estella's where constructs are closely interrelated. Especially in view of her intelligence, Kelly would probably recommend the scientific approach to the solution of her problems.

Adler would notice that what Kelly calls "constructs" have the strong flavor of social involvement. He also would probably credit Estella with relatively strong social-interest development. He would almost certainly see Estella as showing intense striving for superiority, especially in view of a childhood that would have promoted feelings of inferiority. He might illuminate her prototype or fictional goal of becoming a singer with a different light than that shed by the other theorists. He would regard it as a unifying force in her personality, but not a goal that must or should be reached. Instead he would expect that Estella would be in for a shock when her desire to become a singer runs head-on into a reality that makes it unlikely to be fulfilled.

Sullivan who authored a theory founded on interpersonal relations would also notice Estella's strong social involvement. He would see Estella as a heterophilic person with a strong need for tenderness whose interpersonal security is presently far less than maximum. In regard to her son, Sammy would be seen as functioning at the parataxic level. In regard to Estella relationship to her mother, Sullivan would certainly mention the forbidding gestures that characterized her mother's reactions to her. He would likely apply the label "bad mother" to Estella's mother. Unlike other self theorists, Sullivan might see Estella's self-system as relatively well developed in view of her generally solid relations with significant others, except, of course, with her mother.

Horney would see Estella as moving toward people, but probably not to such a degree as to warrant application of the label "neurotic." For one thing Estella does not show the

Estalla Monroe
"compulsive modesty" that is characteristic of neurotic movement toward people. She has, however, succumbed to the "tyranny of the shoulds" and has some distance to go before achieving self-recognition. Horney would also be likely to note the troubling jealousy displayed by Sammy, an unfortunate legacy of his mother's attempt to compensate for her own mother's lack of warmth. Further, she might see Estella as "guilty" of externalization in that she seems to hold her difficult childhood and marriage responsible for her current problems. Rotter would probably disagree, because Estella shows too many characteristics of internal locus of control. Rotter would likely also attribute strong interpersonal trust to Estella in view of her many close friendships.

Murray would see a number of his needs as strongly represented in Estella. For example, there is considerable evidence for n Harmavoidance, n Affiliation, and n Succorance, and some evidence for n Order, n Autonomy, n Dominance, and n Blamavoidance. Obvious presses in her life would include p Affiliation, p Dominance and p Nurturance. Themas would include the presence of friendly, sociable companions resulting in the activation of n Affiliation (p Affiliation > n Affiliation) and a view of her mother as restraining and prohibiting leading to n Dominance (p Dominance > n Dominance).

Erikson would likely see Estella as in transition from young adulthood to adulthood. Due to her failed marriage, she has not yet achieved intimacy (vs. isolation), though her closeness to Sammy is noteworthy. Estella does have several close relationships; nevertheless, she cannot be said to have merged with another adult in a mature romantic relationship. The strength of love will not likely be fully developed in her until she can see herself as becoming one with Rudi or someone else. At present Erikson would probably seen Estella as on the fringes of adulthood. Generativity versus stagnation has not become an issue for her. Whether the strength of care will develop in her is still to be determined. So far she has only shown signs of what Levinson and Sheehy have called the midlife crisis.

In sum, the theorists would likely see Estella as an intelligent, socially and professionally successful person. Nevertheless, they would also see her as a person under construction, not yet complete. Mature romantic love, and even more important her dreams of becoming a singer, are serious issues that are as yet unresolved.

Theorists' Analysis of Estella

Theorist	Concepts used in analysis of Estella
Freud	Oedipus and Electra Complexes, anal retentive, Thanatos, repression, libidinal energy
Fromm	hoarding orientation, necrophilous character, social character, object of devotion, transcendence, mature love
Mischel	delay of gratification, competence(intelligence)/delay link, competencies
Cattell	crystalized and fluid general ability, self-sentiment, ergs
Jung	extravert, persona, individuation, balance between conscious and unconscious, self, archetype, animus, anima
Eysenck	interversion-extraversion scale, ambivert, N (Neuroticism), P (Psychoticism)
Skinner	contingency, extinction, punishment, negative reinforcement, consequences
Rogers	incongruence, self-concept, (actual) experience, ideal self, real self, unconditional positive regard, empathy, positive regard, positive self-regard
Maslow	self-actualization, hierarchy of needs, esteem level, peak experiences, cognitive and esthetic needs, belongingness and love needs
Bandura	Self-efficacy, model, vicarious

Estalla Monroe

experience, performance
accomplishment, modeling

Allport

functionally autonomous, genuine
sense of humor, propriate striving,
rational coping, unprejudiced

Kelly

REP test, constructs, construction
system, extension of the cleaveage line,
subordinate constructs, emergent and
implicit poles, superordinate construct,
scientific approach (therapy)

Adler

social interest, striving for superiority,
feelings of inferiority, prototype, shock

Sullivan

interpersonal relations,
heterophilic, need for tenderness,
interpersonal security, parataxic,
forbidding gestures, bad mother,
significant others, self-system

Horney

moving toward people, neurotic,
compulsive modesty, tyranny of the
shoulds, self-recognition, jealousy,
externalization

Rotter

internal locus of control, interpersonal
trust

Murray

n Harmavoidance, n Affiliation, n
Succorance, n Order, n Autonomy, n
Dominance, n Blamavoidance, p
Affiliation, p Dominance, p Nurturance,
Thema, p Affiliation > n Affiliation , p
Dominance > n Dominance

Erikson

young adulthood, adulthood, intimacy vs
isolation, mature (romantic) relationship, strength, love, generativity vs.
stagnation, care, (mid-life) identity crisis

NOTES

NOTES

NOTES

NOTES

NOTES

NOTES

NOTES

NOTES